Y SERIES IN ANCIENT GREEK PHILOSOPHY

*Anthony Preus, editor*

*Erotic*                                                                    SU

# Erotic Wisdom

## PHILOSOPHY AND INTERMEDIACY
## IN PLATO'S *SYMPOSIUM*

GARY ALAN SCOTT & WILLIAM A. WELTON

STATE UNIVERSITY OF NEW YORK PRESS

Cover image, EROS, by A. Bottini, © Electa 2007


Published by
STATE UNIVERSITY OF NEW YORK PRESS
ALBANY

© 2008 State University of New York

For information, contact State University of New York Press, Albany, NY
*www.sunypress.edu*

Production by Kelli W. LeRoux
Marketing by Michael Campochiaro

**Library of Congress Cataloging-in-Publication Data**

Scott, Gary Alan, 1952–
  Erotic wisdom : philosophy and intermediacy in Plato's Symposium / Gary Alan Scott and
William A. Welton.
    p. cm. — (SUNY series in ancient Greek philosophy)
  Includes bibliographical references and index.
    ISBN-13: 978-0-7914-7583-6 (hardcover : alk. paper)   1. Plato. Symposium.   2. Socrates.
3. Love—Early works to 1800.   I. Welton, William A.   II. Title.

G385.S46 2008
184—dc22                                                                          2007050729

10  9  8  7  6  5  4  3  2  1

# Contents

# Acknowledgments

We would like to take this opportunity to thank several people who have inspired and helped us in completing this book.

Bill Welton wishes to thank his teacher, Charles Burlingame, for teaching him to read closely and to be attuned to the paradox and mystery of Eros in Plato's works. Gary Scott would like to thank his first two philosophy teachers, Dr. Eric Gruver and Neill Cooney, who nurtured the wonder that is the origin of philosophy and who cultivated in their students a healthy skepticism.

Both of us would like to express our appreciation to our teacher, mentor, and friend, Ronald M. Polansky, for showing us the depths and intricacies of the Platonic dialogues. As Aristotle famously said, it is impossible to repay those who have taught one philosophy.

We owe a debt of gratitude to classicist Rik Deweerdt for reading through the penultimate version of the manuscript and for catching a number of typos or outright mistakes. We also want to thank two colleagues who read earlier versions of the manuscript: Francis Cunningham and Paul Richard Blum. We are deeply indebted to Hilde Roos for her tireless efforts as editorial assistant for this project. We wish to express our appreciation to Loyola College's Center for the Humanities for its generous underwriting of some of the costs associated with publishing this book and for buying several copies of the book for the Faculty Author publication library.

Special thanks go to Michael Rinella, Kelli LeRoux, and Michael Campochiaro, from SUNY Press, and our copyeditor, Alan Hewat, and our compositor, Carey Nershi.

We also benefited greatly from the comments of an anonymous referee for SUNY Press, whose criticisms led us to tighten the argument and to show more clearly where and how our interpretation differs from those of our predecessors.

Finally, we wish to thank Jim Lesher for his inspirational presentation on "The Afterlife of the Symposium." Professor Lesher brought together the myriad ways in which the *Symposium* has been interpreted, adapted, performed, and depicted from late antiquity to modern times in various media for various purposes. It has influenced philosophers from Plotinus to Proclus, Augustine, Ficino, and de Unamuno. It has also influenced playwrights and poets from Ben Jonson to John Donne, William D'Avenant, Thomas Mann, and Virginia Woolf. Rubens and Boticelli depicted the party at Agathon's house, and it has inspired composers as diverse as Satie, Bernstein, and Stephen Trask. And it was turned into a musical entitled, "All About Love."

# Introduction

Plato's *Symposium* holds unique interest for modern readers.[1] Arguably, no other Platonic dialogue combines a topic of so central importance to Plato's thought with so dramatic a depiction of renowned ancient characters. Moreover, as we shall show, the *Symposium* offers a distinctive vision of the philosophical life that can provide insight into the underlying unity of Plato's thought. The dialogue also has a number of other features that make it of special importance for the student of Plato.

First, it is one of Plato's two main treatments of *Erôs* (the other being the *Phaedrus*). *Erôs* is a theme crucial to Platonic psychology; and Plato's thoughts on the psyche form one of the foundations for his thoughts on ethics, politics, education, and aesthetics. Under those headings belong his treatments of virtue, law, dialectic, rhetoric, and poetry—concerns that are the themes of most of his work. Thus, if Plato's thoughts on *Erôs* help to clarify his thoughts on human psychology, they also promise to elucidate the better part of his philosophy. Second, the account of *Erôs* presented in Socrates' speech in the *Symposium* connects *Erôs*, the fundamental principle of Platonic psychology, with the metaphysics of the Forms or *Eidē*. As is well known, the hypothesis of Forms also plays a crucial role in Plato's thought. Thus, Plato's metaphysical thought and psychological thought are linked in this dialogue.[2] Hence, *Symposium* provides insight into the relationship between the twin foci of Plato's philosophy. Third, as we will argue, the account of love in this dialogue holds the key to understanding the relationship between what Gregory Vlastos regarded as the more "Socratic" and the more "Platonic" elements in Plato's thought. In what follows we claim to have developed a richer conception of this relationship than the one proposed by Vlastos.[3]

But the interest of the *Symposium* involves more than the centrality of its theme. The *Symposium* is arguably the dialogue that provides the most detailed, varied, and yet enigmatic portrait of Socrates. Although the more popular image of Socrates is drawn from Plato's *Apology of Socrates*,

1

the *Symposium* provides a more intimate perspective, a view of Socrates as he might have appeared to members of his immediate circle in the context of a private dinner party. Of course, information the dialogue offers about Socrates comes through the mouths of other characters (e.g., Apollodorus, Aristodemus, Agathon, and Alcibiades), each of whom has his own motivations and perspectives. Yet one cannot help feeling that Plato is trying to communicate important things about Socrates and not only about his other characters' feelings and impressions of him. The attention lavished upon Socrates in this dialogue is interesting not because it offers any hope of gaining insight into the historical Socrates, but rather because it offers a chance to understand what Plato wanted to say to his contemporaries about Socrates.

In addition to the portrait of Socrates conveyed by the drama of the dialogue itself, in a specific part of the dialogue an account of Socrates is offered by one of Socrates' most notorious associates, the famed Alcibiades. Along with these impressions of Socrates, a more generalized account of the nature of philosophy is offered as part of the teachings of Diotima recounted in Socrates' speech. Since the Platonic Socrates has traditionally been regarded as Plato's paradigm philosopher, a better understanding of what Plato wishes to communicate about Socrates may translate into a richer understanding of what Plato is saying about philosophy as such.

In its treatment of Socrates, the *Symposium* also has much to say about Socrates' relation to other claimants to wisdom in Athens. To take perhaps the most important example, this dialogue is the only place in the Platonic corpus in which Socrates debates two poets, representatives of the two main modes of ancient drama, comedy and tragedy. That this detail is important is surely confirmed by Socrates' remark about comedy and tragedy near the dialogue's close (223d). So, the dialogue makes another contribution to the theme of the rivalry between poetry and philosophy discussed in the tenth book of the *Republic*.

This dialogue also affords a window on Socrates' intriguing relationship to Alcibiades, one of the most significant figures in Athenian history. By the time the *Symposium* was written, its major characters were dead. The Peloponnesian War between Athens and Sparta was long over. Alcibiades had been a key figure in the conflict and had changed his alliance more than once; he had also consorted with the Persians, who, with his encouragement, hoped to exploit the war for their own ends. The war had come to an end in 404 BCE when Sparta defeated Athens and tried to transform her into an oligarchy by installing in power in Athens a small faction of Athenians who became known as "the Thirty Tyrants." Two of these men, Critias and Charmides, had been associates of Socrates and were relatives of Plato. But when they ordered Socrates to bring a foreign resident, Leon of Salamis, for execution, Socrates had bravely resisted their command; and when he had witnessed their injustice, Plato dissociated himself from them. (See *Seventh Letter* 324d–325a where these events are discussed.) Five years after the ouster

of the Tyrants, Socrates had been tried, convicted, and executed by the city of
Athens for impiety and corrupting the youth. Socrates' past associations with
Alcibiades, Critias, and Charmides had much to do with the animus against
him. A significant thrust of the Platonic corpus seems to be devoted to clear-
ing Socrates of the charge of having corrupted these men, and the *Symposium*
seems to number among its other purposes that of exonerating Socrates of
responsibility for the actions of Alcibiades.[4]

The *Symposium* presents a glimpse of the moment just prior to the decline
of Athens. For the conversation at the banquet that forms the heart of the
dialogue is set shortly before Alcibiades sets out to lead the city on the most
ambitious and disastrous military expedition of the war (the Sicilian Expedition), when Athenian imperialism overreached its capacity. The above-
mentioned events would have been recent history to Plato's original audience
of the *Symposium*. The future of Athens in the light of its tragic past would
have been the topic of the day. The role of Alcibiades in these events, and the
question of Socrates' relationship with him, would also have been a matter of
interest and controversy. The various factions at the time were presumably
busy laying blame. The question, "What would be the new role of Athens in
the world?" was bound up with the question of how it should tell the story
of its immediate past and who should be regarded as the heroes and who
the villains in that story. The answers to these questions were linked to the
questions: What should be the city's aims and policies for the future? Where
should it seek its alliances? And what would be its gravest dangers? The *Symposium* presents Plato's perspective on Alcibiades and his relation to Socrates;
the dialogue thus forms one of the few remnants of the controversy over these
pivotal figures.

But the *Symposium* is more than a mere *apologia* of Socrates. It also
affords insights into the limitations of Socrates and even of philosophy itself.
As previously suggested, in presenting another Platonic commentary on the
meaning of Socrates and the meaning of his fate, the *Symposium* also presents
one of Plato's most provocative characterizations of the nature of philosophy.
There are two salient features of philosophy as depicted in the *Symposium*:
the first is that philosophy is fundamentally erotic;[5] the second is that as
erotic, philosophy lies between ignorance and wisdom and also between the
human and divine. Somehow philosophy partakes of each member of these
pairs of contraries simultaneously; at the same time, precisely because it partakes of each, its intermediacy is properly characterized by neither of them.
We believe that the conception of philosophy Plato expresses here sheds light
on the philosophy depicted and embodied in all the other dialogues. Yet, the
*Symposium* is important not only because it enables one to better understand
Plato, but also because it provides an entirely unique perspective on the nature
of philosophy. It is a perspective on philosophy that even after two thousand
years is still not as well known as it should be, and one that holds the key to a
great deal that Plato can still teach us today.

## INTERPRETING PLATO:
## CHALLENGES OF THE DIALOGUE FORM

Plato's works are written in the form of dramas; in them, Plato never speaks in his own voice but only through his characters. Most of the characters are historical; so Plato might be said to have written in the genre of "historical fiction." But in his own time, Plato's dialogues were regarded as belonging to the genre known as *Sokratikoi Logoi* or Socratic Conversations. Writers in this genre included Antisthenes, Aeschines, Phaedo, Euclides, Xenophon, Aristippus, and others.[6] Most of the dialogues are set in the time of Socrates, that is, in the generation *prior to Plato*, so that the action of some dialogues is set in the time of Plato's own childhood or adolescence. This fact already cautions us against being seduced by the verisimilitude of Plato's works into believing that they represent an accurate record of actual events, a kind of philosophical transcription. Since Plato's original audiences often would have known the characters of the dialogues and even, in many cases, their ultimate fates, this historical backdrop adds an extra layer of meaning to the dialogues. Although Plato often uses historical characters whose ultimate fates were generally known to his audience, he often shows us private (and in any case, fictional) conversations between them, thus creating an illusion of being "behind the scenes."

As a result, the Platonic dialogue is a combination of historical fiction, dramatic literature, and dialectical philosophy. We are shown conversations between notorious characters, but with no explicit commentary by the author; Plato stands back from his texts in silence, so as to force the audience to draw its own conclusions. Nonetheless, there are subtle and not so subtle ways in which the silent author "communicates," through his characters, his choice of settings, the dramatic action, and so on. There are specific ways in which the author implicitly shapes the audience's reactions to his texts. Plato does seem to have a "point of view" that emerges as one engages with the dialogues—or rather, as he guides the reader's or auditor's point of view. Nonetheless, it remains controversial just what one is to see from the vantage point Plato constructs. Since Plato leaves us to *infer* his meaning, suggesting more than he *says* explicitly, and since he always speaks through characters (none of whom can simply be identified with him) the difficulties of interpreting Plato have become notorious.

At various times in the history of Plato interpretation one interpretive paradigm or another has been dominant. For a time, Plato was read almost exclusively through a Neoplatonist lens. Then in the course of the last century most interpretations of Plato shared a framework of interpretation that believed that it could trace the development of Plato's thought through a chronological ordering of the dialogues by their dates of composition.[7] According to such developmentalist interpretations, the *Symposium* is usually held to be a middle period dialogue, a work of Plato's prime that represents an important transitional stage in his development.[8]

The tendency of the developmentalist approach was to take the main philosophical protagonist of a given dialogue (usually Socrates) as the "mouthpiece" through which Plato's views were expressed, paying relatively little attention to the possible significance of the dramatic and literary elements of the dialogues. During the last four decades, increasing numbers of commentators on Plato's work have turned away from the "mouthpiece theory" of interpretation.[9] They have seen such a hermeneutic assumption as too limiting and distorting, since the exclusive focus on the words of a single character and the presupposition that those words reflect the author's viewpoint ignores the ways in which dramatic action, context, and the contributions of other characters condition the meaning of the dialogue as a whole. In contrast to the "mouthpiece theory," these interpreters give greater emphasis to the dramatic aspects of the dialogues.

According to this newer school of interpretation, for each dialogue one must explain the choice of characters and setting, the details of the action, and the role of the literary elements in the dialogue. For instance, one should explain why it is that Plato chooses to have some dialogues narrated by a given character while other dialogues are entirely in direct discourse. For those dialogues that have them, one must explain the dialogue's "narrative frame."

The mode of interpretation that takes the dramatic aspects of the dialogue form seriously is especially pertinent to the *Symposium*, easily Plato's most dramatic work. The *Symposium* has more characters with major speaking roles, more obvious action, and also more compelling portraits of famous men than any other dialogue. It also has more levels of narrative complexity than any dialogue but the *Parmenides*.

There have been many attempts in the past to read the *Symposium* from a dramatic point of view, beginning with Stanley Rosen's full-length commentary (in 1968). Recently the commentary of Rosen's mentor, Leo Strauss, has been published, the transcription of a lecture course in political science Strauss offered in 1959. Both of these commentaries represent early attempts to take into account every detail of Plato's text. Nor has it been the Straussians alone who have offered readings that emphasize the drama. As Plato's most dramatic dialogue, the *Symposium* has lent itself to commentaries that try to factor in the literary and dramatic details of the text, such as Daniel Anderson's *Masks of Dionysus*, and more recently, James Rhodes's *Erôs, Wisdom and Silence*. We see ourselves as working in this tradition of dramatic reading.

## THE CONTEXT OF AN ORAL CULTURE

In interpreting Platonic dialogues, it is necessary to bear in mind what is known about their original historical and cultural context. Modern audiences must try to imagine that even in the late Fifth Century BCE, Greece was still predominantly an oral culture, rather mistrustful of the written word. That is to say, the primary carrier of cultural information was the spoken word.

Hence, it is likely that Plato and his contemporaries would have had very different notions of composition and of publication than we have today. "Books," such as existed at the time, were written on scrolls and copies could only be made by hand. At the time Plato was writing illiteracy would still have been widespread. Not long before, writing had been still primarily a convenient way of keeping lists, records, and inventories. To the authors of *sokratikoi logoi* it could well have seemed as though writing was chiefly a way of preserving the spoken word until those words could again be performed or read aloud. In this sense, written works might have been regarded in much the way we think of a musical score; the written text functioned as a kind of temporary housing for works that were meant to be performed or read aloud, not read silently.[10]

The works of the great poets who were the "educators" of the Greeks were usually recited or performed in front of audiences, and generation upon generation of Greeks memorized these tales and rehearsed them frequently. Many people in antiquity possessed considerable skill in memorization, since they would have practiced it from childhood. Plato's dialogues are populated by characters capable of reciting lines from Homer, Pindar, Hesiod, the dramatic poets; and lines from Old and New Comedy. The memorization of these great works was part of any educated Greek's curriculum. Many would also have had extensive experience in public speaking, as a consequence of the fact that all citizens were expected to participate in political deliberation. It would not be an oversimplification to say that to be a man in Classical Greece was to be a "speaker of words and a doer of deeds." Those gathered at Agathon's house would have been as much at home in speechmaking as they were in drinking, as familiar with Homer and the playwrights as with fighting in armor.

## THE DIALOGUE FORM

Commentators on Plato often attempt to answer the question, "Why did Plato write dialogues, especially the richly textured, open-ended kind of dialogues that he composed?" If he had chosen to use them as models, there were many other genres of writing available. There were a variety of forms in which philosophy was expressed in Plato's time, and yet he chose to write Socratic conversations. Why did this particular form appeal to him? In the last four decades increasingly sophisticated and interesting answers to this question have been provided. We will not attempt to say anything novel about this subject in this introduction. We wish only to indicate by a few brief remarks those views with which we have some sympathy.

It seems undeniable that Plato's choice of the dialogue form owes much to Socrates himself; the whole genre of Socratic literature—of which the dialogues are an example—could not have come into being without Socrates. In offering a semblance of the experience of one-on-one investigation with Socrates, the Socratics transpose into writing their culture's orientation toward orality. Plato especially seems to be creating a written image of an experience that he conceives to be primarily a matter of the spoken word,[11] and it is noteworthy that Socrates did not write anything, though he was literate. Moreover, the depiction of philosophy in Plato's texts continually points to the need for the actual experience of the kinds of ongoing one-on-one investigations that are depicted there.

Plato's dialogues seem to owe some of their qualities to the apparent intention to keep alive the sound of Socrates' speech. They pay him homage, stressing his value as an exemplar of wisdom and happiness and his superiority as such over his intellectual rivals. Moreover, the dialogue form is clearly meant to embody Socrates' conversational method, a method that Plato seems to have honored for deep philosophical reasons.[12] But, as Drew Hyland has shown, Plato also uses the dialogue form to remind his audience of the existential/psychological context of philosophy (its "place").[13] By means of the dialogue form Plato can explore the relation between thought and character. He can deal with psychology as well as logic and investigate the complex interrelation between them.

Pedagogically, dialogues can be of value in a number of ways. The dialogue form forces the reader to think for him or herself; the author does not place his personality and opinions on center stage, but instead presents the problems themselves, and various alternative characters discussing them, while holding himself back, remaining silent and anonymous. Such an approach makes it easier for Plato to "get underneath the reader's defenses" as the reader is charmed by the drama and by identification with or alienation from the characters. The presentation of philosophy in the form of a drama can personify some of the reader's views, enabling their consequences to be examined. At the same time, however, it can also lead audiences to look within themselves, to participate in the dialogue, as they are forced to work to understand the text, stimulated by its various conundrums.

Hence, the effect of the dialogue form upon the reader's mind has often been likened to the effect of Socrates upon his interlocutors. Like Socrates the gadfly, a dialogue can stimulate thought; like Socrates the midwife, a dialogue can lead one to give birth to one's own ideas; and like Socrates the stingray, the dialogue can lead the reader to awareness of his or her own ignorance.[14] Furthermore, with dialogues the author can easily introduce conflicting perspectives, having characters commenting on and comparing each other's arguments, and so on. Dialogues can also combine different modes of discourse; Platonic dialogues use drama, rhetoric, poetry, and myth in addition to argument, confronting the different perspectives afforded by these genres with one another, while all of them work together to produce a total effect. Thus, this form of writing lends itself to the nondogmatic, probing, critical approach to thinking that best expresses the nature of philosophy.

In interpreting a Platonic dialogue, one must decide how the various details of the drama relate to each other and to its main themes and arguments. One must provide a plausible interpretation of an element's place

in the overall organization of the dialogue. The goal of interpretation is
to be able to explain the various details in a given dialogue by providing a
plausible and philosophically illuminating account of how all the details fit
together, in relation both to one another and to the central theme, to form a
coherent whole.

Of course, in some cases, just how one should think of the central theme
or themes of a dialogue will not be immediately obvious. But there are several
kinds of clues that should be examined:

1. the setting and the cast of characters;

2. the opening or introductory passages of the dialogue for any clues
   as to the dialogue's concerns;

3. how the philosophical inquiry in the dialogue is initiated, including the actual questions asked in the dialogue, and also the order
   in which they are asked;

4. how the characters themselves characterize their activity, for they
   sometimes have other descriptions of what they are doing than
   just "practicing philosophy," and these descriptions constitute a
   meaningful context for their statements that the author himself
   has bothered to provide);

5. the topics discussed in the dialogue and the relations between
   them, including the progression of topics and how it relates to the
   setting, characters, and to the overall dramatic action of the dialogue;

6. and finally, any other special dramatic or structural clues that may
   indicate what topics are especially important and how the topics are related to one another. Such structural clues may include
   abrupt changes of subject, digressions, interesting juxtapositions,
   and most importantly, any commentary provided by one part of a
   dialogue on another part of the dialogue.[15]

In the balance of this Introduction we present an overview of the characters and major themes of the *Symposium*. This overview will provide an
initial orientation to the text and will touch on the main points that will be
developed in the course of our interpretation.

## SYMPOSIUM'S CAST OF CHARACTERS

The heart of the *Symposium* dramatizes an event that took place in the winter
of 416 or spring of 415 BCE during a second consecutive night of celebration
in honor of the playwright Agathon's victory. Since most of the participants
were hung over from the previous night's overindulgence, the partygoers
establish an agreement at the outset to drink moderately and to spend their
time making speeches in praise of *Erôs*, the god that personifies love.

A few introductory remarks regarding the characters are in order, starting with those whose speeches on *Erôs* are recounted. First there is the young Phaedrus, after whom Plato's other major dialogue on *Erôs* and rhetoric is named. In the *Phaedrus* he is depicted as a lover of speeches (*Phaedrus* 242b), and it is Phaedrus whose passionate desire to hear speeches in praise of *Erôs* establishes the main topic of the *Symposium* (177a-d). It was customary for symposia to have a leader and master of ceremonies, called the *symposiarchos*, or "leader of the drinking." Although no one is explicitly named as symposiarch in this dialogue, there is good reason to suppose that it is Phaedrus,[16] but when Alcibiades arrives, he will take over this role by fiat (see 213e).

Pausanias is the first one to propose that the guests arrange to drink less on this second night of celebration (176a). Pausanias will do his best to defend the practice of boy-love (*paiderastia*),[17] but he does admit that there is a vulgar way of engaging in the practice that must be forbidden. Although it is impossible to legislate loyalty, he will complain that there ought to be a law essentially mandating fidelity, or at least one that ensures some quid pro quo to protect the older lover's investment in the boy. Older and more mature lovers, lovers of psyches and not merely bodies, are capable of distinguishing the right way (the Heavenly Aphrodite) from the vulgar, promiscuous Aphrodite (Aphrodite Pandemos). This heavenly Love should guide the sexual aspects of *Erôs*, if Pausanias has his way.

The next speaker is Eryximachus, the man of science. He is a medical man who uses the cosmology of Empedocles to present his specialist's view of the subject of erotic attraction.[18] He will prescribe moderation to the others concerning the excessive consumption of alcohol at the beginning of the dialogue, and in his speech he will supply the "scientific" perspective on *Erôs*. His account treats *Erôs* as a first principle of explanation grounding all the arts and sciences.

Aristophanes is the famous comic poet, the author of *Birds, Frogs, Wasps, Lysistrata,* and the other remaining representatives of Attic Old Comedy. His play *Clouds* (c. 423), lampooning Socrates, had been performed for more than two decades at the time the philosopher was put on trial. In Plato's *Apology of Socrates,* Socrates credits *The Clouds* with contributing to the climate of prejudice that helped provoke the indictment against him (cf. *Ap.* 18c-e).[19] Yet in spite of this history, in the *Symposium* Plato appears to be fair to his estimable rival in that he provides Aristophanes with one of the dialogue's most entertaining and illuminating speeches.

The other poet in this dialogue is Agathon, the tragic playwright; it is the victory of his play in the Lenean competition that furnishes the occasion for the party, as his home furnishes the setting for it. Although only fragments from his plays have survived, his victory in this competition may well have been seen as crowning the next heir to the tragic tradition most recently led by Euripides and Sophocles.

Then, of course, there is Socrates. Socrates is always presented as an exceptional human being in every dialogue in which he plays a major role; but in the *Symposium* his strangeness and almost inhuman qualities are emphasized as perhaps nowhere else. We are told very early in the dialogue that it was unusual for Socrates to wear sandals (or slippers) or to bathe (174a), which seems to reflect a lack of concern for the body; however, he is clearly in good health, and has a gusto suggestive of physical well-being. He is equally at home when the occasion calls for drinking heavily as he is when it calls for abstinence. He will end up outdrinking everyone else at the party, apparently impervious to the effects of the alcohol (220a; 223c-d). He seems to have thoroughly mastered his desires and to be unconcerned with conventional honors as well (220e). Although Socrates' *daimonion* (or divine sign), a feature familiar from other dialogues, is not explicitly mentioned in the *Symposium*, in his speech he will speak at length about the realm of the *daimonic*; furthermore, he claims love is a great *daimon* and that the one thing he knows is the art of love (*ta erotika*). He is depicted as being subject to strange trances, perhaps also suggestive of his connection to the *daimonic*. In addition to these peculiarities, Alcibiades will emphasize the seductive power of Socrates' rhetoric, his habitual use of irony, the extreme contrast between his appearance and his true nature, the incorruptible character of his virtue, and his likeness to satyrs, the followers of Dionysus.

Unbeknownst to the six speakers on *Erôs*, their conversation will not end with Socrates' speech, despite the fact that the dialogue seems to reach its philosophical apex with the philosopher's recollection of Diotima's teaching concerning the vision of the Beautiful itself (211e–212b).[20] Instead, Plato prevents Socrates (and philosophy) from having the last word by making Alcibiades crash the party after the philosopher has delivered his tour de force. Only Alcibiades speaks about Socrates rather than *Erôs*. But like the other speeches, Alcibiades' speech reflects his own unique point of view and although ostensibly an encomium, it criticizes Socrates at least as much as it praises him.

The notorious Alcibiades was one of the most important but controversial figures of the day. The ward of the great Athenian statesman, Pericles, Alcibiades betrayed Athens and aided Sparta, and this betrayal is considered by many to have been responsible for Athens' eventual defeat in the Peloponnesian War (431–404). Well-born, famous for great physical beauty, notorious for his promiscuity, intelligent and spirited, he would demonstrate his exceptional prowess as a general throughout the war, while gaining a reputation for being a man of dubious, even damnable, character.[21] While aiding the Spartans he helped to bring ruin on his native city; subsequently he left the Spartans for the Persian camp and advised the Persian satrap Tissaphernes to play the Athenians and Spartans against each other. Eventually, however, Alcibiades returned for a time to the Athenian side; amazingly, he was welcomed back, perhaps due to the Athenians' desperation and their recognition of his great prowess as a general. Indeed, Alcibiades' leadership turned the tide of the war and might have secured an Athenian victory had not one of his subordinates acted against orders and allowed himself to be lured out by the enemy to suffer heavy losses. Because of this mistake of his subordinate, Alcibiades was again cast aside and not long after came to an end.

Plato presents Alcibiades as a young man in whom Socrates takes a special interest. Since Plato's dialogues were written after the fates of Socrates and Alcibiades were sealed, even Plato's original audience would have viewed this dialogue's treatment of their relationship through the lens of subsequent historical and political events. Alcibiades represents one of Socrates' most spectacular failures.[22] If the philosopher could have turned this promising man toward philosophy, some of the more tragic and bloody events of the war and its aftermath might have turned out differently. In any case, Socrates' failures with Critias, Charmides, and Alcibiades demonstrate that Socrates himself in some important cases was unable to do what in Plato's *Gorgias* (515e–517a) he criticizes Pericles and other statesmen for failing to do, namely, improve those who associate with him. Indeed, it was in no small part because of these disreputable associations that Socrates would fall under the public suspicion that led eventually to his trial and death.[23]

All of the speeches in the *Symposium*, with the sole exception of the speech offered by Socrates, are examples of encomia, speeches in praise of someone or something. On this occasion, the participants decide to praise *Erôs*, the god of love. As Leo Strauss has noted, the *Symposium* is the only dialogue in which a "god" is the main topic.[24] Socrates, of course, will subsequently be charged with "disbelieving in the gods of the city and introducing strange new gods." One of the issues involved in this charge was Socrates' claim to be visited by a *daimonion*, which many of his time could have interpreted as a "strange new god."[25] Given all this, it is worth noting that in the *Symposium* Socrates will argue that *Erôs* is not a god at all but is instead only a *daimon*. In the *Apology*, Socrates defends his claim to believe in the gods by means of his acknowledged belief in *daimons*. *Daimons*, he says there, are either gods or the children of the gods. In the *Symposium* however, *daimons* are strictly distinguished from gods. They are messengers of the gods, halfway between the human and divine realms.

Yet each of Socrates' companions understands that in speaking about *Erôs* they are not only speaking about a god, but also about a phenomenon of the human psyche. For the feeling of love is the province of the god and the manifestation of his action. The Greek word, *Erôs*, means love as passionate desire, especially sexual desire; but as the dialogue progresses the meaning of *Erôs* will be expanded. In this debate, the meaning of *Erôs* can range from homoerotic sexual desire to a cosmic force of attraction binding the elements of nature into a harmonious whole, and from such "cosmic love" to the fundamental longing humans have for all the kinds of things they lack.[26] This range of meanings explains why a dialogue about *Erôs* will deal with such diverse topics as pederasty, the love of honor, human creativity, and metaphysics.

As the drama unfolds, each of these characters presents his speech, every subsequent speaker trying to expand on or correct things previous speakers had said, or to add something new that other speakers had neglected. The result is a dramatic example of a kind of dialectic, an ever-broadening treatment, not only of *Erôs*, but also of *poiesis* and *sophia*. Yet each account of *Erôs* also reflects the standpoint of the speaker, so that each speaker praises *Erôs* "in his own image." Each speaker conceives of *Erôs* according to his predilections, his own way of life, the role he plays in intimate relationships, and in terms that valorize the virtue he considers most important.[27] But each of these speeches, although no match for Socrates' speech, still has something of positive value to teach about *Erôs* and about the myriad directions in which it leads human beings. Socrates also composes a speech that reflects his own character and way of life; indeed, his speech seems designed to guide its audience to the path of philosophy. Yet in doing so he finds a way to synthesize and celebrate all of the virtues at once (though they undergo redefinition in the process).

## THEMES OF THE *SYMPOSIUM*

A close study of the *Symposium* shows it to have a number of interrelated themes. One such theme is the nature of philosophy as embodied in the character of Socrates. For some reason Plato has chosen this dialogue on *Erôs* to furnish, in the drunken speech of Alcibiades that forms the climax of the drama, the fullest and most enigmatically detailed portrait of his friend and mentor, Socrates. The image of Socrates presented here is unforgettable and hauntingly mysterious. He is depicted as virtuous with all virtue, insulated by the irony that shrouds his superhuman excellence, firmly in the world and simultaneously detached from it, and in all, absolutely unique, like no one known before, as Alcibiades says at 221c-d. Yet, Alcibiades' speech presents both a critique of Socrates and an adoring encomium of him. In the process, it criticizes philosophy as a way of life. Its portrait of the philosopher may be an idealization or an exaggeration—but if so, it is interesting to ask just where the truth is being stretched and for what purpose. Why is Socrates highlighted in this particular way, here, in a dialogue on erotic Love? And why does Plato place this critique of the philosopher in the mouth of the notoriously ambivalent Alcibiades?

The answer must have something to do with the similar features shared by *Erôs* (as described in Socrates' own speech) and Socrates (as depicted by Alcibiades). Diotima's teaching ascribes to *Erôs* certain features associated with Plato's Socrates. It is surely no coincidence that "the art of love" (*ta erotika*) is the one thing Socrates claims to understand (177d-e), a claim made even more notable since it is uttered by a philosopher who is famous for his professions of general ignorance (e.g., at *Apology* 22e–23b). The connection between Socrates and *Erôs* was a commonplace of the *Sokratikoi Logoi*.[28] Moreover, the structure of the *Symposium* as a whole reinforces the connection between Socrates and *Erôs*. The symposiasts offer six consecutive speeches in praise of *Erôs* only to have their contest for the best speech interrupted by Alcibiades, who replaces their praise of Love with his mélange of indictment and praise of Socrates. Hence, in the action of the dialogue, the erotic philosopher, Socrates, comes to stand in for, or instantiate, *Erôs* itself. As Plato depicts him, Socrates is the exemplary erotic.[29]

For all these reasons the nucleus of the *Symposium* is the association of philosophy, in the person of Socrates, with *Erôs*. Thus, the *Symposium* reveals the complex character of Socrates. We suggest that there is a deep reason why Plato reserves perhaps his greatest homage to Socrates for a dialogue concerned with the praising of love as a messenger or *daimon*, a being in-between. On the one hand, it is fitting that a dialogue about love should be the occasion for Plato to celebrate and display his own love of Socrates. But more crucially, Plato's loving portrait of Socrates appears in a dialogue on love because in some way Socrates *is* a kind of *Erôs*, the avatar of philosophical *Erôs*, the paradigm of intermediacy. Yet if this is so, it is only because Socrates is also a unique personification of the spirit of philosophy. At the center of the *Symposium* is a vision of philosophy itself as an erotic enterprise, a practice of intermediacy in the form of Socratic Ignorance. Socrates shows that the philosopher is the one for whom wisdom is dear; but the philosopher cannot claim to possess this wisdom that is prized and pursued.

There are various clues in the dialogue itself that suggest the other major themes that must be taken into account in any viable interpretation of the *Symposium*. We find the following themes:

1. *Speeches about Love by Three Famous Men*—The most obvious theme is of course *the speeches about love* (περὶ τῶν ἐρωτικῶν λόγων 172b2). The attention of Plato's audience is focused on these speeches by the dialogue's narrative frame, which introduces the main body of the dialogue. The narrator Apollodorus is approached by unnamed companions who are interested in hearing what was said at Agathon's party, and their interest is focused on three men in particular, for the only names mentioned are *Agathon, Socrates, and Alcibiades*, as Strauss reminds us (172a-b).[30]

2. *The Relation between Beauty and the Good*—Another theme is introduced at 174a-b by the contrast between Socrates' intention to "go beautiful to the beautiful" (καλὸς παρὰ καλὸν ἴω 174a9) and his claim that "the good go uninvited to the feast of the good" (Ἀγάθων' ἐπὶ δαῖτας ἴασιν αὐτόματοι ἀγαθοί 174b4–5). Strauss points out that Socrates in effect alters the proverb about the good going unbidden to the good in his assertion that he desires to go beautiful to

the beautiful, and suggests that this play with the words "*kalos*" and "*agathos*" announces the problem of whether the ultimate object of *Erôs* is the beautiful or the good.[31]

The whole passage and its adaptations of Homer raise the question of the relative value of Socrates, Aristodemus, and Agathon, which foreshadows the larger theme of the rivalry between Socrates and Agathon or between philosophy and poetry.

3. *The Agōn: Contest of Speeches*—Not only do Apollodorus's auditors want to hear speeches on Love, but these speeches were part of a playful contest between Socrates, Agathon, and the other speakers at the symposium. The contest of speeches dramatizes the contest between philosophy and its rivals, or between philosophic love and other kinds of love.

4. *The Contest (and Mock Trial) Between Agathon and Socrates (Poetry vs. Philosophy)*[32]—This theme is introduced by Agathon's statement (at 175e–176a) that he and Socrates would have to "go to law" concerning wisdom and that Dionysos would judge between them. This comment is clearly meant to reinforce the suggestion of rivalry between Agathon and Socrates and their competing notions of wisdom in particular. Of all Socrates' rivals at this banquet, Agathon has a special role.

5. *The Sacrilege of 415 BCE*—There is a clear allusion implicit in the drama itself to the profanation of the mysteries and the possible desecration of the Herms that occurred in 415 BCE.[33] Strauss thinks that Plato's *Symposium* depicts the Platonic version of the truth of these events.[34] The use of the language of mysteries in the teaching of Diotima related in Socrates' speech, and the use of satyr imagery in Alcibiades' speech are also suggestive of these events. It must also be borne in mind that the profanation of the mysteries was a sacrilege in which Socrates' friends were implicated; thus, these events link to the later charges against Socrates—impiety and corrupting the youth.

6. *Dramatization of the Love of Socrates*—The six speeches on love are surrounded by dramatization of love; for love is exemplified in the narrative frame by Apollodorus's and Aristodemus's love of Socrates and in the final speech by the Alcibiades' love of Socrates.

7. *Philosophy and the Corruption of Political Life (Socrates and Alcibiades)*—The drunken entrance of Alcibiades, who makes the others drink and makes everyone but Socrates drunk, in addition to the roles it plays in relation to other themes, raises yet another theme. This theme is the relation of philosophy to the corruption of politics, or the relation of philosophic *Erôs* to the "drunken" kind of *Erôs*

that rules in political life. At the same time, Alcibiades' drunken
entrance has other roles in relation to two of the themes above. He
is the representative of Dionysus who will judge between Agathon
and Socrates regarding wisdom.[35] He also profanes the mysteries of Diotima's teaching and desecrates the herm-like Socrates.[36]
Special attention must be given to the question of why Alcibiades
is made to play all of these roles at once. There is an inner connection between Alcibiades as representative of Athenian decadence,
as Dionysian judge, and as the perpetrator of sacrilege.

8. *Socrates' Irony and Socrates' Hubris*—Alcibiades also turns his
speech into a mock prosecution of Socrates. He puts Socrates on
trial for hubris. The "trial" between Agathon and Socrates was
also set in motion by a charge of hubris levied against Socrates
by Agathon (175e). Now, in addition to this trial, Alcibiades
"goes to law" with Socrates over Socrates' hubris. Ironically,
Alcibiades' judging in favor of Socrates in the dispute between
Socrates and Agathon over wisdom takes the form of Alcibiades'
accusing Socrates of hubris. There is a deep connection between
Socrates' wisdom and his hubris. The implicit backdrop of these
two fictional trials in the *Symposium* is the trial on charges of
impiety and corrupting the youth that Plato's audience would
have known that Socrates faced. Therefore, the *Symposium* could
be said to involve the interrelation of three trials: the trial over
Socrates' wisdom, the trial on the charge of hubris brought by
Alcibiades, and the foreshadowing of the actual trial Socrates
faced on charges of corrupting the youth and impiety.[37] We noted
already that Socrates' real trial was brought on in part by the kind
of claims about the *daimonic* realm that occur in Socrates' speech
(and elsewhere in the dialogues). There is also a deep connection between Socrates' wisdom, his hubris and his alleged crimes
against the city. Although the *Symposium* is set before the trial
of Socrates, it was composed after Socrates' conviction; thus, the
execution and the fate of Socrates would loom large in the background for Plato's original audience.

9. *Comedy and Tragedy*—All of these themes must somehow relate
to the cryptic suggestion toward the close of the dialogue that the
same poet should be capable of composing both comedy and tragedy (223d).

Finally, all of the above themes must relate to what we take
to be the dialogue's central theme:

10. *Socrates as the Embodiment of Erôs and the Erotic Character of Philosophy*—The dialogue presents six speeches on love, which are
then followed by the unexpected seventh speech about Socrates.

We have noted that, in the last speech, Socrates comes to instantiate the topic of the earlier speeches, *Erôs*. This substitution works
together with other indications to suggest that Socrates is the
embodiment of *Erôs*, the consummate erotic.[38] But Socrates is also
the paradigmatic philosopher, and much of what suggests that he
is the embodiment of *Erôs* lies in what is indicated in the dialogue
regarding the philosophical dimension of *Erôs* and the erotic character of philosophy itself. *Erôs* is said to be a *daimon*, a spirit that
functions as a messenger between the mortal and divine realms,
lying between wisdom and ignorance, possessed simultaneously of
resource and need. But this spirit is depicted as a philosopher, and
philosophy itself is shown to be a form of *Erôs*, participating fully
in its *daimonic* character.

## THE PRAISE OF PHILOSOPHY

The young Plato perceived the horrors and absurdities of political life in
Athens. Socrates' trial and execution by the city was probably only the most
powerful in a series of tragic events, in Plato's view, by which his city suffered partly through its own actions. Plato had seen his city fight and lose a
protracted war for supremacy and empire over the rest of the Greeks; he had
seen his own relatives, at the end of the war (and with Sparta's backing), insti-
tute a disastrous reign of terror aimed at transforming Athens into an oligarchy. At the age of twenty-seven or twenty-eight, he had seen his dear friend,
Socrates, who had impressed him deeply by resisting these same relatives at
great personal risk, tried and executed by his fellow-citizens under the restored
democracy. It is likely that we have Plato's own account of these events and the
conclusions he drew from them in the *Seventh Letter* (324b–326b).

Thus, Plato knew the drawbacks of Athenian oligarchy and democracy
because he had experienced them both firsthand; he understood the characteristic way in which each of these forms of government might become
irresponsible rule. He appears to have been critical of Athenian imperialism
because it implied a misdirected sense of honor and an overweening love of
gain, a greed that bloated the city and turned it from caring about virtue to
the pursuit of material wealth (see for example, *Grg.* 518e–519a and context).
He admired Spartan discipline, but seems to have believed that it aimed too
low, at martial courage, and not at the virtue of philosophical wisdom (see
*Laws* 630d-e, 666e–667a, and the discussion of timocracy in *Republic*, Bk.
VIII). Should not wisdom have a natural right to govern? Should not the
institutions of a political community be aimed at fostering wisdom and uti-
lizing it for the city's well-being?

But if he believed that philosophy was capable of fostering a kind of wisdom, he also knew that a major obstacle to the acceptance of philosophy's value
was the existence of prevalent misconceptions about it. It was the Sophists,

itinerant teachers of rhetoric who claimed to be teachers of virtue, who were responsible for some of these misunderstandings. It is too easy to forget that in Plato's time none of the disciplinary categories used today were in common currency; there were as yet no institutions of higher learning, indeed, no public system of education at all in Athens. Private education consisted in training in the poets, reading, writing, gymnastics, lyre playing, horsemanship, and the arts of war. Studies that we would today call "scientific" such as mathematics and astronomy were undertaken by scattered individuals who might have been collectively referred to by any of several names, including sophists (*sophistai*) and philosophers (*philosophoi*), terms that would have for the most part been used interchangeably. The rhetorician Isocrates, contemporary with Plato, referred to his own discipline as "philosophy" and directly challenged Plato's conception of philosophy.[39] Words such as "philosophy" and "sophistry" were yet to have the fixed meaning that they have today. It was Plato who first formulated the distinction between the conventional rhetoric of the sophists, on the one hand, and, on the other hand, "philosophy," something Plato considered worthy of the "true rhetorician" (*Phdr.* 271b-c) or a "sophist of noble descent" (*Soph.* 231b).

It would be easy for those in Plato's day to confuse philosophy as Plato envisioned it not only with sophistry, but also with the earlier inquiries into nature that had been made by those we now call the Presocratic philosophers. (It is worth remembering that most of these thinkers would no more have regarded themselves as "philosophers" than they would have thought of themselves as "Pre-Socratic"). In his dialogues, Plato had to warn against the dangerous tendencies within these naturalistic inquiries and within sophistry.[40] But he also knew that even the questions raised by his own conception of "true philosophy," formulated by reflecting on the distinctive practice of Socrates, could be threatening to the beliefs of the city. For Socrates' dialectical activities could seem to call into question popular superstitions and the naïve belief in the city's gods.[41] Socrates' appeal to his *daimonion* and his criticisms of the poet's tales about the gods seemed to suggest to many an unconventional view of the divine and, thereby, to offend against the traditional gods and against the traditions and beliefs of the community. Plato was not deterred by Socrates' fate from questioning traditional piety in these and other ways with his own portrayal of Socrates in his dialogues. But the Platonic Socrates' potential danger to the community is something of which both he, the Platonic character, and Plato, the author, seem to have been cognizant (compare *Rep.* 537d–539d and *Ap.* 23c-d). Plato's problem is in part to defend his conception of philosophy from alternatives and from rival conceptions of wisdom offered by the sophists and the poets. At the same time, his problem is to promote philosophy as an alternative form of piety or a means of reforming traditional piety, even while shielding philosophy from the charge that it is impious or dangerously subversive. Yet to say that he wanted to shield philosophy from the charge

that it is dangerously subversive is not to say that he did not regard philosophy as both subversive of conventional opinion and as potentially dangerous
(in the wrong hands) for that reason. He knew the dangers were there and
made no attempt to hide them; yet apparently he believed that the benefits
to be gained from philosophy outweighed the risks.

Given Plato's objectives, as adumbrated above, we should expect Socrates
to be distinguished in the *Symposium* from the other participants, because the
other characters are his rivals in more than just composing praises of *Erôs*.
These speeches are part of a contest (*agōn*) to see who can give the finest
praise of *Erôs*.[42] But the very meaning of such praise is also at stake. What
does it mean to give an excellent speech in praise of *Erôs*?

Although in classical Athens the gift for oratory alone would have
been regarded by many as sufficient proof of political wisdom, the contest
depicted in the *Symposium* is more than just a competition to see who is the
best speaker. For it matters that the speeches in question are not just on any
topic but speeches in praise of *Erôs*. So, not only is skill as a speaker being
tested; the speaker's understanding of love, or of human desire generally, is
also being tested, it being understood that human longing is easily one of the
most significant features of human experience. So each speaker's understanding of life, his practical savvy, and perhaps even his virility is on the line. To
be able to praise *Erôs* well one must necessarily draw on one's own experience
of loving, desiring, and striving.

In terms of the standards governing classical rhetoric it would be enough
if the speech displayed mastery of the beauties of language coupled with
persuasive power. But Socrates, in the remarks that preface his own speech
(201d), would seem to want the others to agree to accept a different set of
standards for judging speeches. Yet it is ironic that Socrates' speech seems
superior not only according to his own philosophic standards, but also, in
many ways, in terms of the twin standards of rhetoric: beauty and power.
Socrates' speech reveals the nature of philosophy and through the superiority
of his speech he demonstrates the superiority of philosophy in life and in the
political wisdom that should guide life. Therefore, the dramatic structure of
the part of the dialogue that contains the six speeches on *Erôs* corresponds to
the process of coming to see the value of philosophy, its distinction from, and
superiority to, its rivals. But then, just after Socrates has presented this magnificent description of the Beautiful itself, the jarring entrance of the inebriated Alcibiades brings the conversation back to earth, reminding us of the
irrational forms of *Erôs* that in fact rule in the political realm.

## SOCRATIC IGNORANCE AND PLATONIC FORMS

On the surface there seem to be two different conceptions of philosophy
in Plato's texts: a dogmatic view and a skeptical view. The dogmatic view
presents philosophy as the knowledge of causes and "Forms" or *Eidē* (that is,

the knowledge said to be possessed by the philosopher-kings of the *Republic*). The skeptical view presents philosophy as the examined life, a Socratic quest that involves a developing awareness of one's own *ignorance*. According to the latter conception, it would seem that philosophy does not issue in knowledge of the Forms, but only in Socrates' "human wisdom," that is, in that awareness of one's own ignorance that has been called "Socratic Ignorance" and is defined as knowing that one doesn't know. This latter conception is associated with Socrates' account of his practice in the *Apology* and is also found ascribed to philosophy as such in Diotima's teaching as recounted by Socrates in the *Symposium*.

According to a developmentalist reading of Plato, these two conceptions of philosophy belong to different periods of Plato's philosophical development. From this point of view, philosophy as the comprehension of Forms is Plato's later conception of philosophy, one that provides a way out of the skepticism of the Socratic position. We are highly dubious about this developmentalist account and in this commentary offer an alternative. In our view, the appearance of a contradiction between the two aforementioned conceptions of philosophy is the result of dubious assumptions regarding the relation between these two themes in Plato's work, the Forms and Socratic Ignorance.

Some accounts of philosophy in the dialogues clearly make philosophy inseparable from the project of coming to know eternal, unchanging realities or coming to possess comprehensive understanding. Given this fact it seems quite odd then that the dialogues never seem to proceed by explicitly *proving* the existence of a relevant Form, explaining what that Form is, and then deducing the relevant consequences from it. Rather, as has often been noted, the theme of the Forms is invariably introduced as a contribution to other discussions, and the specific Forms of the topic under discussion are never *explicitly* articulated. It might be thought that the attempted definitions offered in the dialogues are meant to be verbal formulae expressing the nature of the relevant Forms, but these definitions are either depicted as failing or are at best said to be merely approximate or incomplete.[43] This dichotomy between the view of philosophy as knowing Forms and the philosophizing embodied in the dialogues has partly inspired the work of the Tübingen school, which sees the true content of Plato's philosophy as lying largely in unwritten doctrines.[44] It has also led recent scholars to emphasize the problem of reconciling the form and content of Plato's dialogues.[45]

The history of Plato interpretation can be read as a struggle between dogmatic and skeptical interpretations of Plato.[46] While the most prominent interpretations of Plato have always been those that ascribed doctrines to him, even in the ancient world there were discussions of whether Plato was a skeptic.[47] Since at least Cicero there have been some (in a minority) who think that Plato just presents a variety of different views without taking sides and that Plato has no fixed opinions. Perhaps Plato thinks we cannot have knowledge, and so just encourages the quest for wisdom, without really thinking that we ever achieve it. The difficulty here is to explain what he thinks is gained by philosophy if this is so.

In the secondary literature of our own time, it has become customary to contrast "doctrinalist" with "non-doctrinalist" approaches to the interpretation of Plato. The "doctrinalist" approach takes Plato to be using his dialogues primarily to explain and defend his own views. By contrast, the "non-doctrinalist" approaches are those that either hold that Plato's views are not to be found in his dialogues, or at least that the appearance of such views in the dialogues is secondary to Plato's main purposes in writing them. In exploring a *tertium quid* for reading Plato, it is important to note that the apparently "dogmatic" side of Plato has so far received greater attention than his more skeptical, Socratic dimension.[48]

Many kinds of doctrines have been sought in the dialogues for many reasons. The theme of Forms itself has been viewed as a presentation of Plato's theory. When treated as a theory the presentations of this theme have often been viewed in abstraction from their dramatic context, despite some scholarly complaints.[49] Those who have been inclined to be interested in Plato's so-called "metaphysical theory" have been encouraged by the very conception of philosophy they find in the dialogues to seek Plato's claims to knowledge. Surely, they reason, a thinker who claimed to know eternal truths regarding the essences of things must strive to express these truths in his work. Of course, this argument is utterly circular, for they bolster their interpretation by an illicit appeal to one of the points at issue—just what it is that Plato the author claimed to know. In abstracting the discussions of Forms from their dramatic contexts and in seeking to identify particular assertions of characters with Plato's views, commentators have often paid insufficient attention to the ongoing theme of Socratic Ignorance and the kinds of qualifications it forces upon the philosophical argumentation in the texts.

Yet it seems just as circular, on the face of it, to presume that Socrates speaks for Plato when he professes his ignorance as it is that he speaks for Plato when he discusses Forms. In the case of Forms, one can appeal to the testimony of Aristotle to try to determine Plato's views, and there is evidence that the profession of ignorance was made by the historical Socrates and need not be ascribed to Plato himself. But the fact is that both the theme of Socratic Ignorance and the hypothesis of Forms are prominent in the dialogues, and Plato did precious little to prioritize one over the other. In fact, in the *Symposium* and elsewhere these themes are strangely juxtaposed.

The emphasis on the Forms in certain of Plato's dialogues seems in tension with the choice of Socrates as protagonist and with the importance of the theme of Socratic Ignorance. However, Socratic Ignorance does not disappear from Plato's later dialogues, and this fact is a major problem for the developmentalist account that holds that this theme is a reflection of an early

Plato's dedication to the faithful memory of Socrates. To take one example, the Socrates of the *Republic*, the same Socrates who defends the possibility of knowledgeable philosopher-kings, still professes his own ignorance of such knowledge.[50] The emphasis on the knowledge of the Forms conflicts even more with the explicit claim made in the *Symposium* that philosophy is the love and not the possession of wisdom, and the consequent attribution to philosophy itself (not merely Socrates) of a position between wisdom and ignorance.[51] According to the account of the philosopher provided by Diotima's teaching in the *Symposium*, philosophers *as such* are essentially lovers and not possessors of wisdom. Yet a "vision" of a Form, albeit a rather generic one, figures prominently at the end of the account. This whole account is put in the mouth of a Socrates who still professes ignorance (175e). In both the *Republic* and the *Symposium* then, Socratic Ignorance and a vision of the Forms appear side by side. It should not be overlooked that the theme of Socratic Ignorance receives much more significant treatment in Plato than in Xenophon, the only other Socratic whose complete works are extant. If more of the Socratic writings remained one could better evaluate the extent of Plato's innovations with respect to this theme, but there is no doubt that it is Plato who makes Socratic Ignorance philosophically significant.[52] Those later philosophers who were enamored of this theme all looked back to the Socrates of the *Apology* and other Platonic dialogues.

The developmentalist doctrinalist explanation of the relationship between Socratic Ignorance and the knowledge of the Forms amounts to treating Socratic Ignorance as a theme relevant to Plato's depiction of the historical Socrates or the remnant of Socratic influence upon the young Plato. According to this view, the emphasis upon the knowledge of the Forms comes from the mature Plato and expresses Plato's later epistemological views. From this perspective it may be no more than a contingent fact of history that Plato happened to choose Socrates to be his putative "mouthpiece," thus needlessly confusing issues against his own intentions. Indeed, the doctrinalists can argue that there is no need for confusion about the relationship between the ignorance of Socrates and the potential knowledge of the Forms. Plato has made the relationship between these ideas quite clear in dialogues such as the *Meno*. For there the state of *aporia* in which one becomes aware of one's own ignorance, a state explicitly likened to Socrates' ignorance, is treated as a necessary preliminary to the more advanced stage of philosophical development in which one grasps the knowledge one has initially sought. Led by Socrates through the study of a geometrical problem, the slave-boy passes through an initial phase of perplexity or confusion (*aporia*) and is later brought to the solution.

But bringing in this example to support this explanation overlooks a crucial fact: the "answer" at which the slave-boy and Socrates arrive is only an *approximation*. Socrates has in effect asked the slave-boy to express the square root of eight, an irrational number that can only be approximated.[53]

Emphasizing the approximate or indefinite nature of the knowledge gained in the *Meno*, to say nothing of the learning paradox itself, points us in the direction of those interpretations of Plato that emphasize the importance of nonpropositional knowledge. In light of the idea of nonpropositional knowledge, one can interpret the relationship between Socratic Ignorance and the Notion of Forms in a different manner than the developmentalists. The knowledge of Forms is essentially nonpropositional, and thus necessarily *silent*, as some scholars have suggested.[54] In other words, no propositional expression of the truth will ever be fully adequate to it. Therefore, Socrates' "knowing ignorance" consists in his awareness of his own inability, and that of others, to capture *in words* a truth that may or may not be accessible to humans at a given time in a nonpropositional noetic vision. In line with this view, Socrates could be ignorant with his self-aware ignorance *precisely because he is in touch with Forms* while yet being aware of the inability of the human mind to express the Forms directly in language.

It may be the case, as has been argued effectively by Francisco Gonzalez, that the truths Socrates seeks are expressed indirectly through his very inquiry into their nature, through precisely the failed attempts to express the Forms directly. It is as though the process of trying to attain the ideal and failing helps one understand the mysterious something at which one was aiming.[55] It is arguable that every ideal functions this way; that is, every directly encountered reality to be measured always necessarily falls short of the ideal, whether the ideal in question is the perfection of an exact measurement or the perfection of an ethical standard. To borrow the language of modern mathematics, one approaches the ideal as an asymptote approaches a limit. Plato may have been the first philosopher to note the general character presented by the ideal in our experience—it is experienced as a glimpse of that which eludes our grasp. Dialectic, according to Plato's presentation of it, seems to be set in motion as a progressive approximation to something that eludes final comprehension. It is the human significance of this dialectic that the Platonic dialogue expresses in the form of a unique kind of drama. The dialogues embody a dialectic that provides the tools to reflect on and understand the general character of the ideal that lies at its root. Were it possible for the philosopher to easily and securely grasp a Form and to express its perfection directly in language, it would seem that the dialogic and cryptic character of the dialogues would conflict with Plato's rationalist conception of philosophy; but if the Forms remain elusive, even as dialectic enables the philosopher partially and imperfectly to recollect them, then the dramatic and elusive character of the dialogues make an essential contribution. For as Gonzalez suggests, one understands the Forms when one sees how various attempts at comprehension continually fall short in various ways. The Socratic awareness of ignorance is not contrary to, but inseparable from, a deeper noetic apprehension of the Forms; such an apprehension is a partial recollection of a Form, but for the most part this awareness expresses itself negatively as a greater ability to understand how various attempts to describe the Form fail.

## THE INTERMEDIATE: PHILOSOPHY IN-BETWEEN IGNORANCE AND WISDOM

Although we believe that the idea of nonpropositional knowledge is an important key to a correct conception of the relationship between the Forms and Socratic Ignorance, in this interpretation of the *Symposium* we will focus instead on a related yet neglected aspect of Plato's metaphysics: the notion of "intermediacy." We believe that an examination of this notion, brought together with recent work of other scholars on nonpropositional knowledge in Plato, will help to flesh out the proper understanding of the relation between the Forms and Socratic Ignorance in Plato's dialogues.

In our view, this apparent dichotomy between the view of philosophy as knowing Forms and the embodiment of philosophy in the dialogues is based in part on a misunderstanding of the role of the idea of Forms in the dialogues. The Forms are never presented as dogmatically secure possessions, but rather as glimmering desiderata, the objects of a quest, objects that can inspire us, but which continually elude us in some way. Yet even in order to so elude us, they must also somehow be present to us, open to examination and inquiry. We see Forms, yet we never see them clearly or completely. A comparison of the various dramatic contexts in which talk of Forms appear would show that, in every case, *both our contact with Forms, and our remove from them, is equally emphasized.* Yet contrary to some interpreters, we hold that it is too simple to say that the dialogues never reveal a single Form. The dialogues *do* express Forms—not through specific definitions but through the drama of the dialogues if they are considered as dramatic wholes. One *can* come to see the Form of Justice by reading the *Republic* and one *can* come to see the Form of *Erôs* by reading the *Symposium*. But true to the in-between character of human *Erôs* and philosophy, the glimpse one has of these Forms is always just a glimpse, a partial, elusive noetic insight incapable of faultless and precise formulation in language.

In this commentary, we draw attention to the importance of the notion of "the intermediate" (*to metaxu*) in the *Symposium* and other dialogues. In addition to the intermediacy of *Erôs*, several types of intermediacy will be distinguished, such as the intermediacy of correct opinion, of Recollection, and lastly of philosophy itself.[56] In addition to distinguishing these types of intermediacy, we attempt to show the connections between them. We shall endeavor to show that Plato's use of the notion of "Forms" is misunderstood if it is seen outside the context of such intermediacy. Reflecting on the notion of intermediacy will serve to illuminate the simultaneous connection and tension in Plato's dialogues between their "Socratic Ignorance" and "Platonic Forms."

Recently, some Plato scholars have begun speaking of a *"third way"* of reading Plato, a way that lies between regarding him as a dogmatist and regarding him as a skeptic. According to this approach, Plato may have had views, but imparting his own views is not what he is trying to do in the dialogues. In the dialogues he is *primarily* trying to stimulate philosophical thinking and to turn promising pupils toward philosophy. Plato's intention seems to be to communicate a mode of thinking and examining more than it is to impart a particular philosophical view. To say that this view is generally true does not rule out the possibility that some of Plato's own views and prejudices might still influence his work. A truly "Third Way" reading must not only avoid treating the dialogues as though they were treatises, but should also avoid a merely "skeptical" reading that deprives Plato of any content. Such readings find the "philosophy" of the dialogues in the interrelation between argument and drama.

An effort to find a "third way" of reading Plato that navigates between skepticism and dogmatism, a way that does justice to both the philosophical content and the literary and dramatic features of the dialogues, can also be seen as an effort to hold together the Socratic and Platonic elements in Plato's texts. Such readings seek the unity behind two seemingly opposing conceptions of philosophical wisdom: Socrates' "human wisdom" as the awareness of one's ignorance, on the one hand, and on the other, the knowledge of the eternal realities one might suppose a god to have. Perhaps the notion of *Erôs* as a being in-between, a kind of messenger or go-between, suggests just such a third way, neither stubbornly dogmatic nor ridiculously skeptical. The present interpretation of the *Symposium* will endeavor to show how the tension between dogmatism and skepticism remains in play throughout the philosophical account at the heart of this dialogue. Indeed, Plato builds this "in-between" position into the conceptions of philosophy and the philosopher presented in Socrates' speech.

In fact, Pierre Hadot has recently argued that the *Symposium* provides a distinctively "Platonic" notion of *philosophia*, used to describe the love of wisdom" or the "care for wisdom" and not the possession of it.[57] Hence, Plato's Socrates disavows knowledge—though he remains ever on its trail or "in its draft." In the *Apology*, his role in the city is characterized by him as being in part protreptic—exhorting people to care about wisdom—and in part corrective or remedial—showing others that they are not as wise as they think they are. By contrast with the conceit of wisdom Socrates finds all around him, the philosopher grudgingly admits to possessing only a small, "human" wisdom, which turns out to consist in being ever mindful that he is not wise (*Ap.* 20d, 20e, 21b9, 21d3, 23a-b). In the *Symposium* the characterization of *Erôs* that emerges in Socrates' speech is analogous to the position occupied by philosophy per se and by the paradigmatic philosopher, Socrates, himself. Born of mixed parentage, the hybrid nature of *Erôs* can be expressed philosophically as a kind of being in-between (*metaxu*). The philosopher is desirous of the wisdom she lacks, but at the same time supplied with the resources to pursue it. The position of *Erôs* and the position of the philosopher that Diotima describes are so perfectly analogous that Socrates comes to stand in for *Erôs* when Alcibiades is made to praise Socrates rather than the God of Love. Plato wishes to show through the progression of *Symposium*'s speeches that the truest erotic is a philosopher, and not just any kind of philosopher, but a philosopher like Socrates; so, to underscore this point for his audience, he has Socrates replace *Erôs* in the dramatic *ergon* of the dialogue. Here as elsewhere, Plato conjoins the "negative" experience of recognizing one's ignorance with the "positive" experience of coming to desire the wisdom one lacks. The philosopher, who knows he is ignorant of the most important things, is *well aware* of that ignorance, so that this in-between position of the philosopher might be spoken of as a positive kind of ignorance or as a minimalist sort of knowledge. For *Erôs* in the form of the philosopher's longing for wisdom is a messenger from the divine imparting something of the object of desire through the very desire for it.

This in-between position is elaborated in Diotima's analysis of *Erôs*, which will show that this in-between position describes the structure of human desire. The way in which *Erôs* in general is "in-between" will have to be distinguished, however, from the way in which philosophical *Erôs* is "in-between." For although *Erôs* is described as a philosopher, philosophical *Erôs* is clearly distinguished from other forms of *Erôs* that Diotima discusses. The meaning of this riddle will be explored in our commentary. We hope to explain both how philosophy is erotic and how *Erôs* (in general) is a "philosopher."

Plato's vision of philosophy as love is unique in the history of philosophy. In the *Symposium*, he goes beyond the etymology of the word *philosophy* to suggest that philosophy is not merely a *philia* (friend or friendship) of wisdom, but nothing less than an *Erôs*, an insatiable hunger for a wisdom *that is never finally possessed*. The present commentary is devoted to an elucidation of the meaning and implications of this vision.

CHAPTER 1

# Introductory Dialogue (172a–178a)

## *Functions of Narrative Frames in Platonic Dialogues*

Most of Plato's dialogues are written in direct discourse like dramatic poetry. But some of Plato's dialogues have a narrator who relays the main events of the dialogue.[1] Since the *Symposium* is a narrated dialogue, some account should be taken of the various functions performed by narrative frames in general and by that of the *Symposium* in particular.

Narrative frames allow the author to introduce information about the events in the dialogue that would be impossible, inappropriate, or inconvenient to have characters state aloud in the course of their conversation. The way a dialogue is framed thus provides important information that qualifies in some way the meaning of reported statements and narrated events. Frames can be used to introduce organizing themes that can serve as lenses through which to view the main action of the dialogue. Frames can also be used to create a temporal distance between the audience of the dialogue and the depicted events, shrouding the narrated events in mystery by not allowing the audience to have direct access to them. If the narrated events are set in the past or in another place from the action of the frame itself (e.g., *Phaedo*), the author makes the frame comment on the larger significance of the narrated events by means of the connection between two distinct settings and casts of characters. The frame thus affords Plato one of the devices by which he is able to make one part of his dialogue comment on another.[2] All of these functions are performed by the narrative frame of the *Symposium*.

The narrative "frame" at the beginning of the *Symposium* runs to 174a. It has the effect of "framing" the dramatic action of the party at Agathon's house with a retelling, into which the body of the dialogue is embedded. In the frame, the narrator Apollodorus is approached by unnamed companions who are interested in hearing what was said at Agathon's party. He relates to them that he had only two days ago rehearsed the story for someone named Glaucon, who had also been asking about the same event. Glaucon had heard a garbled version of the story from someone who had heard it from Phoenix, and came to hear a better version from Apollodorus, who Glaucon supposed might have actually been present at the party. Apollodorus corrected him about the timeline—the party had actually occurred many years previously "When we were still children"—and offered to tell him the story as recounted by someone who had been there, Aristodemus—the very man from whom Phoenix had heard the story (172a–173b). The *Symposium* is presented as Apollodorus's second recounting of what he heard from Aristodemus, this time in response to the inquiries of unnamed companions.[3] Thus, the *Symposium* mixes narration with drama, direct with indirect discourse, part of it being narrated and part of it enacted. The frame provides the layering effect through which the events of Agathon's party are presented. With the lens the frame provides, Plato prepares his audience to hear something important, something that could challenge them to change their lives; but the frame also has the effect of reminding his audience that they are at a remove from the real-life events. The layers in *Symposium*'s narration and the temporal gaps between these layers cause the audience to question what its relation to the information and its sources (our narrators) should be. The audience of the *Symposium* should bear in mind that anything Apollodorus says directly to his own audience (e.g., at 222c, where he comments upon the speech just delivered by Alcibiades) would not have been heard by any of the participants at Agathon's house. Such comments do not form a part of the drama of the party, and the drama of the frame is not sufficiently developed at later portions of the dialogue for these comments to possess a dramatic function at the level of the frame-dialogue. But such comments do have a function in relation to Plato's audience; they constitute one of the devices by which Plato is able to make a part of his work comment on another portion of his work. Whenever a Platonic dialogue provides a commentary on one of its own themes or passages, one should consider how the author is making use of this device.[4]

The above considerations raise the question of how the audience is supposed to feel about Apollodorus, since his point of view may be reflected in his narration. Apollodorus is the highly emotional man presented in the *Phaedo* as the most hysterical of Socrates' grieving friends who spend the final hours with him before Socrates is put to death. Some members of Plato's audience might be inclined to relate to Apollodorus as a zealous advocate of philosophy and a lover of Socrates. For them, he would seem to represent a fellow traveler and a kindred spirit. But the way Apollodorus's character is drawn—the self-confessed fanaticism, the proselytism that leads him to insult his audience, the cultic attachment to Socrates—all of this leads one to wonder if he is not the kind of disciple of whom the master is embarrassed. This impression is only reinforced by the way his character is discussed in the *Phaedo*, where his hysteria over the impending death of Socrates is looked upon with distaste by the narrator and where such reactions are remonstrated as "womanly" by Socrates (cf. *Phd.* 117d). Given the supposedly excessive emotionalism of Apollodorus in the *Phaedo*, and given the way he character- izes his enthusiasm for Socrates as a kind of mania at the outset of *Sympo- sium*, (173d7–8) one must ask what Plato has in mind by choosing him as the main narrator of his dialogue.[5]

In considering why Apollodorus is made the narrator, one has to recall that the theme of the *Symposium* is *Erôs*, or passionate desire. Love was char- acterized in the *Phaedrus* as a kind of "divine madness" that brings benefits from the gods to mortals. Is Apollodorus's mania "divine madness"? Apol- lodorus himself surely thinks so; if he did not, he would not be so proud of his insanity. But the fact that Apollodorus regards his madness as divine and even the likelihood that Plato would regard such madness as divine does not mean that the character of Apollodorus is drawn without satire. Socrates in the *Phaedrus* also regards great poets as divinely mad, but that hardly exempts them from his criticism there or elsewhere. Alcibiades testifies later in the *Symposium* to the madness that ensues when one has been "bitten by the snake" of philosophy; yet Alcibiades hardly rates as a character Plato intends his audience simply to admire. Even if Apollodorus's love of Socrates and manic enthusiasm for philosophy speak well for him, the example of Alcibi- ades shows that it takes more than these qualities to make a philosopher. Apollodorus may never have become as bad as Alcibiades, but like certain other of Socrates' friends he shows no sign of excelling as a philosopher and on the contrary shows signs of failing by Socratic standards. Apollodorus is surely meant to make Plato's audiences aware of how far his kind of enthusi- asm is from that about which it is enthusiastic.

To unpack the interpretive problems posed by this dialogue, one should perhaps first ask why these particular characters and this unusual setting were chosen for the exploration of its themes.[6] Plato, here, trusts the narrative to this devotee of Socrates who seems, from what he says in the opening pages of the dialogue, to have undergone an almost religious conversion through his encounter with the philosopher, Socrates (cf. *Phd.* 59a). He says that he rages (*mainomai*, a word that connotes madness) at 173e2, after confessing to hav- ing formerly lived a worthless life as one of those who believed that "philoso- phy was the last thing a man should do" (173a). But having spent three years (172e) in loyal devotion to Socrates, he is clearly dedicated to condemning the misdirected lives of his audience and to exhorting others to become better through the study of philosophy. Whether or not Apollodorus comprehends all, or any, of Socrates' philosophical positions, his zeal for moralizing makes him sound quite self-righteous. "Of course . . . I used to think that what I was doing was important, but in fact I was the most worthless man on earth—as bad as you are this very moment" (173a).[7]

Plato's audience learns that Apollodorus was not in attendance on the extraordinary occasion when Socrates debated the poets, the night when

Alcibiades delivered an unabashed speech about Socrates (172c). The fact that this Glaucon thought that Apollodorus was present that night is proof to Apollodorus that the version Glaucon had heard was badly garbled. Not being there himself, Apollodorus's source for the story of this legendary symposium was the very same source that communicated the story that Glaucon had heard in a garbled form from Phoenix: another follower of Socrates named Aristodemus, a character described as "a real runt of a man" (*smikros*, 173b2).[8] Aristodemus, who seems to imitate Socrates' dress, his habit of going barefoot, and his other strange mannerisms, is presented as a man who was an earlier version of Apollodorus, experiencing previously a case of the same affliction that caused Apollodorus to want to make it his business to know everything Socrates says and does, a concern to which he has now dedicated his life (173a). A little later, when he agrees to retell the story for his unnamed auditors (described as "rich businessmen"), on the way to town, Apollodorus says that his greatest pleasure comes from philosophical conversation (173c). The characterizations of Apollodorus and Aristodemus seem to suggest that cases of fanatic devotion to Socrates were quite typical. These are not very flattering portraits of Socrates' more "obsessed" followers. It could be that one of the functions of Plato's dramatizations is to define what should count as following Socrates in a worthy way and to distinguish it from the devotion of those who would erect a cult of personality around Socrates.

Yet in spite of such reservations about Apollodorus and Aristodemus, Plato presents them as those through whom the story of Socrates at Agathon's party comes down to later inquirers. Aristodemus and Apollodorus, although imperfect, are indispensable as the narrators who provide the only access to the event. Yet this fact creates a distance between the audience and that event. On the one hand, Plato's audience learns that Apollodorus has just had the opportunity to rehearse the whole tale a couple of days earlier. The dialogue opens with Apollodorus saying, "In fact, your question does not find me unprepared" (Δοκῶ μοι περὶ ὧν πυνθάνεσθε οὐκ ἀμελέτητος εἶναι 172a1–2), a point he reiterates a little later (173c1). So the story is fresh in his mind. But he also has flaws as a narrator, perhaps most notably the way he insults his audience at 173a and 173d, as Agathon will later insult his guest of honor (Socrates) in his speech (cf. 195a–196b). Apollodorus tells the businessmen that their affairs are trivial and boring, and calls them "the real failures." He claims to have checked part, but only part, of his account with Socrates, presumably a reliable source (173b). As for Aristodemus, Apollodorus's source for the story, he admits to forgetting some details of the speeches (cf. 178a, 180c) and to forgetting several speeches altogether (180c). He dozes off for part of the evening (223b–c). Yet he is the essential link to the evening's words and deeds for Plato's audience. Put simply, we would not have the story of this infamous drinking party without him. In short, Plato seems to have taken great care to balance the evidence for believing his narrators' accounts with good reasons for viewing them with a critical eye, flushed with skepticism. Their memory lapses and inattentiveness are counterbalanced by the fact that Apollodorus has been able to fill in gaps and to obtain confirmation from Socrates on certain key points, and by the fact that the account is fresh in his mind.

Two different people accost Apollodorus within a few days (sometime between 407 and 399, probably about 404 or 403)[9] desiring to hear the tale of a party that took place more than a decade in the past. This detail suggests, among other things, that Socrates is a notorious personality whose activities were followed closely by many people (and not just by students of philosophy). Plato had some reason to set the main body of the dialogue (the drinking party and the speeches within the frame) twelve to fourteen years before Apollodorus's account of these events and for having the account of these events reported from memory by not one, but two, fallible intermediaries. At a minimum, this setting serves to shroud these events and speeches more densely in uncertainty and mystery. This aura of mystery, in which everything that is revealed seems half-veiled as well, befits a dialogue devoted to *Erôs*. For according to Diotima, *Erôs* itself neither wholly possesses nor wholly lacks what it seeks, just as Plato's audience neither wholly lacks nor wholly possesses access to the events of the symposium. Plato's audience is initially inspired with curiosity for the account of the drinking party, and then offered, in answer to its desire, a cryptic oracle that seems to conceal as much as it reveals. The tale includes tantalizing details that hint at further undisclosed depths—details such as the example of Socrates' trance on the way to the party, or his parting, enigmatic challenge to the poets about tragedy and comedy. The cryptic quality of these details enhances the sense that the audiences' desire to know about Socrates is, like *Erôs* in Diotima's account, a hybrid of resource (*Poros*) and poverty (*Penia*). For that desire is stimulated both by what the dialogue says and by what it does not say, what it uncovers and what it withholds.[10]

The narrative complexity of the *Symposium* results in action and speeches on several levels, and these must be distinguished and kept in mind. We have noted that Apollodorus is narrating the story in about 404 to unnamed listeners. Plato's audiences are allowed, as it were, to "listen in" on this retelling of the tale that is framed by the narrator's "real-time" remarks and actions. But we now know that Apollodorus got the account from Aristodemus sometime between the dramatic date of the *Symposium* (about 416/15) and the date of this retelling. So when, for example, Phaedrus (or any one of the first five speakers) is giving his speech, we must remember that what is said is passed along from the speaker to Aristodemus to Apollodorus to Plato's audience. And the duration between the date of the original speeches and the date of the retelling to which we are privy is about twelve years. The temporal gap between the main body of the dialogue and the retelling of these speeches by Apollodorus is extended further by Socrates' recollections of Diotima's teachings when it is his turn to speak. Socrates will recall the lessons in matters of *Erôs* he claims to have received some twenty-four years earlier. So, when Socrates recalls the series of conversations he claims to have had with Diotima, the narrative structure reaches its greatest complexity. Apollodorus recounts (in 404) that Aristodemus said (some unspecified time earlier) that Socrates told the partygoers (c.416/15) what Diotima told him (c.440). But Plato is believed to have written the *Symposium* sometime in the 380s,[11] which adds yet another layer of temporal remove between the main events of the dialogue and Plato's original audience. The effect of these layers of mediation is to make the audience aware of their distance from the events and to highlight the aura of mystery that surrounds them.

When Aristodemus first encounters Socrates, the habitually barefoot follower finds the master freshly bathed and wearing sandals or slippers. It is notable that Socrates has shod his customarily bare feet and thus that it is Aristodemus who is made to appear more "Socratic" than Socrates on this occasion.[12] This dramatic detail indicates something about Socrates and about Socratic followers such as Aristodemus. First, it shows that Socrates is not so doctrinaire about the simplicity of his usual attire that he will not dress up for a special occasion. But secondly, the very fact that Socrates is adaptable in this way shows that followers such as Aristodemus are focusing on the inessential when emulating external matters such as Socrates' habit of walking unshod.

Socrates says that he is dressed up "in order to go beautiful to the beautiful" (ἵνα καλὸς παρὰ καλὸν ἴω 174a9). In other words, the philosopher explains his attire to Aristodemus by saying that he has to look his best, since he's going to dinner at the house of a good-looking man, the young poet Agathon.[13]

He invites his companion to join him, even though Socrates says he knows that Aristodemus was not invited (174a-b). This exchange occasions a pun on Agathon's name. Socrates rephrases a proverb, which holds that "Good men go uninvited to an inferior man's feast," twisting it to reassure Aristodemus that "Good men go uninvited to a Goodman's feast." Socrates claims that Homer not only corrupted the adage but also insulted or committed an outrage against it (*hubrisai*). Homer did this by making an inferior man, Menelaus, go uninvited to the feast of a superior man, Agamemnon.

Thus, Socrates goes from claiming that he wanted "to go beautiful to the beautiful" to his paraphrase of Homer according to which "good men go uninvited" to the good. It seems that Socrates is replacing the beautiful with the good, or treating the two terms as interchangeable or at least closely related.[14] This dramatic detail foreshadows the way that Diotima's teaching will replace the phrase "beautiful things" with "good things."

But another question is raised by Socrates' remark. One wonders *why* Socrates wanted "to go beautiful to the beautiful." This remark raises the possibility that Socrates is courting Agathon. Plato's dialogue on love might indicate something about Socratic courtship. Certainly, the possibility of a love triangle between Socrates, Agathon, and Alcibiades becomes a subplot later in the dialogue and the intricacy and possible significance of their relationships will have to be examined in the appropriate place.

Socrates' transformation of the Homeric saying also makes the audience wonder who is supposed to be regarded as better and more virtuous among Socrates, Aristodemus, and Agathon. Indeed, Aristodemus modestly claims that he himself is inferior to Agathon and that Homer's version of the saying is more appropriate to his situation than is Socrates' revision. Aristodemus thereby displays that he is overawed by Agathon's fame, or by admiration for his beauty and talent; by contrast, Socrates is not, even though Socrates has uncharacteristically dressed up for the occasion. Later, when Socrates will contrast his own "trivial," dreamlike wisdom with that which Agathon displayed before thirty thousand Greeks, it is quite clear even to Agathon that Socrates is demeaning the poet's wisdom (175e8).[15] All of these dramatic elements raise questions about Socrates' attitude toward the poets, specifically about philosophy's value in comparison with poetry, and thus it is appropriate that Agathon will later suggest that he and Socrates will go to court (*diadikasometha*) regarding wisdom (175e8). All of this dramatic detail serves to prepare Plato's audience to think about the relation between philosophy and poetry, and to think about Socrates the philosopher in his social relations to other intelligent but nonphilosophical men. Aristodemus is afraid that he will appear the inferior in the company of men of letters, and he says that Socrates better think of a good excuse for bringing him. Socrates says, echoing Homer, "we'll think about what to say 'as we proceed the two of us along the way'" (174d). (The more accurate rendering of what Socrates misquotes here is given at *Protagoras* 348d: "When two go together, one has an idea before the other.")[16] But Socrates' preoccupation with some idea causes him to lag behind and become lost in thought, and so he instructs Aristodemus to go on ahead. As a result, Aristodemus is forced to arrive first at the party to which he had not been invited. Thus far the two possibilities mentioned in the text are: that good men go uninvited to a good man's feast, or that an inferior man might come uninvited to a good man's feast (as in Socrates' complaint about Homer's depiction of Menelaus and Agamemnon). There are two further possibilities not previously considered: that a good man might be coming uninvited to an inferior man's feast, or that an inferior man might be coming uninvited to another inferior man's feast. The effect is to invite us to consider these four possibilities: either Agathon or Aristodemus are both good, or both are inferior, or Agathon is good and Aristodemus is inferior, or Aristodemus is good and Agathon is inferior—and it is left to Plato's audience to decide. The question is interesting in that Agathon is a celebrated poet and Aristodemus is a devoted follower of Socrates. Whatever the limitations of Aristodemus with respect to virtue, one wonders whether or not his love of Socrates might give him some claim to superiority over the poet. Hence, the effect of the detail is to raise again an issue foregrounded in the frame—the relative value of the life devoted to philosophy, and the extent to which Socrates promoted a genuine interest in philosophy among his most devoted followers.

When Aristodemus arrives without Socrates, Agathon makes Aristodemus feel welcome, only then to wonder aloud immediately as to the whereabouts of Socrates. Agathon orders a servant to go and fetch the philosopher, but Aristodemus indicates that wandering off alone to think is one of Socrates' habits and that he should not be disturbed (175b). Plato's audience is told that Agathon wanted to send for Socrates many times, but Aristodemus assured him that he would come when he was ready. The philosopher finally came in when the guests were scarcely halfway through the meal (175c).

What is the significance of this episode? Why are we shown Socrates losing himself in thought and being late to the party? Is there a connection between this curious trance and the acts of purification that are betokened by Socrates' bathing before and after the party? One thing that is accomplished by Plato's having Aristodemus arrive before Socrates is that we can learn, via Aristodemus's conversations with Agathon, that such behavior is typical for Socrates.[17] This curious absorption is said to be one of Socrates' habits; it is characteristic of his pursuit of philosophy. The philosopher loses himself in thought and as a result is late for dinner. Not only is he late for dinner, which might be thought to be impolite, but it is perhaps also rude that he lets Aristodemus, who had been invited by Socrates, arrive at the party without him. This behavior makes clear that Socrates' philosophical concerns can cause him to forget about social proprieties or perhaps afford him a sublime indifference to physical concerns such as the need for a meal. (Recall that Socrates is promised a meal and a night of carousing at the beginning of the *Republic*, but the feast turns out to be entirely a feast of words.) In terms of the tripartite psychology of the *Republic* one could say that this detail shows that the wisdom-loving part of Socrates' mind is more powerful than either the honor-loving part or the appetitive part. Furthermore, this whole incident foreshadows the report of a similar incident that Alcibiades will relate later in the dialogue, and this provides Plato's audience with a source for this information independent of Alcibiades' later account. In addition, the whole event further shrouds Socrates in mystery; we wonder what he is thinking, and we are never told. Finally, the event serves to set up an interesting exchange between Socrates and Agathon when the philosopher finally does arrive. Then Agathon's remarks to him indicate that Agathon too wonders what Socrates was thinking, but he receives only a cryptic response from Socrates. Agathon will speak of Socrates' "wisdom," a wisdom that Socrates disclaims, but which Agathon's imagination cannot help conjuring up: Socrates' willingness to separate himself from others by losing himself in thought sets him apart in their eyes. One of the themes of the *Symposium* is that Socrates' peculiarities so distinguish him from others that others begin to regard these distinctions as insulting. Thus, both Agathon and Alcibiades will speak of Socrates' hubris toward others, his remaining aloof and ironic.

Readers of the *Symposium* should constantly recall that our divisions of disciplines and subject areas were not those of the Greeks of Socrates' or Plato's time. The term *philosophoi* did not yet commonly possess a univocal meaning. It was not yet clearly distinguished from sophistry or rhetoric and certainly not from the disciplines that we would today regard as "scientific," such as mathematics or astronomy. The terms *poetry* and *poet* also carried very different connotations than they do today. Poets were men of wisdom, divinely inspired wisdom, and much of Athenian education consisted in the memorization and performance of poetry. Only in this context can one begin to understand what is meant by "the ancient quarrel between poetry and philosophy." Bearing this context in mind also helps one to appreciate the extent to which this rivalry, which Socrates in the *Republic* calls an ancient rivalry, is actually being rendered thematic by Plato, just as was the rivalry between philosophy and sophistry. The *Symposium* is truly unique among Plato's dialogues for its depiction of Socrates in conversation with famous poets, Aristophanes and Agathon. Nowhere else do we see the philosopher debating poets (into the wee hours of the night), and nowhere else are we provided with speeches Plato crafted for them. One must consider what the portraits and the speeches of the poets might tell us about Plato's estimation of poetry, notwithstanding the infamous mention of "an ancient quarrel" in the final book of *Republic*.

Seeing Socrates enter the room, Agathon, all alone on one of the couches, calls out: "Come lie down next to me. Who knows, if I touch you, I may catch a bit of the wisdom that came to you under my neighbor's porch. It's clear that you've seen the light; if you hadn't, you'd still be standing there" (175c-d). This episode and Agathon's statement here confirm that many people regarded Socrates as the kind of person who would not let go of an interlocutor or an idea until he had pursued him or it to the bitter end. Rarely in Plato's dialogues does Socrates walk away from an argument or seek to adjourn a discussion prematurely. But Socrates responds to Agathon by saying that his own wisdom is a shadowy thing at best, as ephemeral as a dream (175d). Upon his arrival at Agathon's house for the symposium, the philosopher famous for his professions of ignorance imputes to Agathon the bright and wonderful wisdom he himself lacks and he ironically suggests that it is he who would be filled by the poet's overflowing wisdom (175e). This remark is one of the key references in this dialogue to the theme of Socratic Ignorance. Much depends on how one understands Socrates' claim that his own wisdom is defective in some way. Clearly, Socrates is being ironic with respect to Agathon's wisdom, as his other remarks to Agathon make clear; but it does not follow that Socrates' remarks regarding the ephemeral and dreamlike quality of his own wisdom are insincere. Indeed, these remarks could very well foreshadow the erotic character of philosophy. Later, in recounting Diotima's teaching, Socrates will suggest that philosophy is essentially the love of wisdom and that as the love of wisdom it cannot be the possession of wisdom. Yet *Erôs* is also said to be a messenger from the Divine; if all *Erôs* plays this role, then certainly the form of *Erôs* known as philosophy does so as well. Indeed, other considerations will suggest that in spite of philosophy's lack of wisdom it is rather more open to the messages of the Divine than are other forms of *Erôs*. For if the *Eidē* or Forms, are divine, and philosophy involves recollections or visions of the Forms, then surely philosophy is the *daimonic* messenger par excellence. But *Erôs* will also be said to both be desirous and possessed of resources and to be both constantly losing and renewing these resources. It possesses this dual nature through its kinship to both Poverty (*Penia*) and Resource (*Poros*). All of these ideas are tied later to the claim that philosophy stands between ignorance and wisdom, having and not having what it desires. It is enough here to suggest that Socrates' remarks about the evanescent character of his "wisdom" and Socrates' trance on the porch may be hints of the paradoxical character of the philosopher's simultaneous communion with and distance from the divinity he seeks.

In addition to minimizing his own wisdom, Socrates also calls into question Agathon's view of how wisdom is obtained, saying, "How wonderful it would be, dear Agathon, if the foolish were filled with wisdom simply by touching the wise" (175d). Socrates thus takes issue with a view of knowledge that is very prevalent even today—the "knowledge-transfer" or transfusion model of learning according to which the teacher can simply put understanding directly into the mind of the learner as though the learner were a passive receptacle. The knowledge-transfer paradigm of the learning process presumes that the teacher possesses knowledge and then simply imparts it to the student. Although this conception may be suitable for some limited kinds of pedagogy, it is not a suitable model for philosophy as Plato's Socrates seems to understand it. In the *Republic* Socrates also explicitly denies that education consists in imparting knowledge in this way, as though one could "put sight into blind eyes" (*Rep.* 518b-c). The Socratic method of question and answer is based on a contrary model of education, according to which the learner must play an active role, even, in a sense, the principal role, in the acquisition of knowledge. In the *Symposium*, Socrates seems to regard Agathon's conception of how knowledge is obtained as almost a hydraulic process. He says to Agathon, "If only wisdom were like water, which always flows from a full cup into an empty one when we connect them with a piece of yarn . . ." (175d). Agathon's mistake will be repeated later by Alcibiades when he admits to thinking that by getting next to Socrates in a sexual way, he will be able to receive Socrates' wisdom and guidance.

It could very well be that the passivity of the student in this model of learning is indicative of the passivity of the audience of poetry; and the image of water flowing from a full cup to an empty one reminds one of an image used in the *Ion* as an image of poetic inspiration, the image of the magnetism flowing from a lodestone to iron rings (*Ion* 533d–534a). One of the differences between philosophy and the tradition of poetic pedagogy in ancient

Greek is that the latter called for a more passive mind on the part of the student, whose psyche was to be shaped via a mimetic relation to the words and deeds of poetry. Philosophy by contrast demands active participation; the benefit to be gained from it demands personal and critical confrontation with and appropriation of the philosopher's way of thinking, examining and arguing, not some particular set of images or propositions. The philosopher's way of thinking is inherently dialogical, open to and indeed dependent on engagement with others in an activity that calls the self into question and subjects it to scrutiny. For these reasons, only those who exercise themselves in thought and inquiry will receive the benefits of philosophy. As with physical exercise, the benefits only accrue to those engaged in the activity. Hence, philosophy can never be a passive, spectator sport. The philosopher, believing that "the unexamined life is not worth living for a human being," needs the dialogue with others as a way of exposing the psyche and turning its vision toward the light.

Not only does Plato write in the dialogue form, but also it is suggested in many dialogues that the conversational method is the best model for learning. Recall again the proverb (taken from Homer, *Iliad* X.224), "When two go together, one has an idea before the other." Socrates alludes to this expression at *Symposium* 174d and quotes it at *Protagoras* (348d). There, Socrates adds this comment: "Human beings are simply more resourceful this way in action, speech, and thought. If someone has a private perception, he immediately starts going around and looking until he finds somebody he can show it to and have it corroborated."[18] This attitude is consistent with the usual procedure followed in the dialogues, in which the partners of conversations are invariably portrayed as searching together. Even in the common case in which one person, such as Socrates, is clearly in control of the conversation, it is continually suggested that in some way the other partner to the discussion is needed. The interlocutors are consistently treated as though they make some important contribution to the inquiry, even though it is not always clear to Plato's audience just how this is so. In Plato's *Seventh Letter*, the language in which philosophical inquiry is described also points to the value of more than one head:

> For this knowledge is not something that can be put into words like other sciences; but after *long-continued intercourse between teacher and pupil*, in joint pursuit of the subject, suddenly, like light flashing forth when a fire is kindled, it is born in the psyche and straightway nourishes itself. (341c-d; Morrow, trans.)

> Only when all of these things—names, definitions, and visual and other perceptions—have been rubbed against one another and tested, *pupil and teacher asking and answering questions in good will and without envy*—only then, when reason and knowledge are at the very extremity of human effort, can they illuminate the nature of any object. (344b-c; Morrow trans.)

In the *Alcibiades* I (132c–133c) Socrates uses the metaphor of an eye looking into another eye, in order to see itself, as the model of the method the psyche must use to know itself. The psyche must look at a psyche, and especially at the part of itself by which it knows and thinks and in which wisdom arises. Here the metaphor of an eye looking into another eye suggests that the psyche needs to encounter the thought of another psyche and the conversation becomes a soul-to-soul conversation.[19] Philosophy for Socrates entails mutual deliberation and shared inquiry, carried on dialectically, through many conversations. Dialogue is a cooperative probing and yielding, an exercise of one's whole character by which each interlocutor puts the other to the test. This exercise presumes that the two inquirers can each lead the other at different stages of the journey. The teacher is like a guide who knows the trail well; she can assist another along the journey, but she cannot presume to know it completely or to have reached the end of what must be a lifelong path. Each person can teach another something by disclosing to the other possibilities of which the other would not otherwise be aware. Now one goes ahead, and now the other, and when the guide guides well, the follower is still permitted to discover for herself what the guide has already discovered. The best guides empower their followers rather than keeping them ever dependent on guidance. Experience on the path affords one the opportunity to pass along certain lessons concerning the nature of the terrain and the attitude most likely to optimize the benefits to be derived from the process. Hence, philosophy entails getting on the road or path, and this introduces another metaphor for pedagogy that is exhibited in the *Symposium*. We shall say more about pedagogy as akin to the relation of guides and followers below.[20]

Socrates says that he can call as witnesses to Agathon's wisdom the thirty thousand people who attended the performance of Agathon's prize-winning play. This comment draws attention to the difference between an impromptu, one-on-one conversation, on one hand, and a rehearsed, mimetic performance in front of a large crowd, on the other. Plato's audience is led to reflect on the contrast between on the one hand a face-to-face or psyche-to-psyche encounter that occurs in a conversation with Socrates and, on the other hand, the act of writing a play, even a prize-winning one, staged before a large crowd. The theme of the contrast between philosophical and poetic/rhetorical discourse will recur in the comments with which Socrates will preface his speech. Agathon will say that he fears speaking in front of his intelligent friends, whereas he did not fear to speak in front of the ignorant crowd. This remark will prompt Socrates to note that it implies that Agathon is worried about getting caught doing something foolish (and perhaps being corrected), but apparently not at all worried about doing something foolish in front of those who would fail to catch him at it.

Socrates suggests that Agathon is more comfortable with show or mere appearance than he is willing to face the truth about the real condition of his psyche. Agathon is comfortable in large crowds because he believes that he appears before them to his best advantage; whereas Socrates had earlier claimed to avoid the previous night's victory party because of his discomfort with large crowds (174a). The exercise of reason in dialectic and the pursuit of truth are more possible in smaller groups that can center their attention on one-on-one dialogue. One could say that large crowds have no capacity for either dialogue or dialectic and that their natural medium is rhetorical persuasion. The philosopher cares nothing for the opinion of a crowd as a crowd, but seeks to elicit from individuals the "one vote" of which Socrates speaks in the *Gorgias*, that is, the voice of reason inside the psyche of a single interlocutor (*Grg.* 471e–472c, 474a-b).

In response to Socrates' comment about Agathon's wisdom, Agathon replies "You are an insolent man [Ὑβριστὴς εἶ] Socrates." He continues, "Dionysus will soon enough be the judge of our claims to wisdom" (175e7–9). This remark is the first of a number of clues that seem meant to indicate how we should understand the action of the main part of this dialogue. Agathon's words introduce the themes of the contest (*agōn*) and the trial by jury, foreshadowing the contest of speeches that is proposed shortly thereafter, a contest that becomes, among other things, a contest over truthfulness between Socrates and Alcibiades later in the dialogue. We shall see that the contest with Alcibiades will take the form of a mock trial in which Socrates is accused of hubris, and in which all of the other speakers are named as jurists competent to judge of Socrates' habitual behaviors and practices. But even before Alcibiades figuratively brings Socrates to trial on the charge of hubris, Agathon is suggesting that he and Socrates will "go to law" (*diadikasometha*) in a dispute over wisdom and that somehow, Dionysus, the god of wine, masks, and theatre, will be the judge of this dispute between them. Any interpretation of the *Symposium* must try to understand the significance of this image in the context of the dialogue as a whole.[21]

Agathon clearly knows Socrates well enough to see irony in what Socrates says. On the face of it, the irony is not obvious—in fact, it could even be that Agathon is "reading into" Socrates' words irony that is not there. It is only because of what we think we know about Socrates from other dialogues that we are inclined to suspect him of irony at this point. But it is also significant that Agathon was probably sincere is saying that he wanted to learn Socrates' wisdom, and when he interprets Socrates as rebuffing him with irony, he probably does at some level feel genuinely insulted, although his remark is surely meant to seem playful. Here is a man who has just achieved a tremendous victory and won the acclaim of thirty thousand Greeks; yet there is something he admires about Socrates. He covets Socrates' companionship and perceived wisdom, a feeling that Alcibiades will later express as well. One must consider the significance of this point. He regards Socrates' remarks as ironic, as though Socrates is holding himself aloof or playing hard to get. He sees pride in Socrates' response, rather than humility. Agathon sees a slight, rather than praise when Socrates acknowledges his acclaim. It is as though Agathon has a sense that the philosopher's wisdom is somehow superior, some higher mysterious secret the mere existence of which threatens Agathon's image of himself. For this reason, Agathon would like to associate himself with the enigmatic philosopher and perhaps to learn his secrets. But this desire does not at all imply an interest in philosophy or even the remotest understanding of what it is. Rather, Agathon seems to be covetous of Socrates' wisdom out of a spirit of rivalry with him, and he seems to want to become more intimate with Socrates so as to find the philosopher's weaknesses and gain an advantage, much as Alcibiades will later report having tried to do.

The apparently playful rivalry between Socrates and Agathon regarding wisdom is perhaps not as playful as it seems; this rivalry surely represents the rivalry between philosophy and poetry (of which Socrates extensively speaks in *Republic*, Bk. X). This conclusion is supported by the remark Socrates makes about Agathon's wisdom having displayed itself before thirty thousand Greeks, which points to a characteristic difference between poetic "wisdom" and philosophical "wisdom": poetic wisdom depends upon or exists in the realm of mere appearance. Moreover, Socrates' remarks about the paltry character of his own "wisdom" are reminiscent of his remarks in the *Apology* regarding his merely "human" wisdom; in both cases Socrates seems to downgrade or belittle his own wisdom, and yet to do so in a way that is simultaneously ironic and sincere.

Socrates is sincere about the limits of his wisdom to the extent that he lacks the divine wisdom that he seeks; but he is ironic to the extent that his search has left him wiser, through his awareness of his own ignorance at least, than those around him. As will be suggested later in connection with Diotima's teaching about *Erôs* and philosophy, it is in the very awareness of ignorance and its concomitant *Erôs* for the wisdom that is lacked that an intimation of that wisdom comes to the psyche as though it were a message from the Divine; yet like Socrates' trance on the porch, the messages of *Erôs* never satisfy the psyche's erotic longing. They simply direct it further along its path. Perhaps one reason why philosophy is to be preferred to poetry for Plato is that rather than being content with images, as is poetry, philosophy belittles its own dream-like status even as it dreams of something beyond dreams.

After the celebrants pour a libation to the god Dionysus, their attention turns to the procedures for the evening's drinking. Pausanias confesses to being hung over from the previous night's celebration and says that he and many others too could benefit from taking it easy on this occasion, and Aristophanes agrees. Eryximachus jumps in to ask how Agathon feels, wondering if he is up for some "serious drinking." But Agathon confesses to having no strength left for anything, and Eryximachus calls this a lucky stroke, since it means that so many of the heavy drinkers are thus incapacitated. Then Eryximachus remarks that Socrates is able either to drink or not to drink and will be satisfied either way (176c). Socrates' ability to drink without intoxication is referred to subsequently (214a, 220a), and the conclusion of the dialogue confirms this estimation of his abilities.

An adequate interpretation of the *Symposium* should explain what it means that Socrates is equally content with either drinking or abstention. Daniel Anderson points out the ambiguity of this detail. Socrates' sobriety might mean either that Apollo protects him, so that he is immune to Apollo's traditional rival, Dionysus; or it might mean that Socrates is always possessed by Dionysus, so that drinking does not alter his behavior. Alcibiades' use of Dionysiac satyr imagery suggests that he at least would opt for the latter interpretation of Socrates; but if Alcibiades is possessed by Dionysus, this could be a case of the god claiming Socrates as his own.[22] Rosen sees Socrates' sobriety as a sign of his unerotic character; we comment on his view at the appropriate place later in this commentary. We think that Socrates' sobriety indicates the superiority of philosophical *Erôs* to other forms of *Erôs*. The "divine madness" of philosophical *Erôs* actually stimulates, nourishes, and protects reason, and when it is strong it can overrule the passions that ordinarily distort reason. Socrates' sound-mindedness (*sophrosunē*) cannot be hindered by excessive appetitive desire or biased by the love of honor or other spirited passion, because Socrates' strongest form of *Erôs* is his love of truth and wisdom.

Eryximachus goes on to dispense his medical advice about the nature of intoxication, the main point of which is that inebriation is harmful to everyone; he says that this is why he refrains from heavy drinking and advises others to do the same. Phaedrus interjects that he always does what Eryximachus says, especially when he speaks as a doctor, and so the guests agree not to get drunk (176d-e). Eryximachus declares it has been so resolved, and then he proposes another motion, namely that they dispense with the flute-girl and engage in conversation. (The legal-political language of "it has been resolved" [δέδοκται 176e4–5] pervades even the discussion of the evening's libations.) We should notice that Eryximachus, who as a physician is a follower of Apollo, has introduced two resolutions that attempt to banish Dionysos, Apollo's rival, from this symposium. This will be no ordinary symposium, to be sure.

All the others agree with Eryximachus's proposal and urge him to suggest a subject for the speeches. He says the idea actually comes from Phaedrus:

> "Eryximachus," he says, "isn't it an awful thing! Our poets have composed hymns in honor of just about any god you can think of; but has a single one of them given one moment's thought to the god of love, ancient and powerful as he is? As for our fancy intellectuals, they have written volumes praising Heracles and other heroes (as did the distinguished Prodicus). Well, perhaps that's not surprising, but I've actually read a book by an accomplished author who saw fit to extol the usefulness of salt! How could people pay attention to such trifles and never, not even once, write a proper hymn to Love? How could anyone ignore so great a god?" (177a-c)[23]

Thus, in the *Symposium*, just as in the dialogue named after him, Phaedrus seems especially concerned with both love and rhetoric, and indeed these are two great forces that are capable of moving the psyches of human beings. Perhaps using Phaedrus to introduce the topic here is Plato's way of reminding us that Phaedrus was moved by love and by persuasive rhetoric to profane the mysteries (with Eryximachus and Alcibiades). In the *Symposium* as in the *Phaedrus* the themes of rhetoric and love are interwoven. Plato wants his audience to be aware of both themes—love, the topic introduced by Phaedrus, and rhetoric, which is emphasized by the contest of speeches and by Phaedrus's remarks about the failure of the poets to praise *Erôs* adequately. Phaedrus's criticism presents a challenge for the speakers. One is reminded here of Adeimantus's remarks concerning the deficiencies of the poet's praise of justice in the *Republic*; in that dialogue Plato clearly uses those remarks to establish a challenge that he intends to meet with his dialogue. He is in effect pointing out that no one has yet accomplished what he is about to do in the *Republic*, namely, achieve the proper praise of justice. Likewise, Phaedrus's remarks here indicate that no one has yet worthily praised *Erôs*, and it is hard not to think that this goal was part of what Plato hoped to accomplish with the *Symposium*. As we have already noted, the *Republic* is also a dialogue that has as one of its major themes the rivalry between poetry and philosophy. So in both the *Republic* and the *Symposium* Plato is displaying the superiority of philosophy (or of his philosophical poetry) over conventional poetry, by succeeding where the poets have failed in the all-important tasks of worthily praising justice and love.

Proposing that they begin with Phaedrus, moving from left to right, Eryximachus asks for the others' approval. Socrates asserts that no one will object to such an idea, adding, "How could I vote 'No,' when the only thing I say I understand is the art of Love [*ta erotica*]?" (177d-e). In what follows we will have to consider the significance of Socrates' claim to understand the art of love.

The prologue ends with Apollodorus reminding his audience that Aristodemus did not remember everything that was said, and that he (Apollodorus) did not remember everything Aristodemus told him, but that he would tell them what he considered most important (178a). This cautionary caveat puts Plato's audience at still further remove from the events that form the heart of the dialogue and serve to underline that this is no mere transcript or word-for-word rendering, for all that Apollodorus relates is what he supposes to be worth relating, and/or what had impressed itself most vividly on Aristodemus's mind. One is led to wonder what Apollodorus is leaving out and what Aristodemus might have forgotten or missed entirely. The total effect of the whole prologue (the narrative frame with Apollodorus plus Aristodemus's account of the events leading up to the speeches on *Erôs* themselves) is to prepare the minds of the audience for a great contest of speeches on love, a contest that may have everything to do with the rivalry between philosophy and other claimants to wisdom, especially poetry—for it is through the contest of speeches that Socrates and Agathon "go to law concerning wisdom."

The six speeches in praise of love that make up the heart of the *Symposium*, should "be heard" through the themes introduced by the narrative frame. One must ask oneself: What is the ultimate significance and outcome of this contest of speeches in praise of *Erôs*? We suggest that the contest is really a contest between philosophy and its rivals. Since each of the speeches not only expresses an understanding of love but each is also an expression of a certain kind of love, one could also say that the dialogue displays different concepts of *Erôs*, ranging between philosophic love and various alternative kinds of love. We must qualify this statement by saying that Diotima's teaching will suggest that all forms of love are in some way philosophical to the extent that the love in a nonphilosophical breast represents the relatively most philosophical element in a nonphilosopher. Nonetheless, the dialogue presents the philosopher's love as being one of a kind. Plato's audience should consider the way in which such a rhetorical contest, a battle of rival praises of love, affords an entry into philosophy simply by juxtaposing alternative ways of being for review. The alternative views of what love is and of what is truly lovable are alternative understandings of the human good, and the need for philosophy grows out of the conflict of alternative understandings of the good. The need for philosophy also grows out of the inadequacy of the rhetoric of praise. By sending away the flute-girl and deciding not to drink excessively, but instead to compare speeches about what is dear to their hearts, the participants prepare the way for the entry of Socrates' philosophical muse.

Plato's audience should also bear in mind the way the entire account of the rhetorical contest is qualified by the other themes introduced in the narrative frame. For instance, one must recall that speeches themselves are objects of interest to Apollodorus and his unknown auditors. Their *Erôs* is directed toward knowing the content of the speeches, not only because they are interested in the topic, but also because they are interested in hearing an account of the views and deeds of certain of the participants. Recall Apollodorus's story of Glaucon's request; Glaucon had mentioned Agathon, Socrates, and Alcibiades in particular, as well as expressing an interest in the speeches on love. The first line of the *Symposium* suggests that Apollodorus's new, unknown companion has made a similar request, since the whole reason Apollodorus claims that he is "not unprepared concerning the things about which you inquire" is that he has just related the same matter to a Glaucon "the day before yesterday." Whether the new companion is interested in the speeches for the same reasons as Glaucon was, presumably Plato would not have included the specifics in Glaucon's request if he did not intend them to color his audience's understanding of the meaning of the symposium. Glaucon's request highlights the roles of Agathon, Socrates, and Alcibiades, and indeed, later in the dialogue it becomes clear that dramatic interaction between these three characters has a special relevance; for they will be exemplifying a kind of erotic triangle, as well as offering successive encomia in the dialogue. Moreover, Agathon will be critical of Socrates, even rude to him, whereas Socrates will reduce Agathon to an admission of ignorance in criticizing his speech as longer on form than on substance. Finally, Alcibiades will criticize Socrates, the only man who has ever made the self-assured Alcibiades feel shame. Also, if one recalls the two "trials" referenced earlier, that between Socrates and Agathon and that between Socrates and Alcibiades, it is safe to say that two of the most important subthemes of the dialogue concern Socrates' relationship to Agathon and Socrates' relationship to Alcibiades respectively. Plato's audience must consider what these "trials" say about the erotic relationship and rivalry between Socrates, Agathon, and Alcibiades.

In addition, we have noted that when Apollodorus relays Aristodemus's account of his meeting with Socrates in the dialogue's frame, another organizing theme is introduced: the question of the relative value of Socrates, Aristodemus, and Agathon. For the question is implicitly raised whether or not Socrates is going as a beautiful man to a beautiful man or as a good man to a good man's feast. Another question is whether or not Aristodemus is a good man or an inferior man who goes uninvited to a good man's feast. All of this begs the further question of whether Agathon truly "lives up to his name" and is really good. These questions foreshadow the disputed theme between Agathon and Socrates over wisdom.

Finally, there is a theme that is not explicitly announced in the dramatic prologue to the speeches, but which would have been in the mind of Plato's audience owing simply to the cast of characters, namely, the profanation of the mysteries and the desecration of the Herms. As we noted above, these were events that transpired in 415, the year in which the party occurred, just prior to the launching of the Sicilian Expedition, and in which three of the present partygoers (Phaedrus, Eryximachus, and Alcibiades) were allegedly involved. Commentators on the *Symposium* frequently wonder what Plato wants his audience to gather from these events. Like others, we see references to these events in the speech of Socrates on love and the speech of Alcibiades on Socrates, and we shall discuss their significance for the interpretation of the dialogue in our comments on these speeches. Adequate interpretation of *Symposium* requires bringing together all these themes and considering the various ways in which they might function together to enrich an understanding of the action and argument of the dialogue considered as a whole.

# CHAPTER 2

# Six Speeches on Love (*Erôs*)

## THE SPEECH OF PHAEDRUS (178A–180C)

Phaedrus is known for being a lover of speeches, as we have noted above. Hence, he is the one who suggests that the partygoers devote time to composing encomia in praise of *Erôs*. According to Eryximachus, Phaedrus should give the first speech because *he* is at the head of the table and because he is, in addition, "the father of our subject" (πατὴρ τοῦ λόγου) on the occasion of this symposium (177d5). In Plato's *Phaedrus*, Phaedrus is shown trying to memorize a speech recently composed by Lysias, the renowned teacher of rhetoric, and later reading the speech to Socrates. In addition to the *Symposium* and *Phaedrus*, he is also present in the *Protagoras* as are all the other speakers in *Symposium* with the notable exception of Aristophanes, the comic poet. (see *Prot.* 315c). Phaedrus was banished from Athens not long after the dramatic date of the *Symposium* (c. 416/15) after he was accused, along with Alcibiades and Eryximachus, of profaning the mysteries.[1]

The speech he composes follows a fairly standard form for epideictic oratory. He gives a short, introductory characterization of the subject at the beginning, supports this characterization with ancillary arguments, goes on to supply examples from the epics and tragedies, and then recapitulates the main points of his account at its conclusion. Phaedrus begins his speech by proclaiming that love is the greatest and most wonderful of the gods, cherished, as he is, by gods and mortals alike. He quotes Hesiod's *Theogony*, the first Greek text to explore the origin of the cosmos, which says that *Erôs* is the third god to come into being, after Chaos and Earth. He goes on to cite Acousilaos and Parmenides in support of his contention that *Erôs* is one of the most ancient gods. According to Phaedrus, human beings receive the greatest gifts from Love, and he elaborates on the good things that he thinks *Erôs* engenders in those who are possessed by it. He will argue that Love inspires people to be courageous and to practice *aretē* (excellence). The ultimate act of Love, in his view, is performed when a lover dies for his or her beloved.

According to Phaedrus, wherever *Erōs* operates, in societies and in more intimate relationships, it is a beneficial social force. Love instills in human beings a sense of shame for shameful actions and a sense of pride in virtuous deeds. And if human beings in general are taught to take pride in courageous and noble actions and to feel ashamed at the prospect of acting shamefully or ignobly, then this powerful social corrective would seem to be even more overwhelming when one is in the presence of one's lover. It is interesting that friendship and romantic love have the power to intensify shame or pride. Shame, pride, and love have a powerful role in shaping people's sense of themselves. In terms of the psychological thought of the *Republic* or the *Phaedrus*, the power of shame and pride are connected with the spirited and honor-loving part of the psyche.[2] The spirited part is the part of the psyche that can be trained to aid the calculative or rational part in its rule over the appetites. Phaedrus's speech is the first of several places in the *Symposium* in which one finds some suggestion of the relationship between *Erōs* and the spirited or honor-loving part of the psyche. Whether or not at the time of writing the *Symposium* Plato had the tripartite conception of the psyche in mind, it is clear that Plato is frequently mindful in this dialogue, as elsewhere, of the power of the love of honor.

As noted in other dialogues, the fear of shame and the love of honor can inspire courage. Thus, Phaedrus muses that if there were a way to form armies and cities from groups of lovers, these would be the best, most excellent cities and the bravest armies. He imagines how courageously a warrior would fight in the presence of, and for the protection of, his beloved. He goes on to recall the cases of Alcestis and Achilles (to which we will return below) to support his argument that Love inspires courage and virtue in those it possesses.

The careful reader will notice that Phaedrus offers only external reasons for doing the right thing, chiefly shame or dishonor in the eyes of others; he offers no intrinsic justification for good or just actions.[3] For Phaedrus, getting caught doing something shameful by one's lover is the most shameful thing of all. Like Agathon later, he will only be concerned about seeming good so as not to get caught and not about really being good.[4] Phaedrus emphasizes the concern of his erotic soldiers with the opinion of their partners; he does not emphasize an internalized sense of shame or dishonor, that is, how one appears in *one's own eyes* as opposed to the eyes of others. Phaedrus may have a sense that there is such a concern on the part of his soldiers as well, but if so, that sense is not made explicit in his speech.

A practical problem for Phaedrus's argument is that it is not clear how erotic attachments could possibly avoid coming into conflict with one's attachment to the community. For it seems human beings treat their loved ones differently than they treat others. If people have to choose between loyalty to their lovers and loyalty to their communities—be it a city or an army—most people would likely choose their near and dear ones. But if they would not choose the community, it is not clear that *Erôs* is suited to serve as the basis for the social bond between people, the kind of social bond needed to link people together within cities and armies. It is precisely this problem that drives Socrates in Book V of *Republic* to attempt to extend the family model to an entire political community. The best that can be said for Phaedrus on this point is that he too, like Socrates in the *Republic*, is imagining a practically impossible case—a situation in which erotic attachment perfectly coincides with the claims of duty (just as Socrates in the *Republic* imagines the coincidence of filial and civic bonds).

Phaedrus's account of *Erôs* conceives of Love in what modern audiences will rightly perceive to be a quite narrow context. The context is the battlefield, and the values and practices of the heroic ethic pervade the speech, as his allusions to the heroes of the epics make plain. Phaedrus conceives of erotic love exclusively in terms of the relationship between an older, wiser man and a younger boy, who serves as the source of inspiration for the warrior's bravery. Initiating the youth into the men's world and functioning as his mentor or teacher were the chief objectives of this practice of *synousia* (literally, "being with"). These mentoring, homoerotic relationships, widely practiced but subject to criticism from some quarters in Plato's Athens, were thought to provide benefits to both parties. But in his speech Phaedrus concerns himself primarily with the benefits that accrue to the younger beloved (*erōmenos*) from the older lover (*erastēs*). His speech celebrates what the older lover gives to the young and impressionable youth, but it does not make explicit what the youth does for the older lover in return. As a result, his account of Love is necessarily one-sided, and because it is both one-sided and restrictive in its context and scope, it is probably fair to say that Phaedrus's conception of *Erôs* is the narrowest of the six speeches in praise of Love delivered in this dialogue.

The kind of erotic attachment in question in Phaedrus's speech is far removed, on one hand, from a modern conception of romantic love as something equal and reciprocal between two people, and on the other hand, from the Christian ideal of Love as *agapē*.[5] In fact, the idea of a love that occurs between equals and is reciprocated in more or less the same way that it is given is not introduced into the *Symposium* until Aristophanes speaks.

In contrast to reciprocal romantic love, in the kinds of relationship between an older man and a younger boy discussed here, each party gives to the other something quite different from what he receives. The older partner (*erastēs*) would teach the younger one how to become a man on the battlefield and a citizen in the city, teaching the youth the requirements of *politikē*. The older lover provides the guidance that helps develop the appropriate senses of shame and pride, grooming the young beloved (or *erōmenos*) for his roles as father, citizen, warrior, tradesman, and so on. But the young beloved provides the older lover primarily with sexual pleasure. Phaedrus, however, is anxious to expand the standard view of the young beloved's role and importance in the relationship.

As someone who himself plays the role of the beloved to Eryximachus (his older lover) in such a homoerotic relationship, it should not be too surprising that Phaedrus highlights the virtues of love from the perspective of the beloved.[6] In Phaedrus's experience, every boy needs a gentle and wise older lover to introduce him to the ways of the men's world, the world of politics, of military arts, and of civic virtue in general. Now, since only male Athenians could be citizens in ancient Athens, it is by no means an exaggeration to say that the world of the ancient Greek city-states was, by and large, a man's world. In absence of a formal system of public education, the education adequate to the requirements of civic life (*politikē*) had to be provided by one's elders. Yet one's own father could only go so far in educating a son for his several roles as citizen, statesman, soldier, and head of household. At a certain point—usually about the age of eleven or twelve—it was widely believed necessary for some adult male besides the father to intervene to guide the boy into manhood. Phaedrus argues that nothing imparts this guidance as well as a man motivated by *Erôs*. For Love inspires one to act rightly and nobly, with a sense of shame, avoiding cowardice and pursuing *aretē* (excellence or virtue) under the tutelage of the more experienced, wiser man. These benefits, in Phaedrus's view, are exemplified on the battlefield where the presence of a young beloved serves to inspire the older warrior to act bravely and honorably at all times.[7] Without the pride born of honor and a sense of shame, "nothing fine or great can be accomplished, in public or in private," according to Phaedrus (178d). Phaedrus cites two examples—one from mythology and one from the *Iliad*—as evidence that *Erôs* motivates people to do courageous and honorable deeds. He cites Alcestis, who was the only one willing to die for her husband, Admetus, when Apollo offered Admetus the chance to find someone else to go to Hades in his place (179b-c). So Phaedrus's first example to support his argument that an older, manlier man will be motivated to fight bravely in the presence of his younger, more effeminate beloved is the example of a woman saving her husband's life.

His other example is the infamous relationship between Achilles and Patroclus in Homer's *Iliad*. After Hector killed Achilles' beloved Patroclus, Achilles was told by his mother, the goddess Thetis, that he had to choose between a short, glorious life, if he avenged the death of his friend, and a long, but inglorious, life as a farmer if he chooses not to take revenge. Of course, he chooses revenge and has to pay with his own life for killing Hector. Phaedrus's use of this example is telling. He argues that Aeschylus, in his tragic rendition of the Homeric tale, got it all wrong: Achilles is really the younger beloved and Patroclus is the older lover, for Achilles was still beardless and the more beautiful of the two. By casting Achilles as the beloved, Phaedrus makes the beloved in these relationships the true hero. In so doing, Phaedrus displays his own self-image and reveals something of his vanity.

Another interesting aspect of this example is that Phaedrus insists that *Erôs* is so powerful a force that it effects human actions even in the case where the loved one has already died (180a). So not only the presence of the loved one, but also the memory or thought of the beloved, can inspire the lover with courage and guide him to act with a sense of shame. Of course, not all lovers are brave enough to die for their beloved, as the example of Orpheus attests, but such characters have no share in honor and they are forbidden to enter the Isles of the Blessed, and instead are made to die at the hands of women (*Symp.* 179d).

In the logic of the heroic/homoerotic relationships within which Phaedrus's argument locates and analyzes *Erôs*, the older lover is presumed to have a kind of wisdom that he can confer upon the youth through regular, daily contact, in exercise, in discussion, in training, and in battle. Since the younger partner must see certain desirable qualities in his lover and want the lover to teach these qualities to him by mentoring him, the youth must actually have some seeds of wisdom and virtue already. But what does the older lover see in the younger beloved? What can the youth do for the older lover who already possesses the knowledge and skills of the man's world? Presumably in the best case, the older lover perceives in his young beloved some potential, some natural gifts, and a solid foundation on which he hopes to build. But beyond the inspiration the young beloved provides to his lover, Phaedrus does not say what the young beloved typically gives to his lover. There may have been men who enjoyed the camaraderie of these associations, who enjoyed teaching a promising and good young man, and who took nothing but pride in the youth's development under his tutelage. But, not surprisingly, sexual relations were also part of the benefit to the lover for his beneficence, and custom seems to have prescribed various boundaries to limit and guide these relationships. For instance, it was considered wrong for the young beloved to give in too readily to the older lover. Disenfranchisement could result in Athens for giving one's self for money. Moreover, the young beloved was not supposed to take pleasure in the sexual side of these associations as the older lover does.[8] Given this stricture, it is appropriate that Phaedrus is discreet: he makes no explicit mention in his speech of the sexual aspect of these homoerotic relationships. Yet perhaps Phaedrus's zeal for praising *Erôs* is itself suggestive of his desire to break out of the conventional limits of the beloved's role.

The last point Phaedrus makes before his summation is quite interesting and might easily be overlooked if one does not attend carefully to what he says. Phaedrus claims that virtue is more honored by the gods when *Erôs* provides the inspiration. But he follows this claim by immediately asserting that the gods cherish more dearly, however, the young boy's love for his lover than they do the lover's *Erôs* for his young beloved, because they are more impressed and delighted with the former than with the latter (180a-b). Since the older man is "more godlike" inasmuch as his *Erôs* is inspired by a god, it is easier, and therefore less praiseworthy, for him to do what he does than it is for the boy to do what he does in the relationship. Thus, Phaedrus highlights the difficulty and at the same time heightens the nobility of the beloved's role.

Now, since Phaedrus plays the role of a young beloved to Eryximachus, one can recognize that he is speaking from his own vantage point and he is championing his own predilections. Here is the first example in the *Symposium* of a speaker valorizing his own way of life in his speech on *Erôs*. For the speakers in the *Symposium* are not merely stating the facts as they see them. Each speech presents a normative view of Love, a view about how *Erôs* ought to be practiced and how it should operate in human communities. Every speech will to a greater or lesser extent paint a picture of a world in which the speaker's values can flourish, a world guided by the virtue that he thinks is the most important in human life. Phaedrus seems to regard courage as the most important of the four cardinal virtues.[9] Phaedrus also emphasizes the role of love in intensifying the concern with honor and shame that can motivate the practice of virtue. But Plato's audience would do well to consider that in addition to inspiring noble action and amplifying the sense of shame, *Erôs* is also capable of making humans shameless and driving them to do the most shameful things. *Erôs* can inspire one to croon under the window of one's beloved. It can make one write bad poetry and behave in other potentially embarrassing ways, as does the young Hippothales in the *Lysis* who annoys his friends with his endless mooning over the title character. *Erôs* might even cause one to do something that compromises one's comrades, one's loved ones, one's country, office, or reputation. So, *Erôs* would seem to be just as capable of leading people to do dishonorable and shameful things as it is to lead them to a sense of honor and shame. But Phaedrus's speech leaves these possibilities out of account. As if in response to this deficiency in Phaedrus's speech, the speech of Pausanias that follows will introduce an important distinction into *Erôs*, splitting it into two by associating it with two opposed goddesses, one heavenly (*Aphrodite Urania*) and one vulgar (*Aphrodite pandemos*). By this means Pausanias will account for both noble and ignoble expressions of love.

The progression and psychology of the speeches teaches us that every person inevitably ends up seeing Love (or desire) as they see the world in general—or, as Aristotle will later put the point: pleasure is the "rudder of our existence." Every person conceives of Love and desire from his or her own point of view. Since human beings always see things from some point of view, situated as we are in space and time, it would appear unavoidable that every view is only a partial view of a larger whole, seen through the lens of the speaker's own character and way of life. Therefore, one must consider the relationship between the logic of the arguments and the psychology of the particular speaker that advances and defends them. One should consider how what each character says is related to the way he lives and to what he values.

In the *Symposium*, Plato is allowing his audience to see *Erôs* from a variety of distinct points of view. The meaning of the *Symposium* can only emerge by comparing and contrasting the points of view of its characters.

## THE SPEECH OF PAUSANIAS (180C–185E)

In his speech Phaedrus made no explicit mention of the sexual aspect of the homoerotic relationships he champions. Perhaps this omission explains why Pausanias's speech begins with this topic, as Allan Bloom points out, for it seems to commence right where Phaedrus left off.[10] The speech of Pausanias immediately and explicitly introduces the sexual dimension of erotic love, the "things of Aphrodite." But Pausanias goes on to distinguish two different Aphrodites, the heavenly one that guides us aright in sexual matters and the common or vulgar one that drives some people to put sexual gratification above all other good things. The speech of Pausanias discloses the degree to which, by the time Plato wrote the *Symposium*, the practice of *paiderastia* had become controversial in Athens. Pausanias claims that the practice is entirely forbidden in Persia and in some Greek city-states. In other places, it seems as though these relationships were not completely endorsed, nor were they entirely forbidden; they existed at the margins of the law and of custom, while remaining accepted cultural practice. Pausanias attempts to put the best face he can on these associations between men and boys, arguing that there is a right way and a wrong way, or a better and worse way, to engage in a paiderastic relationship. But to make this argument, he has to begin by claiming that *Erôs* is complex, rather than simple. By arguing that there are really two Aphrodites instead of one, Pausanias "splits" *Erôs* into two types. He classes the practices he deems good under the heading of the Heavenly Aphrodite and the practices he deems bad under the heading of the Common (or vulgar) Aphrodite.

"It is a well known fact," Pausanias begins, "that Love [*Erôs*] and Aphrodite are inseparable" (180d). But there are really two goddesses named Aphrodite. One is the Aphrodite Urania, or the Heavenly Aphrodite, and the other is the Aphrodite Pandemos, the common, vulgar Aphrodite. Both goddesses are patrons of the sexual aspects of *Erôs*, but the behaviors and practices motivated by the Common Aphrodite are far more indiscriminate and less noble than the behaviors and practices inspired by the Heavenly Aphrodite. Of course, it will be the Heavenly Aphrodite that Pausanias will be defending in his speech. He reminds the audience that, although all of the gods are deserving of honor and must be praised, we must distinguish these two very different ways in which the *Erôs* for sex can be practiced, according to which of the two Aphrodites is its patron or partner.

The argument Pausanias makes begins with a general premise that sexual relations, like human actions in general, are neither good nor bad in and of themselves; their value depends on how well or badly they are performed. He claims that none of the three activities—conversing, drinking, or singing—is inherently noble (*kalos*); everything depends on the way the act is performed. If it is performed nobly then it is noble, but if it is performed improperly, then it is base (*aischros*; 181a4). The same holds true for sexual relations, according to Pausanias. Contrary to what Phaedrus's argument had seemed to imply, it is not *Erôs*, as such, that is worthy of praise; rather, *Erôs* is praiseworthy only when it produces noble sentiments and honorable behaviors in human beings. One might imagine that Pausanias was thinking of all sorts of counter-examples during Phaedrus's speech, examples of occasions when people (even leaders of great nations) have done the most shameful and ridiculous things under erotic passion. Phaedrus was trying to convince the audience that *Erôs* always (or for the most part) inspires a sense of shame in human beings, but Pausanias seems aware of the fact that their erotic impulses can just as easily drive people to do disgraceful, extreme, and most shameful things.

Pausanias wants to differentiate these two different ways in which "the things of Aphrodite" can be pursued in order to make a better defense of *paiderastia*. He will go on to argue that while the bad ways of engaging in them should justly be abolished, the good way of practicing them should be legitimized, rather than throwing out the proverbial baby with the bathwater on account of the behavior of the bad practitioners. He will defend the principle of justice or fairness, for he seems to regard this virtue as the most important one in human affairs.

According to Pausanias, the *Erôs* of the Common Aphrodite is so indiscriminate that its followers will even go with women as well as with men. They will be more interested in the body than in the mind; moreover, they will be attracted to the most unintelligent, since they care only about the consummation of the sexual act whether the courtship is carried out nobly or otherwise (181a-b). The followers of the Heavenly Aphrodite, on the other hand, will behave in the contrary way; they will pursue males of promising intellect and character and pursue them in an honorable fashion. The reason for the difference between the two Aphrodites, Pausanias explains, is that the Common Aphrodite is younger and is a mix of male and female, but the Heavenly Aphrodite is older and is purely of male origins. Thus, it is natural for those under the sway of the Heavenly Aphrodite to fall in love with boys. Being mature and thus freer of the "lewdness of youth" ensures that this Heavenly *Erôs* will not be so smitten by a beautiful body alone, nor will it be inclined to chase very young boys. The lover moved by the Heavenly Aphrodite will be attracted to boys about to become men, to boys, that is, who have begun to develop a mind of their own. This Aphrodite prefers a stronger, mature, and more developed character as the object of its attention. Upon such a worthy youth, a man guided by the Heavenly Aphrodite would bestow everything he could in order to nurture him toward manhood (181c-d).

With a tone of moral indignation Pausanias claims at 181e that "there should be a law" forbidding affairs with really young boys. Such a law is meant to prevent injury to one of the parties, but the modern reader of this speech may be surprised by which party Pausanias's proposed legislation is primarily intended to safeguard. For it is not the vulnerable youths who are to be protected by the law so much as it is the older lover, who needs to have his investment safeguarded against youths who would later spurn their mentors/patrons.[11] If one gets involved with a boy who is too young, one cannot know what kind of character he is investing in, and thus the tremendous investment of time, energy, and money spent to tutor, arm, and educate him might be completely wasted. Hence, a law forbidding affairs with really young boys appears necessary to protect the older lover's investment, in Pausanias's view. He goes on to argue that he would permit these more mature (Heavenly) relationships to develop beyond the traditional cutoff point prescribed by convention: the first appearance of a beard. The relationship between Pausanias and Agathon lasted well beyond this stage and other practitioners of pederasty may have viewed its unusual length with suspicion.

Whereas Phaedrus spoke from the perspective of a beloved in such a homoerotic relationship, Pausanias, who was widely known to be the older lover of Agathon,[12] here reveals his concern to defend the interests of the lover in such a relationship, the role he himself occupies. He does not think that men should have to risk such an investment without any hedge against being rejected or betrayed by the boy on whom he has lavished his time and affection. Perhaps this almost comical twist in the speech is designed to bring out the irony in Pausanias's argument. For in a mentoring, pedagogical relationship between such an older man and a youth, it is the younger man who not only has the most difficult role in the relationship, as Phaedrus pointed out, but who also must act from the more laudable motive. The youth is presumably interested in wisdom, virtue, and whatever other skills and knowledge the older man might be able to confer upon him through their regular association; but the older man presumed to possess this wisdom and virtue appears to be interested primarily in satisfying his sexual desires. So not only must the youth be capable of perceiving that the older man has some wisdom to teach him, but he also must already have a healthy share of virtue inasmuch as he desires the nobler end.[13] Plato seems to underline this irony that the younger partner, presumably in need of wisdom and virtue, behaves more nobly than the older man, who is presumed to have virtue and nobility.

It seems clear that the "spin" Pausanias puts on these practices represents his best efforts to formulate a rational justification for his own predilections.[14] But his speech is also concerned with justice. He argues that not getting involved with a boy until the boy has reached puberty and is getting a beard should help ensure that the lover's attraction is well placed. For this will not just be an attraction for the boy's body but also an attraction for his psyche. But, of course, young men of this age will also be less vulnerable to exploitation or mistreatment than would the younger boys pursued by the vulgar lovers. So Pausanias's law would protect both parties, saving the well-meaning heavenly lovers from wasting their affections and saving the young boys from unscrupulous vulgar lovers. He highlights the fact that the existence of this latter kind of person is precisely what has necessitated laws against adultery, rape, and so on. The lovers who are dragged about by the Common Aphrodite are incapable of self-restraint, so an external restraint is required, and the law supplies this restraint (181e). Pausanias worries that the lack of boundaries or restraints on the part of common lovers has led some people to conclude that it is disgraceful to have sexual relations with any male whatsoever (182a). For Pausanias, such a conclusion would be a case of throwing the baby out with the bathwater, an unnecessary overreaction that would produce unintended harmful consequences of its own.

Next, his speech surveys attitudes about the practice of *synousia* in various neighboring communities. The laws governing such practices are said to be most complex in Athens and in Sparta. In Persia, Pausanias says, love affairs between men and boys are entirely forbidden, because the rulers cannot tolerate the strong bonds of friendship between men and boys that are forged in such relationships. Philosophy, sport, and love are specifically named as activities that produce such bonds, loyalties that are in conflict with allegiance to the state. Pausanias gives as an example in support of this point the two lovers who attempted to kill the tyrant Hippias in the late sixth century. (Although Harmodius and Aristogiton failed in their attempt to bring him down, Hippias was overthrown three years later and the two lovers received the credit for this.)

Outside of Persia, Pausanias explains, *paiderastia* is sometimes forbidden and sometimes permitted, even encouraged (182a-d). From 182d to 183d, he goes on to survey various customs of his own city, but there seems to be disagreement about whether Pausanias overstates his case regarding Athens' tolerance for the practice of boy-love. Xenophon, a former general and writer of Socratic dialogues, thought he did (Compare Xenophon, *Symposium*, ch. 8, 27–35, *Conversations of Socrates*, 263). There is likely to be hyperbole when Pausanias claims at 183c that his countrymen do not even consider a lover's vows binding and that there is immense freedom in Athens that allows lovers to disregard their responsibilities.

Pausanias uses his survey of the various customs regarding pederasty to argue for a middle ground between the complete endorsement and the total abolition of the practice. He claims that to abolish it altogether would produce cowardice and leave young men to lust for power, but on the other hand allowing all forms of such associations would cultivate a "general dullness and stupidity" (182d). He claims that the kind of balanced view of the subject he advocates is already enshrined in Athenian customs. According to Pausanias, in Athens it is considered more honorable to declare one's love, especially when one is in love with a noble youth, than it is to keep it a secret. The lover, according to Pausanias, is encouraged in every way; conquest is deemed noble, only failure is shameful. His countrymen praise the most extraordinary acts performed by a lover, acts that would be disgraceful if done for any other purpose (182e–183a). Lovers do the most ridiculous and humiliating things and yet no blame attaches to their behavior because everyone recognizes that *Erôs* is the driving force in these cases. Pausanias asserts that the gods will even forgive a lover for breaking his vows, so powerful a force is *Erôs* understood to be in human life. This part of Pausanias's speech seems to conflict with his first point that what makes an action noble is that it is performed in a noble way; for now he seems to suggest that no action is so disgraceful that it may not be forgiven in a lover. But presumably Pausanias does not intend to go so far, for his point is that this approval is only one side of the Athenian attitude. The other side is that there are several kinds of restrictions on the practice of *paiderastia* in Athens. Such restrictions include the fact that boys have hired chaperons or pedagogues to protect them when they go around the city. Moreover, boys who get involved with men are often ridiculed insufferably by their peers, and their elders do not prevent them from joining other boys in ridiculing those who do engage in the practice, nor do they reproach them for ridiculing them. Furthermore, Pausanias explains, it is considered shameful to yield too quickly to a suitor, and we have already noted that it is even cause for disenfranchisement to be seduced by money or political power into giving one's favors to someone with whom one is not in love. Pausanias takes the apparently conflicting attitudes to the practice of pederasty as proof of his distinction between two types of Aphrodite and two corresponding types of love. The Athenian customs welcome and approve of the "heavenly" form of love and set restrictions upon pederasty designed to discourage the earthly and vulgar variety. In Athens, he says, the rituals of courtship have been transformed into a competition, and the various obstacles and standard phases of the courtship are designed to allow only the honorable kind of association to develop fully.

Pausanias summarizes his position by concluding that, in his opinion, "love is like everything else, complex: considered simply in itself, it is neither honorable nor a disgrace—its character depends entirely on the behavior it promotes. To give one's self to a vile man in a vile way is truly disgraceful behavior; by contrast, it is perfectly honorable to give one's self honorably to the right man" (αἰσχρῶς μὲν οὖν ἐστι πονηρῷ τε καὶ πονηρῶς χαρίζεσθαι, καλῶς δὲ χρηστῷ τε καὶ καλῶς 183d6–8). The vile man, of course, has already been identified as the Common or Vulgar Lover. But here Pausanias adds another quality to the Heavenly kind of Love: a man moved by it will be a lover for life, loving with a permanence to match the more stable character of his more mature beloved (ὁ δὲ τοῦ ἤθους χρηστοῦ ὄντος ἐραστὴς διὰ βίου μένει, ἅτε μονίμῳ συντακείς 183e5–6).

"Our customs, then, provide for only one honorable way of taking a man as a lover," Pausanias declares, and it requires the union of two principles: the principle of *Erôs* and the principle of virtue. This point suggests that one must be a lover of virtue, in general, so that virtue guides the erotic attraction to one's young beloved (184b-d). "[T]hen, and only then, when these two principles coincide absolutely, is it ever honorable for a young man to accept a lover" (184e). So it is not reprehensible, in Pausanias's opinion, to give one's self for virtue; that is, if a young man puts himself at another's disposal because he believes he can learn from him, then this is "neither shameful nor servile." What is more, Pausanias defends the young man's actions even in cases where one is *deceived* about the lover's goodness or wisdom. He asserts, "[I]t is noble for him to have been deceived" (185b), because he was motivated by the right desire. Pausanias believes his mistake exhibits that such a young man would "do anything for the sake of virtue [*aretē*]." He concludes: "It follows, therefore, that giving in to your lover for virtue's sake is honorable, whatever the outcome" (185b). This argument is a very convenient one for a wolf to make, for it suggests that the young boy has nothing to lose in surrendering to the sexual advances of the man, as long as he does so from a sincere desire to acquire virtue.

When one considers what Pausanias stands to gain by such an attitude, it calls into question his claim to be interested primarily in virtue.[15] When lover and beloved make virtue their primary aim, this is the work of the Heavenly Love, a benefit to cities and citizens alike, according to Pausanias. But it may well be that Pausanias is only using virtue as a cloak for his real interests in the practice of pederasty. His attempt to characterize Athenian customs as a "golden mean" between excessive license and total prohibition may simply be a convenient rationalization. His law against pursuing very young boys is made primarily with an eye to his own interests. When he claims that it is noble for youths to trade sex for virtue and that it remains noble to do so even if the youth is deceived, his high-minded talk about virtue begins to seem a rather thin disguise for his own predilections.

## THE SPEECH OF ERYXIMACHUS (185C–188E)

Owing to his position at the table and to the fact that the speeches are proceeding from left to right (cf.177d), Aristophanes is supposed to speak next. But Aristophanes complains of hiccups and asks for help from Eryximachus, the doctor. He proposes an alternative to Eryximachus: either cure me or take my turn (185d). Eryximachus offers to do both things, and prescribes a series of cures for the comic poet's hiccups: holding his breath, gargling, and finally inducing a sneeze. These dramatic details raise several questions for the interpreter. Why does Plato assign hiccups to Aristophanes at this point in the dialogue? What is the point of the reversal of order between Aristophanes and Eryximachus that forces the doctor to speak before the comic poet?[16]

In his comedies, Aristophanes often made jokes that involved bodily functions, and in fact, in his play, *The Clouds*, he lampoons Socrates by making several such jokes.[17] Might Plato be turning the tables on Aristophanes in his own version of the Dionysian theater by depicting him suffering hiccups and then being cured by gargling and sneezing, three noisy phenomena involving bodily passages? Such low humor has a particular role in the Old Comedy of Aristophanes. What makes such humor funny lies in the incongruity between human pretension and human reality.[18] In *The Clouds*, Aristophanes showed that the airy philosopher remains subject to the physical realm in its coarsest forms despite his attempt to spend his time contemplating more elevated subjects. By thus subjecting his Socrates to physical degradation, the comic poet unveils what must have seemed to him as the absurdity of the philosopher's life, which is made to appear even more ridiculous because of its arrogant disregard for social conventions. He who would regard himself as higher than other men may be brought low, his pretensions undercut by his mammal body. Plato's use of "low humor" here, if it pokes fun at Aristophanes, does so in a way that still reminds us of the serious side of such things as bodily functions by putting them in a medical context. Aristophanes too, no less than the philosopher he lampoons in *The Clouds*, is subject to the strictures of the body; he is not one whit superior to the philosopher in terms of his relation to the body. His body can sabotage him, as hiccups prevent him from taking his rightful turn at speaking; he is made to experience how the body can inhibit him from pursuing the things of his concern. But there is more to this dramatic episode than a Platonic response to low comedy.

In the movement of Plato's drama, Aristophanes' case of hiccups might also serve to undermine the seriousness of Eryximachus's speech. As one reads silently the doctor's scientific pronouncements on right living and health, on order and harmony, modern readers must imagine the speech's counterpoint;[99] for, as we learn by comparing 185d-e with 189a, the doctor's words would have been punctuated by Aristophanes' hiccups, gurgling, breath holding, and finally an explosive sneeze. These potentially comical bodily eruptions no doubt undermined the serious, sometimes pompous, and overly pedantic, tone of Eryximachus's speech.

One might well ask whether it is Aristophanes or Eryximachus who is more directly the butt of Plato's joke. The reversal in order poses a challenge to Aristophanes as well as to Eryximachus, because, when it is his turn to speak, the comic poet's account of the origin and nature of *Erôs* now must somehow top the doctor's speech and the all-embracing cosmic role it assigns to *Erôs*. But if Aristophanes' speech can rise to this challenge, it will indicate something important about Plato's ultimate estimation concerning which character comes out worse in this dramatic reversal. Indeed, the fact that Aristophanes will be cured of his hiccups by following the doctor's prescription may be Plato's way of putting Eryximachus's proficiency as a doctor beyond question, thereby placing his account in a more favorable light. How often in real life does it happen that a doctor prescribes a cure for his patient, as Eryximachus does for his table companion, and then gets to watch the regimen prove successful in the space of a half an hour?[20]

Eryximachus is a physician, a man learned in the "natural philosophy" of his day; he is the ancient equivalent of a "man of science." So it should be no surprise that his speech on *Erôs* reflects his point of view as a specialist in medicine and his interest in natural phenomena in general. For Eryximachus, Love is not a phenomenon that occurs solely between men and boys.

*Erôs* is not merely a human emotion on Eryximachus's view, but a principle of the "cosmos," that is, of the natural "order of things." The doctor draws on both the philosophy and the medical counsel of Empedocles, for whom Love (*Philotēs*) and Strife (*Neikos*) were the fundamental forces responsible respectively for the growth and union, and decay and dissolution, of all things. Love brings all matter together and Strife pulls it apart. In framing *Erôs* as a cosmic force like attraction and repulsion affecting all material things, Eryximachus clearly expands the discussion of *Erôs* in the dialogue beyond the scope of Phaedrus's and Pausanias's speeches. The physician in the group appeals from the outset to his own expertise, medicine, which has taught him that love is not just a feeling experienced by humans, but is a force operative in all life and in all bodies, that is, in all things. Love even directs things in the domain of the gods. But Love is also a deity for Eryximachus, as it seems to have been for Empedocles; for the Greeks impersonal cosmic forces of nature could be called "gods" without implying that they assumed a human form. Eryximachus's speech also echoes ideas that some of Plato's philosophical protagonists endorse in other dialogues, such as the view that health is a kind of harmony or orderliness within the body. So to whatever extent Eryximachus's views may be taken up into the dialectical movement of the dialogue or superseded later in the *Symposium*, they should not be dismissed out of hand.

Eryximachus builds upon Pausanias's distinction of *Erôs* into two *Erotes*, expressing a desire to extend Pausanias's insight that *Erôs* possesses a double nature (186a) to all living things in the *kosmos*: plants, animals, human beings, and the gods. But Eryximachus will define his two Erotes differently than Pausanias's uranian and pandemic loves. Eryximachus contrasts the double-natured *Erôs*, desire (*epithumia*), with *Erôs* as concord (*philia*), which does not have a double nature because it is defined as a reconciliation (*philia, homonoia* 186e1–2) of opposites, or "contraries." The characteristics of *Erôs* as desire will be exemplified in medicine and the characteristics of *Erôs* as concord will be illustrated through music. The two loves can be seen in the effects of contraries in healthy and sick bodies. Konstan and Young-Bruehl have argued that Eryximachus's account relies upon significant aspects of medical doctrine, current at the time, in particular, the practices set down in the Hippocratic treatise *On Regimen*.[21] They show that Eryximachus's account is really quite sophisticated, presenting Eryximachus's syllogism as follows:

P1   Health and sickness in the body are different and dissimilar things;

P2   Dissimilar things desire and love dissimilar things; (therefore,)

C    the healthy and the sick have different kinds of love (that is, love dissimilar things," 40).

They go on to show that Eryximachus introduces a different kind of "Love" at 186D. "Up to this point," they write, "the argument has been straightforward enough. The two components of the double Love are distinguished both by their objects and by the kinds of bodies in which they inhere, healthy bodies desiring things that are good for them, sick ones the reverse" (40). Eryximachus explains the doctor's art as follows:

> A good practitioner knows how to affect the body and how to transform its desires; he can implant the proper species of Love when it's absent and eliminate the other sort whenever it occurs. The physician's task is to effect a reconciliation and to establish mutual love between the most basic bodily elements. (186d)

If sick bodies desire bad things, they must be made to desire what is good for them. Eryximachus explains that the doctor must be able to turn antipathy in an organism into congeniality. And as Konstan and Young-Bruehl put it, "The meaning of Love here is not and cannot be the same as it was earlier in the speech, and the difference is in fact signaled by what amounts to a new definition." At 186d6, Eryximachus uses the word *philia*, while *Erôs* had been previously understood as *epithumia* (desire). This new definition of *Erôs* stresses contrary elements that can be brought into friendship or concord with one another, reconciled with one another by the doctor who knows how to do this. Operating under the patronage of Asclepius, the doctor must be capable of instilling "loves" that are absent and plucking out ones that are excessive. So the *Erôs* understood as the reconciliation of contraries that produce concord or friendship is differentiated from *Erôs* understood as two different kinds of desires.

According to Eryximachus, medicine is just a science of the effects of love on the body with respect to filling and emptying. The physician's art is partly a diviner's (*mantic*) art, for it is the art of the physician to distinguish healthy from unhealthy love. By "loves" in the body Eryximachus means the forces of Harmonia and the forces of Strife—the relationship of contrary elements within the bodily whole. The physician is able to promote attunement while mitigating discord in the body, creating or preserving an attunement between these forces. This point becomes clearer when Eryximachus says that a doctor's job is to establish a reconciliation and love between the body's basic elements.

According to Eryximachus's Empedoclean understanding of the world these basic elements are contraries, pairs of "opposites" such as hot and cold, bitter and sweet, wet and dry. The Presocratics already recognized that change happens between contraries. Whenever anything changes, they would argue, it changes along some continuum or other that ranges between extremes; the extremes are treated as "contraries" rather than contradictories because although they cannot both be present in a thing at the same place and time, they *can* both be absent. Cold and hot are contraries. For instance, something can be *neither* extremely hot nor extremely cold—as when it is simply lukewarm—but nothing can be *both* extremely hot and extremely cold *in relation to the same thing at the same time*. Of course, things that fall on a continuum between the contraries hot/cold can in a sense be "both hot and cold" but only in the sense of being a mixture of heat and cold that is neither extremely hot nor extremely cold. The more a thing passes from one contrary, the more it moves toward the other. The contraries are in a sense then naturally in opposition—each drives the other out when it enters into a thing. For example, increasing heat in a thing drives out the previous cold, and vice versa. Yet since things always fall somewhere within the range of various contraries, everything can be seen as a mixture of contraries, and the states of any given thing can be understood as a precise proportion of one contrary to another.

The health of an organism too can be seen as a kind of balance or "attunement"; whatever the optimal or healthy condition of a thing is, it can be seen as a balancing, or a "harmonia," of the opposed contraries. Such a balance will characterize the healthy love or harmony throughout the cycles of build up and release. Healthy Love occurs when the forces of Strife are controlled and ordered by the forces of *Erôs*, that is, when one contrary is brought together with another into an attunement. This attunement may be seen as constituting a kind of "love" or concord between them. Right love would involve the right kind of mixture, with the elements present in the right proportion to produce the "healthy" state; wrong love would be disorderliness, the effect of Strife in the cosmos.

Moderation is the virtue the doctor thinks is most important. Hence, just as Eryximachus had counseled the others earlier in the evening to be moderate in the consumption of alcohol as a corrective for having drunk to excess on the previous night, he argues here that the Healthy Love is a moderate love.

It seems clear that Eryximachus, as a follower of Apollo's order, sees himself as combating Dionysus and his forces of chaos. Yet it is surprising how "out of balance" his account is, judging from the minor role he assigns to Strife. (Not surprisingly, almost the first thing Aristophanes will do in his speech is to tell the story of how Zeus bisected the original human beings, reminding everyone of the power of division as a force, which Eryximachus had soft-pedaled in his speech.)

From Eryximachus's medical perspective, *Erôs* is the force in nature that attracts the dry to the moist, the hot to the cold, and the bitter to the sweet. Applied to human relations, this logic might imply that the male seeks the female and vice versa, an argument that will not serve Eryximachus in the defense of pederasty. Nor does he appear to notice this implication of his argument. He ignores completely love between individuals, since his profession concerns itself primarily with the effects of love in the body. As Anderson rightly notes: "Somewhere along the line—even though Eryximakhos is

Phaidros' lover—the concept of love as a relation between two individuals has disappeared" (*Masks of Dionysos*, 39). Eryximachus also seems unaware of the threat of renewed Strife implicit in the principle of attraction of like for like,[22] a principle that would seem to pose a strong challenge for the physician claiming expertise at balancing or attuning these opposing forces. So, as Anderson has shown, while our physician argues within a largely Empedoclean framework (augmented by Heraclitus and the Hippocratics), he does not grasp the effect of entropy on the overall picture of an Empedoclean universe.

Eryximachus mentions and uses the statements of poets and Presocratics even while saying things that suggest his intellectual distance from, and superiority to, them (see, e.g., his disagreement with the poets at 186e). His remarks about the poets suggest that he does not often agree with them. In this, Eryximachus reflects a certain type of "scientific" character. The poets claim to be divinely inspired; they embody the traditional wisdom. The type of man Eryximachus is, someone who sees himself as possessing specialized knowledge gained by inquiry and who is undoubtedly skeptical of the poets' claims to inspired wisdom, will invoke poetic wisdom only with reservation. Nor is a man who is in love with the dry clarity promised by naturalistic explanations likely to approve of obscurity in a philosopher. He is specifically critical of Heraclitus's famous obscurity. He charges that Heraclitus spoke imprecisely when he described harmony as the reconciliation of discordant notes (187a). He goes on to clarify what he supposes Heraclitus meant to say: "Heraclitus probably meant that an expert musician creates a harmony by resolving the prior discord between high and low notes" (187a-b).[23] Eryximachus does not shy away from claiming that everything—physical education and farming, poetry and music—can be explained in terms of the mixtures of contraries. In his discussion of music in particular it becomes clear that the Healthy Love is a concord of opposites. Music is the art of the effects of love on rhythm and harmony. Harmony resolves the opposition between high and low notes, while rhythm is the mixture or loving concord of fast and slow. He considers these effects in two spheres: composition, which is the creation of new verses and melodies, and musical education, which teaches the correct performance of musical compositions. The good love in music, produced by the Heavenly Muse Urania—the muse associated with philosophy in Pausanias's speech (and also at *Phaedrus* 259d)—is the love felt by good people or by people who might be improved in goodness by love.[24] This muse clearly links back to Pausanias's Uranian Aphrodite. The other kind of love, the negative kind of love, is the love associated with the muse Polyhymnia, the muse of many songs, who is characterized as being "common and vulgar." This muse is reminiscent of Pausanias's Aphrodite Pandemos. Eryximachus says that people must be careful to enjoy the pleasures of this muse without slipping into debauchery; they must find a way to receive the pleasure without the harm. He compares this to regulating the pleasure of eating by means of medicine. That is, just as a healthy diet requires that one restrain one's self from indulging to excess the pleasures of junk food, so too one must beware of using pleasure alone as a standard in music.[25]

Next, Eryximachus broadens his account to explain that these two species of Love are everywhere—not only in all areas of human life, but even in the seasons. The elemental pairs of contraries "hot/cold" and "wet/dry" blend together in various ways to effect not only seasonal changes, but also the weather as such and the conditions of agricultural production. The wrong kind of love brings about plague, blights, diseases, frost, hail, and so on. One sees here the ecological side of Eryximachus's thought; the world around us is regarded as a living creature governed by the same energies that govern human beings. It seems to be implied that there is always some state of love, never simply an absence of love; love never goes away, but it can be properly or improperly channeled.[26]

Perhaps most foreign to twenty-first-century ears is Eryximachus's claim that astronomy studies the effects of love on the movements of stars and the seasons. "Seasons" (τῶν ὡρῶν 188a1) here must refer to the seasonal movements of the constellations. With this assertion, Eryximachus has broached the subject of Love's role in relation to the divine, since the heavenly bodies were thought of as gods. So, in keeping with the earlier claim that Love even governs dealings among the gods, Eryximachus begins to move in the direction of the gods—taking up next the relations between the gods and mortals. For the rites of sacrifice and divination that govern the communication between gods and mortals is also the province of Love. Eryximachus thus anticipates in a slight way what Diotima will say later in Socrates' speech. *Erôs* will indeed have everything to do with the communication between men and the gods according to Diotima's teaching. The role of *Erôs* in the relation between the human and the divine is an important theme in Plato but occurs nowhere more explicitly and yet enigmatically than in the *Symposium*.

Even with sacrifice and divination, both proper and improper loves can arise, and here it would seem especially crucial to have the right kind of love. Eryximachus places the origin of impiety in following the wrong kind rather than the right kind of love; humans should follow the right kind of love in every interaction with the gods and with parents. Eryximachus does not consider the simple absence of *Erôs*, as though there could be no such thing; the impious person, perhaps even the atheist, is not someone with no love in relation to divine things, but someone with the wrong kind of love. Perhaps Eryximachus means that everyone reveres something, so that those who do not believe in the traditional gods will make a "god" out of something else— perhaps money, pleasure, or conventional honors. According to Eryximachus, divination is the science of Love in this sphere, the sphere of justice and piety. Thus, Eryximachus does discuss virtues other than moderation; but since even these virtues are based on the harmony of contrary elements, even these virtues would seem to be species of moderation.

Eryximachus emphasizes the greatness and the variety of love's power; he suggests that it may even be called absolute. He adds enigmatically that it is "even greater when directed at the Good."[27] Eryximachus concludes by saying in summation that *Erôs* gives us happiness and good fortune, the bonds of human society and concord with the gods.

Eryximachus's speech is one of the more comprehensive in its understanding of the variety of the phenomena of love; only the speeches of Aristophanes and Socrates are comparable. Eryximachus has articulated a view of *Erôs* as a natural force at work throughout the cosmos and in every sphere of human life. Not only his own art of medicine, but all human art is said to depend on understanding the healthy and diseased loves that produce the good or bad conditions of things. Mastery of love provides the key to the knowledge required to balance or to harmonize all things. Yet Eryximachus's conception of *Erôs* as a natural principle or a cosmic force that extends throughout the natural world is influenced by or borrowed from pre-Socratic and Hippocratic sources; despite its philosophical rigor, Eryximachus's speech is arguably the most derivative of the six speeches on *Erôs* in the *Symposium*.[28] Eryximachus seems to represent a kind of intellectual temperament that is still familiar today: the sort of specialist or expert who filters everything through the lens of his or her expertise and becomes too narrowly focused, unaware of how the part he or she studies is related to the whole. Plato's Eryximachus illustrates how a narrow focus can create a kind of intellectual myopia. He completely identifies with his profession, so much so that his own identity or personality is assimilated to it. His scientific naturalism succeeds in removing everything remotely erotic from his speech on *Erôs*, as his account of Love focuses exclusively on its biological side while leaving out its human dimension. There is nothing romantic or "sexy" about Eryximachus's discussion of *Erôs*; his speech describes sexual relations in terms that more closely resemble the workings of a hydraulic pump than an affair of the heart.[29]

As he brings his account of *Erôs* to a conclusion, Eryximachus tells Aristophanes, whose hiccups have finally been cured, that he (Aristophanes) can "complete" (ἀναπληρῶσαι, literally, "fill up") the argument, unless the comic poet intends to take a different approach (188e3). The doctor acknowledges that he might have left something out, although he did not mean to do so. Aristophanes' speech can be seen in part as a correction of the narrowness of the specialist, Eryximachus.

## THE SPEECH OF ARISTOPHANES (189A–193E)

Plato's audience learns (at 189a) that Aristophanes has overcome his hiccups, but only after applying the full range of remedies that Eryximachus had prescribed at 185d-e. This is implied by (1) his earlier promise to follow Eryximachus's instructions (185e), (2) the fact that Eryximachus's instructions put the remedies in a sequence, and (3) the fact that he now says the problem was not solved until he had applied the sneeze treatment (189a). One must imagine that while Eryximachus was speaking, Aristophanes was holding his breath, gargling, and finally sneezing. Aristophanes' bodily disruptions would indeed have created a strange counterpoint to Eryximachus's speech about the concord of Love in the body. As if to drive the point home, Aristophanes wonders aloud that the noises and ticklings associated with sneezing were able to restore the order and concord that for Eryximachus constitute the healthy kind of love (189a). This remark of the poet's is surely meant to be comical; the poet is offering himself as a counterexample to the Hippocratic theory of orderly (*kosmion*) Love (189a3).[30] Eryximachus, not surprisingly, takes Aristophanes to be clowning and reacts defensively. His response reminds the audience that Aristophanes is a comedian and that it might therefore have to expect something comical from him. Eryximachus, the follower of Apollo, threatens to keep watch on Aristophanes, a follower of Dionysus; his concern for order puts him on guard for anything laughable in the latter's speech. Aristophanes says that he is not worried about saying something laughable (γελοῖα), which would be appropriate to his muse, but about saying something ridiculous (καταγέλαστα) (189b6–7). In other words, he hopes his audience will laugh with him, rather than at him.

It is surely no accident that both Eryximachus's and Aristophanes' callings are mentioned at the outset of their speeches. We have noted that every speech in the dialogue reflects something of the speaker's *character*, yet the speeches of Eryximachus, Aristophanes, and Agathon also reflect their *occupations*, occupations with which Plato, as a philosopher, had to come to terms. The fact that Aristophanes the comic playwright is followed immediately by Agathon the tragedian—thanks to the reversal in the order of speeches caused by Aristophanes' hiccups—is also surely no accident. Given the cryptic remarks regarding comedy and tragedy made to these two characters by Socrates at the end of the dialogue (223c-d), Plato surely creates this reversal of order in part to bring the tragic and comic poet together and place their speeches closest to that of Socrates. Thus, the order of the last three speeches on *Erôs* foreshadows Socrates' debate with the poets at the party's end (see 223d).[31] The theme of the speeches at Agathon's house may be *Erôs*, but philosophy's relation to tragedy and comedy is one of the main themes of Plato's *Symposium*. Ultimately the two themes are related; one will best understand philosophy's relation to tragedy and comedy by understanding the relation of each of them to *Erôs*.

But one should also wonder why Plato did not simply establish this order of speeches from the beginning. For Plato did not merely group Aristophanes and Agathon together; rather, he has Aristophanes and Eryximachus change places. This switch is partly explained by the decision to inflict Aristophanes with hiccups, and we have already suggested some possible reasons for that choice. But there may be yet further reasons to make Eryximachus and Aristophanes trade places.[32]

Aristophanes sidesteps Eryximachus's suggestion that he "fill in" (ἀναπληρῶσαι) what Eryximachus had begun; rather, he announces that he will take a different approach from either of Eryximachus or Pausanias. They had missed the real power of *Erôs*, who cares for and benefits the human race more than any other god does. If people knew Love's real power they would have built the greatest temples and made the greatest sacrifices to him.

Whereas Eryximachus's account of *Erôs* was naturalistic or scientific, Aristophanes speaks in mythic, pious terms. This approach befits the criticism made by the historical Aristophanes against the hubris of the Sophists and of naturalistic philosophy (a criticism seen in *Clouds*). Aristophanes' prominent mention of temples and sacrifices at the outset of his speech is only the first sign of his concern with piety. Eryximachus, in contrast, had subsumed sacrifices under more universal principles, the same principles one can observe in physical bodies and their coarse urges and ailments. He also suggested that medicine is a kind of divination (188c-d).

Aristophanes claims that Love is "the most philanthropic god," that is, "the friendliest to men" (φιλανθρωπότατος), standing by humans and curing their ills. Aristophanes indicates that he expects the others to pass on the teaching he relates to them (189c8–d1). His proselytizing zeal seems to foreshadow Socrates' remarks at the end of his own speech (212b-c), where he says that being persuaded by Diotima of love's great value he tries to persuade others and exhorts them to honor matters of love. Aristophanes' and Socrates' speeches are the only two that seem to be offered in a proselytizing spirit. This parallel between their speeches suggest that these two speeches are especially fit for general or public consumption; Aristophanes and Socrates are both particularly interested in the moral improvement of others. Many have felt that these two speeches are the most impressive of the speeches on love in the *Symposium*.[33]

Aristophanes hearkens back to the primordial hidden beginnings; a golden age when there were three kinds of humans, not just male and female, but three sexes in all (189d-e): man, female, and the "androgynos," the "man-woman" or hermaphrodite. This suggestion of "three sexes" already provides enticing material for Aristophanes' comic imagination. More comical still is the shape he ascribes to the original humans and their mode of locomotion (189e–190b). The original humans were round, with four arms and four legs, having one head with two faces and four ears. They also had two sets of sexual organs although, as Aristophanes mentions later, they propagated on the ground (191b).[34] Even these original round humans were capable of sexual reproduction then, but apparently they did not have the desire we call *Erôs*, for Aristophanes' myth is a myth of its origin. These beings could walk equally well in either direction, and when they had to move quickly, they could do cartwheels (190a-b). This fantastic description accords well with the comic playfulness of the historical Aristophanes.

After this humorous prelude, Aristophanes explains that the males were offspring of the Sun; the females of the Earth, and the male-female combinations were offspring of the Moon. The Moon is said to "partake in both" male and female, but perhaps the thought is also that the Moon combines qualities of both the Sun and the Earth. Being descended from these heavenly deities explains why the first humans were spherical, yet sharing this property of being spherical with their divine parents makes the offspring seem more ridiculous than divine.[35]

These original humans had great strength and ambitions. They dared to attack the gods.[36] Zeus and the other gods did not want to wipe out the humans as they had the giants before them, because they wanted the sacrifices and the worship that humans provide. This detail suggests that the gods are in a way dependent on humans and also that the original humans were at one time pious enough to make sacrifices and worship the gods.

Comedy often functions by tying our pretensions to our low and absurd origins; by bringing together these opposites, our pretensions are shattered and we achieve a kind of healing clarity. Here Aristophanes brings together the secret human desire for mastery with a beginning that shows that this desire is associated with a monstrosity. He thereby suggests that human beginnings were at one and the same time both grand and ridiculous, or that the first humans were grotesque and laughable in proportion to their hubris, in a way that contradicted their pretensions. By associating human beings with such origins, he serves to undercut human pretensions now to counteract any tendency toward hubris humans may still retain.

Aristophanes' myth has been compared to the myth of the Fall of Man in Genesis.[37] It explains the unsatisfying or problematic aspects of the human condition as the result of a punishment for a primordial impiety. According to Aristophanes' story, the gods are threatened by increasing human power, but they do not want to lose the plentiful sacrifices they might obtain from the humans. Zeus's plan addresses both considerations; by cutting the humans in half he at one and the same time weakens them and multiplies their number, so that the gods can expect even more sacrifices from them in the future (190c-d). Somehow the mere reduction from whole to half, from four-legged to two-legged, greatly reduces their power, so much so that this reduction is not offset by their increase in numbers. Their power must be more than halved, for it is unclear that only halving their power while at the same time doubling their number would have the effect of rendering them harmless, if they had truly been harmful before. But the gods never had much reason to fear the human assault, as the ease of Zeus's act shows. If humans are not pious, they will be halved again, forcing them to hop around on one leg (190d). Once more the idea of two-legged humans as halved creatures having to learn to walk on only two legs, combined with the vividly ridiculous image of hopping one-legged people, adds to the coarse comic effect of Aristophanes' words. Aristophanes is careful to say that the humans' faces must be turned toward their wound so that they can see what their folly has wrought. The navel is the place where the skin of each halved human is drawn up and sewn together by Apollo, to whom Zeus assigns the job of tending to the halved creatures. Some wrinkles of skin are left as a reminder of their transgression and punishment (190e–191a).

Aristophanes' comic tale, with its characteristically Aristophanic flight of fancy, is the tale of an original condition from which human beings fell through an act of hubris. Daring to vie with gods, humans were reduced to a condition much less than their original one, and they live under the threat of yet further bisection if they dare to step outside their mortal bounds again. Thus, Aristophanes' speech conveys a serious moral lesson, even as do the similarly imaginative plays of the real Aristophanes. Plato has provided a fitting speech for his Aristophanes, a speech that, as K. J. Dover has shown, combines elements of tragedy, philosophy, and folklore.[38] Whereas Pausanias and Eryximachus, each in his own way, splits love in two, Aristophanes takes this idea one step farther and tells of the actual splitting in two of original human beings. His account makes clear that Aristophanes believes that respect for the gods is the most important virtue human beings can possess, for it was impiety that caused the original beings to be bisected, and the threat of further splitting is intended to keep people respectful and pious.[39]

This mythic backdrop is now used to explain the phenomenon of *Erôs* and the curious longing it involves. According to Aristophanes, each and every human being is longing for a lost original wholeness—in the terms of the image, for the "other half" from whom each was originally severed and whom each now requires to "complete" him or her. This conception of *Erôs* certainly has much in common with a romantic notion of love with which we are still familiar today: the idea of the lover as the "missing piece" of our life which will somehow complete us, the "other half" without which we cannot be whole. Aristophanes is the first to introduce into the conversation the idea of romantic love, a love that is more reciprocal and equal than love as conceived by Phaedrus, Pausanias, and Eryximachus.

The curious view of Aristophanes also implies that the loved one is in a sense not *another* at all, but simply a missing part of one's *self*. Aristophanes compares the human being to the *symbolon*, half of a broken coin, each half of which is kept by different people as a token of friendship or a means of surety; "[E]ach of us is the *symbolon* of a human," he says (ἕκαστος οὖν ἡμῶν ἐστι ἀνθρώπου σύμβολον 191d3–4). What each halved human longs for is not truly a distinct other at all, but rather part of an original lost self. All longing for others is explained as an instance of the longing for what has been taken from us, a longing for what we lack. All attraction for another person, on this view, is a species of the primordial human desire to be whole again, reunited with what originally belonged to us but which was taken from us long ago.

In this way, Aristophanes uses his myth to explain not only human longing but its seemingly futile nature; what all humans long for—to be rejoined into one—is something they never really can have. So an element of tragic unfulfillment remains in all love.

Aristophanes also uses the three original types of human to explain the different objects of sexual desires: attractions of men for men, women for women, and women and men for each other. Interestingly, all heterosexual love is said to descend from the third sex, the hermaphrodite (ἀνδρόγυνον, 191d7). But, according to Aristophanes, men who are attracted to men are the manliest men because they are descended from the original males (192a). He could also, but does not, say that women who are attracted to women are the most feminine of all women because they are derived from the original female who was all-woman. Instead, he makes them into courtesans whose aloofness toward men is apparently taken as a sign of lesbianism (191e). Nonetheless, Anderson points out that against Phaedrus's and Pausanias's exclusive focus on homoerotic *Erôs*, Aristophanes at least includes discussion of heterosexual attraction as a natural human desire. The comic poet seems to say at 191c that only heterosexual pairings could propagate, while the other two, unable to reproduce, would only be capable of receiving momentary satisfaction that would allow them to get on with their business.[40] But there is no reason to think that Aristophanes is not serious about his praise of homosexuality. He claims that all politically powerful and ambitious men are really attracted to males and that they only marry and have children to satisfy local custom (191e–192b). But when Aristophanes anticipates that Eryximachus may jokingly try to apply his words to Agathon and Pausanias and responds that perhaps Agathon and Pausanias do happen to be "male by nature" (193c), there is certainly some humor at their expense. The implied compliment, that Pausanias and Agathon are especially manly, contradicts what is known of Agathon.[41] In any case, even other practitioners of pederasty would have viewed the unusual length of the relationship between him and Pausanias with suspicion. Aristophanes may be ostensibly flattering Agathon and Pausanias but the irony of his comments would not have been lost on the others.

According to Aristophanes, Zeus now feels pity for the pathetic creatures he has thus produced and as a kind of afterthought invents human sexual reproduction. Aristophanes seems to emphasize how silly humans are, if an aspect of themselves that they regard as so fundamental is the product of a divine afterthought. The original humans used to cast their seed on the ground to reproduce. If this was sexual reproduction outside the body, as the cicada example suggests, then one must suppose that the male/male and the female/female combinations needed each other in order to reproduce. But such procreation would have been without sexual desire, since it is the origin of *Erôs* that Aristophanes' myth endeavors to explain. Indeed, the reproductive process must have been a cool, rational act, or else impelled by an autonomous, passionless instinct and carried out without much feeling. In Aristophanes' account, in contrast to that of Eryximachus, Strife appears *before* Love; the bisection precedes the longing for one's lost half. Thus, Aristophanes seems to argue that Strife is more fundamental than Love, whereas Eryximachus had put the stress on the other side of Empedocles' view, focusing on Love as a harmony and ignoring the important role Empedocles gave to Strife.[42]

According to Aristophanes' story, Zeus must turn the genitals around to the side of the wound. In so doing, Zeus also invents interior reproduction, which enables the male/female pairs to reproduce and male/male pairs to enjoy a certain kind of sex (191b-c). Aristophanes leaves out female/female relationships. Only now, after having sex, can they get on with their lives, whereas before they were even allowing themselves to starve because they could not join with their other halves in "sexual union" (191b). But since sexual union is not really the original wholeness they seek, it is not clear why it is supposed to heal them; it is somehow the next best thing, the nearest possible approximation to their true desire (191d, 192c-e, 193d). Aristophanes cannot mean literally that one is only drawn to one's original half, for of course, we are only distant descendants of those original humans and were not actually severed ourselves. What is more we find ourselves attracted to many people, not just our unique "missing half." The myth at most "explains" the attraction for a specific gender, but not which specific people one will find desirable.

Aristophanes describes the mysterious attraction of *Erôs* and the longing for union implicit in it. He mentions that every human *psychē* wants something and yet doesn't even know what it wants. "It's obvious that the soul of every lover longs for something else; his soul cannot say what, but like an oracle it has a sense of what it wants, and like an oracle it hides behind a riddle." (ἀλλ' ἄλλο τι βουλομένη ἑκατέρου ἡ ψυχὴ δήλη ἐστιν, ὃ οὐ δύναται εἰπεῖν, ἀλλὰ μαντεύεται ὃ βούλεται, καὶ αἰνίττεται 192c7–d2). In comparing the psyche's sense of what it lacks with the oracular power of divination, Aristophanes foreshadows the teaching of Diotima in Socrates' speech according to which *Erôs* is a messenger from the gods. Oracles are messages from the gods, but it is notoriously difficult for mortals to properly interpret them. Emanating from the gods, such messages have validity and a hold on mortals that they cannot deny; but coming from the gods, they transcend what mortals understand. Divination leads mortals in a direction that mere intelligence could not take them. So too, in the case of love, something has a hold on the lovers, but they do not yet know what it is. Only in the fullness of time will the true meaning of the "oracle" that is *Erôs* be revealed.

Aristophanes claims that if Hephaestus asked two lovers if they wanted to be joined into one they would jump at the chance (192d-e). What is perhaps most important about this story is that it takes a god to voice the longing of the lovers; they themselves do not realize what it was they had wanted until they hear it articulated by the god. In real life most humans would not think to say that they wanted such a union; yet if they reflect upon the secret logic of their love, such an outcome would seem to be a figurative expression for what they most desire.[43] Love, on Aristophanes' view, is the attempt to restore our original wholeness. Sexual intercourse is the best humans can do for now, but it holds out the promise of a return to lost unity (193c-d). Thus, Aristophanes suggests that love is a second-best expedient and that it points to something even better (192e–193a, 193c-d). The best thing of all would be reversion to the primal nature (ἡ ἀρχαία φύσις 192e, 193d) or finding the other half (see 193c). But the best *among available circumstances* is that which is nearest to this original state, and that closest approximation is to find the love (παιδικῶν) who is "according to one's mind" (193d).

In closing, Aristophanes commands his companions (twice within a few lines—193b-c and 193d) not to make a comedy of his speech. It would seem the comic poet is asking to be taken seriously. His seriousness here may be part of his comedy, but he also is suggesting that the audience should try to see through the obviously comic qualities of the speech in order to grasp its deeper truth, a truth that is more tragic than comical. One must look deeper, beneath the laughable surface, to the serious underlying meaning, the moral or existential message of the speech. Some commentators have suggested that Plato has crafted for Aristophanes a tale that is at once comic and tragic.[44] The thought of round, eight-limbed beings or the prospect of humans hopping around on one leg brings laughter, but the speech also has a tragic side. For the odds are not good that anyone will find his or her perfect match, the one person who can complete them and make them whole again. Even if one was lucky enough to find him or her, one might not really want to be joined and have one's individuality dissolve. But even if one did desire it, one will almost assuredly be disappointed, for, Aristophanes' pious hopes to the contrary, the lost wholeness does not seem likely to be recuperable. Aristophanes' account captures a primordial tension in human longing. For humans do long to unite, and yet it would seem that the desire has an absurd quality, insofar as the desire to lose one's separate self in union seems to negate the very subject that desires it. And insofar as the speech points to a longing that stretches beyond any person, beyond any simple remedy or fulfillment, it suggests that all human beings will feel insatiable longing. Yet Aristophanes does hold out the "greatest hope" that if humans are sufficiently pious Love may restore them to their original nature (193d).

Aristophanes' speech may have indeed "filled in" gaps left by Eryximachus's speech. For Aristophanes *Erôs* is constituted by a primordial schism, not cosmic harmony. Unlike the doctor, the comedian emphasizes the human aspects of love. Rather than employing a naturalistic approach, exploring nature's laws and elements, Aristophanes' approach is mythic, the story of humanity's fall through an original act of hubris and impiety. Thus, Aristophanes' account is religious and poetic whereas Eryximachus's account had been naturalistic or scientific; Aristophanes' view is also more pessimistic about human nature and the nature of love. At the same time, however, Aristophanes' speech is less reductionistic than Eryximachus's speech; Aristophanes does not forget human feelings but takes them as his cue. Whereas Eryximachus had stressed moderation and order and had displayed his pride in and reliance on his Apollonian art, Aristophanes stresses piety and human dependence on the gods, in devotion to his muse and to his patron deity Dionysus. Of all the speeches thus far, only Aristophanes deals with all forms of human erotic attraction. Only Aristophanes' image of bisected humans stresses the mutual attraction of love as opposed to the asymmetry of lover and beloved characteristic of Greek pederasty. Although Aristophanes began his speech by announcing that love is most beneficial to humans, it seems that his myth makes love the result of a punishment, an ever-present reminder of human imperfection and our subordination to the divine. But such is precisely Aristophanes' pious point—Love benefits human beings by reminding them of their imperfection and their subjection to the divine. The relation of *Erôs* to the divine is another point that will be taken up and transformed by Socrates.

## THE SPEECH OF AGATHON (194E–198A)

A brief interlude reminds the audience that only Agathon and Socrates have yet to speak. Aristophanes says that he is eager to hear what Agathon and Socrates will say (193d-e); Aristophanes himself is well aware that Agathon and Socrates, the two remaining speakers, were both lampooned by him in his plays (in *Thesmophoriazusae* and *Clouds*, respectively). He therefore has reason to be concerned that they will take this opportunity to retaliate by attacking his speech.

Eryximachus says that he would worry about Socrates and Agathon having something left to say, except for the fact that he knows they are skillful in the art of love (193e). This remark gives Socrates a chance to express his misgivings about having to speak after Agathon, whereupon Agathon accuses the philosopher of trying to inflate the audience's expectations. If the audience expects more than Agathon can deliver and if Socrates delivers far more than he promises, it will cast Socrates' speech in a better light. Agathon can see that Socrates' praise of his abilities is ironic, but rather than contemplate the underlying ground of that irony, Agathon would rather impute to Socrates petty intentions.

Socrates responds that in order for him to suppose that such a ploy would work, he would have to have forgotten how brave Agathon was in the dramatic contest that Agathon has just won, when he spoke before the large numbers of Athenians. The implication is that since Agathon is such an accomplished poet, as proven by his victory over other playwrights, he should easily be able to endure the pressure of his impending performance here. Agathon notes that an intelligent person would find a few intelligent people more frightening than a crowd of fools. Although Agathon distinguishes between the wise few and the many fools, a distinction also made by Socrates, his remark has further implications that are not lost on Socrates. Apparently, Agathon regards the audience of his award-winning tragedy as foolish. He implies that he would say different things to them than to his friends here at the drinking party. Thus, this exchange also relates to the contrast discussed earlier, the contrast between making speeches or performing something rehearsed for a large audience, on the one hand, and an intimate engagement in a Socratic conversation, on the other. It is quite a different thing to write or perform impressive poetry than it is to be able to answer questions and defend one's positions extemporaneously. When it is Socrates' turn to speak, the philosopher will cleverly subvert the demand to give a standard rhetorical speech by recalling a series of conversations he had with a wise woman Diotima. Thereby he smuggles in his preferred question-and-answer manner of conversing.

A crucial difference between these modes of discourse is brought out by Socrates' reply to Agathon. The reply is twofold. First, he points out a contradiction in what Agathon has just said—namely, that the crowd of "intelligent" men whose opinion Agathon is worried about now were also part of the larger crowd Agathon was addressing in the amphitheater. Second, Socrates points out that if Agathon means that he would be ashamed of doing anything ugly (or shameful) only in front of wise men, he is implying that he *would not* be ashamed to do anything ugly or shameful in front of ordinary people (194d). This inference seems to show that Agathon is more concerned with *appearances* than he is with *reality*—that is, he is more worried about getting caught doing bad or foolish things than he is with actually doing them.[45]

Phaedrus, wisely seeing that this remark of Socrates' could lead to one of the philosopher's characteristic rounds of cross-questioning with Agathon, jumps in to warn the young poet against answering Socrates' remark (194d). If you get a conversation going with Socrates, he says, we will never get to hear the rest of the speeches. He also makes the remark that this outcome would be fine by Socrates who cares only for conversation, and Phaedrus does not fail to add that Socrates is especially fond of conversation with handsome boys. This comment raises the question of the motivation behind Socrates' activities. There are, of course, other statements in this dialogue (and elsewhere in the Platonic corpus) that suggest that Socrates had some kind of prurient interest behind his practice of seeking out young boys for discussion. These remarks are augmented by certain ways that Socrates himself sometimes describes his relationship to his partners. For instance, *Gorgias* 481d and *Charmides* 155d make it clear that Plato wants his audience to be aware that Socrates is capable of erotic attraction to the young men he meets. But these indications are in tension with the spirit of Socrates as it is depicted in the dialogues and especially with the account of Socrates given by Alcibiades later in the *Symposium*. Clearly this problem is connected to the meaning of

Socrates' claim to have expertise in matters of love. It should be recalled that associations of Socrates with *Erôs* could be found in other Socratic writers besides Plato. The problem of Socrates and *Erôs* is related to the problem of the relations between *Erôs* and philosophy. These problems will be better addressed after an examination of Socrates' speech on love.

It is Phaedrus's duty as the symposiarch to get a speech from both Agathon and Socrates. His interruption at this point to remind them of their duty may be saving Agathon from a Socratic cross-examination, in which the kinds of embarrassment Agathon seems to be worried about would be likely to result. So we can imagine Agathon secretly breathing a sigh of relief as he begins his speech. The savvy members of Plato's audience may suspect that it is easier to perform before thirty thousand people a work one has rehearsed to perfection than it is to submit to an ad hoc examination of one's way of life at the hands of Socrates.

Agathon is the first of the speakers to spend some time at the outset discussing what the procedure for praising love should be. Aristophanes had criticized the approach of the previous speakers, but he did not really explain the principle behind his own method of praising love. Agathon attempts to state the principle he is following, one that he contends will render his speech superior to all of the others. Agathon declares that the previous speakers did not really praise *Erôs*, the god, himself, but only the gifts that he gives humans (that is, the speeches did not touch on what *Erôs* is, in itself, but only praised it for its effects). Agathon claims that he will explicate what *Erôs* himself is like, what qualities the god himself possesses. According to Agathon, the proper method for praising anyone is first to say what his qualities are, the qualities for which we praise him, and only then should one go on to describe the positive effects he produces as a result of having these qualities. This procedure reflects, albeit dimly, the Socratic dictum that in speaking about something one must first define it, in order to know what it is in itself, before trying to determine its other attributes (*Meno* 71b, *Rep.* 354b-c). But in claiming to speak about the qualities of *Erôs* before discussing Love's gifts, Agathon is *not* saying that he will *define Erôs* (that is, say *what* Love is) before enumerating *Erôs's* attributes. To do that he would either have to define the phenomenon of love or the god of Love, and Agathon is very far from trying to do either of those things. Hence, Socrates would still have reason to complain that Agathon is trying to explain what *Erôs* is like before understanding what *Erôs*, in itself, is.

According to Agathon, all gods are happy, but *Erôs* is the happiest of all because he is the most beautiful and the best. The reason why he is the most beautiful god, according to Agathon, is that he is the youngest; this is in direct opposition to what Phaedrus had said when he claimed that *Erôs* was among the oldest of the gods.[46] One might ask what it means that Love can be thought of as old or young, among the oldest or the youngest. To say that he is among the oldest of the gods suggests that *Erôs* is the source of all the other forces in the universe; love is the primordial force. To say that Love is young is to ascribe to *Erôs* himself qualities associated with his effects: *Erôs* is associated with the vitality of youth, and *Erôs* makes the one who feels his power feel young. It was a commonplace of ancient philosophy that the cause of something possesses the property that it causes other things to possess. The idea is that in order for a thing to bestow something on another, it must first possess what it bestows. So if *Erôs* causes vitality in others, then by this logic, *Erôs* should possess vitality himself. It is ironic that, after beginning by insisting that he will be the first to praise *Erôs* for what he is rather than for his effects, Agathon will then define what *Erôs* is entirely in terms of its effects. Agathon will ascribe whatever qualities are associated with the effects or the objects of *Erôs* to *Erôs* himself.

Recall that Agathon is the beloved of Pausanias; like the speech of Phaedrus, the beloved of Eryximachus, Agathon's speech places *Erôs* in the role of a beloved (the object of the lover's desire), that is, in *his own role*.[47] Agathon sees *Erôs* not as the paradigmatic lover, but as the ultimate object of Love; he conceives *Erôs* as the most beautiful beloved. Even though Socrates will correct this feature of Agathon's speech, Agathon's speech does implicitly raise the question of the relation between beauty and *Erôs*.[48] The problem of beauty is not something that is simply dropped when Socrates returns to the conception of *Erôs* as a lover; rather Socrates' speech will ultimately be as much, if not more, about beauty and its essential role in understanding the nature of Love. Closely associated with the question of the relation between *Erôs* and beauty will be the question of the proper object of *Erôs* and of the relation of *Erôs* to that object.

One of the ways that Socrates will criticize Agathon's speech will be to say that Agathon has ascribed to *Erôs* itself attributes that are really possessed by some of its objects. But however valid this criticism might be, Agathon's approach does have some merit. It makes a certain sense to say that one knows what Love is through the phenomena in which it manifests itself or that one understands *Erôs* better by considering the characteristics of its objects. Thus, Agathon's personification of *Erôs* in terms of the qualities of the objects of *Erôs* can provide some insight into *Erôs*.[49] It is also interesting to note, however, that Agathon ascribes to Love features he thinks he himself possesses in great abundance compared to Socrates.

To understand how Agathon personifies *Erôs* by attributing to *Erôs* the properties of its objects, consider the way Agathon claims to prove that *Erôs* is young. *Erôs* is young because it flees old age. *Erôs* hates the old and will go nowhere near it. *Erôs* loves the young and is one of them, following the principle that attraction occurs "like to like." *Erôs*, says Agathon, is forever young. But to express the matter literally, one would say that erotic desire is more typical of youth than it is of old age, and that the youth tend to be more erotically desirable than the elderly are. Since the objects and subjects of *Erôs* are typically young, Agathon ascribes youth figuratively to *Erôs* himself.

Apparently, the god frequently visited the young and beautiful Agathon. Indeed Agathon's promiscuity is famously ridiculed in Aristophanes' play *Thesmophoriazusae*. When an old man named Mnesilochus says that he does not know Agathon, Euripides retorts: "You may not know him, but you have had sex with him" (line 35).[50] No wonder Agathon left Athens, as Apollodorus reminded the rich businessmen at 172e. No wonder, also, that Socrates and Aristodemus rephrase Homer in such a way as to raise the question whether Agathon is or is not a good man, as his name implies. The same promiscuity with which Agathon is characterized by Aristophanes is evidenced in the *Symposium* by the fact that Agathon flirts with both Socrates and Alcibiades right in front of Pausanias.

In order to refute the tradition that makes *Erôs* ancient, a primordial force, Agathon goes back to its sources (cited by Phaedrus), Hesiod and Parmenides, and claims that the deeds they recount, on account of their violence, could only have happened under Necessity, not under *Erôs*. If Love had ruled then, there would have been peace and brotherhood among the gods, as there is now that Love is king. Here *Erôs* replaces Zeus, the traditional king of the gods. It would seem that Agathon is presenting a view of cosmic progress. Violence transpired under the reign of Necessity, according to Agathon; the tales of previous poets indicate that violence also transpired under the reign of Zeus, whom Agathon does not mention here. Only under the reign of Love is there no violence. It would seem that Agathon would like to reform the way his fellow Greeks think about the gods. Once again one finds in what Agathon says a faint reflection, almost a parody, of what Socrates says in other dialogues. For Socrates will say that human beings should not ascribe bad things to the gods (*Rep.* 379a–380c; *Euthy.* 5e–6c). But whereas Socrates denies that gods can make war on one another, Agathon can imagine gods warring, but not under Love's rule. In any case, it is characteristic of Agathon's worldview that the past was worse than the present. His view thus contrasts with Aristophanes' view, according to which the past was a golden age in which humans existed in a higher state and from which they were expelled by divine punishment. Agathon's attitude suggests a certain shallow optimism and complacency in Agathon's character. The victorious poet believes that he is blessed and has everything he needs, and this conceit is reflected in the picture he paints of *Erôs* according to which *Erôs* is a god possessed with every positive attribute.

In addition to youth, Agathon ascribes many other characteristics to *Erôs*. He argues that Love is delicate because Love only walks on what is soft—the characters and psyches of men and gods and, in particular, in soft and gentle natures, as opposed to harsh ones. *Erôs* has a fluid and supple shape, for he can enfold a psyche and withdraw surreptitiously. *Erôs* is good-looking and avoids anything ugly; between Love and Ugliness there is war. (This claim seems to slight his guest, Socrates, implying as it does that the physically ugly Socrates would have no experience with Love and would, therefore, be unqualified to speak about it, contrary to the philosopher's claim that this is indeed the one art he is proficient in.) Love has an exquisite complexion, because the god consorts with flowers—including "flowers" in the extended sense of bodies that are in youthful "bloom."

After surveying the "physical" attributes of *Erôs*, Agathon proceeds to the ethical character of the god. Love is just, causing wrong to no one and being wronged by no one; for violence, being opposed to Love, comes nowhere near it. *Erôs* doesn't force himself on those subject to him; rather, they surrender willingly. This remark illustrates something about the way Agathon thinks of justice. What is just is that to which people have *consented*, what they have enacted by agreement, and thus, according to Agathon, the conventions are kings of society. On the one hand, this view associates justice with freedom and a submission to authority that is consensual or voluntary; on the other hand, Agathon's view would seem to make law and justice purely matters of convention, mere human agreement without any further standard. That justice is merely conventional is a view Plato's Socrates vigorously opposes in other dialogues (as does the Athenian Stranger of Plato's *Laws*). Plato's protagonists are not legalists. If there were no standard against which human laws or agreements could be measured, there would be no such thing as a bad or unjust law. Such legalism would imply that those who have the power to make the laws determine what is just; thus, the meaning of justice would be relative to a given legal system. If there is no such thing as an unjust law, there could also be no such thing as an unjust society. This equation of justice with the conventional is another way in which Agathon's speech about *Erôs* reveals more about Agathon than it does about *Erôs*. The emphasis on convention in this part of his speech supports the conclusion that Agathon is concerned with the superficial and the merely apparent, the realm of opinion, rather than with knowledge or wisdom. Because he is concerned with pleasure and ease, he cannot be bothered to think through the implications of his statements.

Agathon continues ascribing each of the virtues to *Erôs*. Love also has "the biggest share of moderation." If moderation is taking just the right amount—not too much and not too little—then this suggestion involves an oxymoron: in Agathon's account, Love seems to take *an immoderate share of moderation*. Moderation, for him, is power over pleasures and passions, and no pleasure is more powerful than *Erôs*. On the one hand, for Plato the idea that true moderation can be merely a matter of being ruled by the most powerful of all passions could be a misunderstanding, since this view is critiqued by Socrates in the *Phaedo* (68e–69a). On the other hand, however, there *is* a sense in which virtue, as Socrates understands it, *is* a matter of being ruled by a single passion—the passion for wisdom.[51] There may be some truth to what Agathon says, if it is understood in a different way than Agathon understands it. Desire *for the right thing* may be the only force capable of overcoming the temptation that is desire for the wrong things. But Agathon seems to be thinking of romantic love, so that he is regarding a situation in which one overcomes certain dangerous desires by means of another stronger desire *that is equally dangerous* (the kind of circumstance critiqued in the *Phaedo* passage cited above). True moderation in the Platonic sense is not merely the rule of a single desire, but the rule of a single desire of the right kind, a desire for the highest object.

For Agathon, *Erôs* is brave, because not even the god of war, Ares himself, can stand up to *Erôs*. He refers to the myth in which Ares is smitten with Aphrodite, and her jealous husband, Hephaestus, traps the two of them while they are making love. Agathon uses the myth to claim that Ares has no hold on *Erôs*, but *Erôs* does have a hold on Ares; *Erôs* is therefore more powerful than Ares, the bravest of all the rest, and therefore *Erôs* must be the bravest of all. Once again, as in the case of justice and moderation, the speech of Agathon displays his misunderstanding of a virtue. It is a misunderstanding of bravery to think that being more powerful makes one brave; confidence inspired by the knowledge that one has more power might not be the same thing as bravery (compare Aristotle, *Nicomachean Ethics* 1116b5–24). Agathon's desire to outdo everyone causes him to see all of the virtues through jaundiced eyes. Yet even in this case there is a sense in which Agathon's account has some truth to it; in common with Phaedrus, Agathon forges a connection between *Erôs* and bravery, and love can indeed inspire humans to face dangers. To be sure, Love in the form of the love of honor may be at the heart of bravery. (More will be said on this topic in the speech of Socrates.)

Agathon's desire to outdo all of the other speakers—including the last speaker whose speech he has not yet heard—is evident, for Agathon brings into his account each of the four virtues that had just been lauded one at a time by the four previous speakers. Phaedrus celebrated courage, Pausanias defended justice, Eryximachus promoted moderation, and Aristophanes' tale advocated piety. Agathon will defend wisdom; but he takes as his task, that is, as the task of the wise and good, to clarify all the other virtues, and he attributes all five of these virtues to *Erôs*. Mark Moes nicely explicates just how Agathon hopes to outdo the others (foreshadowing Alcibiades' desire to outdo Socrates) in his account of the virtues in the following passage:

> In his description of *Erôs* as the most virtuous (read "powerful") of the gods, Agathon presupposes an understanding of the cardinal virtues as personal traits that enable their possessors to dominate others. In his account *Erôs* is *just* because everyone willingly "serves" him (195c). *Erôs* is *temperate* because temperance "rules over" desires and pleasures, because *Erôs* offers the greatest pleasure and so "rules over" all the lesser pleasures (196c). *Erôs* is courageous because he "overpowers" even Ares the god of war (referring to the story in Book 8 of the *Odyssey*). *Erôs* is *wise* because he inspires poetry and art in anyone who is touched by him.[52]

Since Agathon's pretensions drive him to find a way to ascribe every possible virtue to *Erôs*, he cannot forget perhaps the most important of them
all, wisdom, which is the only virtue not celebrated thus far by the previous
speakers, although each was implicitly staking a claim to it. Agathon points
out that he is honoring his own profession as Eryximachus did the medical
art, as he goes on to make *Erôs* into a poet. That being a poet is the first sign
of Love's wisdom shows us how highly Agathon thinks of his art. People in
Agathon's time generally believed that the gods inspired poetry. The poets
were thought to have a kind of almost supernatural wisdom. That these two
ideas might be in conflict—that the poets were inspired, on the one hand,
and that he poets possessed wisdom, on the other hand—would not ordinarily occur to most people. It took a Socrates to point out the conflict between
these ideas, as he does in Plato's *Ion*. In Socrates' day people looked to the
great epics of Homer to get their sense of things, to find the models by which
to shape their lives. Classical Athens was a society that had only recently
made the transition to literacy from orality, and in many respects it was still
in transition. Poetry functions in oral societies to preserve and to transmit
important knowledge, as well as to prescribe the behaviors expected of various members of the community. In these and other ways, poetry functioned
in the ancient world as a repository of cultural information, and it was seen
as a source of the greatest wisdom. It is this high status of poetry, and the
authority it was granted as a kind of knowledge, that Plato's dialogues challenge in several places, most notably in *Republic* X.

Agathon proves that *Erôs* is a poet by the same method he has been
using all along; he ascribes to *Erôs* any property associated with the effects
or objects of *Erôs*. So, since love inspires poetry in people, Love must be a
poet; Love grants poetic power through inspiration, and one cannot give
another a power one does not possess oneself. Agathon may be thinking of
the model of teaching: Love teaches the art of poetry when it inspires poetry.
The teacher cannot teach what the teacher does not understand. But some of
the other discussions of poetry in Plato's dialogues show that it is questionable whether inspiration can be thought of as a form of understanding (the
*Ion*, for instance, examines these issues; see also *Apology* 22b-c).

Who can doubt, Agathon says, that *Erôs* is responsible for the production
of all animals? But rather than thinking of *Erôs* as some kind of elemental
force, in the manner of Eryximachus, Agathon thinks of *Erôs* is an anthropo-
morphic god who displays his craft-knowledge and poetic power through his
ability to make these natural things. Diotima will build upon Agathon's reference to the creative impulse in her teachings, as related by Socrates; poetry
in the narrow sense of "versification" is just one branch of poiesis in a broader
sense that includes all kinds of production. Hence, Agathon continues by
immediately jumping back to the example of human production, claiming
that all artisans have *Erôs* as their teacher, since the only truly successful
craftspeople are those who love their craft. (The speech of Agathon and the

other speeches before the speech of Socrates, whatever misunderstandings they might contain, also show how important love is by delineating the variety of phenomena for which it is responsible.)

Agathon then goes further and claims that *Erôs* taught even the gods their knowledge of the arts. *Erôs* taught Apollo archery, medicine, prophecy, the Muses music, Hephaestus bronze-work, and Athena weaving. *Erôs* even taught Zeus the governance of gods and men! If the gods are conceived as purveyors of these various crafts, as they usually were, then it is natural to assume that they too must love their crafts and that their love is also integral to their perfect grasp of them, as is the case with human beings. Thus, Agathon is able to make this inference from mortal phenomena to the nature of the gods. This inference falls under the same assumption or way of thinking that has governed his discourse throughout—the confusion of the mortal and the immortal, of love with the properties of the things loved, and of appearance with reality. Diotima's teaching, transmitted through Socrates' speech, will suggest that these three confusions are deeply connected because the three oppositions involved are ultimately one.

Agathon returns to his earlier claims that the gods once quarreled during the reign of Necessity, but that *Erôs* took over and settled these disputes. Then Agathon prepares to end his speech by summing up, reminding his listeners of key points and drawing the conclusions he wants especially to impress on them. *Erôs*, he says, is the most beautiful and the best and is the cause of other things being such (197c). Once more, something that Agathon says is reminiscent, though only dimly, of something the Platonic Socrates might say. For Socrates sometimes suggests that Forms give particular things properties that the Forms themselves somehow perfectly possess, that is, that they make particular things somehow "like" them by conferring on them their own properties. What many modern interpreters call "Theory of Forms" is a metaphysical view that has been cobbled together out of suggestions in Plato's texts, and, given the nature of Plato's writings on the Forms, it is impossible to be sure what his considered views on the Forms really were. The claims that Forms are somehow "like" the particulars that "participate" in them and somehow possess the same properties that they grant to particulars are highly controversial claims, and many doubt whether Plato ever held these views, or if so, whether he held them throughout his career.[53] But the claim that there is something, *Erôs*, that is most beautiful and best and is responsible for other things being such is clearly reminiscent of the language of Forms. If Agathon's point is taken another way, however, it is even less than a dim and uncomprehending reflection of the Forms; for given that he is talking about *Erôs*, he might mean that people seem to be beautiful and best when viewed by others through the eyes of *Erôs*. If that is what he is intimating, then this is another case in which he suggests that appearances are everything. If only those people seem beautiful and best whom we love, and all it really means to ascribe beauty and virtue to someone is that they possess such an appearance to the eyes of love, then beauty and virtue would be products of subjective opinion.

For his finale, Agathon waxes poetic, breaking into meter and adopting some of the rhetorical tricks popularized and taught by the famous sophist-rhetorician Gorgias of Leontini. According to Agathon, *Erôs* "gives peace to men and stillness to the sea, lays winds to rest and careworn men to sleep. Love fills us with togetherness and drains all of our divisiveness away. Love calls gatherings like these together. In feasts, in dances, and in ceremonies, he gives the lead. Love moves us to mildness, removes from us wildness" (197c-d).

The idea in this peroration seems to be that *Erôs* is responsible for peace and for togetherness. Agathon invites people to join *Erôs* "in the song he sings that charms the mind of god or man" (197e). This idea of singing songs to charm the psyche and to redirect for the psyche's benefit the feelings of love is also found in the Platonic dialogues in other contexts. The Athenian Stranger in the *Laws* for instance, makes an important use of the idea of using incantations to charm the psyche (659d-e, 664b-c, 665c) as does Socrates in the *Phaedo* (77e–78a).

Agathon closes by saying that his speech is meant partly in fun and is partly serious. The contrast between the serious and the playful, as well as their ambiguous mixture, is found throughout Plato's corpus.[54] Agathon's speech is another example of a Platonic fusion of the serious and the playful, put in the mouth of a tragic poet (as Plato earlier put an even more obvious example in the mouth of Aristophanes).[55] Agathon's speech is comical for its vacuity, its pretense, and its clever word plays; it is seriously sad because much of this comedy is unintentional. It also seems to leave everyone but the young outside the influence of *Erôs*. It is also the most overtly self-congratulatory of any speech so far. Yet it will not take long for Socrates to call Agathon's understanding of *Erôs* into question.

For the Greeks, to say that Love is a god does not mean that love is not also at the same time a human emotion, for the human feeling of love is considered just the manifestation or work of the god. So in praising the perfection of *Erôs* as he does, Agathon is also praising the human experience of *Erôs* as an experience of fullness. Socrates in contrast will make *Erôs* something quite different from a god, and the human experience of *Erôs* for Socrates will be characterized by a longing for something that is lacked. The fullness Socrates also finds in love will be inseparable from this lack; as in Aristophanes' tale, the joys of love for Socrates will be tainted by dissatisfaction, at least until Love achieves its pinnacle, its fullest bloom.

## INTERLUDE (198A-199C)

According to Aristodemus (who, it will be recalled, is the one who conveyed the story of these speeches to Apollodorus), everyone vigorously applauded

Agathon's tour de force. Agathon's clever word-plays and his use of other rhetorical devices have had their intended effect, and he has been quite successful with most of his audience. Yet it will become obvious, if it is not already, that Agathon's speech is almost entirely vacuous, from the point of view of philosophy. Like Agathon himself, the speech is longer on appearance than on substance. Part of the reason that what Agathon says about *Erôs* remains at the level of superficialities is that he is not really concerned with the real truth or meaning of what he is saying. Rather, he seems to be focused on making a beautiful speech according to popular standards, despite his pledge to go to the heart of the matter. With only rhetorical conventions for his guiding principle, Agathon again demonstrates why he is more comfortable with an ignorant crowd than a wise one, explaining perhaps why he earlier suspected that he should be embarrassed to speak before wise men. Socrates ironically suggests that it should now be obvious why he was afraid to follow Agathon. If Socrates has anything to fear, it should only be from the poor taste of an audience that has just found Agathon's speech so pleasing. But Socrates would be afraid only of saying or doing something ugly or shameful, even in front of fools, for it is not the opinion of his audience that really matters to him, but the truth. Yet Socrates is a master of rhetoric himself.

His concern for the truth on this occasion causes Socrates to be put in the less than gracious position of having to criticize his host. He begins ironically, but his seeming praise falls away quickly. Socrates comments on the beauty and variety of Agathon's speech, but then suggests that the only truly exceptional part was its ending; at the same time he makes clear that the peroration was heavily indebted to Gorgias for its rhetorical techniques. Socrates fashions a wonderful play on the similar words *Gorgias* and *Gorgon*, the mythic monster who turned men to stone the instant they looked at her. Socrates puns that he was afraid Agathon was going to use the Gorgias-head (symbolizing the hypnotic and incapacitating power of Gorgias's rhetoric) to paralyze and incapacitate him.[56]

The philosopher waxes ironic, lamenting: "I realized how ridiculous I'd been to agree to join with you in praising Love and to say that I was a master of the art of love, when I knew nothing whatever of this business, of how anything whatever ought to be praised" (198c-d). This remark refers back to 195a, where Agathon boasted that he has a method for praising that works with any subject. But Socrates goes on to criticize Agathon's speech so thoroughly that it is clear that he finds very little of redeeming value in it. Moreover, although the philosopher will say many things in his speech that dispute points other speakers have made, Agathon is the only speaker made to endure a brief cross-examination by Socrates. Agathon is the only one whom Socrates brings to an admission of ignorance or perplexity (*aporia*) in this dialogue.

Socrates continues his rebuke of Agathon:

> In my foolishness, I thought you should tell the truth about whatever you
> praise, that this should be your basis, and that from this a speaker should
> select the most beautiful truths and arrange them most suitably. I was quite
> vain, thinking that I would talk well and that I knew the truth about praising
> anything whatever. (198d)

This is doubly ironic. On the one hand, what Socrates has just said—that
one should tell the truth and suitably arrange the most beautiful truths—is
plausibly the truth about praising anything whatever; if you don't tell the
truth about something you cannot *really* be praising *it*. On the other hand it
was Agathon, not Socrates, who actually made the claim that he knew the
"truth about praising anything whatsoever," so Socrates is also pointing up
Agathon's vanity and the fact that the tragic poet has a different conception
of truth than the philosopher does. Socrates continues:

> But now it appears that this is not what it is to praise anything whatever;
> rather it is to apply to the object the grandest and the most beautiful quali-
> ties, whether he actually has them or not. And if they are false, that is no
> objection; for the proposal, apparently, was that everyone here make the rest
> of us think he is praising Love—and not that he actually praises him....
> [Y]our description of him and his gifts is designed to make him look better
> and more beautiful than anything else——to ignorant listeners, plainly, for of
> course he wouldn't look that way to those who knew. (198d–199a)

Socrates accomplishes a number of things at once with his opening move.
First, he calls into question the notion of "praise" accepted by the other speakers, suggesting that they are building their praises on falsity rather than on
truth. Of course, although he does not pursue the point, this would in effect
mean either that the other speakers were liars or that they themselves did
not know the truth about love. In ironically calling their technique an "art"
Socrates playfully suggests that they were aware of what they were doing, and
were deliberately lying about love. But this is a playfully ironic suggestion;
the other speakers are merely ignorant of the nature of love.

Yet Socrates could be indicating something subtler. Not only are the other
speakers ignorant, but their misconception of the nature of true praise has
caused them even to *lack concern* with the truth about love. The truth, from
the point of view of their conception of praise, is too mundane to be bothered
about—rather, each speaker had conceived his task as one of impressively and
skillfully attributing to *Erôs* greater attributes than did his predecessor. This
strategy climaxes in the speech of Agathon; and in Socrates' opinion, the
speech was all form and no substance. In calling attention to his assumption
that the point was to tell the truth about the thing being praised, and not to
falsify or conceal, Socrates raises an issue that will be even more prominent
later in the dialogue: just how is one supposed to get at the truth of a matter and communicate it to others. This question will be a source of dispute
between Alcibiades and Socrates a little later.

A related question raised by Socrates' ironic beginning is the question of the extent to which the other speakers thought that they were being "artful" in speaking. The other speakers no doubt thought they were being "artful," that is, in showing off their competence at speech making, even though none of them claims to be a professional rhetorician of the sort Socrates critiques elsewhere. But the poets, Aristophanes and Agathon, are interesting cases. For surely poets think of themselves as having an "art of speaking"? Even the claim to be inspired by the Muses did not prevent poets from thinking of themselves as having an art at the same time, which is why Socrates has to push the point that these claims seem incompatible in the *Ion* (533e–535a) and in the *Apology* (22b–c). In the *Gorgias*, Socrates calls poetry "rhetoric of the theater" (502d). In that dialogue Socrates distinguishes between true and false arts (463b–465d), and between good and bad species of rhetoric (503a-b). Those distinctions should be kept in mind here.[57]

Socrates makes it clear that he had agreed to take part under a mistaken assumption about the meaning of praise, or the standards to be used in praising. By this means he renegotiates the terms of his participation and announces that he will be operating under a different conception of what constitutes praise. Therefore, his speech must be judged by different standards than the speeches of the others. This move illustrates the way that philosophy introduces a new set of standards into discourse based upon principles that are radically different from those employed in poetry and rhetoric as traditionally understood. Socrates says: "I'm not giving another eulogy using that method, not at all—I wouldn't be able to do it!—but, if you wish, I'd like to tell the truth my way. I want to avoid any comparison with your speeches, so as not to give you a reason to laugh at me" (199a-b). He is asking to be evaluated by different standards than those under which the others competed, but he has also made it obvious that he believes that his standards are really the best ones. A further irony is that Socrates' speech will also be more beautiful than the others, as well as being truer from a Platonic point of view.

At this point, Socrates asks Phaedrus for permission to ask Agathon a few little questions, so that when he has Agathon's agreement he can speak on that basis. The exchange that follows between Socrates and Agathon is similar in its style to Socrates' usual sort of philosophical activity in the dialogues. Socrates' cross-examination and refutation of Agathon highlights a contrast between the format of long speeches demanded on this occasion and the mode of a Socratic conversation.[58] Here we note briefly some of the key differences between long speeches and the short question-and-answer method preferred by Socrates.

From a survey of the various contexts in which the issue of Socrates' conversational method is discussed in Plato's works, we can say that Socrates prefers the question-and-answer method for several reasons. First, with the question-and-answer method, one is able to obtain another's assent or understanding and assent step by step, a procedure likely to minimize misunderstandings and achieve the maximum clarity. It also allows points of disagreement to be taken up as they arise and permits both parties to be clear about points of agreement and disagreement. Second, the constant appeal to the other for their opinion through the stages of an argument forces the interlocutor to think more actively about the matter and actually to participate in the investigation. By contrast, long speeches place their audience in a more passive role; their effect can be more mesmerizing than stimulating. Furthermore, long speeches can be hard to follow; the speech rolls on and develops its points with no room for questions. One is not invited to examine specifically each step in the chain of argument and to keep track of inferential relationships, as one is asked to do by Socratic conversation. The question-and-answer method, in contrast to mere speechifying, puts the burden of inquiry on the interlocutor, not just on the speechmaker. With the question-and-answer method, Socrates says in the *Republic*, both parties act as lawyer and member of the jury, pleader and judge, in mutual deliberation or inquiry (*Rep.* 348a-b). Both parties in such conversations must exercise their analytic and argumentative skills as well as the ability to hear and to assess their interlocutor's arguments. Finally, there is one other possible benefit to the one-on-one form of conversation conducted by means of the question-and-answer method, and that is the way in which Socrates seems to form an ad hoc, and usually short-lived, community of inquirers with his conversation partners. Such a conversation may even engender friendship, as happens in the case of Socrates, Lysis, and Menexenus in Plato's *Lysis*.

## SOCRATES QUESTIONS AGATHON (199C–201C)

Socrates begins by claiming to admire Agathon's stated approach, which was that one should first show the qualities of Love himself and only then speak of his deeds. As suggested above, Socrates can see in this procedure a reflection of his own insistence on the priority of the "What is X?" question. Socrates holds that one should first answer the question "What is X?" before investigating the various attributes of X. Accordingly, his interaction with Agathon is aimed at laying bare the nature of *Erôs*; but he does not proceed directly to the question "What is *Erôs*?" Instead, he begins his first exchange with Agathon by asking whether Love is love of something or of nothing. He clarifies this question by referring to another term of the same type, "father"; the type in question here may be called "relational terms," that is, terms that imply a relationship between two things. A father is a father *of* someone; similarly, love is always love *of* something. If Socrates were asking about a father, "is he a father *of* something or not?," the appropriate answer would be that a father is a father of a son or a daughter. Socrates uses "mother" and "brother" as additional examples. The "mother" example shows that two different terms can be related to the same things—"mother," like "father," is related to "son or daughter." The "brother" example provides a different relationship, but remains within the sphere of the family, a principle arena of love, but not the sort of love that had been in the forefront up to this point. *Erôs*, unlike *philia*, is not commonly thought of as applying to family members, but these examples remind Plato's audience that human love takes many forms. Having established that fathers, mothers, and brothers are fathers, mothers, and brothers *of* someone, Socrates wants to know the answer to the parallel question: Is love the love *of* something or nothing? Of something, Agathon is sure.

The argument thus far has made the simple but crucially important point that love is a relational term: one cannot speak of love without implying that the love has an object, that it is felt in relation to something or someone. There is no such thing as love that has no object; that is, there is no such thing as love that is love of nothing. Socrates' questioning of Agathon continues: "Then keep this object of love in mind and remember what it is. But tell me this much: does Love desire that of which it is the love, or not?" When Agathon answers in the affirmative, Socrates next wants to know if *Erôs* actually *has* what he desires and loves at the time he desires and loves it. He gets Agathon to agree that one only desires something of which one is in need—if one did not need it, one would not desire it. He asks the rhetorical questions, "Would someone who is tall want to be tall? Or someone who is strong want to be strong?" Agathon agrees that such a one would not, and so they seem to have already agreed that desire is only of that which is lacked, because no one desires what he already has. But shortly thereafter Socrates will qualify this conclusion (200c-d).

Thus far Socrates has established that love has an object, but that it does not possess its object, but rather longs for it as something that it currently lacks. Next, he will qualify this in such a way as to account for apparent counterexamples (200c-d). For might not a strong man want to remain strong, a fast one fast, or a healthy one healthy? Socrates' answer to this is as follows: when someone says, "I'm healthy and that's just what I want to be, I'm rich and that's just what I want to be, or I desire the very things I have," Socrates will point out that what one wants in these cases is to go on possessing in time to come the things one already possesses. Desire here means: "I want the things I have now to be mine in the future as well." So even in this case it turns out that the lover desires something he does not already possess; what he desires that he does not have is the future possession of what he has now. The conclusion they reach is that anyone who desires "desires what is not at hand and not present, what he does not have, and what he is not, and that of which he is in need" (Καὶ οὗτος ἄρα καὶ ἄλλος πᾶς ὁ ἐπιθυμῶν τοῦ μὴ ἑτοίμου ἐπιθυμεῖ καὶ τοῦ μὴ παρόντος, καὶ ὃ μὴ ἔχει καὶ ὃ μὴ ἔστιν αὐτὸς καὶ οὗ ἐνδεής ἐστι 200e2–4).

The above argument shows that humans, as temporal beings, lack the continuity, the extension into the future, of what they take to be good. This lack is similar to the lack or need introduced in Aristophanes' speech by our lost other halves. It might seem that the future in Socrates' account replaces the lost past in Aristophanes' account; but the need for immortality, which will soon be discussed, is in a way bound up with a lost "origin" for Socrates as well. This origin is not temporal, however; as something outside of time, it transcends the dichotomy between past and future. Philosophy's devotion to this atemporal origin is what enables it to transcend the simple dichotomy between the conservative (preserving the past) and the revolutionary (preparing the future). Aristophanes was the conservative who accused Socrates of subversive innovations. But philosophy in its Platonic guise, and in any guise in which it pursues reason's grasp of eternal truths, is at once conservative and revolutionary, neither wholly one nor the other. For the eternal is not new, but neither is it simply the old as such. The eternal does not depend on history or progress, but it can ground innovation as well as the status quo. Thus, even revolutionaries can appeal to eternal principles. The eternal may have been grasped in the past, but it is ever available to confirmation by direct intellectual apprehension, and so it becomes a standard by which independent reason can evaluate traditions rather than take them on faith. Yet insofar as the wisdom of the past has managed to capture some insight into eternal principles, it can never be simply dismissed by philosophy in favor of what is merely new.

Socrates sums up at 200e–201a the two points that have been made thus far: Love is love of something (200a) and what Love loves is what he lacks (200e). Next, Socrates makes a third point about *Erôs*; he refers back to Agathon's speech to draw in the point that Love loves what is beautiful. But if *Erôs* is a desire for beauty and never for ugliness, and *Erôs* loves what he needs and does not have, then love needs and does not have beauty.

But there are several problems with Socrates' reasoning here. First, Love could possess its *own* beauty, but desire some *other* beauty that it still did not possess. Even so, Socrates' point that Love does not desire the beauty it already possesses would be well taken. Love would have a lack of beauty insofar as it desired beauty, but this fact would not establish that Love was not beautiful in any respect. Second, according to the general point Socrates made previously, there is a sense in which Love could desire even the beauty that it itself possess. For Love could be beautiful and *yet want to go on being beautiful*. Socrates now ignores the possibility he had admitted before. Perhaps this possibility would not have helped Agathon, to whom it would have also seemed impossible that Love could ever lose the beauty it possesses. If it were impossible for Love to lose its beauty, it would seem to have no need to *desire* its continued possession of beauty. For in that case the continued possession of it would be assured. In any case, it is clear that Socrates does not legitimately establish the point that love cannot be beautiful, for it does not follow from the claim that love must lack *in some sense* the beauty it desires. Even though Socrates does not fairly establish the claim that Love is not beautiful, his argument does bring out that claim that Love is a desire for something that is in some sense lacked. This claim, which will be important in the teaching of Diotima that Socrates will relate, is true enough even though it does not really establish that Love is not beautiful. The claim that Love is not beautiful is also important for what Socrates wants to argue, but it will be qualified by what he will say later on. For *Erôs* will be assigned an intermediate status between the mortal and the immortal; this intermediate status will imply that *Erôs* must be related to both beauty and ugliness in some way.

Socrates finally gets Agathon to admit that he did not know what he was talking about in his speech when he said that love was beautiful.

After having "shown" Agathon that Love is not beautiful, Socrates tells Agathon that his speech was beautiful anyway, as if to console him. Then Socrates immediately asks Agathon if he thinks good things are always beautiful as well. Socrates is not asking whether beautiful things are always good, but the possibility of a close association between goodness and beauty seduces the beauty-loving Agathon, who also happens to be widely acknowledged to be beautiful as well and whose name, after all, is Greek for "good." After Agathon replies that good things are indeed beautiful, Socrates concludes that if Love needs beautiful things, and all good things are beautiful, Love needs good things as well.

The previous inference does not follow as stated, for it has not been said that all beautiful things are good and it could be that the beautiful things Love needs are all non-good beautiful things. All good things might be beautiful, without all beautiful things being good. In fact, Socrates implied that it is not the case that all beautiful things are good when he criticized Agathon's speech for being beautiful, but not good. So if Love needs beautiful things and good things are beautiful, it does not necessarily follow that Love needs good things, if we could suppose that the beautiful things that Love needs are non-good beautiful things. But perhaps the underlying thought is that if good things are beautiful, and if Love lacks *all* beautiful things (which need not be the case), he must also love good things, all of which are agreed by Agathon to be beautiful. It follows, then, that Love would lack those beautiful things that are good, as well as those that are non-good. As noted previously, however, the mere fact that Love desires beautiful things does not really show that Love lacks all beautiful things. Love may possess some beautiful things, but still desire others that it lacks. Likewise, Love could possess good beautiful things, but lack and desire non-good beautiful things, on the basis of what has been said so far. What will eventually rule this possibility out is that, according to the teaching of Diotima to which Socrates will appeal in his speech, Love is not really desire for the beautiful ultimately; instead it is ultimate desire for the good. Yet it remains true that just as in the case of beauty so too in the case of goodness there is a hole in the argument. For Love could possess some goodness and still lack other goodness that it desires; or it could desire the continued possession of the very goodness that it already has but also wishes to preserve. These possibilities would still be in accordance with Socrates' and Agathon's previous agreements.[59] Yet none of these holes prevent Socrates from at least arguing that *Erôs* is not good or beautiful enough to be a god. For according to Socrates a god could lack no form of goodness. Nor would a god have to desire the continued possession of his own good, being assured of it.

Socrates convinces Agathon that, lacking and needing beautiful things, Love lacks and needs the beauty of good things. Agathon says he cannot challenge Socrates—but he seems to mean that he is unable to beat Socrates in a verbal battle. "Let it be as you say," suggests that he is surrendering without really being convinced of the point he concedes. But Socrates insists that it is the "truth" that Agathon finds impossible to challenge, whereas it would be easy to challenge Socrates.[60] This exchange is perhaps Plato's way of signaling that that point in question has not been established here but that it is still true in some sense; he may be indicating that the claim that Love lacks the good is a mere true opinion. Human love certainly does lack some good because the very existence of desire implies imperfection. To the extent that *Erôs* is a personification of human desire, the imperfection of desire would be sufficient to deny *Erôs'* divine status, from the point of view of Plato's Socrates. But Socrates' response to Agathon invites the reader to consider whether what Socrates has argued is indeed the truth or only Socrates' opinion. If some of the conclusions in question are easy to challenge, as they seem to be, they are simply Socrates' opinions. But although the *reasoning* may be suspect, certain of the *conclusions* may be undeniably true in any case; and then, qua true, the conclusions, as opposed to the reasoning intended to support them, will be impossible to refute.

## DIOTIMA QUESTIONS SOCRATES (201D–203B)

Socrates lets Agathon go (201D). Next, the philosopher says that he will try to give a speech about *Erôs* he once heard from a wise woman, one Diotima of Mantinea. Socrates credits her with teaching him the art of love. Since the art of love is the only matter Socrates claims to understand (177d-e), this amounts to crediting Diotima with teaching him all he knows.[61]

One wonders if the art of love is not the very thing that makes Socrates Socrates, that is, whether the strange knowledge it involves is not bound up with what he calls in the *Apology* his "human wisdom," that is, his ever-present awareness of his own ignorance (20d–23b).[62] It could be that this art of love is the secret lore that enables Socrates to carry out his god-given mission by means of his method of cross-examination.[63] For in this method he makes others like himself, numbing them as though he were a stingray, and bringing them into his own confused condition with respect to many kinds of questions (see *Meno* 80a-d). In this way, he awakens in others a desire for knowledge, a love of wisdom akin to his own. This awakening of love could be part of the erotic art that Socrates claims is the only thing he understands.[64]

In any case, Socrates claims that it was Diotima who led him to understand *ta erotika*, and in her cross-examination of him, she seems to have guided Socrates to the truth about love in the same way that Socrates often leads others with his question-and-answer method. Indeed, Socrates even indicates that his refutation of Agathon was modeled on Diotima's earlier refutation of him (201e). Thus, by invoking the memory and teachings of this mysterious figure, Socrates also is able to craft a conversation in place of a monologue. By doing so, he is able, as it were, to smuggle in his preferred question-and-answer method of conversing and thereby avoids merely presenting another long speech.

The use of the character Diotima has been the subject of much scholarly discussion. It is sometimes asked whether she is a real, historical person or an invention of Plato's imagination.[65] Others ask whether the character *Socrates* makes her up on the spot to fit the demands of this occasion. Socrates may have invented her on the spot, since her teachings happen, so conveniently, to provide the philosopher with a way of refuting points other speakers have just made. But there is no way completely to rule out the possibility that she is based on someone real, and that Socrates picks and chooses aspects of what he learned from her. At the same time, Socrates is permitted to refute other speakers, while admitting that he too used to think some of the things the other speakers still believe. In any case, Socrates offers scanty information about her. She was wise about many things; she is said to have put off the great plague that swept Athens in 430 for ten years by telling the Athenians what sacrifices to make.

Thucydides' *History* should make us wonder if forestalling the plague for ten years would amount to a claim of authoritative wisdom.[66] By putting off the plague until 430, she would have caused it to occur during the siege of Athens, and Thucydides suggests that the plague was more devastating owing to the close quarters in which the citizens were forced to live by that circumstance.[67] If Plato had this in mind, he might be warning his audience not to trust uncritically what Socrates is telling us through Diotima. But it is not clear that Plato has this inference in mind. Moreover, Diotima's forestalling of the plague would still be admirable, even if it falls short of preventing the plague from coming altogether. It seems unlikely that Plato would expect his audience to hold Diotima responsible for the plague's eventual onset or for the living conditions in force at the time. Whatever one might try to infer from the claim that she delayed the plague, one must try to interpret the significance of Diotima in terms of her role in the *Symposium* considered as a whole.

The decision about how to understand Diotima's role—in particular, whether we should understand her teaching about *Erôs* as a conception endorsed by Plato or as offered in some way for criticism—is a key question to be wrestled with by readers of the *Symposium*.[68] Unfortunately, there is no way to know at the outset which answer is the true one. But there are certain obvious features of Diotima's role in the dialogue that probably should guide its audience. First, Socrates' recollection of her teachings makes Socrates' speech arguably the most interesting and the most brilliant up to this point. Second, its superiority seems to be highlighted; Plato appears to have written the drama in such a way as to make his audience see that Socrates' speech surpasses the others. The fact that Socrates' speech is the last of the speeches on *Erôs* puts weighty demands on Socrates' shoulders, and this positioning itself is telling. Third, although Plato does not fail to have Aristophanes ready to make a rejoinder of some kind (212c), her teaching seems in many ways entirely consistent with other themes in the dialogues. Unfortunately, the fact that aspects of Socrates' speech are consistent with things said in other dialogues would only prove something, on its own, if we assumed that Plato could never criticize ideas he presents favorably elsewhere, an assumption that seems false.[69] It is therefore possible that Plato incorporated subtle criticisms of elements of Diotima's teaching into the drama of the *Symposium*, even if those elements do agree with what his philosophical protagonists say elsewhere. Even if Socrates' speech is more "brilliant" than the others, that need not imply that Diotima's teachings are true, though this would then undercut his criticism of Agathon quite severely. And we must remember that although Socrates' speech is the last of the speeches on *Erôs*, it is not the last speech in the *Symposium*; hence, Socrates and Diotima—the two philosophical characters in the dialogue—are not given the last word. Yet as we will see, her account of *Erôs* incorporates elements of the earlier speeches, as though it is meant to synthesize their best points, but also offers criticisms of the earlier speeches as well; and perhaps because of her teachings, Socrates' speech is the most detailed of the speeches on *Erôs* and the one with the most "Platonic" and philosophically involved content. Coming at the end of the speeches on *Erôs*, Socrates' account of Diotima's teaching seems intended to outshine all the earlier speeches on human desire.

We believe that when Socrates presents her teaching Plato's audience is supposed to see it as marvelous and profound, and to feel that it contains truth. But this impression may only be intended to be the audience's first impression, not necessarily a view that can survive thinking about the puzzles that the remainder of the dialogue presents. Plato seems to write dialogues that contain puzzles that provide a new perspective on the dialogue as a whole when one thinks about them. These puzzles lead his audience to a deeper level of insight. One puzzle with which any serious reader must contend is the problem of the relation of the speech of Alcibiades (and of the dramatic action that precedes it) to the teachings of Diotima. Until we have thoroughly considered that question it would be premature to attempt to write the last word on Diotima.

Socrates says that he will give his speech on the basis of Diotima's teaching and that he will use what he and Agathon had just agreed upon as his starting point. Following Agathon, Socrates concurs that one should first describe what *Erôs* is and what he is like and only afterward praise his works (201d-e).[70] Socrates had made the same claims about *Erôs* to Diotima that Agathon had just been making—that love is a great god and is one of the beautiful things—whereupon Diotima had refuted him in the same way as he has just refuted Agathon. Socrates puts himself in Agathon's place, consoling Agathon with the knowledge that the philosopher himself had once believed what Agathon now believes. Socrates thus perhaps lessens the sting of the refutation he has just meted out to his young host.

Socrates' recollections of his tutelage by Diotima represent one of the very few places in Plato's dialogues where Socrates is depicted in the role of a student at the feet of a teacher and actually shown learning something about a subject. In most dialogues, Socrates expresses his seemingly sincere hope that he will learn something from his interlocutors, but Plato's audience often has the sense that he has heard nothing new about the subject matter by the end of a given conversation. It is also significant that Socrates' teacher is a woman, especially given the context.[71] Symposia were all-male events, the only woman present being the flute-girl who is sent away at the beginning of the dialogue. When Socrates introduces this strange mantic from Mantinea in his speech, she plays the role of priestess rather than the role of a courtesan or flute-girl; yet she is a priestess of matters of *Erôs* (*ta erotika*). As his teacher in matters of *Erôs*, she might be responsible for the fact that Socrates will be better able to charm his followers with his voice than could the satyr Marsyas with his flute (215b-d). In true dialectical fashion, Socrates uses Diotima's teachings to incorporate some aspects of the previous speeches into the fabric of his own account, while refuting other aspects of what previous speakers had said.

As Socrates recalls his lessons at the feet of Diotima, we learn that she had shown him that it is a mistake to think of love as a beautiful god. Socrates asks what he is to think of *Erôs* in that case; if he is not beautiful and good, is he then ugly and bad? Diotima points out that this binary logic creates a false dichotomy, because there is an intermediate possibility that Socrates is overlooking. *Erôs* could be neither wholly beautiful nor completely ugly, but something in-between the beautiful and the ugly. The idea that love could be in-between the beautiful and the ugly, just as true opinion lies in-between wisdom and ignorance, introduces what is perhaps the most important and "pregnant" idea of Diotima's teaching and Socrates' speech: the idea of the in-between or intermediate (*metaxu*). The intermediate is in-between two opposites; strictly speaking, the intermediate is neither of the opposites, but in another sense it somehow partakes of both opposites at once. In the passages that follow, Diotima exploits this idea in several ways. She ties this understanding to the idea that *Erôs* is a Spirit (*daimon*), in-between gods and mortals. According to Diotima, spirits are *messengers*, not only *existing* in a category between gods and mortals, but also *moving* between them as well—literally acting as go-betweens in their role as messengers. Spirits bridge the gap between what is permanently divided, that which can be joined together in no other way than through such intermediaries: the divine and human realms. Diotima's teaching contains the beginnings of a philosophy of religion, among other things.

Besides introducing the suggestive idea of *Erôs* as a spirit or messenger, this teaching about love links an account of human striving in all its manifestations, on the one hand, to an account of the ultimate nature of things on the other. Put another way, it connects what has been taken as Plato's psychological thought with what has traditionally been taken to be his metaphysics of participation. As a result, the teaching of Diotima's seems to form an essential link between two dimensions of Plato's thinking that together constitute what were once called "the twin pillars of Platonism": what the dialogues say about the human psyche and what they say about the notion of Forms.[72] One might also say that linking these twin pillars here ties together the practical and theoretical aspects of philosophy.

*Erôs* is neither a god nor a mortal but a *spirit*, or *daimon*. Spirits are intermediaries existing in-between gods and mortals and acting as messengers that relay the prayers and sacrifices of mortals to the gods and the commands and gifts of the gods to mortals. What does it mean to call *Erôs* a "spirit" and to ascribe to him this in-between (*metaxu*) status and messenger-role? If human *Erôs* itself is a spirit, then it is not wholly or simply human; but Diotima is including all human desire under this rubric. Inclusion of human *Erôs* in the realm of the *daimonic* seems to imply that humans are rendered more than human, although less than divine, by virtue of their desires. It also suggests that human desires are linked to the divine. It might seem as though this connection to the divine could only be true of those "higher" desires, that is, the more intellectual or spiritual desires. But Diotima's teaching suggests that somehow *all* desires are connected to the divine, although some are connected more and others less directly. All desires have some relation to the divine but some desires are closer to the divine than others. It is helpful to keep in mind two contrasting aspects of her account. The image of the *daimonic* messengers is an image of *connection* between *opposites in tension*; it is an image that involves both schism and a bridging of the gap created by the schism. One must try to keep each of the connected opposites involved in *Erôs* in mind and to see how they are given a place in Diotima's thought, or else her subtler points may be badly misunderstood.

*Erôs* is a messenger, and as a messenger it leads or guides human striving toward the objects of human desire. That *Erôs* functions as a messenger also means that in the very process of desire, the desiring one is led closer to what he or she values. One receives a "message" from the object of desire in this sense: the object of desire informs and shapes the character of the desire, and the desire informs and shapes the psyche of the one desiring. Whether the object of desire is real or illusory, it has an impact on the desiring one. To say that *Erôs* is a messenger means that one receives a share of the object of desire through the very desire for it.

All desire betokens some kind of lack, something that one wants, needs or has at present and wishes to retain in perpetuity (In the last case what one "lacks" is a guaranteed future possession of what one possesses now). But far from being simply a negative sign of one's privation or need, *Erôs*, because it is always guided toward some object, embodies within its very desiring a hint about fulfillment. Put another way, since all desire is directed toward something, when one becomes cognizant of desiring, one is usually also cognizant of what is desired. There may be cases in which one does not know what one wants; but even in these cases, one's desire is a standard that determines what one does *not* want, that is, one can discover that some things fail to satisfy the desire. The more intensely one feels the desire, the more intimately one is linked to the object of desire.

As an example, consider the loving memories of lost loved ones. In remembering loved ones, one feels somehow closer to them; they are present even in their absence. All objects of love have a kind of "presence" in the heart of desire. One can be inspired by the objects of love and admiration, and through the very desire for them, gain a kind of access to them or gain a share of their beauty. The greatness of the loved object is reflected by the heart that loves it (cf. *Rep.* 500b-d). The figure of Socrates suggests that the unalloyed love of wisdom can provide a kind of intimation of wisdom, a relation to wisdom that inspires Socrates' search and keeps him free from false pretensions. Socrates' awareness of his own erotic longing for the wisdom that he lacks allows him to know the important difference between what he knows and what he does not or cannot know. He is somehow aware of the possibility of wisdom he does not possess, and he is in love with that possibility; whatever does not seem to measure up to that wisdom falls short of his desires. Although he remains unable simply to possess the wisdom that he seeks, he maintains himself in constant connection with his erotic longing for wisdom. By being in pursuit of wisdom rather than believing himself to be in possession of it, he acquires the "human wisdom" of which he speaks in the *Apology*. This characterization of Socrates' erotic relationship to wisdom will be confirmed by what Diotima says about philosophers in general.

The connection forged by *Erôs* goes in both directions. When one prays for strength or for guidance, human needs or desires are projected toward the gods; but hidden in the desires themselves are hints of the very guidance and gifts that are sought. This communication between mortals and gods occurs through the medium of *Erôs*. Humans desire the gifts of the gods, and somehow, through this very desire, are guided by the gods. The object of desire informs the desire itself, and the desire has an impact on the psyche.

But clearly the idea that human desire contains both longing for the gift and a way of receiving it must be qualified. Hungering for food does not necessarily bring one nearer to food; but it does stimulate one to seek food because the desire prompts one to think of the desired object. In the case of less obviously physical desires, desires that are often considered "spiritual" such as the desire for beauty or the desire for knowledge, the inspiration provided by the prompting of desire can be more substantial. One has some idea of the object of one's desire; desire enlivens that idea in one's mind. That idea then becomes a source of guidance. It must be something like this account that is intended in saying that *Erôs* is a messenger from the gods. What complicates the matter further is that even the purely physical desires, such as the desire for sex, contain some relation to the "higher" or so-called spiritual desires, according to Diotima. Even physical desire can lead one toward an appreciation of beauty that can eventually go beyond physical pleasure. The power of the object of love to inform the psyche through the psyche's very desire for it can be seen if one considers the diverse effects on mind, body, and behavior had by diverse objects of desire. Human life becomes quite different depending on which of the following is the fundamental object of longing: food, money, sex, pleasure, comfort, family, power, creative expression, honor, wisdom, God, or the attempt at some combination of these loves. No matter what the object of one's love, love informs one's life.

In the *Symposium Erôs* is said to be a messenger from the divine; it inspires those it possesses. In Plato's other major dialogue on *Erôs*, the *Phaedrus*, *Erôs* is also said to be a kind of divinely inspired madness (244a–245c). The *Phaedrus* clearly links love with the idea expressed in several dialogues that all learning consists in "recollecting" our prenatal knowledge of the Forms. This knowledge is said to be "recollected" in the sense that it is not learned from experience, not based upon experience; rather, experience only serves to "remind" us of the Forms. In the *Meno* and the *Phaedo* this notion of recollection is associated with the belief in reincarnation; there it is said that humans recall what they have learned in a previous life. In the *Phaedrus* this period of existence is depicted as belonging to a period of disincarnate existence before our psyches were associated with our current bodies. However literally or metaphorically one understands these presentations of Platonic recollection, one thing that they seem to indicate is that in order to understand the world of our experience we must already possess some knowledge of the Forms; but this knowledge is sufficiently obscure and confused that it is as though we have forgotten what we once knew. And yet we must retain some sense of what we are seeking in order even to be able to mount a meaningful inquiry into it. For instance, in order to formulate a definition of anything, say, an elephant, we must already have some sense of what is and is not an elephant before the discussion begins; failing this, one would have no sense of what one is trying to define. This idea appears in various ways throughout the dialogues. For example, Socrates does not know what justice is, but he can understand enough about it to come up with a counterexample that his friends will accept, as when they all see that giving a weapon back to a madman would not be just (*Rep.* 331c, 331e–332a). That is, Socrates and his friends must have some limited sense of what kinds of phenomena would count as just and unjust even if only to be able to propose definitions that are supposed to cover these phenomena. They must have some sense of justice even in order to see that these definitions fail by failing to cover all the phenomena or by including inappropriate phenomena. All of this implies some prior, latent grasp of "Forms," that is, some implicit, as yet inarticulate sense of the matters under investigation.

Love is related to recollection in part because the desire to learn, the hunger for knowledge, is vital in providing the motivation to learn.[73] When we feel our *Erôs* for knowledge, we may make the requisite mental efforts and begin to recollect. But it seems also that love is already bound up with ideas, with logos; we have desires for something or other, our desires have objects. These objects of desire need not be physical objects, of course; we can desire feelings, knowledge, states of affairs, etc. But whatever we desire has an ideational content, a Form, a whatness that makes it what it is. In our longing itself, therefore, there must appear an intimation of the Form of what we desire.

## THE SPEECH OF SOCRATES (202B–212B)

### PHILOSOPHY AND INTERMEDIACY: *ERÔS* AS HYBRID AND MESSENGER

Agathon and Socrates had both contended that *Erôs* was beautiful and good (201e). But Diotima asks Socrates if he has not observed that there is something between wisdom and ignorance (ἔστιν τι μεταξὺ σοφίας καὶ ἀμαθίας 202a2–3; μεταξὺ φρονήσεως καὶ ἀμαθίας 202a9), which turns out to be correct opinion (ὀρθὴ δόξα 202a9). Then Diotima claims that *Erôs*, just like correct opinion, is also something "in between." Initially, *Erôs* is placed between the beautiful and the ugly because it lacks beautiful and good things and accordingly cannot be a god (202d). Instead of being a god, *Erôs* is held to be a *daimon*. According to Diotima, the *whole* of the *daimonic* lies between the divine and the mortal (202e).

Before going farther, we must briefly reflect upon what is being said here. *Erôs*, which for the Greeks was both a deity and the human experience of love or desire in general, is somehow between the divine and the mortal, according to Diotima. The love humans feel is not merely a human or mortal thing; rather, it is somehow above the level of merely human being. Yet this love that humans feel is by its very nature not something divine either, for it involves a lack and the divine lacks nothing. So, according to Diotima, Love, by its very nature, both links mortals to and separates them from the divine.

Notice that thus far, a type or object of *Erôs* has not even been specified; what has been said here of *Erôs* has been ascribed to *Erôs* in general. In what follows it will become clear that *Erôs* includes *all forms of human desire*. In a very condensed way, Diotima has just made an amazing claim about the whole of the human condition—namely, that *all* human desire somehow lies between the mortal and the divine realms and links them together. This interpretation will be borne out by what follows.[74]

Beginning at 202e6, Diotima interprets the power or function of *daimones* in general:

> They interpret and carry messages to the gods from humans and to humans from the gods—the entreaties and sacrifices from the one group, and the commands and the returns made to sacrifices from the other. Furthermore, being in the middle region between both they fill this region, so that the whole is bound together with itself.

Diotima goes on to associate every art that links the humans to the divine with these daimonic powers, such as all prophecy and priestly knowledge of sacrifices, rituals, incantations, oracles, and magic/sorcery. She also says that God never mingles with the human, but that all instruction and communion of gods and humans both in waking and sleeping, is on account of these *daimones*. So our whole access to the divine depends on the mediation of these "*daimones*" of which *Erôs* is one.[75] Whoever is wise in these ways is said to be a "daimonic man" (*daimonios anēr* 203a5). All other arts—common arts and crafts—are "vulgar" by comparison.

One might suppose that being in between the divine and the mortal would be a state of neutrality that has no relation to either side. However, the first indication that this is not so is the power of *Erôs* to *communicate* between the two sides. As a communicator between both sides it must bear messages from each. This messenger role implies that it must somehow be in contact with and reflect each side. Furthermore, the function of the *daimonic* is to somehow bind the mortal and the divine realms together into a whole. The communication afforded by the *daimonic* unifies the elements, but without merging them. As part of that which makes possible the relations between these domains, *Erôs* must possess an intimacy with both sides.

The idea that *Erôs* reflects both the mortal and the divine is reinforced by the story of *Erôs*'s birth from his "parents," Poverty and Plenty (203b3ff). *Erôs* partakes in certain respects in the natures of each of his parents, which are exact opposites. As a result of his parentage, he is not merely between the ugly and the beautiful, or between the divine and the mortal, but between many other related pairs of opposites. For example, *Erôs* is said to be poor and yet resourceful (his resources are always returning and ebbing away), neither mortal nor immortal, living and dying by turns, and neither wise nor ignorant, but both desirous of and possessed of wisdom (203d6). Clearly, this in-between condition is not merely a case of neutrality. Rather, being in-between and being neither member of a pair of opposites in this context means having a share in both of them, as the dual parentage of *Erôs* shows.

The idea that "that which is neither shares in both" was already dimly prefigured in Diotima's remarks about correct opinion. Correct opinion is neither knowledge nor ignorance precisely because it is similar to each: just like knowledge, it encounters being; and just like ignorance, it is unable to give an account of itself (202a4–8).

## PHILOSOPHY AS DAIMONIC

Diotima then adds that *Erôs* moves "between wisdom and ignorance as well." (σοφίας τε αὖ καὶ ἀμαθίας ἐν μέσῳ ἐστίν 203e5); the same language is used here as was used of correct opinion (cf. 202a3). This remark provides the occasion for her to elaborate on the nature of philosophy as such:

> No god loves wisdom or desires to become wise—for he is wise—nor if any-one else is wise, does he love wisdom [θεῶν οὐδεὶς φιλοσοφεῖ οὐδ᾽ ἐπιθυμεῖ σοφὸς γενέσθαι—ἔστι γάρ—οὐδ᾽ εἴ τις ἄλλος σοφός, οὐ φιλοσοφεῖ 204a1–2]. But again neither do the ignorant love wisdom or desire to become wise. For this very thing is difficult about ignorance, that not being beautiful or good or wise, one seems to one's self to be sufficient. For he who does not think he is in need will not desire that which he does not think he needs. (204a1–7)

Therefore, none of the gods is a philosopher, according to Diotima. But the wise are not the only nonphilosophers; for Diotima explains, "[N]o one who is ignorant will love wisdom either or want to become wise" (οὐδ᾽ αὖ οἱ ἀμαθεῖς φιλοσοφοῦσιν οὐδ᾽ ἐπιθυμοῦσι σοφοὶ γενέσθαι· 204a3–4). The truly ignorant are ignorant of their ignorance, and as a result, they are content with themselves although they are not beautiful nor good nor wise.[76] This sort of ignorance is contrasted with the love of wisdom.

But the lovers of wisdom are also not wise, but ignorant as well, though in another sense. The whole difference between the lovers of wisdom and the truly ignorant consists in the fact that those who are ignorant are unaware of their ignorance. As Diotima says: "For what's especially difficult about being ignorant is that you are content with yourself, even though you're nei-ther beautiful and good nor intelligent" (αὐτὸ γὰρ τοῦτό ἐστι χαλεπὸν ἀμαθία, τὸ μὴ ὄντα καλὸν κἀγαθὸν μηδὲ φρόνιμον δοκεῖν αὐτῷ εἶναι ἱκανόν 204a4–6). Given the features that separate the gods on the one side and the ignorant on the other side from the philosophers, one can see that the philosopher too is ignorant, but unlike the ignorant spoken of here, is aware that he or she is in need. Awareness of ignorance, knowing that one doesn't know, is what motivates the search for wisdom. Interestingly then, Diotima ascribes to philosophy itself a characteristic that readers of Plato have come to associ-ate with Socrates, namely Socratic Ignorance; for Diotima's description of the philosopher as such is surely the same as Socrates' description of his "human wisdom" in the *Apology* (ἀνθρωπίνη σοφία *Ap.* 20d8). [77]

The younger Socrates of the *Symposium*, understandably confused at this point, asks Diotima (at 204a-b) who the lovers of wisdom are, if they are neither the wise nor the ignorant? Diotima says that it would be obvi-ous even to a child: "[T]hose who love wisdom fall in between those two extremes" (οἱ μεταξὺ τούτων ἀμφοτέρων 204b1–2). Those who allow their ignorance to propel them to seek wisdom are truly the lovers of wisdom, or philosophers (204b).

But what Diotima means at 204a by something that is in-between ignorance (ἀμαθίας) and wisdom (σοφίας) seems very different from the in-between state of correct judgment (or "right opinion" or "true belief") ( Τὸ ὀρθὰ δοξάζειν 202a5;ἡ ὀρθὴ δόξα 202a8–9). Earlier, at 202a3, Diotima had suggested that correct judgment lay between wisdom and ignorance (τι μεταξὺ σοφίας καὶ ἀμαθίας), "between 'understanding and ignorance," just a few lines later (μεταξὺ φρονήσεως καὶ ἀμαθίας 202a9). She characterizes this intermediate state as "judging things correctly without being able to give a reason" for one's opinion. The fact that such judgment or opinion somehow grasps the truth is said to separate it from ignorance while still falling short of complete understanding owing to its unreasoning character. But when she says that those who love wisdom—the philosophers—fall between the extremes of wisdom and ignorance (204a), we should be guided in our interpretation by the reasons why the Gods and the ignorant are said not to be lovers of wisdom. The gods already possess wisdom and therefore are not in want of it, whereas the ignorant are not aware of their need for it and so do not desire it either. Since the Gods do *not* love wisdom because they already are wise, and the foolish do not love wisdom precisely because they think they are wise, and therefore are unaware of their lack (204aff), a lover of wisdom can be neither wise (with the wisdom of the Gods) nor ignorant (with the ignorance of those unaware of their ignorance). On the one hand philosophers do not possess wisdom, for if they did, then, like the gods, they would not need to seek it. But on the other hand, neither are philosophers so ignorant as to believe that they already possess the wisdom they lack. Instead, being in-between these two states, philosophers share in wisdom just enough to be aware of their own ignorance and to understand their need to seek the wisdom they lack. But note once again that being in-between involves sharing in both: the philosopher must be ignorant of what the gods know, and yet must possess a self-awareness greater than that of the merely ignorant who do not love wisdom. The philosopher *partakes of ignorance to the extent she lacks wisdom*, and also *partakes of wisdom to the extent that she is aware of her ignorance and indeed allows that ignorance to spur the desire for wisdom*. Thus, the position in which the philosopher finds herself mirrors the position that we discerned in the case of correct opinion. Both *Erôs* and correct opinion, are characterized by this peculiar "having and not having," for "that which is neither shares in both," since it seems to have aspects of both ignorance and wisdom, possession and lack of what is desired. Moreover, this description of the philosopher clearly applies to *all philosophers as such*, according to Diotima.

That the philosopher by nature must be situated between wisdom and ignorance seems to run counter to the view that philosophical knowledge would consist in grasping Forms, if the knowledge of Forms is conceived according to the standard rationalist paradigm of self-evident a priori knowledge that establishes its own certainty. Diotima's teaching, its context, and the nature of the Platonic dialogue itself as a literary form of conveying philosophical truth, all provide some reason to doubt that the philosopher's grasp of Forms should be understood simply according to this traditional model. Exactly how the philosophical knowledge of Forms might depart from the standard interpretation we hope to clarify through our discussion of Diotima's teaching and its relations to other themes in Plato's texts. But from the start one should bear in mind a central interpretive problem, namely, how to square what is said here about the nature of philosophy not only with what is said about the philosopher's knowledge of Forms in other dialogues, but also with what is said later in Socrates' presentation of Diotima's teaching about the vision of the Beautiful in which philosophical *Erôs* culminates. One might well wonder whether or not the vision of the Beautiful described later will somehow cancel or revise what was said earlier about the nature of philosophy. We will argue that both the intermediate nature of philosophy and the possibility of philosophical *Erôs* culminating in the vision of a Form are possible and that these notions are compatible with one another. The vision of the Form must be understood in such a way that it does not cancel the intermediate nature of philosophy.[78] Perhaps there is a kind of self-evidence that does not imply certainty, since the a priori evidence in question amounts to a noetic insight into something that is never fully or adequately grasped, but that nonetheless is capable of guiding the understanding in philosophical investigation. We will develop this suggestion in what follows.

If one connects what Diotima has said about philosophy with what was said previously about *Erôs*, one may see that philosophy *as such* is between ignorance and wisdom precisely because it involves desire for wisdom, and such desire implies a certain kind of lack of what is desired. We say "a certain kind of lack" because from what has been agreed upon by Agathon and Socrates (200b-e), it is in a sense possible to both possess something and desire it. But in that case the *continued possession* of something is still lacked, and this continued possession is, strictly speaking, what is desired. Because temporal creatures can be thought of as "lacking" their futures, that is, lacking any guarantee that they will continue in the future to possess what they now possess, there could be wise philosophers, but just not philosophers who could afford no anxiety over the retention of their wisdom. However, it is interesting that Diotima does not bring this possibility out. Indeed, she seems to contradict it with her insistence that philosophers are neither wise nor ignorant. It should be recalled that not only are philosophers said to be between wisdom and ignorance, but also the wise and the ignorant are said to not desire wisdom, that is, they do not philosophize. The wisdom of the wise that Diotima is discussing here, wisdom in the strict sense, is precisely that divine wisdom with which Socrates contrasts his human wisdom in the *Apology*. The gods presumably are wise in such a way that precludes their being desirous of wisdom, because their ongoing possession of it is assured. Diotima does not merely speak of the gods, however, but of anyone who is *wise*. The point to be made here is that the extremes of wisdom and ignorance as conceived here are given a special sense. The wisdom that philosophers lack is a wisdom that could not be lost; a given philosopher could conceivably be temporarily wise or wise in a limited respect. Such wisdom may or may not seem to go beyond Socrates' "human wisdom" as it is represented in the *Apology*. As long as the philosopher lacked any aspect of wisdom, he or she could still be a lover of wisdom in those respects in which he or she was still aware of lacking wisdom. But certainly, then, such a philosopher would be less and less of a philosopher the more he or she knew. Therefore, ultimately it remains true that *qua philosopher* a philosopher would still live in an intermediate state between ignorance and wisdom.

But it is not even clear that true wisdom can exist in any other way than as a whole. Plato's epistemological thought revolves around this paradox: that partial knowledge seems to be possible, and yet as long as anything remains unknown, or especially as long as the Good remains unknown, any so-called "partial knowledge" might be corrigible, subject to modification if what is still unknown should come to light. Surely this idea is an important feature of the ocular metaphors of the Cave Allegory in the *Republic*; clarity of vision is a matter of degree, and the philosopher's "eyes" are said to need to adjust when exiting the Cave. It is only when the philosopher sees the Sun that his or her eyes have fully adjusted. Anything seen prior to that point may have been seen somewhat dimly and incorrectly. Yet not even at that point does the philosopher become infallible; for according to the Cave allegory the philosopher's eyes need to readjust when returning to the Cave. Presumably the mistakes made on the way out of the Cave are caused by lack of familiarity with the Forms (whether they be mistakes made about Forms or mistakes made about particulars) and the mistakes made on the way into the Cave or in the Cave before the eyes have readjusted are mistakes caused by having to relate formal knowledge to the confusing sensory awareness of particulars. In any case, the fact that the philosopher is depicted in the Cave Allegory as spending so much time with imperfect vision in a state of transition between realms, a transition that is a matter of degree, suggests that even in the *Republic's* account of coming to know the Forms and coming to apply this knowledge to the world, the philosopher exists in an intermediate position. Of course, the intermediacy in the *Republic* may seem to be an intermediacy of a different kind than that initially depicted in the *Symposium*. Diotima is speaking of the philosopher's epistemic state and desires vis-à-vis the gods and the truly ignorant, and not speaking about an ontological intermediacy between a realm of shadows (particulars) and daylight objects (Forms). But clearly the ontological dimension of the intermediacy is expressed in the *Symposium* as well via the contrast between the mortal and the divine.

As the "love of wisdom" all philosophy must involve *Erós* and all philosophers must have *Erós* for wisdom; apparently the "philia" involved in "philosophia" is a form of *Erós*. For by definition philosophers are those who desire wisdom, and Diotima's teaching includes this desire as a species or stage of *Erós*. Philosophy, as a form of *Erós*, must also in some way unite the divine and mortal realms.

## THE MYTH OF *POROS* AND *PENIA* (THE BIRTH OF *ERÓS*)

As previously stated, the role of messenger that travels in both directions accords *Erós* a certain duality. Diotima fleshes out this implication of her teaching with the story of the birth of *Erós*, in which the conflicting natures of his parents are used to explain *Erós's* dual or hybrid nature. *Erós* is born from two opposed parents, Resource or Plenty (*Poros*) and Poverty (*Penia*), and shares partially in the nature of each. The parents of *Erós* met and conceived their child on the day of Aphrodite's birth. Resource, having feasted, and being intoxicated with nectar, falls asleep in the garden of Zeus. Poverty decides to sleep with him and conceive a child by him—with the intention of thereby relieving her lack of resources, that is, obliging Resource to support her and her child. This detail is actually important, because it points to the natural tendency of what is lacking to be guided to whatever can supply what is lacked. This principle, that whatever lacks is led to seek what it lacks, is so fundamental that it precedes the birth of *Erós* in Diotima's theogony, and yet this principle will be embodied in the account of *Erós* as well. The naturalness of the tendency of that which is lacking to seek that which can fulfill the lack establishes a natural hierarchy, a natural ordering, and lays the groundwork for a natural principle of limit, as we shall see.

Because *Erós* is the product of the union of two such opposing natures as Resource and Poverty, and because *Erós* the offspring reflects features of each parent, *Erós* has a paradoxical or seemingly contradictory hybrid nature.

> [H]e is tough and shriveled and shoeless and homeless, always lying on the dirt without a bed, sleeping at people's doorsteps and in roadsides under the sky, having his mother's nature, always living with Need. (σκληρὸς καὶ αὐχμηρὸς καὶ ἀνυπόδητος καὶ ἄοικος, χαμαιπετὴς ἀεὶ ὢν καὶ ἄστρωτος, ἐπὶ θύραις καὶ ἐν ὁδοῖς ὑπαίθριος κοιμώμενος, τὴν τῆς μητρὸς φύσιν ἔχων, ἀεὶ ἐνδείᾳ σύνοικος 203c7–d3)

This imagery suggests transition, a passing from one place or state to another, and indicates that *Erós* comes unbidden to people's homes and impedes their daily business. *Erós* is always in need. But *Erós* is also "a schemer after the beautiful and the good" (ἐπίβουλός ἐστι τοῖς καλοῖς καὶ τοῖς ἀγαθοῖς 203d4–5). (Note that both beauty and goodness are referred to here.) On account of his father's influence, *Erós* is also "brave, impetuous, and intense, an awesome hunter, always weaving snares, resourceful in his pursuit of intelligence, a lover of wisdom [*philosophōn*] through all his life" (ἀνδρεῖος ὢν καὶ ἴτης καὶ σύντονος, θηρευτὴς δεινόσ, ἀεί τινας πλέκων μηχανάς, καὶ φρονήσεως ἐπιθυμητὴς καὶ πόριμος, φιλοσοφῶν διὰ παντὸς τοῦ βίου 203d5–7).

## ERÔS AS PHILOSOPHER

Not only are the philosophers lovers of wisdom, but according to Diotima, *Erôs* itself is a philosopher. Diotima makes it clear that *Erôs* is to be numbered among the philosophers (ὢν ἂν εἴη καὶ ὁ ″Ερως 204b2) and it is by virtue of being a philosopher, a lover of wisdom, that *Erôs* is said to be between ignorance and wisdom. Because wisdom (*sophia*) is among the most beautiful things and *Erôs* is concerned with the beautiful, "it is necessary that love [*Erôs*] be a philosopher, and being a philosopher to be between wisdom and ignorance" (204b4–5).[79] This reason is clearly dependent on the earlier claim that *Erôs* must in some sense lack whatever he desires, and *Erôs* desires wisdom. This follows from the idea that *Erôs* desires *all* beautiful things, and wisdom has been established as one of the most beautiful things.

Because *Erôs* is a philosopher, he is a lover and not a possessor of wisdom throughout his whole life. Since all humans as such have *Erôs* and continue to have it while they remain alive, this claim presumably means that no human passes beyond this state of being a seeker. Yet clearly this also cannot mean that all humans are by nature philosophers, even though they all possess *Erôs*. One can well ask why it is that Diotima calls *Erôs*, the genus of which philosophy is one species, *a philosopher*. *Erôs* for wisdom should be just one especially important species of *Erôs*. It is not at all clear how the genus can belong to one of its own species.

Plato is using features of a species of love, philosophy, to bring out characterstics of love, the genus in general. By this means, he points to the ways in which philosophy is like other loves and other loves are like philosophy, thereby helping to bring out the essence of *Erôs* that manifests in all of its diverse forms. But perhaps this image of *Erôs* as a philosopher is also meant to suggest that all human desires have an inner connection to philosophy. Such a connection might be found in the idea that one needs to reflect on desires to attain wisdom. Or perhaps the connection is that the restless and insatiable character of human desire can eventually lead humans to reflect philosophically. Yet the best explanation may be that it is the beauty of wisdom that links philosophy to all other objects of desire; for somehow all else that *Erôs* desires is seen as beautiful as well, and in the course of Diotima's teaching philosophical wisdom will prove to be especially close to the Form of Beauty Itself. For Diotima, all love is essentially of the Beautiful, and more ultimately, of the Good; the Beautiful and the Good are found in the aspects of things we truly desire. Therefore, anything that more perfectly embodies that desired quality (or qualities) is more fundamentally an object of desire.

This point establishes a natural hierarchy among the desires, based on a hierarchy of entities that more perfectly (or less perfectly) embody Beauty and Goodness. Thus, to say that all desire is philosophical may be only to say that all desire is putatively aimed at some form of the Good.

*Erôs* is also called a "genius with enchantments, potions, and clever pleadings" (δεινὸς γόης καὶ φαρμακεὺς καὶ σοφιστής 203d-e), as he had earlier been characterized as a weaver of snares and "an awesome hunter" (θηρευτὴς δεινός). These images point to the power of *Erôs* to influence minds for better or for worse, healing or harming them with its "potions," ensnaring them in desire, coloring their perceptions, shaping their beliefs. (To realize the lasting appeal of these images, one has only to think of popular songs, songs that assure that "Love is a drug," so that one can be "Addicted to Love," or that liken love to "that old black magic.") Like drugs and magic, *Erôs* can alter perceptions, exert influence, and have a powerful effect on health. Philosophy too can alter perceptions, influence decisions, and affect health. Philosophy can work magic and have a medicinal effect. Indeed, in other texts Plato's philosophical protagonists are pictured as hunters, and Socrates himself is sometimes likened to an enchanter.[80]

Initially, Diotima indicates that philosophy is a kind of love. Then it becomes clear that Love itself is a philosopher. In other words, philosophy is a participant in Love that is uniquely capable of revealing deep truths about the generic nature of Love, that is, about the Form of Love. Philosophy is a species of Love that has a special role or privileged place among the species of Love; as becomes clear in Diotima's later teachings, philosophy is the highest form of Love; as her image of *Erôs* as a philosopher suggests, it is also that form of love in which the nature of Love is most transparently revealed.

## THE INTERMEDIATE AS NEITHER AND BOTH

*Erôs* is not itself beautiful and good, but desires the beautiful and good things it lacks. Yet, if all that Diotima has said is to be taken seriously, *Erôs* should also participate in wisdom, and along with wisdom, in beauty and goodness, to some extent. For *Erôs*, as messenger and guide between the divine and mortal realms, and as the child of *Poros* and *Penia* partaking of the nature of both of his parents, must be *between* all that it desires and the conditions opposed to its desires, and so must partake of all of these opposing conditions at once. Agathon had tried to make Love into a God and a Beloved; but that would be to deify the merely human, since human beings are fundamentally erotic beings, longing for that which they do not possess or for the continued possession of that which they cannot retain. In contrast, Diotima's view is subtler. On the one hand, she recognizes a great gulf between the human and divine. She says, "God cannot mingle with man" (θεὸς δὲ ἀνθρώπῳ οὐ μείγνυται 203a1-2); it takes a *daimon* to cross the gap between the divine and the mortal realms. Yet, *Erôs* is just such a *daimon* and thus bridges the gap, that is, serves as a messenger, forming a medium of communication between gods and humans. *Erôs* then provides humans with a link to the Gods. Hence, *Erôs* also guides mortals by communicating to them something of the divine perfection. To vary the metaphor as Diotima herself does, *Erôs* also partakes in the qualities of his father, Resource (203d, 204b). Therefore, he finds some guidance from the traces within himself of the objects of his desire; and yet this guidance must occur in spite of poverty he inherits from his mother.

This contrast between Resource and Poverty that Diotima ascribes to *Erôs* represents the resource and poverty in the human experience of desire. What is especially significant is that the region between extremes partially participates in both extremes. By sharing in both extremes it involves a paradoxical having and not having rather than being merely empty. This same idea that the intermediate involves traces of both extremes is seen in the metaphor of *Erôs* as a messenger. For the message from the divine is not the divine itself, but it is a kind of guidance from the divine that puts one in touch with divinity.

Thus, the Poverty and the Resourcefulness of *Erôs* are bound together almost as one. But does Diotima want to say that *Erôs* possesses *at all times* the features of *both* parents, or does she think that *Erôs alternates* between their contrasting characteristics? Actually, *both* of these possibilities are somehow correct and are equally suggested by the text. That *Erôs* experiences resource and poverty by turns is indicated explicitly at 203e, where the use of the "*tote men*, . . . *tote de*" construction suggests two separate occasions (ἀλλὰ τοτὲ μὲν τῆς αὐτῆς ἡμέρας θάλλει τε καὶ ζῆ, ὅταν εὐπορήσῃ, τοτὲ δὲ ἀποθνῄσκει 203e1– 3). Moreover, transition is also suggested by the words that follow (πάλιν δὲ ἀναβιώσκεται διὰ τὴν τοῦ πατρὸς φύσιν 203e3). The words that follow next, however, suggest that the transitions from the state of resource to poverty and back again happen so continually (ἀεὶ) that one could say that *Erôs* is in neither condition at the same time (τὸ δὲ ποριζόμενον ἀεὶ ὑπεκρεῖ, ὥστε οὔτε ἀπορεῖ Ἔρως ποτὲ οὔτε πλουτεῖ, σοφίας τε αὖ καὶ ἀμαθίας ἐν μέσῳ ἐστιν 203e3–5). The resources of *Erôs* are "always" ebbing away, and the upshot is that *Erôs* is (in general) *neither* rich nor poor. Note too that being *neither* poor nor rich is associated with being in the *middle* between wisdom and ignorance in the words that follow. But being in neither of these states implies that one is in a way in both of them; for to the extent that *Erôs* is losing resources it will be like the poor, and to the extent that *Erôs* always has resources to lose it will be like the resourceful.

But to say that *Erôs* has the features of both parents at once is not to collapse the distinction between *Erôs*'s two parents or between the objects of our desire and the felt longing for them. It is not that the same desire also possesses the object that answers the desire, for that would simply fulfill the desire and negate it as a desire. Rather, it is that the longing for the object itself contains an *intimation of the object*; and that intimation *shapes the desirer through the longing for the object*. Through our longing for *that* object, *as opposed to some other object*, we become who we are. For instance, who or what someone admires reveals a lot about one's character; what one desires, that to which one aspires, indicates much about who one is even if one never fulfills one's dreams. For one's desires and dreams certainly shape one's life. For example, one may never wholly possess wisdom, but may become a better, "wiser" person by caring about it and allowing the desire for it to guide one's life. Since some people are guided by the basest or most destructive desires, desires that lead them to unhappiness and/or vice, it is clear that to live an excellent life it is not enough to desire just *anything*; it seems to matter very much *what* one desires. So the *nature* of the object is informing one's life, one's psyche, *through* the *love* for the object.

The power of the object of love to guide and shape the psyche of the one loving is what is meant by the "resource"-side of love. The fact that love remains a longing for what one does not possess is what is meant by the poverty-side of love. According to Diotima's "phenomenology" of *Eros*, resource and need are bound together in the *daimonic* message of love.

### THE MEANING OF LOVE AS MESSENGER; HOW DESIRE PARTICIPATES IN ITS OBJECT

Diotima next accuses Socrates of having previously thought of *Eros* as a beloved rather than as a lover (204c). The conception of *Eros* she is criticizing is Agathon's confusion of *Eros* with the objects of *Eros*. Diotima indicates that this way of understanding *Eros* is misguided. *Eros* is a seeker, a follower of beauty and goodness. He is thus the lover, as opposed to the beloved or what is sought, and as such *Eros* lacks the beautiful and good traits that it loves. But humans are creatures of love. As suggested earlier, for Diotima our very being is constituted by desire; the description of Love is at the same time a description of the human condition. Like *Eros*, human beings are beings in need, lacking what they need. Yet they do not simply lack it altogether; just as *Eros* somehow participates in his father's nature, human desire must involve an intimation of what is desired or else one would not seek it at all.[81]

Diotima's teaching is that the human experience of love is a messenger, delivering messages from gods to humans and back again. One must try to understand how love can be a messenger between gods and humans. This metaphor only makes sense if we see love as somehow consisting in *both* the entreaties from mortals to gods *and* the responses from the Divine. The simultaneity of messaging in both directions is implied in the dual parentage and hybrid nature of *Eros*. *Eros* is not only an intimation of the divine but is at the same time an entreaty from the mortal sphere. Desire is both entreaty and response, both prayer and providence. If one tries to unpack the imagery and to ask what it means, phenomenologically speaking, to say that love is such a messenger, it seems to mean that humans are somehow in contact with that which they desire through their very desire for it. For the object of desire has the power to inform the psyche *through the psyche's very desire for it*.

Through love the lover can have some form of "participation" in the object of love; but one might well consider how this kind of "participation" is different from the notions of "participation" associated with Platonic Forms. To express it simply, when a thing participates in its Form it becomes an instance of that Form, that is, it becomes an instance of the property of which that Form is the essence; but in contrast, when one desires a beloved, or for that matter even a steak sandwich, one does not thereby become an instance of one's beloved, or of a steak sandwich.

Yet there is a link between these two kinds of participation that needs to be explored. Sometimes one *can* become a participant in X by desiring X, and one may take on some features of what one desires. For instance, the desire for goodness may already improve someone, giving them at least a slight share in goodness; likewise, someone's desire for holiness may move them in the direction of holiness. That such an idea may not be too far from Plato's mind can be seen in what he makes Socrates say at *Republic* 500c-d, where he speaks of the philosophers admiring the Forms and *thereby becoming more orderly like them*.

Yet desire alone is often not enough to ensure one's participation in the quality desired. Perhaps one is not guaranteed to become good by merely desiring to be good; certainly one cannot become beautiful according to conventional standards merely by desiring to be, nor can one become a neurosurgeon merely through desiring to be one. And yet even so, one is changed by desire; and the way desire changes one depends upon the character of the desire. Furthermore, one aspect of the character of the desire has to do with the object of the desire. A desire for X may change one in different ways than a desire for Y, in virtue of the fact that X and Y themselves are different. Even if one does not through one's desire for X come to share in the properties of X or take on any X-ness, still the nature or essence of what is desired does leave a characteristic mark upon the one who desires it. The desire for wisdom makes one a philosopher, whereas the desire for an excessive amount of food would only make one a glutton. Desire enlivens the idea of the object of desire in one's mind, and the idea becomes a source of guidance; or to put it another way, the object of love shapes the desire, and the desire itself shapes the psyche. Human life becomes quite different depending on which desire moves the psyche.

## FURTHER MYSTERIES: THE POINT OF *ERÔS* (LOVE'S OBJECT AND USE)

So far, Diotima has been teaching of the *character* and *parentage* of *Erôs* (*Erôs's* character and his parentage being bound together by her account). Next, Socrates asks her: "What use is Love to human beings?" (204c8). Diotima initially replaces Socrates' question "What use is Love to human beings?" (ὁ Ἔρως τίνα χρείαν ἔχει τοῖς ἀνθρώποις) with the question, "What is the point of loving beautiful things?" (*Tί τῶν καλῶν ἐστιν ὁ "Ερως*). Thereupon, she immediately replaces this question in turn with another question: "The lover of beautiful things has a desire; what does he desire?" (*ὁ ἐρῶν τῶν καλῶν· τί ἐρᾷ;*) This question is presumably meant to lead down the path that answers the former questions. If one could understand *what* the lover of beautiful things *loves*, one could then understand *why* love is of beautiful things and of what *use* love is to humans.

To this question of what the lover of beautiful things desires, Socrates answers that the lover of beautiful things desires them to become his own (*Γενέσθαι αὐτῷ* 204d7). In Socrates' initial view then, the desire for beauty is a desire for *appropriation* of beautiful things. But apparently such an answer does not seem fundamental enough to Diotima; she asks: "What will this man have, when the beautiful things he wants have become his own? (*Tί ἔσται ἐκείνῳ ᾧ ἂν γένηται τὰ καλά;* 204d8–9). When Socrates says that he does not know how to answer this question, Diotima proposes replacing the word *beautiful* (*καλοῦ*) with the word *good* (*ἀγαθῷ* 204e). She then asks what the one who desires good things desires. To this Socrates responds in the same way as before, that the lover of good things desires that they become his own. Again Diotima asks the follow-up question: "And what will he have when the good things he wants have become his own?" (*Καὶ τί ἔσται ἐκείνῳ ᾧ ἂν γένηται τἀγαθά;* 204e5).

This replacement of the love of beautiful things with the love of good things and the way Socrates responds to the two formulations should be pondered. One must contemplate this transition in the light of the three questions elaborated above: What is the use of love to humans? What is the love of beautiful things? What does one who loves beautiful things love? This last question was supposed to lead down the proper path, but now it seems that this question leads to a dead end. Although Socrates can answer this question itself by saying that the lover of beautiful things desires that they become his own, he cannot answer the question what the lover of beauty will have when the beautiful things become his own. Socrates is not able to go far enough along this route; he is unable to go deeply enough, to get to what is truly fundamental. So his guide, Diotima, suggests a new route: she brings in the word *good*. One must consider why Plato bothers to portray Socrates' puzzlement, and why Diotima's replacement of the word *beauty* with the word *good* is depicted as the way out of the impasse. Perhaps goodness can somehow explain, in a way that beauty alone cannot, the answer to the first two questions: "What is the love of beautiful things?" and "What is the use of love to humans?" For the question that Socrates cannot answer—the question of what the lover of beauty gains by gaining possession of beauty—is another way of phrasing the question, "What is the point of desiring beautiful things?" Socrates' inability to answer this question shows that in order to answer the question about the point of beauty one must go beyond beauty. It would seem that to explain the function of love in human beings, even just erotic love, requires going beyond beauty. When the word *good* is put in its place, suddenly and magically, as it were, Socrates can answer the parallel question: when one possesses the good things one seeks, what one gains is happiness, understood as well-being (*eudaimonia*). Goodness is more fundamental, or of greater pertinence than beauty in explaining why human beings love what they do. Thus, beauty will be judged by the standard of the Good, not goodness by the standard of beauty.

Here one should reflect on a certain way of thinking that is embodied in the Socratic ethics depicted in the dialogues, one that plays a role in Plato's psychological thought and also forms the background for Diotima's teaching. According to this way of thinking, all people desire the good, and in desiring the good, they desire their own happiness. These fundamental assumptions are certainly controversial. The "good" and "happiness" seem to be treated as though they were univocal concepts; but it is by no means clear that all humans want some single X, the same X, throughout their lives, the same X that all other humans want. And if they did want some X, why call it "the good," or why call it "happiness," or why believe that the "good" and "happiness" are either the same thing, or related in such a way that the pursuit of the one is for the sake of the other? Socrates often seems to treat the claim "all humans desire the good" as though it were trivially true, that is, as though it meant "all humans desire something, and 'the good' by definition is whatever it is that they all desire"; similarly, it often seems as though "everyone desires happiness" is treated in the same way. "Happiness" is a word that has no definite content at the outset of the discussion and seems to be used as a variable to indicate whatever it is that all human beings desire; and then "the good" could be defined as whatever it is that is responsible for the attainment of "happiness." But it should be noted that this way of thinking brings in unannounced several controversial assumptions. Among these assumptions are the following: (1) that everyone wants one single ultimate goal throughout their lives to which all of their other desires must be related as means to a further end; (2) that this ultimate end is not only stable throughout an individual's life but that it is fundamentally the same (in some sense ) for all human beings; (3) that this fundamental goal, if it exists, is entitled to the name "the good" as though it had something to do with conventional virtue or morality; and (4) that this ultimate goal is also tied to happiness, so that everyone's desire is egoistic to the extent that each person is concerned with their own happiness and well-being; and finally (5) that achieving the good implies achieving happiness and achieving happiness requires achieving the good. Although these assumptions are far from uncontroversial they are important features in Socratic ethics and Platonic psychology.

For one thing, these assumptions indicate a natural hierarchy of desires. For if all desire desires one ultimate object, and all other objects are simply desired as means to this ultimate object, then the desires for merely instrumental objects are in a way subordinate to the desire for the ultimate object. Put this idea together with a Platonic notion of participation, and the objects of desire can be related not merely as means to ends, but also as participants possessing a desired quality to the Forms that engender those qualities in them. Moreover, if it is a given quality of an object that makes an object desirable, then presumably anything that more perfectly embodies that desired quality is more fundamentally an object of desire; and the quality itself, or perhaps the Form of which the embodied quality is just the reflection, may be seen as an even more ultimate object of desire. So, a natural hierarchy among the desires is established. Some desires come closer to expressing the psyche's ultimate desire than others do.

Moreover, if the good of the psyche is to fulfill, or to come as close as possible to fulfilling, its ultimate desire, then perhaps it is better for the psyche to be governed by its ultimate desire, as opposed to being governed by subordinate desires but without being aware of their proper relation to the ultimate desire; for a psyche that devotes all its energies to the continuous pursuit of its ultimate desire may have a better chance at fulfilling it or coming as close as possible to doing so than would one that gets distracted and confused by the pursuit of secondary goals, taking them for primary. But then if it is good for the psyche to be ruled by its ultimate desire, or those desires that best reflect the underlying desire behind all desire, then it would be good for the psyche to be ruled by whatever part of the psyche contains such desires. Since each part of the psyche is associated by Socrates in the *Republic* with a specific kind of desire, the natural hierarchy of the desires recalls the natural hierarchy of the parts of the psyche discussed there. Therefore, Socrates' or Diotima's assumptions can be taken to imply the existence of a natural ordering of the psyche that constitutes its well-being.

In speaking of a "natural ordering" in this context, however, one does not mean an order in the psyche that actually or normally obtains, one that obtains "naturally" from the time of a human being's birth; rather, one is speaking of the order of the elements in the psyche that *would* produce its well-being *if* they did obtain, just as in speaking of what is "naturally" healthy for a human body, one is speaking of a relationship between the body's elements that need not normally obtain at the birth of a human being. Indeed, just as physical excellence is healthy and conducive to the well-being of the body without at all being a "normal" state that arises spontaneously without effort, so too the excellence that constitutes the health and well-being of the psyche does not arise spontaneously and without effort either. Nonetheless, the possibility of such an order of the elements of the psyche that would constitute its well-being is the basis of the moral psychology discussed in the *Republic* and hinted at in other dialogues, such as the *Gorgias*. The importance of this moral psychology to all of Plato's ethical, political, and educational thought should be borne in mind as one examines the ground of this psychology in Diotima's teachings of *Erôs*.

One could doubt the various assumptions outlined above; for instance, one could doubt whether everyone wants one single ultimate goal throughout their lives to which all of their other desires must be related as means to a further end. Furthermore, one can doubt whether this ultimate end is fundamentally the same (in some sense) for all human beings. Moreover, if there is such an end, it is not clear why one should call that end "the good" or even "happiness." If one supposes that all humans do possess a shared goal, calling it "the good" may suggest that it is a moral objective, and calling it "happiness" may suggest that it is a self-interested goal. Yet the "good" is often presumed to be a self-interested goal in the dialogues, in the sense that it is often assumed that by the "good" one intends something that is good for oneself, something that would be truly advantageous for one.

When Socrates in the *Republic* tries to show that the life of justice (as species of ethical goodness) is the life of happiness, he is clearly trying to show that the virtue in question is advantageous for its possessor. It seems to be constantly suggested that the person who does not know or believe that virtue is advantageous for him will not pursue virtue. The wearers of the Ring of Gyges would pursue vice precisely because they would see it as being in their self-interest; thus, to answer the challenge posed by the story of the Ring, Socrates must show that justice leads to happiness and is thus advantageous to its possessor. These details suggest that Socrates believes that all people are self-interested and that any moral difference between them is a matter of their possessing more or less correct views about what will truly be in their interest.

But these details also indicate how Plato or Plato's Socrates would account for the apparent diversity of human desires. From Socrates' point of view, most people would agree that human beings love what at least *seems* good to them, where "good" is understood in the sense of what is advantageous to them, that is, what will make them happy; but what seems good or advantageous to some is not what seems good or advantageous to others, and it is possible for people to simply be mistaken about what is in fact advantageous to them. But if one desires something that seems to be X in virtue of its appearance *as* X, then just as in the case where one desires something as a means to X, so too in this case one is actually desiring X in a more fundamental and authentic sense. For if one desires Y *merely* as an appearance of X, or if one desires Y *merely* as a means to X, then one ceases desiring Y as soon as it fails to appear to be X, or in the other case, as soon as it ceases to be a means to X. So, in addition to the relation between *ends* and *means*, and in addition to the relation between *Forms* and their *participants*, there is also a relation between the *reality* of X and an *appearance* of X; in each case the latter is in a certain sense naturally subordinate to the former, in the sense of being desired because of it or for its sake. All of these relationships play a role in establishing the natural hierarchy of desire that plays such a crucial role in Diotima's teaching and in Socrates' moral psychology. Moreover, the last two types of relations go a long way to enabling Plato to account for the possibility of one fundamental desire underlying all the apparent diversity of human desire. They also account for the special privilege of that one special desire versus all the different specific desires that occupy the forefront of human consciousness. For humans do seem to desire particular objects in virtue of their qualities, and those qualities always possess a kind of generality in the sense that they can be embodied in more than one thing (at least theoretically); thus, diverse particulars can manifest the same quality by sharing in the same Form, and despite their many differences can be desired in virtue of that quality that they share. So the Form-particular relation can serve to explain the hidden unity behind human desires; humans all desire the same Form or whatever embodies that Form, and diverse particulars can embody that Form in infinitely different ways and to different degrees. Moreover, the appearance-reality relation can function in a similar way, since there may be multiple divergent appearances of a single reality; thus, Socrates can believe that all desire the true good or the true happiness, but that each precisely for this reason must seem to desire whatever he or she believes (however mistakenly) to be the true good or the true happiness. As a result, the unity of desire is refracted through the prism of participation and through the prism of illusion; and insofar as the participants are thought of as mere "images" or in a certain sense "illusions" of the truth of the Form, or insofar as human illusions are based on exclusive attention to particulars and an ignorance of their Forms, these two prisms can be seen to be related. But this unity within diversity and the natural hierarchy it makes possible is precisely what gives normative authority to certain elements within the Platonic psyche.

We have here put forward an account of the relation between the desire for the good and the other human desires that seems to be rather different from the interpretation of Plato's view offered by Charles Kahn. Kahn resists what he calls a "Freudian analogy" according to which "we might interpret Platonic *erōs* as a common pool of motivational energy, to be distributed between Plato's three parts of the psyche in such a way that more for one means less for another."[82] For Kahn it is only the desires of the rational part, and to a lesser extent the desires of the spirited part, insofar as they can be influenced by reason, that are so flexible. It is this "metaphysical desire" that can be redirected and that, depending on how it is directed can either reinforce or subtract from the essentially fixed desires of the appetitive part. According to Kahn:

> The notion implied by the theory of sublimation, of object-neutral desires leaving the channel of bodily pleasure to direct themselves toward learning, is strictly incompatible with the psychology of the *Republic*, according to which each part of the soul has (or is) its own distinctive desire, defined by the object in each case. . . . The desires of the *epithumetikon* cannot be transferred to a more noble object; they are defined by what they are a desire for. . . . The

analogy to irrigation leads Plato to write as if it were the same epithumiai that are diverted from one channel to another. However, if we are to remain true to Plato's conception of desire as individuated by its proper object, we must understand that "desires inclining strongly in one direction" means that a certain type of desire is strengthened by erotic reinforcement; whereas "they abandon the pleasures of the body" means that the corresponding appetites have been devalued, deprived of the erotic charge, and hence weakened. What one values most is what one practices and pursues, and this becomes stronger; what one values less is consequently neglected and diminished.[83]

Kahn is correct that there is a part of the psyche that does indeed truly desire sensual, physical pleasure and the fulfillment of sexual desires, etc. It is natural and good for that part of the psyche to desire such things, since it is part of that element's proper functioning. But that appetitive desire that is truly aimed at sensual gratification is aimed at a limited good; when the desire goes beyond the limit of the proper gratification of the desire, it always conflicts with rational desire (the desires of the rational part of the psyche) over how much is too much. This point is the point at which the psyche leaves behind desire for true participants in the good and instead desires— or seems to desire—their mere *eidola* (their mere shadows, merely apparent goods). This refraction of desire through false belief is what Kahn considers to be the seduction and improper channeling of rational desire. What Kahn sees as the distinct and fixed objects of desire of the subordinate parts of the psyche are in one case participants in the Form of Good at which the rational part is and ought to be directed. For the rational part, in desiring our good, also desires the fulfillment of precisely those desires of the lower two parts of the psyche the fulfillment of which would be good for the psyche as a whole. But in another case these objects, to the extent that they are excessively desired relative to a given psyche, are merely *apparent* goods—and given the analysis above, there is a plausible sense in which such apparent goods are not really or ultimately what is desired. To the extent that the lower parts desire more than they should—and they always do in a unenlightened soul—they present a false image of the good to the rational part, and it is this influence of the lower elements upon the rational part, through the flattery of pleasure and the false images of the good, that Kahn takes to show the flexibility of rational desire and its complicity in its own seduction. It is true that Diotima does not reduce all desires to one desire; she does not suppose that desires are neutral and object-less until channeled in a specific direction. But neither are the objects even of the lowest element, appetitive desire, wholly without connection to the metaphysical reality sought by the higher part of the soul. For they are either true participants in that reality, or false images of such participants, and in either case they are related to that reality.

Diotima asks what one who loves good things will have by possessing these good things. Socrates thinks the answer to this question is easier: he will have *eudaimonia*, or well-being. Diotima's response acknowledges the special place of *eudaimonia* in human life when she says, "There's no need to ask further, 'What's the point of wanting happiness?' The answer you gave seems to be final" (205a). Socrates accepts the answer as true from Diotima, whereupon she asks him if he thinks that the love to have good things is always common to all human beings, and Socrates replies that it is.

Then Diotima asks why, given that the love for good things is common to all, we do not say that everyone is in love, for it would seem that everyone loves and strives for *eudaimonia* (205b). One might well ask what this question means. So far, Diotima has suggested that all love for beautiful things (and really, all love as such) is at bottom a love to possess good things always. Now she explains that everyone possesses this love, but that we do not always call them lovers, that is, we do not always call this love "love" in every case where it appears. According to her view, everyone is possessed of love at all times, and furthermore everyone, in the end, loves the same thing: the possession of good things in perpetuity. But then Diotima wants to know why we discriminate among certain forms of this love and reserve the term *love* for these forms alone.

Diotima states that people reserve the word *love* for one special kind of *Erôs*, calling the other various forms of desire by other names (205b).[84] As though to respond to Agathon, she draws an analogy to the use of the word *poetry* (*poiesis*), that is, "making" or "creating," which can refer to any kind of creation or production whatever. Everything responsible for bringing something into being from nonbeing is a kind of poiesis, including the creations of every craft; thus all craftspeople are poets. But not all craftspeople are called poets; instead, we give them other names, giving the name of *poetry* only to the products of the Muses and the name *poet* only to those who bring those works into being. It is the same way with *Erôs*: only one part of *Erôs* is recognized as love—the other forms of desire, while still being really *Erôs*, are given other names (205b-d) while the name of *"Erôs"* is reserved for only one of them. Every desire for good things and for happiness—Diotima gives the examples of moneymaking, love of sports, and philosophy (205d)[85]—is a kind of *Erôs*; but none of these desires is called "love," and none of those who practice these things are called lovers, although in fact they are.

Diotima has now led Socrates to a name for the ultimate goal of human desire—well-being (*eudaimonia*)—and suggested that this fundamental desire is the bond of unity that runs through all the varieties of desire. All individual human desires are at bottom aimed at happiness. To modern ears "happiness" has a connotation of subjectivity that is inappropriate, however. What constitutes this well-being is no mere matter of subjective opinion; rather, it is an objective condition of the psyche akin to health. Therefore, *Eudaimonia* is better translated as "well-being."

The human *psychē* (mind or soul) seems to be an intermediary being in Plato's "metaphysics": neither as immutable as the Forms nor as ephemeral

as matter.[86] This intermediary status of the psyche is fitting given the intermediate status of *Erôs*. Psyche, the life-force, seems to be that element in
becoming that longs for being, or that element in the mortal that longs for
immortality, that is, it is the *psychē* that is characterized by the erotic longing
for what it lacks. At *Republic* 580d–581c, Socrates presents the three parts
of the *psychē* in terms of philia. There is the part that loves money and gain
(φιλοχρήματον καὶ φιλοκερδὲς 581a6–7), the part that loves victory and honor
(φιλόνικον αὐτὸ καὶ φιλότιμον 581b2) and the part that loves learning and
wisdom (φιλομαθὲς δὴ καὶ φιλόσοφον 581b9). But it is clear that the types of
"*philia*" involved in these three cases are kinds of longing for what is lacked,
forms of *Erôs*.[87] This point is nicely confirmed by the fact that the desires for
all three things are explicitly mentioned by Diotima as forms of *Erôs* (even
moneymaking, χρηματισμὸν, at 205d4; also honor-love, φιλοτιμίαν 208c3, and
philosophy, φιλοσοφίᾳ 210d6), and also by her general point about the excessive narrowness of the ordinary understanding of *Erôs* (205a-d). So human
beings are by nature lovers, and this love is channeled in these three different
ways.[88] The unity behind these various forms of desire is that *Erôs* is always
desire for good. If one understands "good" in this context to mean what is
beneficial or advantageous for one, then it is plausible to say that everything
desired at least *seems* good or beneficial to the one desiring it. At least, to one
with a desire it would seem advantageous to have that desire fulfilled in the
absence of any countervailing desire.

    This characterization of human desire as aiming for what at least *seems*
good erodes any hard antinomy between reason and desire, since for the Platonic Socrates all reason aims at the achievement of the good as well.[89] For
Socrates, all desire has a cognitive component, insofar as humans desire what
at least *appears* good to them. That the object of desire may not in fact be
advantageous, although it may seem to be so when one experiences the desire
for it, is a point that plays a central role in Plato's psychology.

    The difference between reason and desire in this respect is that reason
is better equipped, if it is properly trained and employed, to find the truth
about the good and therefore to find the true good. Reason has to critique
the appearances of the good that are implicit in desire, to determine which of
these appearances are capturing the truth. Reason has to move beyond mere
appearances of the good so as to apprehend the reality of the good. Reason
then has the function of correcting desire, correcting the judgments about
the good implicit in desire, and therefore redirecting or reeducating desire.
Yet reason itself is ideally guided by a special kind of desire, the desire for
truth. This desire for the truth in its most philosophical form, as the kind of
divine madness of which the *Phaedrus* speaks, can open the mind to apprehension or "recollection" of the truth.

    In Diotima's view, all have the same goal: all desire the Good. But most
humans are mistaken about what the goal is; they think the goal is something
physical or some kind of honor. Mistaking the goal causes evil. Thus, one

can use this Platonic psychology to explain the Socratic paradox that all evil is ignorance. For it might be held that even the most deliberate and willful evil is done with the intention of securing the wrongdoer's good, but that such evil will always fail to secure the true good, the proper ordering of the soul's elements. Moreover, when humans make these mistakes they are not getting what they really want, that is, the true good; thus, one also obtains an explanation for the Socratic paradox that all evil is involuntary. Again, even if an evil is done "deliberately" it is done with the intention to benefit oneself, but this intention is not what is evil in the action, since all persons naturally share this intention; what is "evil" in the action is the fact that, not only can one's desire not be fulfilled by this means, but that one has actually done something counterproductive to one's happiness without meaning to do so. In other words, the "evil" in the action consists in a *mistake* about what actually will benefit one. But such mistakes are by definition involuntary. The true good is what is really desired, for the false goods are desired only qua the appearance of the good, that is, only in the belief that they are advantageous in some way. Therefore, desires for false goods are ignorant desires.[90] But the actions one performs in ignorance are involuntary in the same sense that a mistake, in the strict sense of the word, is involuntary.

So, according to Diotima's teaching, the only true object of *Erôs*'s longing is the Good. But this Good is not what it seems to be at first; thus, human desire takes on many forms depending on the level of one's consciousness.

## *Erôs* and the Natural Order of the Psyche's Objects

Socrates got Agathon to admit that he did not know what he was talking about in his speech when he said that love was beautiful. To claim that *Erôs as such*, that is, *qua desire*, already possesses beauty, in Socrates' view, would be like claiming the absolute perfection of the human psyche. Such a claim would miss the fact that desire qua desire points beyond itself to an object in which it seeks its satisfaction. If *Erôs* already possessed beauty (in every respect), it would seem to have what it desires already. Human longing and human striving would come to an end, for humans would already have all those things for which they long. At times it may be difficult for humans to admit their needs and imperfections; yet only by doing so, by admitting that there is something greater for which to strive, can one hope to make real progress.

Take as an example, Socrates' admission of his own ignorance. It seems humble on Socrates' part to admit the failings of his knowledge, yet it is precisely this admission that opens him up to the philosophical quest. Socrates' awareness of his own imperfect understanding is bound up with his longing for perfect understanding. It may not be realistic to strive for perfection, since doing so sets a standard higher than humans can actually achieve. But ignoring that inner need for perfection and refusing to imagine what would count as perfect limits one's awareness to what is already known to be possible; thus, refusing to be guided by one's desires for perfection leads to complacency. The mysterious, unattainable perfection for which *Erôs* longs is like a horizon ever-receding before us, forever challenging us to transcend our current limitations.

Yet this same *Erôs* tempts humans to treat as final something less than that which they desire. Wishful thinking often causes one to treat as "perfect" something that one already possesses, in effect trying to eliminate neediness by wishing it away, attempting to escape imperfections by ignoring them. An important form of human *Erôs* is the love of one's own.[91] One can love one's own either by caring for what is good for one's own or by believing that what is one's own is already as good as it can be. For Agathon to claim that *Erôs* already possesses beauty, in Socrates' view, is tantamount to claiming that one is already perfect. By realizing that *Erôs* longs for what it lacks, Socrates is pointing out the imperfection of *Erôs* qua *Erôs* and placing perfection above human beings. It will become clear that for Socrates no one invents perfection, and it is only in the light of perfection that all that is imperfect can be properly understood and assessed. In Diotima's teaching as related by Socrates, it is of the very nature of human beings to be the kind of beings that strive for goods beyond themselves.

The deeper meaning behind the claim that Love is not beautiful is that the object of desire is in some sense higher than the desire itself. The desire is merely a means to the object of desire, and the desire naturally yearns for the possession of the object of the desire; desire is "a way of being that calls out for another way of being."[92]

Human limits are revealed through desires, for desires *do* indicate the lack of something. One may in a sense possess what one desires, but not in the same sense in which one desires it. Desires also provide human beings with direction and standards—setting up the goals by which humans guide and evaluate themselves. The process of fulfilling their desires is rendered complex by the fact that human beings are gripped by many conflicting desires. For this reason the fulfillment of certain desires often entails the frustration of other desires, and of course some desires per se may be harmful, unhealthy, illegal, or unethical. But if there were nothing outside a given desire at which it aimed, if a desire could somehow exist without a definite object, that desire would in one sense have no natural limit. "Limit" can be understood in a variety of senses. Desire that is only temporarily satisfied is in one sense unlimited, for it will always recur. In another sense, however, desire does have a natural limit insofar as it has an object and a satisfaction point at which it aims, even if its satisfaction is always partial or temporary. Because any given desire points to something beyond it that would fulfill it if it could be achieved, reason can find a principle of limit in the idea of this fulfillment by which to measure the achievement of the desire.

But desires could also be limited in another sense; for the fulfillment of one desire may limit one's ability to fulfill other desires. Since different desires aim at different objects, one might assess and rank desires if one were able to measure or rank their objects and their corresponding satisfactions. Every "prioritization" of one thing or activity over another is an instance of ranking desires; moreover, one thereby determines limits for the subordinate desires, since one has in effect decided that the desires for the object of higher priority are to come first.

The existence of objects of desire enables people in principle to rule and order desires, if they are capable of ordering the objects at which their desires aim. But the problem of circularity and relativity looms again; for any ranking of one object of desire over another seems to presuppose the priority of one desire from the outset. The need to fulfill one desire, a desire of higher priority according to the ranking of its object, might set a limit to the fulfillment of another desire, a desire with an object one deems of lesser importance or urgency. But it is unclear how one determines which object has a greater importance or urgency in the first place. But the idea that it might be possible to rank objects of desire is connected to that idea that desire is desire for something lacked; for in Socrates' account of Love, the objects that have the higher priority are objects for which the psyche *is most truly longing*. The "lower" objects of desire are desired *only as a means* to the "higher" objects, although the psyche is usually unaware of this crucial fact.

In showing that Love is not beautiful but longs for beauty, Socrates is suggesting that a certain object of desire is higher than the desire itself. It is not clear that this is always the case; it is not clear that food is "higher" than the human desire for food. The object of desire is "higher" than the desire itself only in the sense that the desire is not *itself* desired by us, but rather the *satisfaction* of the desire is desired by us. The object of desire is desired as a means to such satisfaction. Desire does not desire itself qua desire but only its satisfaction; thus, it desires the object that would satisfy it rather than itself qua desire. If one is hungry and is offered a choice between food and further hunger, then (other things being equal) one takes the food. The case where other things are not equal, where there is something else at stake—for instance, when one turns down food and values hunger instead because one is engaged in a hunger strike—is also a case in which one desire has set a limit to another and the other desire in question is valued for the sake of its object. Thus, such a case is also a matter of deciding that the object of one desire has a greater importance than the object of another. So, in the case of the hunger strike, one has prioritized one's cause over the satisfaction of physical appetite; the desire given a higher priority sets limits to the satisfaction of the lower-priority desire. But Socrates' argument about Love's lack of beauty is really only intended to point out that desire points beyond itself and implies that there is something beyond desire itself that is valued and that makes possible desire. The arguments that will discriminate and prioritize different objects of desire come later.

Thus far, several senses in which one might find a hierarchy in desires have emerged: (1) the object of a desire has a natural priority in value over the desire itself ; (2) similarly, anything desired as an end has a priority over what is desired merely as its means; (3) moreover, what is really desired has a priority over what is only desired through a mere appearance of, or a mistaken belief about, what is really desired. Similarly, (4) the quality itself in virtue of which one desires an object might be thought to have a kind of priority over the objects that merely embody that quality. For to say that a given quality is that "in virtue of which" one desires an object implies that one would not desire that object were it not for its possession of that quality (or that one would not have desired it in the same way, although perhaps one might have desired some *other* quality in it); it also implies that one would have desired any other objects possessing that same quality equally as well (other things being equal), and that one would have desired objects in proportion to the amount of that quality they possessed (again, other things being equal). Finally, in addition to all of the above ways in which a kind of natural order might be found in one's desires, there is also (5) the simple need, discussed above, to rank and priori- tize one's desires, for desires pull in different directions and the satisfactions of some preclude the satisfactions of others. This means that desires *force* choice upon one, including choices of which desire to heed and which to resist and of what attitude to take toward one's own desires. Even if there were no "natural" way of ordering the desires, it would seem that humans would have to invent some way of doing so. If humans are motivated by a desire for their own indi- vidual and/collective well-being, presumably they would use their understand- ing of the conditions of such well-being to help them rank and prioritize their other desires. Indeed, many desires do seem to be desires for what appears to constitute or to be means to well-being; and it is the qualities in virtue of which these objects seem to constitute well-being or to be a means toward it that seem to be what one is really desiring in desiring the objects, but desiring them precisely as a means to well-being or as instances of well-being.

Diotima's view is that there is one most basic desire, a desire that is the ultimate source or root of all the other desires. This desire is the desire for the good—for *our own good*, that is, our desire to *possess* what is good completely and for all time. All other objects of desire are desired only for the sake of this final good. So in spite of the apparent variety of conflicting inclinations within human beings, there is one common desire that is shared by all people: the desire for *eudaimonia* or well-being.

This desire would not amount to much of a common standard if it were true that well-being is simply a subjective state or feeling of "happiness" and that each person is able to invent his or her own brand of happiness from scratch. But from Diotima's point of view, well-being for the psyche is some- thing analogous to a healthy state in the body. Being healthy is not merely a matter of subjective opinion. Something similar is being claimed about *eudai- monia* as a psychic state. If one could really create happiness out of nothing on the basis of a subjective feeling, it would be fairly easy to achieve happiness by willing it into existence. But as it is, people have to expend considerable effort pursuing genuine happiness. They may even be wrong about what will make them happy. The recalcitrance of a resisting reality and the realization of one's errors are modes in which the objectivity of the world manifests itself to human beings. The surprise that one feels when one's expectations are disappointed combines both the recalcitrance of a resistant reality and the realization of the error involved in one's former expectations. The unavoidable but previously unknown and unforeseen implications of one's thoughts, desires, and commitments also testify to the "objectivity" of truths, including truths regarding human happiness. Humans may have to change their *attitudes* in order to promote their own well-being; moreover, even a change of attitude can often be achieved only at the cost of considerable effort. The need for effort shows that well-being is rooted in certain objective conditions. "Well-being" implies living and faring well, that is, it depends upon how human beings live their lives. Clearly, *eudaimonia* differs from any merely subjective mood or feeling of elation.

In much ancient philosophy it was held that happiness could be won through working on the *psychē*. For happiness or *eudaimonia* was conceived as an objective condition of the mind or psyche that one had to work to create, just as one cannot become a great athlete or musician by mere wishing but only by great and sustained efforts. The goal of *eudaimonia* entails a certain ranking of desires and some method by which to differentiate true goods from those apparent goods that turn out to be harmful. Since human beings do not desire everything for the sake of everything else, but rather desire some things for the sake of others, it must be possible to determine a hierarchy of desires. One would rank desires according to the superiority both of their objects and of the aspects of one's self exercised by pursuing them. Their relation to the ultimate goal of all human desire would determine the superiority of certain objects of desire and of certain parts of the psyche. Those objects would be superior and those parts of the psyche best that are most essentially involved with the ongoing possession of the good. But clearly, the employment of such a standard for the ranking of desires requires a clearer understanding of the good.

## THE DIALECTIC OF SELF AND OTHER: ONE'S OWN VERSUS THE GOOD

Next, Diotima turns to the criticism of an important point of Aristophanes' speech: the idea that all human beings desire their "other halves," that is, some lost part of themselves. In handling this point she will also be clarifying a troubling issue: What is the relationship between the desire for the good as such and the desire to make the good one's own? According to Diotima,

> [A] lover does not seek the half or the whole, unless, my friend, it turns out to be good as well. I say this because people are even willing to cut off their own arms and legs if they think they are diseased.... I don't think an individual

takes joy in what belongs to him personally unless by "belonging to me" he
means "good" and by "belonging to another" he means "bad." That's because
what everyone loves is really nothing other than the good. (205e–206a)

It would seem that Diotima has unequivocally stated that the good is the
most fundamental or ultimate object of desire. The desire for the good is even
deeper and more fundamental than the love of the self, since she holds that
people only love the self or a part of the self to the extent that they believe it
to be good. People also love possessions to the extent that they believe them
to be good; the self is merely the most intimate of one's possessions, as *Laws*
726 suggests.

But when one desires something, one automatically desires to *possess* it in
a certain sense; even when one desires that an event happens, one might be
said to desire *to possess a world in which that event happens*. Perhaps one never
desires something good for someone to whom one bears no relationship; at
the very least, once one has a *desire* for something, even if it is for another's
sake, the fact that one *has* the desire and would be *satisfied* by the desire's
satisfaction now gives one a *personal* stake in the matter. Thus, from a certain
point of view, desire is always for one's self, since it is always the desire to
possess the good *for one's self*, or to experience the satisfaction of one's own
desire. But if this line of reasoning makes any sense, it qualifies what Diotima
has just said. True, one only desires to possess something because it is good,
and one does not even desire to possess one's most intimate possessions, even
parts of one's self, unless they are good; however, if something *is* good, then
one does desire *to possess it*, to make it *one's own*. Therefore, it would seem that
the desire for self is in a certain sense just as fundamental as the desire for the
good. This conclusion seems to be confirmed by the following exchange:

"Can we simply say that people love the good?" (ὅτι οἱ ἄνθρωποι τἀγαθοῦ ἐρῶσιν)
"Yes" I said.
"But shouldn't we add that, in loving it, they want the good to be theirs?"
(ὅτι καὶ εἶναι τὸ ἀγαθὸν αὑτοῖς ἐρῶσιν). (206a3–7)

Having established that the ultimate human desire is for what is good,
and moreover the possession of the good, Diotima adds the final important
qualification: *Erôs* desires to possess the good forever (καὶ οὐ μόνον εἶναι, ἀλλὰ
καὶ ἀεὶ εἶναι 206a9). This point will have tremendous implications in what
follows. Here ends Diotima's initial discussion of the object of *Erôs*.

## THE DIALECTIC OF SELF AND OTHER:
## GIVING BIRTH IN BEAUTY TO POSSESS THE GOOD FOREVER

Next, Diotima asks a series of questions: "How do people pursue (this object)
if they are truly in love? (τῶν τίνα τρόπον διωκόντων αὐτὸ), "What do they do
with the eagerness and zeal we call *Erôs*? (καὶ ἐν τίνι πράξει ἡ σπουδὴ καὶ ἡ

σύντασις ἔρως ἂν καλοῖτο;), and finally, "What is the real purpose of desire? (τί τοῦτο τυγχάνει ὂν τὸ ἔργον; 206b1–3). The last question is related to the question that Diotima has been addressing for some time now: "What is the use [χρείαν 204c8] of *Erôs* to humans?" The *chreia* of *Erôs* is related to its *ergon*. Her series of questions suggests that one can understand the real purpose of desire, that is, the function of desire in human beings, if one looks at how people in love behave, or at what they do with their desires. The next phase of Diotima's teaching that Socrates recalls will tie the ultimate goal of desire—possessing the good forever—to the so-called "function" or "work" (*to ergon*) of love, "giving birth in beauty," or reproduction.

When Socrates says he would not be her student if he already knew the answers, Diotima adumbrates her solution: the real purpose of *Erôs* is "giving birth in beauty, whether in body or psyche (ἔστι γὰρ τοῦτο τόκος ἐν καλῷ καὶ κατὰ τὸ σῶμα καὶ κατὰ τὴν ψυχήν 206b7–8). It should be noted that the *ergon* (the function or work) of desire is different from its ultimate goal; its *goal* was to possess the good forever, but its *work* turns out to be "to give birth in beauty."

Diotima begins her exposition of this connection with the startling statement that "all of us are pregnant, Socrates, both in body and in psyche" (κυοῦσιν γάρ, ἔφη, ὦ Σώκρατες, πάντες ἄνθρωποι καὶ κατὰ τὸ σῶμα καὶ κατὰ τὴν ψυχήν 206c1–2). Since Diotima says that *all* humans are pregnant, she clearly means something unusual by such "pregnancy." In pregnancy in the ordinary sense, a woman gives birth to an offspring that is an image of its parents; a new life is created to replace the old. In the extended sense of pregnancy Diotima is proposing, a person will give birth to offspring that are his or her "images" and these images will be new creations that in some cases at least are replacing what is old. Diotima's account will seek to explain all kinds of human creativity under this heading of "pregnancy and birth" (ἡ κύησις καὶ ἡ γέννησις 206c7–8). Bodily pregnancy will be tied back to the *poiesis* she had spoken of earlier; *poiesis* was said to include all forms of bringing things into being out of nothing (205b–c). The works of the poets will constitute spiritual offspring, another type of begetting. Through bodily pregnancy, physical life is extended indefinitely; through pregnancy of psyche, spiritual or mental life is extended indefinitely.

Diotima's next point is that nothing can give birth in the ugly, but only in the beautiful.[93] By making this point, Diotima is bringing beauty back into the picture, and beginning to further clarify its relation to the good. One desires what is beautiful for the sake of the good;[94] but one desires beauty in particular as that which stimulates human beings to give birth, and/or that which provides the fitting place in which to give birth, the appropriate womb in which conception or fertilization can occur. But Diotima has not yet indicated why giving birth is good. She says that all human beings are pregnant, but she has yet to explain why and in what sense all humans (males and females) are pregnant, and why birth, as opposed to abortion, is a good thing. Diotima's teaching will supply a nonobvious answer to the question of why reproduction is good, an answer that in a sense also explains why and in what sense all people are pregnant.

It is helpful to consider in outline the underlying structure of Diotima's teaching about *Erôs* and reproduction. People desire the good, and desire to possess it forever; for the sake of the continued possession of what is good human beings desire reproduction, and for the sake of reproduction they desire beauty. Beauty will be good then, *only insofar* as it enables people to reproduce successfully in a way that provides the good things, and the ongoing possession of good things, that *Erôs* ultimately seeks.

But there is also a reason why reproduction depends upon the Beautiful; it is because reproduction is "godly," "an immortal thing for a mortal animal to do" (ἔστι δὲ τοῦτο θεῖον τὸ πρᾶγμα, καὶ τοῦτο ἐν θνητῷ ὄντι τῷ ζῴῳ ἀθάνατον ἔνεστιν 206c6–8). Ugliness is out of harmony with the divine, but beauty is in harmony with the divine (ἀνάρμοστον δ' ἐστὶ τὸ αἰσχρὸν παντὶ τῷ θείῳ, τὸ δὲ καλὸν ἁρμόττον 206d1–2). Here one may conjecture that the beauty that inspires both creativity and reproduction is itself "godly." In the *Phaedrus* Beauty is said to be the most visible Form (*Phdr.* 250d-e), a Form that reminds humans of the other Forms and so inspires love, which there is called "divine madness." In the *Phaedrus*, good poets are also said to be divinely mad, divinely inspired. But the highest manifestation of divine madness is the true philosopher's longing for the contemplation of Forms; this longing is a kind of inspiration because it involves "recollection," a greater awareness of Forms and a corresponding transformation of the psyche. Thus, the role of Beauty in the *Phaedrus* may serve to clarify why it is that Beauty is said to be in harmony with the divine in the *Symposium*, and why it thus plays such an important role in reproduction and creativity, the modes through which mortal creatures approximate as close as possible to immortality.

Creativity and reproduction—as modes of poiesis, bringing things into the process of Becoming—are ways in which the world of Becoming, the empirical world, relates to the realm of Being, that is, the realm of the Forms. For to bring forth from Nonbeing into Being in the process of Becoming is the onset of *participation*. In Becoming both the onset and the cessation of participation are always occurring as elements of the physical flux pass into and out of participation in given Forms. It is out of love of the Being in things, despite the impermanence of their earthly manifestations, out of love of the Beauty of Being that shines through those manifestations, that creativity and reproduction bring new things into Becoming. To express it theologically, Diotima says that the goddess of childbirth—*Moira* (Fate) or *Eileithuia*—is Beauty. Drawing near to beauty, animals are joyful and give birth, but drawing near to ugliness they experience pain and do not give birth. Beauty releases those who are already "pregnant" from their pain, and this release is why Beauty is valued. But what Love *really* wants is not Beauty, according to Diotima (206e). Rather, she now calls it "reproduction and birth in beauty" (*Τῆς γεννήσεως καὶ τοῦ τόκου ἐν τῷ καλῷ* 206e5). Yet, reproduction is not a final or fundamental answer either. For Diotima asks why *Erôs* is concerned with reproduction.

Diotima's account then passes on to the cause of desire. She gives a description of the kinds of phenomena to be explained: the pangs of desire animals feel when in heat, and the frenzy and fearlessness of animals protecting their young (207a-b). Humans, she points out, might see reasons for behaving this way, but it is unclear what can explain this behavior in irrational animals. Socrates does not know the answer and is chided by Diotima for not knowing it; she chides him probably because the previous teaching that love involves the desire to "possess the good forever" implies the answer Socrates should now know. Socrates only says that he knew he needed a teacher and asks her to continue her lesson (207c).

Among animals, she explains, the cause is the same as with humans—mortal creatures desire immortality. The desire of *Erôs* that wants to "possess the Good forever" implies the desire for immortality (*ἀθανασίας δὲ ἀναγκαῖον ἐπιθυμεῖν μετὰ ἀγαθοῦ ἐκ τῶν ὡμολογημένων, εἴπερ τοῦ ἀγαθοῦ ἑαυτῷ εἶναι ἀεὶ ἔρως ἐστίν· ἀναγκαῖον δὴ ἐκ τούτου τοῦ λόγου καὶ τῆς ἀθανασίας τὸν ἔρωτα εἶναι* 206e8–207a4). Reproduction is the way that mortals can partake of immortality.[95]

At this point, if not earlier, Diotima's account of *Erôs* has become an account of nature as well, just as Eryximachus's account had been. The only way mortal creatures can partake of immortality is through reproduction: leaving behind a new young one in place of the old (207d). But by this Diotima does not mean merely reproduction in the ordinary sense of the term; she includes in "reproduction" the regeneration of individual animals, as portions of their bodies die and are replaced as they grow from youth to old age. Human beings as well go through this same process, and do so in the psyches as well as in their bodies; "manners, customs, opinions, desires, pleasures, pains (and) fears" are constantly changing, coming to be and passing away in one's *psychē*, just as old cells in the body die off and new ones are born, in the course of a lifetime. The question of personal identity is raised: each of these living creatures is said to be the same, but in reality there is constant change of the creature's components. Living creatures are said to be alive, while parts of them perish and are replaced (207d-e). Therefore, we might be said to be partly dying and partly being reborn all the time—a point Diotima does not bring out, but a process that is implied in her account and that fits with the character of *Erôs* as dying and being reborn continually.

With respect to the *psychē*, it is not merely emotional states and mere beliefs that suffer this fate, but knowledge does too (207e–208a). Individual items of knowledge need to be refreshed by study because they are continually being lost through forgetting. It is not the *content* of the knowledge that necessarily changes, not the changing of the truth as an objective condition of things, but knowledge as a psychic state, that is, it is the firmness of one's

grasp on knowledge that perishes and must be replaced. For how imperma-
nent the truth was would depend on the truth in question. Nothing Diotima
says here rules out the possession of eternal truth; it simply rules out the lasting possession of eternal truth without the aid of study to renew knowledge.

Diotima says, "And in that way everything mortal is preserved, not, like
the divine, by always being the same in every way, but because what is depart-
ing and aging leaves behind something new, something such as it had been"
(τούτῳ γὰρ τῷ τρόπῳ πᾶν τὸ θνητὸν σῴζεται, οὐ τῷ παντάπασιν τὸ αὐτὸ ἀεὶ εἶναι
ὥσπερ τὸ θεῖον, ἀλλὰ τῷ τὸ ἀπιὸν καὶ παλαιούμενον ἕτερον νέον ἐγκαταλείπειν
οἷον αὐτὸ ἦν 208a7–b2). With these words, Diotima's contrast between divine
and mortal is linked to the contrast between Being and Becoming familiar
from other Platonic dialogues. She adds: "By this device, Socrates . . . what
is mortal shares in immortality, whether it is a body or anything else, while
the immortal has another way" (ταύτῃ τῇ μηχανῇ, ὦ Σώκρατες, ἔφη, θνητὸν
ἀθανασίας μετέχει, καὶ σῶμα καὶ τἆλλα πάντα· ἀθάνατον δὲ ἄλλῃ 208b2–4).[96]
The replacement of each temporal being with another being that is yet an
image and offspring of the one before is the way that mortal things share in
the immortality of the divine—an immortality not of the individual, who is
just a temporal stage or a series of temporal stages, but an immortality of the
underlying idea.

Since humans are beings of *Erôs*, and since *Erôs* is the striving to possess
the good forever, in striving for the good humans owe their very being to the
Good. Any Form functions as just such a good for whatever temporal thing
participates in it. The temporal things may not always possess "desire" as we
understand it, but they do have a conatus toward Being seen in their tendency
to persist through time, for this persistence means that they continue to manifest the pattern of the Form that makes them be what they are. Of course,
since the essence of Becoming is change, sooner or later temporal things
cease to participate in the relevant Forms and dissolve. It is as though the
world of Becoming were alive—with a World-Soul—and its temporal change
were a futile striving to unite with the timeless stability of its pattern—as
though the Good of the Forms drew their various Becoming participants to
them by inspiring *love* in them. Moreover, in seeking their own good through
their desire for the Good and the Beautiful that are *timeless*, humans seek
*immortality*; and this desire for good then leads to and governs reproduction
and creativity. These processes of reproduction and creativity prove to be the
continuation of the self through images of itself. Indeed, the self itself at any
one time consists of these images, each replacing the other—the images *are*
the self. What makes them continuous, part of the same self, is that each is
the image or offspring of the one before it and bears its nature into the future.
Just as a Form manifests in its countless changing particulars, the self, in
striving for its own good, manifests itself as countless changing particulars,
each the offspring of other such changing particulars. A *commonality* manifests in, or is shared between, a parent and her offspring; likewise between an

artist and her works; and likewise in each temporal stage of a changing thing or self. Although this commonality is not in every case what Plato would call a Form, still these various kinds of unity-within-diversity seem to be linked by Diotima's teaching, for Diotima is likening physical reproduction to creativity and lumping the regeneration of individual creatures in with both.

She closes this part of the lesson by emphasizing the distinction between the mortal and the immortal. Change, the replacement of the old with the new, is foreign to that which does not exist in time. The zeal of desire is a zeal for immortality, and for the permanent possession of the good, unlimited by time.[97]

Amazed, Socrates asks her, "Is this really the way it is?" Diotima responds, "in the manner of a perfect sophist" (ὥσπερ οἱ τέλεοι σοφισταί 208c1). This phrase seems to express a deliberate duality in Plato's presentation of Diotima. The literal meaning of "perfect sophist" sounds positive, suggesting "*sophia*" or wisdom, but the connotations of "sophist" in Plato's work raises suspicion. Calling her a "perfect" sophist emphasizes her "knowing" or "prophetic" status; but the use of the word *sophist* in this context is also an ironic reminder that one would have to be suspicious of any human claiming to know such things. In other words, the phrase brings to mind the following alternative: "Either Diotima's teaching is more than human, graced with prophetic insight inspired by the gods, or Diotima may be professing what she cannot actually know."

Diotima immediately goes on to link what she has been saying to the phenomenon of the love of honor.[98] The desire for honor is particularly important in Plato's reflections on human psychology, and it is connected with the spiritedness that forms the second and intermediate part in the *Republic's* account of the psyche (*Rep.*, Book IV, 439e–441c). Diotima exclaims that one would be amazed at the irrationality of those who pursue honor, were one not to bear her teaching in mind and if one did not realize that those who pursue honor are in a state of love or desire. Again we see the breadth of this notion of *Erôs* as the desire for the possession of good things; in this case the immortality implied in the possession of the good forever comes to the forefront. Here the pursuit of honor is treated as a form of *Erôs* as the desire to possess the good forever. The honor-lover desires honor, but honor that lasts forever, or as long as possible. As Diotima puts it: the honor-lover desires to "lay up glory immortal forever" (καὶ κλέος ἐς τὸν ἀεὶ χρόνον ἀθάνατον καταθέσθαι 208c5–6).

Honor-lovers will face any danger for this immortality, even more so than for their children. This claim suggests the superiority of the spiritual offspring through which honor-lovers seek immortality when compared to biological offspring. This theme of the bravery born of honor-love seems to reprise what had been noted in connection with earlier speeches—that love can make one fearless and that love can be connected with the pursuit of honor. Indeed, Diotima brings up examples that had been employed earlier by Phaedrus: Alcestis dying for Admetus, Achilles dying after Patroclus. She even mentions a new example: Codrus, the legendary last king of Athens, who she says "died so as to preserve the throne for his sons" (208d). Diotima says: "I believe that anyone will do anything for the sake of immortal virtue and the glorious fame that follows; and the better the people, the more they will do, for they are all in love with immortality" (οἶμαι ὑπὲρ ἀρετῆς ἀθανάτου καὶ τοιαύτης δόξης εὐκλεοῦς πάντες πάντα ποιοῦσιν, ὅσῳ ἂν ἀμείνους ὦσι, τοσούτῳ μᾶλλον· τοῦ γὰρ ἀθανάτου ἐρῶσιν 208d7–e1). If this claim of Diotima's reflects Plato's point of view, it should be clear that such a passion must be crucial to Plato's understanding of human psychology; and there are many indications in other dialogues that Plato does indeed accord a central place to honor-love.

The ability of honor-love to overcome fear is linked to its ability to aid reason. For it can be trained to overcome all other desire (not just fear); and yet, while it can overcome all other desires, it is itself capable of being influenced by rational persuasion. One could say that there is one desire that does have a natural priority over the love of honor and can outdo it: the Socratic love of wisdom. The source of this priority lies in the fact that the love of honor depends upon ideas about honor, ideas that can be made the subject of rational criticism, so that rational reflection can modify the shape that the love of honor is to take. Honor depends upon ideas, and specifically, it depends upon some conception of what is to be valued, of the good. But the love of wisdom can call into question conventional views of the good and the honorable and can bring the mind into larger and fuller reflections on the meaning of the good. Owing to its capacity to be influenced by reason and its ability to overrule other desires, the spirited part of the psyche, associated with the love of honor, is said in the *Republic* to be the natural ally of the calculative or rational element, which, according to the psychology of virtue presented there, ought to be ruling the psyche. But there are many indications throughout the Platonic corpus that Plato is aware of the power and equivocal nature of the spirited element and of the importance within that element of the love of honor. One sees this idea especially in the insistence in the *Republic* that the guardians be highly spirited but that their spiritedness should be properly moderated by a balance of musical and gymnastic education.[99]

Those who love honor are prepared to spend money, to suffer, and even to die. This suggests the power of the love of honor to overcome certain "natural" impulses—to overcome the love of gain and the fear of death, in particular. The fact that the love of honor can overcome the love of gain and the fear of death is one reason why Socrates in the *Republic* regards the spirited part of the psyche (the honor-loving part of the psyche) as the natural ally of the rational part of the psyche. Socrates points to the ability of the honor-loving aspects of human character to resist the lower appetites (*Rep.*, Book IV, 439e–441c). The honor-loving part of the *psychē*, in the form of the fear of dishonor, can enable us to overcome desire (*Laws*, Book I, 647a-b) as well as fear. For instance, we may starve ourselves on a diet, denying bodily appetites, owing to a feeling of shame or the desire to be "honored," that is, admired, for our appearance. Therefore, honor-love is naturally the ally of the calculative part of the psyche in its struggles with appetites and fears, since rationally informed honor-love can enable one to resist desires and fears. Of course, Plato is also keenly aware of the ability of improperly directed honor-love to subvert reason rather than serve as its ally, as many of his dialogues make clear. This theme of the importance and yet danger of honor-love runs throughout the *Symposium* and will be revisited in our conclusion.

## SPIRITUAL PREGNANCY AND BEGETTING

Next, Diotima makes a distinction that is vaguely reminiscent of Pausanias's distinction between the Heavenly and the Vulgar Aphrodites and the associated Loves; but Diotima's distinction is between the pregnancy of body and the pregnancy of psyche. Those who are pregnant in body "turn more toward women and pursue love in that way" (οἱ μὲν οὖν ἐγκύμονες, ἔφη, κατὰ τὰ σώματα ὄντες πρὸς τὰς γυναῖκας μᾶλλον τρέπονται καὶ ταύτῃ ἐρωτικοί εἰσιν 208e1–3). Diotima is thinking of men here; she speaks of them thinking to acquire immortality "through begetting children" (διὰ παιδογονίας 208e3).[100] Those who pursue their love in this way are also said to be "those who are pregnant in body" (οἱ μὲν οὖν ἐγκύμονες, ἔφη, κατὰ τὰ σώματα). So, the sex drive in men seems to be connected with male fertility, which is treated here as a kind of pregnancy. Because they pursue *Erôs* in this way, they are said to provide themselves with immortality through childbirth. Thus, Diotima responds to Eryximachus's scientific way of accounting for Love, at bottom, as a process of "repletion and depletion" (πλησμονὴν καὶ κένωσιν) of the body (186c7); but her view will not be merely a naturalistic account of reproduction; she will accommodate both physical and spiritual productivity in her view. At the same time, from a view of *Erôs* as desire and need she will derive a view of *Erôs* as engendering and bestowing.

Diotima proceeds next to speak of those who are pregnant in psyche—or more exactly, "even more pregnant in psyche than they are in body" (οἳ ἐν ταῖς ψυχαῖς κυοῦσιν ἔτι μᾶλλον ἢ ἐν τοῖς σώμασιν 209a1–2).[101] This group seems to lack nothing in physical fertility, but to have an additional level of fertility. They are pregnant with "what is fitting for a psyche to bear and bring to birth" (ἃ ψυχῇ προσήκει καὶ κυῆσαι καὶ τεκεῖν· 209a2–3), namely, "wisdom and the rest of virtue" (φρόνησίν τε καὶ τὴν ἄλλην ἀρετήν). When Diotima claims that "all poets beget, as well as all the craftsmen who are said to be creative" (ὧν δή εἰσι καὶ οἱ ποιηταὶ πάντες γεννήτορες καὶ τῶν δημιουργῶν ὅσοι λέγονται εὑρετικοὶ εἶναι· 209a4–5), this line is surely meant to announce that the phrase, "wisdom and the rest of virtue," is meant rather loosely, as it must be if it is to cover the full range of human creativity. For, at least from the

Platonic point of view, only the true philosopher begets true wisdom and true virtue. As will become clear in what follows, in the end Diotima's teaching adheres to this Platonic idea. Nonetheless, one should note that at this stage in her presentation the poets and craftsmen are said to beget "wisdom and the rest of virtue." There is a kind of wisdom and virtue that poets and craftsmen can beget, and even such wisdom and such virtue have a value. That value remains even if it is the case that when compared to true philosophic wisdom and virtue that of the poets and craftsmen seem to be mere semblances (as will appear in what follows).

But Diotima is careful to point out the "greatest and most beautiful part of wisdom," which, she explains, "deals with the proper ordering of cities and households, and that is called moderation and justice." Someone psychically pregnant with these things "from early youth" will, at the appropriate age, "go about seeking the beauty in which he would beget" (209b). He is naturally more drawn to beautiful bodies than ugly bodies, just as pregnant creatures in general are (even though his pregnancy is pregnancy of psyche), and he is even more drawn to the combined beauty of psyche and body. It is again being assumed in this part of Diotima's speech that the relationship is homoerotic, but it is unclear whether this emphasis is somehow essential to her point or merely a concession Socrates is making to his audience or that Diotima is making to Socrates. In any case, if such a spiritually pregnant man finds a man beautiful in both body and psyche he then becomes filled with "ideas and arguments about virtue—the qualities a virtuous man should have and the customary activities in which he should engage." The beauty of the other man leads the pregnant one to try to educate him (209c). Thus, Diotima is connecting *Erôs* and the reproduction born of *Erôs* with education, and with a form of education that is not merely the kind of education provided by the poets and the craftsmen, "who are said to be creative." Diotima continues: "But by far the greatest and most beautiful part of wisdom deals with the proper ordering of cities and households, and that is called moderation and justice" (209a). (One might wonder whether Diotima's claim here is really her last word on the question of the greatest wisdom. For her final revelation of the higher mysteries of *Erôs* may suggest otherwise.)

In common with the beautiful young man the educator nurtures the newborn offspring of virtue. Their bond is stronger than that of the parents of human children because their offspring is more beautiful and more immortal than a merely biological offspring. "Everyone would rather have such children than human ones," Diotima claims, and everyone envies and admires the great poets like Homer and Hesiod because their immortal "offspring" provide their creators with lasting fame ("immortal glory and remembrance") (209c-d). She then names Lycurgus and Solon, the lawgivers of Sparta and Athens respectively, as examples of such begetters. In their cases the immortal offspring is not poetry in the conventional sense, but good laws, the basic principles which bind the community together and express the beliefs and values its citizens share. So when Diotima later speaks of the love of constitu-tions and laws in her description of the ascent of love, she may have in mind those laws that embody the psyche of the body politic. This example is a key to the kind of "begetting of virtue" Diotima has in mind.

## HIGHER MYSTERIES: THE LOVER'S ASCENT

Yet after all this, Diotima next indicates that she has not yet revealed the final purpose of *Erôs*. She says that even Socrates could come to be initiated into the lower mysteries of Love. But the purpose of all this begetting when it is rightly done is a "final and highest mystery" (τὰ δὲ τέλεα καὶ ἐποπτικά) and Diotima claims to be unsure whether or not Socrates is capable of following her in what comes next (210a).[102]

To guide the discussion toward the "greater mysteries" of *Erôs* Diotima first explains the order of proper progress in the practice of *Erôs*. The true lover "must begin in his youth to devote himself to beautiful bodies" (ἄρχεσθαι μὲν νέον ὄντα ἰέναι ἐπὶ τὰ καλὰ σώματα 210a5–6); "he should love one body and beget beautiful ideas there; then he should realize that the beauty of any body is brother to the beauty of any other and that if he is to pursue beauty of form he'd be very foolish not to think that the beauty of all bodies is one and the same" (210a–b). Notice that the begetting of beautiful ideas, and the spiritual pregnancy it presupposes, are there from the very outset. Diotima is not beginning with a purely sexual relationship, although the stage at which one loves a particular beautiful body nowhere precludes sexual relations and a love at this stage would begin as a physical attraction.

Next, the lover should pass from the love of one beautiful body to the love of all beautiful bodies by realizing that all beauty of body is kindred (210b). Diotima probably does not mean that one should go from monogamy to sexual promiscuity. Rather, she is referring to the first dim realization on the part of the lover that all physical beauty is similar in kind. Beauty has a common nature in all its manifestations, the Beautiful Itself, in which they all participate and that renders them all beautiful. Ultimately, the lover will be led to see that this nature is not itself physical and not itself localized in space and time. This realization does provide a certain liberating perspective that frees one from excessive attachment to one manifestation of beauty, but on the other hand does not imply complete indifference or aloofness. This love of "all beautiful bodies" may include, for all we can tell, the appreciation and enjoyment of physical beauties completely outside the sexual context. In any case, we are not told that the lover of all beautiful bodies will actually seek to beget in them all. In fact, the effect is rather the reverse: his desper-ate pursuit of a single beautiful body comes to an end, and the lover becomes chastened to that extent, not more promiscuous. As long as the lover loves only once, it might seem as though Aristophanes was right and that this "first love" is his missing "other half." But if the lover falls in love a second

time, he or she may realize that the beauty of one body is very much like
the beauty of any other, and the beloved seems somehow less extraordinary
and unique. In fact, one could say that the equal desirability of all beautiful
bodies, together with the impossibility of pursuing them all, forces the lover
to a new level—he must seek new criteria of beauty, for the beauty of body
alone would pull him in many incompatible directions. Diotima merely says,
"After this he must think that the beauty of people's psyches is more valuable than the beauty of their bodies" (μετὰ δὲ ταῦτα τὸ ἐν ταῖς ψυχαῖς κάλλος
τιμιώτερον ἡγήσασθαι τοῦ ἐν τῷ σώματι 210b6–7). She does not explicitly
indicate why this transition happens; but perhaps, as suggested above, it is
because "the beauty of all beautiful bodies" is "one and the same" (ἕν τε καὶ
ταὐτόν) (210b3). With the perception of this unity the lover must now grad-
uate to a beauty that is far rarer and somewhat closer to the single nature of
Beauty that explains the beauty of all beautiful bodies.[103] Diotima also does
not dwell on why this next step is necessary because it is taken as obvious
that the more lasting beauty of psyche is more important than the beauty of
body, which is bound to fade. But it is not just a question of temporal lon-
gevity, but of the affinity of the beauty of the psyche for, or its greater metaphysical proximity to, the intangible nature of Beauty that can explain the
common beauty of diverse bodies. Diotima's ladder of love moves from the
things that we begin loving toward the source of what is lovable about them.
When the lover-initiate comes to appreciate and place more value on the
beauty of psyches, this is also when, through doing so, he comes to appreciate the beauty of those things that form the psyche—laws and practices, customs and activities, and finally, knowledge. At the level of knowledge, the
lover is guided not merely by a single example of beauty, but begins to grasp
the generality or universality of beauty, the identity that suffuses its diverse
forms, as it is manifested in the beauty of ideas. The beauty of ideas appears
as a "great sea of beauty" (τὸ πολὺ πέλαγος τετραμμένος τοῦ καλοῦ 210d3–4)
and beholding this sea fosters the growth of many further beautiful ideas
and theories (θεωρῶν πολλοὺς καὶ καλοὺς λόγους καὶ μεγαλοπρεπεῖς τίκτῃ καὶ
διανοήματα ἐν φιλοσοφίᾳ ἀφθόνῳ 210d4–6). Philosophy is born here. Philosophy then, is a very advanced form of *Erôs*, an elevated kind of loving and
begetting. Only after being nurtured by this process, guided by philosophy,
does the psyche at last come to a vision of its true goal, the ultimate object of
erotic striving (210d–e).

At 211a–b Diotima describes the highest object of love, which appears
to be a "Form (*eidos*)" or Idea, the Form of Beauty itself. It is a deep question
to ask in what sense the Form of Beauty can be the highest object of love, if
what love really longs for is "to possess the good always"; for one might wonder if the ultimate object of *Erôs* is Beauty or the Good.[104] Diotima seems
to indicate that the psyche comes as close as it can to "possessing the good
always" precisely through its vision of Beauty Itself. To sort this out, we
should recall that to possess the good always implies immortality and that

the mortal being's way of approximating to immortality is through "giving birth in beauty." But the mortal being only desired immortality as a means to "possessing the good always." This link suggests that the mortal being comes as close as possible to "possessing the good always" by "giving birth in beauty." The vision of the Beautiful turns out to be the ultimate way of "giving birth in beauty," since this vision will inspire great fecundity on the part of the psyche that has it. Such a psyche will give birth to true (as opposed to merely apparent) virtues. So it would seem the closest humans can come to "possessing the good always" is to have the vision of the Beautiful Itself.

Readers of Plato inevitably wonder: What is the relation between the vision of the Beautiful depicted here and the vision of the Good Itself discussed in the *Republic*? In the *Republic* the quest of knowledge seems to culminate in the contemplation of the Good as the source of all intelligibility; in Diotima's account, the love of beauty, which is also the desire for goodness, a desire to possess the good forever, culminates in a vision of Beauty Itself. According to Socrates' account in the *Republic* it would seem that the Form of Beauty, like all other Forms, must somehow depend for its being and its intelligibility on the Form of the Good. In the *Symposium Erôs* is said to be ultimately the desire for the Good, for its perpetual possession. Given these facts, it would seem that according to Diotima's teaching as well the vision of the Beautiful is meant to lead on to the vision of the Good. Unfortunately, further problems lurk here. Since the vision of Beauty gives rise to true virtue, it would seem that by contemplating Beauty Itself the philosopher comes to participate in the Good and to possess particular goods that also participate in it. The Form of Beauty seems to be accorded a special relationship vis-à-vis the other Forms in the *Phaedrus*, and in the *Symposium* it would seem to have a special relationship to the Good. Beauty, as the Form that is the most apparent in the sensible world, inspires the love as divine madness that leads on to the Forms (*Phaedrus*); in the *Symposium*, Beauty manifest in the world is the divine element that stimulates the desire to "give birth" physically and spiritually, but such reproduction is a manifestation of the desire to "possess the Good forever." Beauty initially appears as the object of *Erôs*, but Diotima teaches that *Erôs* is ultimately a desire for goodness. Yet this goodness seems to manifest in the psyche through the perfection of psyche's love and its attainment of the vision of Beauty Itself. Whereas Beauty is the harbinger of the Forms, provoking the *Erôs* that is the messenger of the Forms, the divine madness of their inspiration, that is, their recollection, the Good is the "sun" that is the source of the Forms and is somehow also responsible for their ultimate comprehension. Plato has not simply identified the Good and the Beautiful in his texts, but explores their intimate relationship to one another and to the remaining *kosmos* of Forms, with reference to which they each play a special role.

Whatever Beauty itself is, it is not just another beautiful thing. Diotima explains that this beauty neither comes to be nor passes away; rather, it always is (πρῶτον μὲν ἀεὶ ὂν καὶ οὔτε γιγνόμενον οὔτε ἀπολλύμενον 210e6–211a1). Unlike the particular beautiful things one finds in the world of change (cf. *Rep.*, Bk. V, 479a-b), this Beauty is not beautiful only in some respects and not in others. This beauty is not subject to the relativity to which ordinary beauty is subject, but remains beautiful in every respect and from every point of view (οὐ τῇ μὲν καλόν, τῇ δ᾽ αἰσχρόν, οὐδὲ τοτὲ μέν, τοτὲ δὲ οὔ, οὐδὲ πρὸς μὲν τὸ καλόν, πρὸς δὲ τὸ αἰσχρόν, οὐδ᾽ ἔνθα μὲν καλόν, ἔνθα δὲ αἰσχρόν, ὡς τισὶ μὲν ὂν καλόν, τισὶ δὲ αἰσχρόν 211a2–5). Nor does this beauty appear "in" anything (οὐδέ που ὂν ἐν ἑτέρῳ τινι, οἷον ἐν ζῴῳ ἢ ἐν γῇ ἢ ἐν οὐρανῷ ἢ ἔν τῳ ἄλλῳ 211a8–b1). For it is not the beauty "of" anything, not of anybody, and not even of any account or knowledge (οὐδέ τις λόγος οὐδέ τις ἐπιστήμη 211a7). This beauty exists "itself by itself with itself" and is "always one in form" (ἀλλ᾽ αὐτὸ καθ᾽ αὑτὸ μεθ᾽ αὑτοῦ μονοειδὲς ἀεὶὸν 211b1–2). This beauty is that in which all other beautiful things share, and indeed, it is that which makes them beautiful. When the beautiful particular things come to be or pass away or change, this beauty is unaffected. It is clear that she is speaking of a Form, for were one to replace the word *beauty* with a variable, her description would seem to accord with a generic description of a Form. The Form of F (a) neither comes to be or passes away, and (b) remains unaffected by the generation and destruction of the things that participate in it; the Form F is (c) always F, that is, always just what it is to be F, and as such (d) it is not F in some respects and not-F in others, for it is just the standard of F-ness in terms of which the relative Fs in the world are defined. A Form F is (e) not to be confused with any of the details of the particular Fs in which it is manifest, that is, the Form F is not the F "of" anything; it is not a mere instance of F-ness, but F-ness itself. As such it is (f) "itself by itself with itself, always one in form." Finally, it is (g) that which all particular Fs share in that makes them all Fs—it is their "F-ness" itself.[105]

Diotima's description seems generic in that it tells one no more about Beauty than it would about any other Form; in fact, such a generic description of the formal nature of a Form tempts one to think that here one is gaining an intimation of the very Form of Form Itself. Since the Good also has some claim to be considered as the Form of Form Itself, the vision of the Beautiful may be being described in such a way as to penetrate into the fundamental nature of Form-ness that all Forms share, thereby offering veiled hints about the Form of the Good that grounds their being and renders them intelligible. In addition to having the generic properties (a)-(g) just listed, the Form of the Good is a unity that enables the Forms to be and makes them knowable, just as each Form not only possesses (a)-(g) but enables its particulars to be and makes them knowable. In each case there is a "harmonization" of disparate properties in a particular to form a noetic whole, and in each case the "harmony" is derived from the Form's very unity; each Form too is a "harmony" because it is a unity that organizes noetic differences. The idea of the Good that is manifest in both Forms and in good particulars is just the idea of such an order or harmony, one that constitutes the being and intelligibility of whatever partakes in it. Each Form is a good, a participant in the Good, and each Form is what enables its participants to be good in turn; a particular participates in the Form of the Good by properly or fully participating in its own Form. Forms and their particulars may each be good, but in a differing sense; a particular may be good to the extent that it accords with the order of its Form; but the Form is good as an instance of order that grants being and intelligibility to other things, thus encapsulating what is essential to the nature of the Form of the Good as that which in turn grants being and intelligibility to the Forms themselves.[106]

But one should also not forget that the entire previous presentation of Diotima's teaching and the discussion in the *Phaedrus* (to say nothing of the *Greater Hippias*) have each said some more specific things regarding the specific nature of Beauty as well. The Form of Beauty is a Formal participant in the Good, having properties (a)-(g) above like all other Forms, also sharing in the nature of Goodness like all other Forms by being a unity that enables its participants to be and that renders them knowable precisely as such participants, a unity that is a harmony of noetic differences; yet Beauty also has these properties in such a way that it is more manifest to the senses and speaks more directly to the human psyche and its *Erôs*, thus functioning as a mediator between the psyche and the Forms. Beauty is a mediator by virtue of its stimulation of *Erôs*, *the* mediator par excellance, and by stimulating *Erôs*, beauty stimulates reproduction and giving birth in beauty.

But the properties Diotima *explicitly* ascribes to the Form of Beauty (properties (a)-(g) above) are not just properties of this Form, but of any Form, and indeed we can understand these properties by thinking about universals or "kinds," without having to adopt any "theory" of Forms. To see this, consider the following example: imagine a set of five humans and three dogs. To the question, "How many *kinds* of things are there in this set?" it makes sense to answer "Two," namely, human and dog (as opposed to answering "eight," as we would were we asked for the number of *individuals* in the collection). Now this answer is not changed, that is to say, the *number of kinds involved* is not changed, by adding or subtracting any number of humans or dogs (as long as the number remains above zero). Furthermore, the natures of the kinds—the properties of each kind as a kind—are completely unaffected by the changes and fates of the particular individuals falling under the kinds. If a human diminishes in size or grows old, the kind "human" remains unaffected. This example gives one a sense of the kind of unchanging and timeless quality Diotima wants to ascribe to the Form of Beauty Itself. *What Beauty is* has nothing to do with *which* specific instances of beauty there may happen to be in the world, or with *where* or *when* they are glimpsed; the nature of beauty is unaffected as the particular beauties change. The Form of Beauty is the nature of beauty or the what-ness of beauty, in which all cases of beauty have a share.

To understand the absolute character of Forms versus the relative character of the particulars that partake in them, it helps to remember that according to this view the particulars have their properties by virtue of their participation in Forms. Moreover, the Forms function to some extent as a standard, or yardstick. The Form is absolutely F because it provides the standard by virtue of which F is ascribed, whereas particular things may be more or less F—and hence relatively F—according to whether they share to a greater or lesser extent in the Form. Particular beauties can be more or less beautiful, or beautiful in one respect and not in another; but the nature of beauty itself cannot vary in its beauty (i.e., *in its being the nature of beauty*) in any way, since it *is* precisely the nature of beauty itself, that which determines what beauty is. The particulars are beautiful by *sharing* the property of beauty. The Form of Beauty is beautiful by *being* the nature of that property.

There is some discussion in the literature on Plato about a problem that might seem to arise from the claim that the Form of Beauty is beautiful. It seems that in saying that Beauty itself is beautiful we are treating the Form as though it were just one more beautiful thing among others. But if the Form of Beauty is beautiful, it must be beautiful in a different way than particular beautiful things are. The particular things receive their beauty by participating in the Form, but the Form of Beauty does not receive its beauty from elsewhere—it *is* beauty, all beauty, the beauty that is in all beautiful things; it does not merely "*have*" beauty as a property.

When one correctly progresses through the stages of love and "begins to see this beauty" (τὸ καλὸν ἄρχηται καθορᾶν) then, according to Diotima, "he has almost grasped his goal" (σχεδὸν ἄν τι ἅπτοιτο τοῦ τέλους 211b6–7). Note the "*schedon*." One could well wonder what remains before the end is completely realized. Perhaps the Form of Beauty is akin to the Form of the Good and leads one on to it.[107]

At the end of her account Diotima reiterates the various stages of the true lover's progress leading to the final lesson in which one learns (γνῷ αὐτὸ τελευτῶν) "just what it is to be beautiful (ὃ ἔστι καλόν 211c8–d1). The life of beholding this Beauty, according to Diotima, is the kind of life a human being should live.[108] Having once seen Beauty itself, all lesser beauties, whether of gold, clothing, boys, or anything else, pale by comparison. Diotima does not fail to note how powerful is the effect of erotic desire for physical beauty; it leads the lover to desire to be with and gaze on the beloved to such an extent that the lover would gladly forego, if he could, all other satisfactions and needs (211d-e). Recalling the power of ordinary physical beauty to evoke such powerful desire, Diotima then indicates that the power of Beauty Itself would be much greater, once it were seen. It is as though, in Diotima's teaching concerning the stages of the true lover's ascent, Beauty performs a "striptease"; the audience is supposed to have reached a fever pitch of spiritual excitement as she invites us in imagination to gaze upon the naked essence of Beauty Itself, divested of its earthly dress, the various particulars through which it ordinarily appears (211e–212a).[109]

Only by looking at Beauty Itself in the only way it can be seen—by the mind alone—will the lover be able to beget true virtues as opposed to images of virtue. This claim perhaps implies that the wisdom and virtues generated by the poets and craftsmen are not the "true virtue" of which she speaks, but instead are mere "images of virtue."[110] Indeed, when one is in touch with images of beauty one gives birth to images of virtue (εἴδωλα ἀρετῆς), but when one is in touch with true beauty (the Form of Beauty Itself) one gives birth to true virtue (212a). This claim of Diotima explains a great deal about how we are to understand the levels of virtue—or the distinction between true virtue and images of virtue—implied in this passage. Some so-called virtue is born of the love of something less than Beauty Itself and the philosophical knowledge that the love of Beauty Itself implies. These "virtues" may be created by the love of gain or the love of honor in the conventional sense of these notions; such virtue is based on mere "true opinion," laws and customs or even non-philosophical knowledge. But these virtues are pseudo-virtues, semblances of the true virtue. True virtue can only be based on contact with Beauty Itself and the philosophical knowledge that it implies (see also *Phaedo* 69a-d).

The last cryptic remark in Socrates' account of Diotima's teaching is that the gods love those who have given birth to true virtue (i.e., those who are in touch with Forms) and that if any human being could become immortal, it would be such a one (τεκόντι δὲ ἀρετὴν ἀληθῆ καὶ θρεψαμένῳ ὑπάρχει θεοφιλεῖ γενέσθαι, καὶ εἴπέρ τῳ ἄλλῳ ἀνθρώπων ἀθανάτῳ καὶ ἐκείνῳ 212a5–7). This remark either offers hope for personal immortality to one who has practiced philosophy ("the practice of death" as it is called in the *Phaedo*) or else perhaps, consistently with Diotima's earlier claims, it means that such a human being has achieved the highest form of "reproduction," giving birth to spiritual offspring of the highest rank, so that such a one participates in immortality to the highest degree possible for a mortal being. Perhaps contact with timeless Forms offers the psyche a kind of "participation" in timelessness in the midst of time, the closest mortals can come to immortality.

Having presented Diotima's account, Socrates claims to have been persuaded by it and testifies that he tries to persuade others of it. Apparently, Socrates' being persuaded and persuading others about these things is the result of his having learned and being able to teach the art of love, the one art he claims to know and which he credits Diotima with teaching him. *Erôs*, according to Socrates, is the best helper humans can have in acquiring virtue; for this reason he practices the rites of love and commends them to others. The claim that "*Erôs* is the best helper in acquiring virtue" may point to the importance of proper motivation in any achievement or education. The acquisition of virtue would be no exception. One has to *want* it; that is, first one must learn to *desire* the beauty of virtue, and then one will be naturally drawn to practice it.

## PHILOSOPHY AS THE ART OF LOVE

*Erôs* is a *daimon* and as such has this function of bridging between the mortal and divine. Philosophy involves *Erôs*. Philosophy, as the *Erôs* for wisdom, is thus a *daimon* devoted to wisdom. Philosophy, as a *daimon*, is a messenger involved in the communication between the mortal and the divine. The in-between state of philosophy is a form of the mediation between the divine and the mortal that constitutes the task of *daimon*es. Yet Diotima also depicts *Erôs* as a philosopher, suggesting that the form of *Erôs* known as philosophy is somehow connected to all other forms of *Erôs* and that the nature of *Erôs* in general becomes especially manifest in philosophy, its highest form.

But not only is philosophy a kind of love and not only is Love a philosopher—philosophy is also *an art* of love. Socrates is a student of Diotima, and Socrates' philosophical practice *is* the teaching of Diotima applied. Diotima's image of the philosopher is surely embodied in the character of the ignorant Socrates depicted in Plato's dialogues, a philosopher who has the human wisdom of knowing that his own wisdom is worth little or nothing compared with that of the gods (*Ap.* 20d-e, 21b, 21d, 22d, 22e, 23a-b.) Hence, Socrates is the perfect embodiment of the philosopher that Diotima describes because he seeks wisdom all his life while claiming never to have attained it. Socrates is truly erotic, embodying both the intermediate nature of *Erôs* and its concomitant duality. For philosophy as Socrates understands it is the practice that leads himself and others to the "human wisdom" of self-aware ignorance, a "wisdom" that expresses both the intermediacy and duality of *Erôs*. Such wisdom is neither the wisdom of the gods nor the ignorance of those unaware of their own ignorance, those who do not seek wisdom. Being neither divine wisdom nor the vulgar ignorance, the "human wisdom" engendered by philosophy is in a way both ignorant and wise. Moreover, when one considers the more "Platonic" accounts of the nature of philosophy that appear in the dialogues, one finds that the philosopher is still in an intermediate position; a denizen of the realm of Becoming (itself an intermediate ontological condition between Being and Nonbeing), the philosopher attempts to "recollect" the Forms. Yet such recollections generally seem to remain partial. According to the Cave Allegory of the *Republic*, philosophy is a long and laborious transition from the shadows of Becoming to the light of Being; but at every point in this transition one is in an intermediate state, as the "mind's eyes" slowly adjust to the light of the Forms or to the darkness of the Cave. There are reasons as well to see Socrates' philosophical practice as the art of love he claims to have learned from Diotima. This art is the one thing he claims to know. Moreover, his interactions with his interlocutors can be characterized in terms of Socrates' leading them to love the right thing, wisdom. By making them aware of their need for wisdom, he awakens in them the philosophical desire to seek wisdom.

We believe that in Diotima's words Plato reveals something of the way he himself thinks of philosophy, and for this reason Diotima's teaching clarifies and illuminates all other aspects of Plato's work, including his use of the dialogue form. Philosophy is the highest form of the *daimon, Erōs*; as such philosophy is itself *daimonic*, and thus finds itself between the mortal and the divine, always attempting to mediate between them. This in-between character of the philosopher's stance is reflected in what the other Platonic dialogues have to say about philosophy and the philosopher. One sees this in-between character reflected in Socrates' characterization of his "human wisdom" in the *Apology*, a wisdom born of the sense of his own ignorance; but even in Plato's supposedly more mature epistemological and metaphysical ideas, those having to do with the hypothesis of Forms and the idea of Recollection, one sees that the philosopher is given the same intermediate position. The Forms are the divine realm of which the highest messages of *Erōs* speak, in both the *Symposium* and the *Phaedrus*; the philosopher recollects the Forms through love, and as the dialogues make abundantly clear, such recollection never finalizes itself in absolute knowledge. For both Plato and all of his philosophical protagonists (Plato's Socrates, Plato's Parmenides, the Eleatic Visitor, the Athenian Stranger, and Timaeus) remain seekers until the end. One should see that both the conception of philosophy as Socratically ignorant and the conception of philosophy as a vision of the Forms appear together in the teachings of Diotima. That is because a "vision of the Forms," or the "recollection" of the Forms is never capable of eradicating Socratic Ignorance, or if it can do so, can do so only at the end of a journey so long that the journey itself accounts for the primary, most obvious and prevalent character of philosophy. Even when Plato's metaphors provide a vision of the destination, they do so for the sake of characterizing philosophy as a path to that end; until one has done with philosophy one remains on the path, and Plato, it would seem, remained a philosopher to the end.

If philosophy is the highest mode of the same art of love that Diotima taught Socrates, then the same art of love seems to be embodied in Plato's practice as the writer of the dialogues, for the dialogues are expressions of *Erōs* that are designed to have an educational effect upon their audiences in part through the awakening and channeling of *Erōs*. A quick survey of the conception of virtue and education presented in the dialogues reveals that according to this conception both virtue and education have everything to do with the channeling and ordering of desire. For instance, according to the tripartite psyche account of the virtues in the *Republic*, the most virtuous psyche is that in which the proper part of the psyche and its desires rule (*Rep.* 580d–583b). According to the definitions of virtue and education in the *Laws*, virtue is the state of *symphonia* between the rational and irrational elements in the psyche that occurs when the psyche has been trained to love and hate the right things, that is, when the desires of the irrational elements have been brought into line with the rational element; and education is the art of making the psyche love and hate the right things (*Laws* 653b–c). Hence, Plato's whole conception of education is concerned

with what Michael Despland called "the education of desire."[111] Even the
higher education of the guardians in the *Republic*, although it is certainly
not reducible to the rhetorical manipulation of desire, could not transpire
were it not for the love of truth that the guardians are to cultivate and that
inspires their search for knowledge. Love is the medium in which recollection of the Forms can occur; no student learns well without intense interest
in her subject.

Moreover, since philosophy and recollection are so closely associated by
Plato with the divine madness or the *daimonic* messenger that is love, it is
quite clear that as a philosopher Plato's art must be Diotima's art. Moreover,
the idea of the intermediacy of *Erôs* illuminates the unusual character of
Plato's writing. It has been noted that the dialogues possess philosophical
content but in such a way as to leave the audience unsure of the convictions
of the author. This feature of the dialogues is surely a result of Plato's concern not so much to report his own findings as to stimulate the thinking
of his audience and to lead them onto the path of philosophy. Everything
about the dialogues themselves is reminiscent of the depiction of *Erôs* by
Diotima; they seem to possess and to lack, to be full and empty at the same
time; they are full of suggestions, ideas, questions, possibilities, but they
lack dogmatic solutions or easily understood presentations of the author's
positions. They awaken *Erôs* in the audience, stimulating longing for truth
while providing an intimation of it, and yet they never fully satisfy that
longing, only intensify and channel it in various directions. They tease and
seduce their audience with questions and hints, drawing it into deeper and
more comprehensive views of the subject matter, but never culminate in any
attempt at a final account. It is possible that if one gazed into the dialogues
long enough one would one day glimpse a Form, and perhaps, with persis-
tent reflection even find oneself having an increasingly vivid awareness of
ultimate reality; but if so, it would be the result of one's diligent use of the
dialogues to cultivate one's own *Erôs*. The Forms are always recollected out
of one's self, out of one's *Erôs*, and the author of the dialogues well understands that his work merely provides the opportunity, an opportunity that
comes to nothing without the efforts of the audience. Plato understands
as well that those efforts, and whatever glimmers of truth may result from
them, cannot be replaced by any sort of dogma. The dialogues are cryptic,
and, like the Erotic Socrates of the *Symposium*, they present an exterior very
different from how they look when one has opened them up and glimpsed
inside. Yet they seem to go on forever opening. In this the works of Plato are
better able to express the essential nature of philosophy itself than are the
works of many other philosophers. Since the notion of intermediacy seems
so useful in helping us understand the peculiarities of Plato's writing, one
should think that in Diotima's teaching, if anywhere, one is gaining insight
into Plato's own view of philosophy. Any interpretation that tries to sever
Socrates (or even Plato) from Diotima's teaching will be incapable of doing

justice to these connections and harmonies between Diotima's teaching and the content and form of the dialogues, including their portrayal of Socrates.

To encourage further reflection about the connections between Diotima's teaching and Plato's other portrayals of the paradoxical duality inherent in philosophy, we will return to this discussion in the Appendix. We shall consider further the themes of Socratic Ignorance and the Recollection of Forms as they appear in other dialogues. The Appendix will show how these apparently opposed themes in fact reflect the duality of the philosophical *Erôs* discussed in Diotima's teaching. The fact that Diotima's teaching of the duality of *Erôs* can help to make sense of the connection between apparently divergent themes in Plato's text—namely, Socratic Ignorance and the Recollection of Forms—bolsters our claim that Diotima offers unique insight into Plato's conception of philosophy.

## THE ROLE OF DIOTIMA AND HER TEACHING IN THE *SYMPOSIUM*

Plato's audience must consider what Plato might want them to understand by Socrates' appeal to the character and teachings of Diotima. First, although Socrates is constrained by the occasion to deliver an encomium rather than to engage in dialectical philosophy, he nonetheless succeeds in smuggling his question-and-answer method into his speech, for by recalling the teaching of Diotima he can relate the salient parts of a series of dialectical conversations he claims to have had with his teacher on "*ta erotika*." Second, introducing Diotima as his guide in erotic matters frees the philosopher from having to praise his own characteristics and his own chosen vocation directly, as others had done. Third, Plato's audience learns that Socrates possesses his knowledge of the art of love, the only thing he claims to understand, as a result of Diotima's guidance. The account of this teaching in the art of love casts a new light on Socrates' accustomed philosophical activities, and leads to the conclusion that the truest erotic is the philosopher who recognizes his ignorance and permits this awareness to motivate and guide him in the search for wisdom.

Finally, it must be significant that Diotima is a "wise woman from Mantinea," a prophetess and not a philosopher.[112] She does speak of philosophy as well as many other things, but as a divinely inspired prophetess; as such, she could be seen as a representation of Wisdom itself, and her teaching a philosopher's dream of what a wise person, as opposed to a mere philosopher, might say.[113] But there is a dilemma: on the one hand, in other Platonic dialogues such divine inspiration does not qualify as knowledge or wisdom, but at best as true opinion; and yet on the other hand, Diotima is supposed to be Socrates' teacher in the one art he claims he truly *knows* (177e). So apparently she *is* transmitting a kind of *knowledge*. Perhaps she personifies the positive or "resource" side of *Erôs*, while Socrates in his role as her ignorant student represents the "poverty" side.[114] Diotima is playing the role of the father, *Poros*, to Socrates' portrayal of the mother, *Penia*. The duality of *Erôs* is expressed in these two sides of Socrates' speech—the critical side teaching humans that they lack wisdom, and the evocative, positive side articulating this very lack into an account of being and of the fundamental impulses of human nature. Hence, Socrates' very speech parallels the nature of the *Erôs* it discusses. In any case, one should not forget that the *Erôs* of philosophy, embodied in the mature Socrates, is somehow in-between wisdom and ignorance, the gods and mortals, resource and poverty, and therefore reflects both sides of each of these contrary pairs. If Diotima's teaching represents the "resource" dimension of Socrates' *Erôs*, at the same time it points to a higher mystery, a "resource" that *Erôs* still lacks, the vision of the Beautiful Itself. Thus, Diotima's teaching brings the "poverty" of *Erôs* to mind as well.

Socrates introduces Diotima when it is his turn to give a speech, perhaps because someone absent is needed to speak the truth that is always absent, that is always lacked, and yet that insinuates itself in the present. The wise woman is "present in the mode of absence" just as the Forms that the philosopher seeks are "present in the mode of absence" in human longing. Diotima, as the one "present in the mode of absence" at the symposium, should be different in a fundamental and relevant respect from those present. Thus, she is a woman, representing what appears from a male perspective as an unbridgeable otherness; and she is wise, someone who has perhaps attained what from the point of view of most mortals can at best be glimpsed and struggled toward. She is a mysterious figure, and mystery implies a concealment that hints at hidden riches. Hence, she is presented as a hierophant and mystagogue, a priestess of Mysteries in the process of initiating Socrates.[115] Her prophetic guise is utterly appropriate to the way that *Erôs* communicates, as a *daimon* and messenger that moves between the mortal and divine realms.

Let us now take stock of the more important points of Diotima's teaching. In one sense, she indicates that humans are fundamentally not simply egoistic; it is not, at bottom, ourselves that we love. Instead we love the good. But on the other hand, everyone wants the good to be his or her *own*; each one wants to *possess* it. This point implies that an element of egoism is inescapable in any desire. The good that transcends the self and that inspires people to step outside themselves as they now are, is at the same time a good all people desire. But people desire to possess it, that is, to take it into themselves and make it their own. As a result, Diotima's account captures a tension in human desire between egoistic and anti-egoistic tendencies.

This tension is responsible for certain conundrums about love and friendship. For instance, in seeking lovers or friends, one might wonder whether it is more natural for people to seek those who are like oneself, those with whom one is compatible by virtue of sharing things in common with them (thus perhaps affirming one's ego, supporting one's current conception of one's self); or whether it is more natural to think "opposites attract" and that people seek from another what they need and what they lack in themselves.

It seems that human beings have both experiences, and the tension in love to which Diotima is pointing seems to illuminate this fact.[116] The things that one already pursues one takes to be good; one is guided by one's love of honor, that is, one's need for recognition and approval and self-respect, and thus, it is likely that one will seek affirmation from others who are like-minded and share one's values. But on the other hand, each person experiences needs that seem to require one to seek out the resources of others, and so one naturally looks to others to fill deficiencies in oneself. The desire for a good that one lacks pushes one outside the bounds of one's current state and leads one to seek things from others; but one's desire to possess the good for oneself tempts one to make one's possessions, beliefs, loves, etc., into the goods that one desires, and so to evaluate the world and others in terms of their proximity and accommodation to oneself.

*Erôs* is the passion to bring self and other together where the "other" desired is really the good. Socrates' presentation of Diotima's teaching responds to Aristophanes by arguing that human beings would get rid of any part of themselves if they thought it was good *for them* to do so; but since the "for them" is always there, the self is not completely transcended. Nonetheless, if one considers the sort of good that one desires for oneself, it seems that each different type of good desired presupposes a different way of defining oneself. Consider the contrast in Book IX of the *Republic* between the gain-lover, the honor-lover, and the wisdom-lover (*Rep.* 580d–581c). These are three different sorts of people living three different sorts of lives. The differences between them are created by the differences in what they desire. For humans define themselves by their loves and desires, their dreams and goals. Who one is can be redefined when one's desires are redefined. This redefinition can happen by ascending the stages of Love's progress as Diotima describes it; this process is a maturation of desire produced by deepening awareness, attention, or knowledge. That is, one's views about what is good determine one's views about who one is, about what is in one's interest, and about what counts as true honor. All these views shape one's notions of identity. Moreover, every notion of who one is also implies some idea of the good. If one's view of oneself depends on one's understanding of the good, and one's view of the good depends on one's understanding of oneself, then knowledge of the true good would lead to true self-knowledge. Knowledge of both the good and the self would be intimately bound up with the knowledge of *Erôs*; for the self is essentially composed of different types of *Erôs*, and the good is the ultimate object of *Erôs*.

The definition of *Erôs* that has emerged from Diotima's teaching might be phrased as follows: *Erôs* is a *daimonic* messenger between the mortal and the divine, full of poverty and resource, longing for a good that it lacks, desiring to possess that good forever, and thus seeking immortality through "giving birth in beauty," that is, through creativity that is inspired by beauty and that is expressed through beautiful forms. As a *daimonic* messenger, *Erôs* can lead one to a greater awareness of the divine, of a divine good that the psyche can behold and in which it can participate, but which it can never simply be. One understands *Erôs* when one understands its in-between status, its essential longing for something that it lacks, and the various objects of *Erôs* and their relation to one another. Through such understanding one comes to see that all the various objects of *Erôs* are really means to the ultimate object of *Erôs*, the good. When one learns the nature of one's deepest desire one has come to a deeper self-understanding. So, in coming to understand the true object of one's most fundamental desire, one comes to understand both the true good and oneself as well.

It is Socrates' knowledge of *Erôs* that makes Socratic self-examination such a powerful form of self-cultivation. Only reflection that confronts one with one's own ignorance can awaken a desire for wisdom and its beauty, a desire that, transforming *Erôs*, redirects it toward the objects it has really been blindly seeking all along. Only reflection on the mysterious source and nature of the beauty shared by physical things can lift one above the absorption in and fascination with physical desire by evoking a sense of philosophical wonder. Philosophy can elevate and guide human beings above concern with material desires and conventional honors, if only for limited periods of time. This capacity of philosophy is not contradicted by the fact that individual thinkers may more often than not, consciously or unconsciously, subordinate their thought to these lower desires. That only shows that individual thinkers do not often fulfill the promise of philosophy.

In the *Phaedrus* beauty is said to be the most visible of Forms here in the world of change (250d). According to the myth of the "super-celestial" (*hyperouranian*) realm presented there, beauty leads human beings to recollect the other Forms they once beheld before their imprisonment in a physical body. Beauty has the power to kindle in humans the divine madness that is *Erôs*; this divine madness is a form of inspiration. The divine inspiration of *Erôs* leads human beings to "recollect" the Forms. Yet, of course, this is merely another way of speaking about the function of *Erôs* as a messenger from gods to mortals. Beauty speaks to the human mind of a higher realm. If one pursues beauty where it leads attentively, it leads higher and higher. In the *Symposium* it leads in the direction of the true good, away from those pseudo-goods that merely appear good from a limited perspective, but which turn out not to be good.

According to Diotima's teaching, everyone wants the real good. No one says, "Give me a pseudo-good so I can have the illusion of happiness." But everyone will do whatever he or she *thinks* is going to propel him or her toward the true good. The implication is that those who are mistaken about what the supreme good is will be trying to obtain something other than what they really want; they spend their time mining fool's gold.

Hence, there is an ambiguity in love. In one sense, love can be directed at various things, and sometimes at wrong or inappropriate objects; but in a deeper sense love's true aim is always "the good," one's own happiness. When one loves any object one always seeks the true good through it, *so that one's desire is in fact divided*: one desires the true good and one desires X (the immediate object) *as a means to the true good*. In one sense, one loves and wants the object at which one's desires are actually directed, that is, whatever *seems* good. But at the same time, in another sense one desires *only* the good—for one desires the present object *only* because one believes, however wrongly, that it is a means to what is truly good for one. Therefore, a hungry person might feel desire for a bowl of fruit until she realized that the fruits were artificial. The original desire remains in one sense, for she is still hungry, but in another sense, the desire has changed, no longer being directed at the plastic fruits. If one were fully to recognize *with one's whole being* that the thing one desires is not going to satisfy one's desire, one would cease to desire it. But if one's desire really is fundamentally for one's own good, then *if one recognized with one's whole being* that the thing one desires *is not beneficial for one*, one should cease to desire it as well. The cases that seem to be counterexamples to this claim, cases where one believes one is acting against one's better judgment, are not really counterexamples, because even in those cases a part of oneself still believes that one's choice is beneficial. For instance, the cigarette smoker may know that she is risking her health but at the same time believes that it is more beneficial for her at the moment to alleviate the discomfort of nicotine withdrawal. The immediate discomfort has the effect of magnifying the good of immediate relief, making it appear of greater worth than the avoidance of long-term health problems that might not manifest and that in any case are difficult to imagine in their proper proportions.[117] Therefore, when one chooses pleasure over one's long-term benefit, some part of oneself, namely the part that desires to experience the pleasure, takes the pleasure to be a benefit, even if one tells oneself at the same time that one is being foolish and self-destructive. For Socrates, the conquest of a foolish desire over our better judgment is always really the victory of ignorance. People say that they cannot resist their desires, but it is the *foolishness* of the desire that is the problem. The foolishness seems to have more strength than "better judgment" because at some level one's own mind is fooled. For the foolishness of the temptation is insufficiently appreciated and the wisdom of the better judgment is insufficiently understood. So, from Socrates' point of view, such choices are involuntary, in the same way that making a mistake is involuntary by definition. Socrates would not deny that one may have a feeling of being "overwhelmed" by desire, but he would hold that such a feeling only arises on account of the power of ignorance in one's psyche. For the desire that "overwhelms" one is itself based on a mistaken perception or understanding, and if that misunderstanding were cleared up the desire would dissipate. Human motivation is related to understanding; one is motivated to act well to the degree that one properly appreciates the value of a good action. So what seems like "weak will" is really the ignorance of the good. When one chooses something other than one's true good, one acts contrary to one's own ultimate desire, but in the (conscious or unconscious) belief that one is pursuing it.

From this point of view, one can understand the Socratic paradox that evil is ignorance, and that, as ignorance, evil is involuntary. All people, good and evil, are trying to find the good, but the evil do this foolishly and therefore unsuccessfully. In this sense, virtue is knowledge. Thus, one can find a ground in Diotima's teaching for the so-called "Socratic paradoxes"—"Evil is ignorance" and "No one willingly does evil"—that Socrates defends in other dialogues. The key is the belief that desire is always governed by what one believes to be the good (for one). If one desires whatever is good for one and it should turn out that what is good for one is the life of virtue, then one in fact desires virtue whether one is aware of it or not. Although one might deliberately break the law, in doing so one is generally mistaken about how to achieve one's own good, and one does not make a mistake about one's own good voluntarily. In a sense, then, what makes the lawbreaking involuntary is not that it happens contrary to volition, but the fact that the volition is formed in ignorance—since one has made a mistake in believing that one may obtain the good through the act. In fact, according to Socrates, one has harmed oneself without meaning to do so. If one truly understood that one was harming oneself through evil, one would never do it, according to this view. To the obvious objection that self-destructive behavior does occur, Socrates might claim that even apparently self-destructive behavior is indulged in, paradoxically, for the sake of benefit to oneself. For there are a variety of things a self-destructive person might believe that they gain through acts of self-destruction.

One can also see from Diotima's account how love becomes dangerous. Because all people desire to make the good their own, people are very easily led through a kind of wishful thinking to want to believe that what is "their own" is therefore the good. Here is the source of what is ordinarily called egoism; it is an attempt to make reality into what one wishes it to be, and to treat the current forms of one's desire as already possessing their object. This egoism is also the fundamental human illusion that seems implicit in Agathon's deification of love. There are many examples of taking what is one's own to be the Good itself. One has only to think of the human tendency to treat one's own country, one's own group, one's own creed or point of view, one's own current lifestyle, and so on, as sacrosanct and inviolable. In general, human beings seem to care more about the fate of their own things, friends, families, countries, etc., and less about the fates of things of others. But along with this greater concern for one's own good comes a tendency toward wishful thinking that easily leads people to overestimate the value of what is one's own, or a tendency to have a bias in one's own favor. Hence, it is easy to ascribe to oneself, one's friends, one's family, or one's country a higher value relative to others than it may actually have. All forms of the ignorance that takes itself for wisdom belong here. This condition of the psyche prevents one from living the examined life, since one will not seek for a wisdom or a good that one believes one already possesses (see *Philebus* 48d–49a, where Socrates speaks of three ways of not knowing oneself or one's own goods). Ordinary ways of seeking honor are tied to this phenomenon. In pursuing conventional honor, one accepts certain conventional symbols—awards for bravery or virtue, applause, achievements—as indicative of one's possession of the good one seeks.

At lower levels of Love, according to Diotima, Love is not truly aware of what it ultimately desires. What it desires is the true good, which would lead to the true happiness. All things at the lower rungs of the ladder of Love may have some intrinsic value—Diotima never denies that—but they are ultimately desired as a means to happiness. When they are taken as ends in themselves that are not directed toward any further end, that is, when these instrumental or intermediate goods are believed to be sufficient in themselves for happiness, they become obstacles to genuine well-being.

According to Diotima, the supreme good for humans that would constitute human happiness is a relation to something timeless or eternal. The supreme good for humans is not the Form of the Good but a relation to it that constitutes participation in it. The Good in Itself (which is akin to the true Beauty of which Diotima speaks) is literally *without time*, for it stands outside of past, present, and future. What is truly divine, for Diotima, seems to be timeless. But mortals, however, exist in time. Mortals are constantly changing, replacing old elements of themselves with new elements, both at the level of the body and at the level of the psyche. It is only by replacing the old with the new that mortals continue through time; continuing through time is as close as mortals come in ordinary life to the immortality that is timeless. Thus, Diotima indicates that reproduction of all kinds—all forms of replacing the old with the new—is how mortal beings imitate, or attain a share of, genuine immortality. This account also relates to the Platonic notion of "participation"; the particulars that share in Forms are always temporal beings and their "participation" consists in the continual replacement of old temporal stages of themselves with new stages that somehow are "images" of those they replace, in part by virtue of somehow sharing in the same Form. Of course, the mystery of participation still remains at the level of the temporal stages, since they must already "participate" in a Form in order to constitute "images" of their predecessor stages, and participation also involves multiple "images" of a Form existing simultaneously.

It is because the supreme good is timeless that one wants to possess it forever. That is to say, human beings want to possess it by sharing in it, and thereby sharing in its immortality. But mortal creatures cannot literally make themselves timeless. So the desire for the timeless reality creates in people a desire to imitate its immortality through reproduction. Diotima includes in reproduction all forms of creativity. Creating offspring is the mode of immortality most readily available to animals, but longer lasting even than one's children are great works of art and literature, monuments to great heroes and so on.

Another, more direct way to think of the desire to possess the good forever is as follows: if something is good, and it stops, that is bad. So clearly, the greatest good imaginable would be everlasting. But the good does not do one much good if one does not possess it in some sense or have some relation to it that confers some goodness on oneself, that is, that makes one happy. So ultimately, one wants an everlasting good that one may possess everlastingly. But if one is going to possess it forever, then one has to be immortal. Therefore, at bottom, one desires immortality. This desire for immortality is also at the root of the desire for fame and reputation, just as the desire for the good as such is at the root of the love of honor. Being honored or loved can help one believe that one is good; the love given or the honor accorded affirms one's goodness, or even constitutes a feeling of goodness. Moreover, one has a tendency to believe that honor will provide one with a kind of "immortality" if one is remembered by posterity.

The desire for honor also provokes humans to create, to produce great works and deeds. Each of these creative endeavors is an attempt to capture some reflection of the Good. Each is also an offspring that expresses something essential of its creator and to which one can be as attached as people are to their own children. People seek to be affirmed, and even to become immortal, through their works. Inspired by the beauty that guides them toward the eternal good they seek, humans "give birth" creatively in an attempt to touch that divinity, and to share in its timeless nature in the only way temporal beings can. The need for perfection, for all the good one does not possess, for eternity—this need is a messenger that both leads and links human beings to what they do not have. This same *Erôs* allows them to be guided by the messages and inspiration they receive from the divine realm. This same need, both as an impulse to transcend what one currently is and as communion with and transformation by what is already beyond the order of Becoming, enables people to be creative.

*Erôs* gets human beings to risk themselves—for instance, in the form of brave acts born of spiritedness. In contrast to the acquisitive, appetitive part of human beings that wants to consume, the part of human beings that loves honor is spendthrifty: it expends itself, but for the sake of some higher, nonmaterial gain: respect, awe, love, power, honor, and so on. Hence the honorlover seeks whatever convinces him of his worth, his possession of the good, and whatever seems to secure him immortality.

According to Diotima, the good people desire is timeless, but the closest mortals can come to it is through reproduction. The desire to possess the good forever is what leads people to creativity and honor seeking. But she ranks the forms that this desire to create can take. Just as spiritual reproduction seems superior to biological reproduction, so too are the different forms of spiritual creativity ranked. Highest of all spiritual endeavors, in her view, seems to be that of the philosopher who is led to see the nature of Beauty itself. Apparently, as love progresses, it advances toward what is most desired; and what is most desired is what makes other things desirable. So each stage of love's progress ascends toward the cause of the stage below it, that is, toward whatever it was that bestowed the desirable qualities on the lower stage. Therefore, beautiful customs and laws stand higher than beautiful psyches, because beautiful psyches are shaped by beautiful customs and laws; which embody, we might say, the soul of a body-politic. And beautiful studies stand higher than beautiful customs and laws, because the best customs are shaped by beautiful studies. Higher than these beautiful studies is the highest study of Beauty itself, culminating in a vision of the very Form of Beauty.[118] This vision is itself "creative" or "reproductive," inspiring the desire to "give birth in beauty" and leading the philosopher to "give birth" to true virtue (212a).

The philosopher will seek to educate others in the practice of philosophy, a practice that leads to virtue and the culminating vision. Education too is an example of spiritual fertility, according to Diotima (209b–e). She highlights the examples of poets and lawgivers as educators; yet her closing remarks, other Platonic dialogues, and Plato's own practice, all suggest that philosophers will strive to become legislators and to rival and surpass the poets in education.[119]

With her depiction of the culminating final vision, Diotima places the life of philosophical inquiry above the life spent seeking conventional honors. The good that mortals truly seek is timeless. But the good that humans can possess in closest approximation to the timeless good does not involve the possession of anything external or any socially conferred honor, for it would be a tenuous well-being that depended upon external things or upon the recognition of others. Instead, the human good consists in a certain way of life, something more fully within one's power to effect. Calling this life "philosophical" or saying that it involves "contemplation" should not be misconstrued to mean that it is a life that is narrowly "theoretical." The philosopher's life demands the transformation of the whole person through practice of dialectic, that is, through the kind of spiritual exercises exemplified in the conversations of Socrates. From Diotima's point of view, this life consists in drawing ever closer to the supreme or ultimate good.

In the view set out by Diotima, there is one sense in which people can give themselves the good, but in another sense they cannot. People can open themselves up to the Good and can allow themselves to be guided by it; but only by following after a perfection they cannot create themselves and by obeying its dictates can they attain genuine well-being. The lower levels of Love, the objects of ordinary desire, if focused on excessively, might all be seen as failed attempts to give oneself the true good, failed attempts to find the Good at the level of what is merely mortal and changing. When people try to make what is already "their own" into the Good, or when they try to find the Good outside of themselves on the level of physical objects or conventional honors, they are doomed to failure. For Diotima, the highest good for which the human being is longing is the transcendent Good known only to the lover of wisdom. Changes of fortune affecting merely temporal goods will seem relatively unimportant to one who knows that the supreme good is timeless, and that one's happiness depends only on pursuing the wisdom that comes from the apprehension of timeless beauty. Temporal goods may retain significance, but only as conditions of the possibility of a life devoted to philosophy; and the philosopher demands relatively little from the temporal world.

Since obtaining the supreme good for Diotima seems to imply living the life of a philosopher, those who are uninterested in living a life that includes self-examination are ignorant of their deepest longing, their own unique potential. If one understood that self-knowledge and right living was the path to the ultimate fulfillment of one's deepest desire, one would desire excellence through the philosophical life. Therefore, it is only because of ignorance that philosophy is neglected.

In recounting his own initiation, an initiation his role as seeker and lover of wisdom has enabled him to undertake, Socrates is initiating others. Socrates is an expert on *Erôs* not merely because he has been taught by Diotima, but because his own experience of directing his desire toward the most noble and lasting objects has given him deep and complex understanding of a longing that somehow can convey features of that for which it longs. Indeed, Socrates' own longing for wisdom through his continual contact with ignorance has imparted to him a kind of "human wisdom." Perhaps his human wisdom is the human inflection of the wisdom of the gods that remains beyond him. For although he does not possess divine wisdom, it is the awareness of that very lack, and the implied awareness that there is something lacked, that constitutes the limited wisdom that he does profess to have. His love, as a longing for what it lacks, is a messenger.

## FROM LOVE AS NEED TO LOVE AS RESOURCE

Diotima's teachings about *Erôs* have often been seen to fall short of capturing all that is meant by the word *love* in contemporary times. One drawback of taking "*Erôs*" as the fundamental impulse of the human psyche and understanding human love as such a desire to possess the good is that it seems to leave out a more altruistic sort of love. Whereas *Erôs* is "egoistic" in its need to possess, and whereas it only transcends the "self" for the sake of an other or not-self that the self desires *to possess*, there is a kind of love, it is said, that is concerned solely for the good of the other. It is not merely that this love is self-forgetting in its absorption in the desire for the other, as *Erôs* can be; it is not merely that this love is willing to risk or to sacrifice part of the self for the sake of a relation to the other, as *Erôs* can be; rather, there is a kind of love that does not desire to possess or to gain from the other, but merely to serve the other and bring about the other's good. This giving love is sometimes identified with the Christian concept of *agapē*, brotherly love.[120]

Another defect that has been found in Diotima's conception of love is that it seems to deny the finality of the love of individuals; according to her (or Plato's) conception, one loves others only for the sake of loving the Divine, the Forms (or perhaps one's own good, to be obtained through one's association with Forms). On this view, beloved individuals seem to be at best merely the stained glass through which the light of love's true object shines. This feature of Diotima's teaching has been thought to account for a certain frigidity in the psyche of Socrates and a certain inadequacy in his relationship to others. He is thought to care for them only for the sake of their usefulness to him in his own dialectical practice of philosophy and not for the sake of their own development or on account of any of their unique personal qualities. It is as though, critics allege, Socrates needs only a generic interlocutor; he does not need lovers or friends.

One can see a certain similarity between these two criticisms. They both find in Diotima's view a rather narcissistic view of love. For every desire is based on the psyche's fundamental *Erôs*, an *Erôs* that is concerned with the psyche's own possession of its own good. Both the other as an other (according to the first criticism) and the other as an individual, along with everything else in the world of particularity and change (according to the second criticism), are rendered merely "instrumental," mere means to the psyche's own end—and given the inessential nature of any given one of them, any given one of them would be a relatively dispensable means at that.

But both of these criticisms, whatever truth they may contain, fail to do justice to an aspect of Diotima's teaching. For Diotima does take some account of the generous or giving aspect of love through her views about spiritual reproduction and the psyche's need to "give birth in beauty." For although *Erôs* desires to possess the good forever, this need generates in the psyche *a need to give*—for humans can only approximate to the immortal possession of good through giving birth in beauty, and giving birth in beauty implies a munificent bestowal upon mortal objects of care and concern. The psyche desires to generate its own offspring, to reproduce its "image"; but it finds it can only do so with the aid of other psyches, who are each of them desiring to generate their own images as well. Ultimately, a human can give nothing but herself, and it is in such giving that her psyche finds its greatest gain. It is true that on Diotima's view humans do not give gratuitously, as though with the grace of an all-sufficient God; rather, humans have a *need* to give, and thus giving is still grounded in human need. But from this need comes a munificent concern for the other as genuine as from any other impulse.

One sees these ideas clearly embodied in Diotima's conception of philosophical pedagogy. The lover who beholds the Form of Beauty Itself is inspired to give birth to true virtue, not mere images of virtue (212a); but this remark hearkens back to the earlier discussion of those "pregnant in psyche" who sow their ideas and arguments about virtue in the psyche of beautiful youths and together with them nuture their shared offspring: "Such people ... have much more to share than do the parents of human children, and have a firmer bond of friendship, because the children in whom they have a share are more beautiful and more immortal" (209c-d). These words of Diotima suggest that the strength and intimacy of a relationship based on shared philosophic pursuits are if anything present in it to a greater degree than they are in ordinary relationships. It is true that at this point she is speaking of those spiritually pregnant in general, and not specifically of philosophers, but her later remarks about the philosopher giving birth to true virtues, and the grounds on which the spiritually pregnant are said to have a superior bond—namely, the superiority of their offspring—combine to suggest that the bond between two philosophers, or between a philosophic mentor and her disciples, would be especially profound.

Although *Erôs* is *ultimately* directed at the Good, *Erôs* is also *genuinely* directed at earthly objects since those objects can have various degrees of participation in the longed-for transcendent object of desire. To the extent that earthly things *have the potential to* participate in that object, they become themselves genuine objects of desire. The need to give birth, the creative impulse behind the teacher's motive, is born of the desire to possess the good forever, and reproduction on this view therefore amounts to the desire to bring the good as much as possible into the mortal realm. Moreover, the "offspring" imagery suggests that one will care for these temporal goods one is bringing about *as a continuation of one's own self*, one's bid for immortality. Hence, one cares powerfully for the other. In *Erôs* we have a longing to promote the good on earth that is similar to the Demiurge's creative impulse in the *Timaeus*, but for the fact that the Demiurge creates *out of his goodness*, whereas humans create out of a *desire* for the good (for the immortal possession of the good) *that they* (to a certain extent) *lack*. Yet the very desire for the Good contains a message and inspiration from the Good, that is, the Good's nature is communicated to humans to an extent through their desire for it; humans participate in the Good to some extent through their desire for it, and do so the more perfectly the clearer they become about the nature of the object of their ultimate desire. The idea that the Divine, that is, the Good, communicates to mortals through love clearly links Diotima's doctrine of *Erôs* with the *Phaedrus'* notion of divine madness through which, according to Socrates, the greatest benefits come to mortals (*Phaedrus*, 244a). This connection between the Divine and mortal objects of desire provides an incentive to care about another's good and to identify the other's good (or the other's progress toward the good) with one's own. Diotima's view of *Erôs* is no more deficient than any *religious* view of love, for example, one that holds that "we must love God with all our heart and soul and our neighbor as our self" or even one that holds that we find God in the other. There is no reason that, having the highest vision of Beauty Itself (or the Good, or the Forms generally), the initiate will not be inspired to "give birth in beauty" and to sow the seeds of virtue into the souls of youth.

## DIOTIMA'S TEACHING IN RELATION TO THE EARLIER SPEECHES

The earlier speeches prepared Plato's audience for Diotima's teaching, and her teaching brings together and unifies disparate points made by the earlier speakers.[121] Phaedrus's speech emphasized that love is the one passion that is able at times to overcome the fear of death and so make people capable of bravery, and thus of real goodness, which often requires bravery. The implication is that love enables us to see beyond our limitations and brings us closer to immortality. Pausanias distinguished different kinds of love, according to their distinct objects; he sees that the experience of love differs with different objects. At a minimum, love comes in spiritual as well as physical forms. For Eryximachus, *Erôs* is cosmological as well as human, and functions as a principle of explanation. *Erôs* brings together elements in the larger universe, and the love of humans must be seen in that context. Aristophanes' speech reminds us that *Erôs* involves an insatiable longing to be whole or complete, and this incompleteness and the yearning it provokes are of the essence of being human. All desire derives from the longing to be made whole, but it is of the nature of human existence to be incomplete, insofar as there is a future story still to be written. In Agathon's speech the properties of love are confused with the properties of its objects. Such confusion is a mistake, but it also represents a truth: desire does somehow *communicate* something of that object. Truly loving admirable things can make one more admirable; and loving despicable things makes one despicable. And yet, as Socrates goes on to point out, the distinction between love and its object never wholly collapses.

Thus, taken together, the previous speeches highlight these properties of love: (1) Love enables human beings to overcome the fear of death and thus to break beyond the self; (2) Love has both bodily and spiritual forms; (3) Far from being merely a human emotion, Love exists also at the cosmic level and stretches throughout the natural world; (4) It involves a yearning incompleteness that is never fully fulfilled; But (5) Love in some sense comes to reflect the objects by which it is guided. All of these aspects of *Erôs* are captured at once by Diotima's account in Socrates' speech. She explains the self-transcending quality of *Erôs* and its ability to overcome fear of death more fully than Phaedrus does. Diotima's teaching concerning the stages of love and her distinction between biological and spiritual reproduction allow for the levels distinguished by Pausanias, the Heavenly as well as the Earthly Aphrodite. Her view of *Erôs* is every bit as cosmological as that of Eryximachus, and it is capable of subsuming his other main points. She has delved even more deeply into the yearning incompleteness of love than did Aristophanes, but at the same time provided a critique of his notion of "lost wholeness." Finally, she articulates an understanding of *Erôs* that is contrary to that of Agathon, but her teaching also brings out the hidden grain of truth in Agathon's speech. For *Erôs* on her view is a messenger, and by bringing messages from the divine it can, in its highest forms, help the lover to come to possess (however imperfectly) some of the qualities of the supreme beloved. The ability of the perfect lover to become more like the beloved is represented by the fact that Socrates, the consummate embodiment of philosophical *Erôs*, will actually come to replace *Erôs* as the object of praise in the next speech, the speech of Alcibiades. Like the *Erôs* that he embodies, Socrates points beyond himself to a beloved of ultimate value; but precisely by being such a paradigm of *daimonic Erôs* with his own divine message for humankind, he becomes a reflection of that higher good of which his whole being has become a sign.

In some ways, Socrates' speech, with its account of the teaching of Diotima for whom love is also a universal natural force, builds on the good suggestions in the speech of Eryximachus. But Socrates' speech also incorporates the concern with the human and religious domains that one sees in the speech of Aristophanes. This synthesis of the concerns of Eryximachus and Aristophanes suggests that philosophy "completes" science. For Socrates modified and improved philosophy after the nature philosophy of the Presocratics had been corrupted by the teachings of certain sophists regarding nature and convention; Socrates showed that philosophy can understand nature in a way that supports, rather than undermines, the political concerns of justice and moderation. Whereas Aristophanes declines the invitation simply to fill in the speech of Eryximachus, starting as he does from a different ground, the philosopher's speech will synthesize the rationalism of Eryximachus and the piety of Aristophanes.[122]

At the same time, Socrates synthesizes Aristophanes and Agathon. The insatiable longing of *Erôs* that Aristophanes had noted is preserved, although according to Diotima's teaching the psyche longs not for a soulmate, but for the good. Yet Agathon's insight that *Erôs* partakes of goodness is preserved, although not in such a way that would make desire itself the possessor of what it desired, thus denying its essential character as a longing for what is lacked. If human distance from the good brings out the comic character of human existence, while human participation in the good in spite of inevitable limitation and lack is what constitutes tragic nobility, then by the doctrine of *Erôs* Socrates synthesizes the comic and the tragic. Socrates has shown that his wisdom is superior to Agathon's because Socrates understands *Erôs* better. Socrates' deeper understanding of *Erôs* is able to do justice to both the comic and tragic aspects of life.

Socrates' "speech" demonstrates differences from and superiority to the encomia of the other speakers. It shows why *Erôs* should be guided by the love of wisdom. His speech does this by relating the love of wisdom to all other forms of erotic/creative endeavors and showing philosophy to lie at the summit of them all. At the same time, Socrates reveals the common object of all these activities or practices and makes the case that philosophy alone best attains it, however imperfectly it does so. The "speech" further explains the nature of philosophy as *daimonic*. All forms of erotic desire are *daimonic*, and function as spirits or messengers according to Diotima; but one must imagine that, in coming so near to the ultimate goal of all *Erôs*, philosophy is especially *daimonic*. The messenger becomes even more of a messenger as it does a better job of conveying the message.

Since the message is always *only a message* from another region, it never succeeds in *transporting* one to the other side, to the realm of Being or the divine. But one *can* be guided by the message of Being here in the world of Becoming, in Time, by attending to and caring for one's own *Erôs*. As Eryximachus had suggested earlier and as Diotima's teaching reaffirms, the proper care of the self consists in cultivating the right form of *Erôs* in one's own character. Such cultivation is clearly embodied in the dialectical practice of Plato's Socrates and in Plato's own literary art.

# CHAPTER 3

# The Entrance and Speech
# of Alcibiades (212c–222c)

## THE ENTRANCE OF ALCIBIADES

The introductory dialogue (or Prologue) and the speeches of the first six speakers (Phaedrus, Pausanias, Eryximachus, Aristophanes, Agathon, and Socrates) serve to get the audience excited about philosophy as it appears in contrast to its rival claimants to wisdom—conventional virtue, the study of nature, and poetry. This protreptic part of the *Symposium* corresponds to the kind of experience that would make a young poet burn all of his poetry and devote himself to philosophy (as, legend has it, Plato did after he became interested in spending time with the historical Socrates). The glorious vision of the Beautiful Itself in which Socrates' speech culminates awakens the *Erôs* in Plato's audience, filling the audience with the divine messages that *Erôs* brings. But then, just after Socrates has presented this magnificent description of the Beautiful itself, the jarring entrance of the inebriated Alcibiades pulls the conversation back to earth, reminding us of the irrational forms of *Erôs* that in fact rule in the political realm.

The author of the last speech in the *Symposium* does not even arrive until after Socrates concludes his magnificent speech. The dialogue might well have ended at the point at which Diotima holds out the promise that after a lifetime of following *Erôs* in the right way, the true lover may be permitted a glimpse of the Beautiful itself. Employing the language of initiation typical of the mystery religions, the almost ethereal passage in which Diotima describes how the vision of true beauty yields real virtue and a share of immortality is clearly the apex of the dialogue. Hence, it might have seemed fitting to allow the philosopher to have the last word on the matter and to have ended the dialogue at its highest height. But Plato does not permit the dialogue to end here, choosing instead to have Alcibiades, handsome military general and

155

ward of Pericles, crash the party and unsettle the lofty mood reached just prior to the end of Socrates' speech.

The applause and cheers for the philosopher's performance made it impossible at first for the guests to discern who was causing the ruckus outside in the courtyard. "All of a sudden" the noise intensified as a group of drunken revelers arrived, and Agathon sent his servants out to see who was there. Alcibiades was heard shouting, already inebriated and demanding to be taken to Agathon. It is reported that a flute-girl and several friends among the merrymakers half-carried Alcibiades to the door, by which point he managed to stand up under his own power. He is crowned with a wreath of ivy and violets and has ribbons in his hair (212c-e). Violets had been a symbol of Athens since Pindar's fragment linked the two forever in verse[1] and were also symbols of Aphrodite; ivy was the preferred headdress of another character notorious for being disruptive—Dionysos.[2] Such attire is altogether appropriate for Alcibiades on this occasion; in his drunken condition, he comes as an emissary of Dionysus. The contrast between this drunken street troupe and the wholly intelligible world spoken of at the end of Socrates' speech could not be more extreme. The entrance of Alcibiades will also be seen to jeopardize the sobriety of the hungover men gathered at Agathon's house, for Alcibiades will soon appoint himself "symposiarch" or "leader of the drinking" and insist that everyone join him in his state of intoxication (213e). Although in his speech on Socrates Alcibiades will charge the philosopher with hubris and playfully put him on trial before his companions, he also plays the role that Agathon had said Dionysus would play; his remarks on Socrates will decide the dispute between Socrates and Agathon regarding wisdom.[3]

To fully appreciate the significance of Alcibiades' entrance and speech within the dialogue as a whole, one must consider how these developments relate to the culminating vision of the Beautiful Itself in Socrates' account. If one considers the historical context within which Plato would have been writing his philosophical dramas, it is clear that Alcibiades is partly emblematic of the virtues and vices of imperialistic Athens. He evokes the memory of the city's fate in the war. Plato probably sees the war and the city's loss of the war as direct results of the citizens' failure to undertake proper self-care. As Socrates implies in the dialogue that offers a rationale for his whole life's mission, the Athenians' failed to put the care of the *psychē* above the care for money, power, honor, and pleasure (*Ap.* 29c–30c, 37e–38a. See also *Gorgias*). Bringing in Alcibiades here is, among other things, a way for Plato to remind his audience of what is at stake in connection with the issues of *Erôs* and philosophy.

The original audience of Plato's *Symposium* would have been mindful of the fates of its characters. As we noted in our introduction, the conversation at the banquet appears to take place right before Alcibiades sets out to lead Athens on its most daring and ambitious military expedition of the war. According to Thucydides' account, Alcibiades was the initiator of the

Sicilian invasion; while Nicias, the other general, was opposed to sending forces to Sicily, because he thought the expedition was too risky. Not long after his appearance at this drinking party, the expedition to Syracuse would set out and Alcibiades would be summoned back home to answer charges of defacing the Herms and profaning the Eleusinian mysteries, the notorious sacrilege of 415 BCE. Rather than returning to Athens, however, Alcibiades defected to Sparta, and his advice aided them in defeating the overextended Athenians, bringing disaster on the Athenian invasion of Syracuse that he himself had instigated. Although Alcibiades would later return to the Athenian side and almost succeed in turning the tide, it was still partly as a consequence of the demoralizing loss of men and resources in the Sicilian Expedition that Athens would eventually lose the war. After the oligarchy of 411 fell, the leaders of the Athenian generals urged Alcibiades to return and take command of the fleet in Samos. He did, and almost tipped the scales back in their favor. He was welcomed back into the city in 407. But four months later, as a result of one of his subordinate's failing to take orders, the Athenians suffered a loss and dismissed him once again. In 404, when the city was on the verge of defeat, there were still calls for and rumors of another return; but he was killed that same year.[4]

After a siege Athens would fall. The Spartans would install the oligarchic Athenian faction known as the Thirty Tyrants. And on account of his former association with some of the Tyrants and with Alcibiades, Socrates would come under suspicion as a corrupter of youth, leading ultimately to his trial and execution under the restored democracy. All of these facts would have been well-known to Plato's original audience. Hence, this dialogue presents a glimpse of the moment just prior to the beginning of the end for Athens' Empire.

At the time Plato was composing the *Symposium*, long after these events, the future of Athens, in the light of its tragic past, would have very likely been a prime topic of debate, and Plato is surely responding to these recent events through his drama. The role of Alcibiades in these events, and the question of Socrates' relationship with him, would also have been a matter of great controversy.

Plato's presentation of Alcibiades (who in many ways reflects the city he betrayed and almost saved) and of Alcibiades' relation to Socrates should be viewed against this backdrop. Plato's presentation of Socrates' character and mission is shaped by Plato's wish to contribute to the debate about the meaning of these historical events. Although nothing prevents Plato's account from at the same time containing some historically accurate material, we should be mindful that his presentation of Alcibiades, like his presentation of Socrates, is not strictly a historical biography. Yet it is no doubt owing to Socrates' actual aims and activities that Plato believes he can turn back to them to draw lessons for the Athenians of his generation. Plato may have thought that it was not too late for the next generation to turn to philosophy. The lesson of the Platonic dialogues for Plato's time was surely that those who can do so should live the philosophic life. But those incapable of philosophy should respect and honor the philosophers, giving them a role in the governing of the city as educators, advisors, lawgivers, or gadflies, if not as rulers.

At the same time, however, the dialogues suggest Plato's awareness of the tragic improbability of the philosopher's success in the effort to overcome human folly, naked hubris, and the love of victory (*philonikia*). The character of Alcibiades and his speech in the *Symposium* show what happens when *Erôs* is misdirected. Like the Tyrannical Man of the *Republic*, Alcibiades' life shows that *Erôs* can be quite dangerous and destructive, unless it is aimed at the right objects and diverted away from others. It is worth repeating that the Athenian Stranger in the *Laws* says that education is a matter of directing the psyche to love and to hate the right things as opposed to the wrong things (*Laws* 653b-c). Socrates makes the same point in the *Republic* when he explains that education is not a matter of putting sight in blind eyes, but in turning one's vision (and, we might infer, one's care or concern) toward the right things, that is, those things that are truly good (see *Rep.* 491d-e, 518b-c, and 519a-b). For right action seems much easier to achieve if one desires (and therefore takes pleasure in) what is good. A similar conception of virtue and vice also clearly follows from the discussion of the types of psyche in *Republic* IX (580d–581c). This need for *Erôs* to be properly directed implies further that *Erôs* will be duly limited; the virtuous person will not let his desires be limitless and he will not cultivate desires for base or wicked things. But Alcibiades' acquisitive *Erôs* is representative of that of imperial Athens— greedy for honor, for power, for gain, filled with hubris, in short, incapable of order or restraint.[5]

It is not enough for Plato to show the danger of Alcibiades' character and the motivations Alcibiades shares with the Athenian people, but he must also analyze the defects involved. In analyzing Alcibiades' case, he must both justify Socrates' interest and association with the promising young man and also explain the failure of this promise and the implications of it for the understanding of Alcibiades and Socrates that he wants to present. That this character appeared worthy of Socrates' attention seems to interest Plato, as evidenced from the fact that he devotes a dialogue to conversations between the controversial general and the controversial Socrates (viz., the *Alcibiades* I).[6] The relationship between them is also underscored in the *Gorgias* when Plato has Socrates say that he has "two loves: philosophy and Alcibiades" (*Grg.* 481d). Additionally, Alcibiades comes to the defense of Socrates' position in the *Protagoras* (336b-d; 348b). Through Alcibiades' account of his relation to Socrates in his *Symposium* speech, and through his interaction with Socrates in the dialogue, one sees that Alcibiades is noble enough to have some appreciation of the value of Socrates. After all, he has had a glimpse of Socrates' goodness that eluded the perception of most people. Nonetheless, Alcibiades is tragically unable to overcome his own character and his attachment to the

Athenian demos because he is unable to overcome his desire for honor and the "things of the city." This perception might be reinforced by the doubts Socrates expressed at the end of their very first conversation about Alcibiades' ability to resist his love of adulation and flattery. (See *Alc.* I, 135e.)

The real question, from the perspective Plato is creating, is not why Socrates failed with Alcibiades, but how he could have thought that he might succeed with this character. Clearly, Socrates knew that he would have to compete with what in the *Republic* he calls "the greatest sophist," the corrupt upbringing offered young men by the conventional values of Athens itself (*Rep.* 492a-e). It is remarkable that Socrates was able to get through to Alcibiades at all, that is, that he could cause this brilliant young ward of the legendary Pericles to question himself and even to feel ashamed of himself. Such a feat is quite remarkable when one realizes that nearly every other voice Alcibiades would have heard would have been flattering rather than critical.[7] His beauty, intelligence, and talent were unsurpassed, and he certainly had no shortage of supporters or conspirators. The Athenians were willing to choose him as general for an extremely important expedition, an expedition they mounted on his advice. Moreover, even after this disastrous event, the failure of which had much to do with betrayal by Alcibiades, Athens was willing to forgive him and accept him as leader again later in the war. Alcibiades was not a man who was used to accepting criticism and censure, but one who demanded honor; when he did not get it, he changed sides. With this background in mind, one must consider the way the entrance and speech of Alcibiades alters the mood of the *Symposium*.

That the drunken Alcibiades should crash this symposium at which Socrates has just finished telling the others of his initiation into erotic matters by the priestess Diotima is highly symbolic. Recall that it was to answer the charges of defiling the Herms and profaning the mysteries for which Alcibiades was called back from the Sicilian expedition. Alcibiades' crashing of the party and his drunken speech on Socrates constitute the true version of his sacrilege. He profanes the mysteries of *Erôs* and the "herm" that he attempts to deface is the satyr-like Socrates.

Diotima had herself employed the language of the Mysteries. It might be supposed that her philosophical version of the mysteries was already a profanation of the traditional Eleusinian rites, to say nothing of Socrates' revelation of these mysteries to his friends who have undergone no special initiation. But it would be better to consider Socrates' speech itself as an attempt to initiate his friends into the mysteries of *Erôs* and it is this attempt that is profaned by the incursion of Alcibiades. Alcibiades too employs the language of initiation and mystery at 218b. Superficially, he seems to take more care than Socrates about the status of his listeners, asserting that he will only speak to those who share the mania and Bacchic frenzy of philosophy, and telling the "profane" to close their ears. But Alcibiades' use of the language of the Mysteries is just a sign that he profanes the mysteries of Diotima by an unwitting mockery that destroys their elevating effect and drags the party back down to earth. Thus, the action of the dialogue is foreshadowing the charges that will be brought against him later. Both he and Socrates use the language and symbolism of the mystery religions to make their distinct points, one about *Erôs* and the other about the Bacchic frenzy produced by philosophy and about the true nature of Socrates. But since the highest form of *Erôs* according to Diotima is also philosophy, and Socrates is the exemplary philosopher, there is a connection between these topics. If Socrates had just been engaged in initiating the others into the mysteries of Love, with a vision of the philosophical life at their center, Alcibiades' speech seems to be a comic presentation of some of the same material. It is because Alcibiades profaned these mysteries, the mysteries of philosophy, that he was doomed to exile from the philosophic life, the true city (*Rep.* 595a) that might have been his, but that he was doomed to betray.

Plato's audience soon learns that Alcibiades, who, like Socrates, was not in attendance on the first night of celebration, has come to crown Agathon, "the cleverest and best looking man in town" (212e). He asks those gathered whether he should simply transfer the crown he is wearing to Agathon's head and then leave, or stay and join the party. The others agree that he should stay, and they bid him to take a seat. Agathon calls for Alcibiades to sit next to him, and the already inebriated Alcibiades, ribbons covering his eyes, makes his way, like a blind man led by his friends, to Agathon's couch. Since the headband of ribbons had now slipped down over his eyes, rendering him unable to see that Socrates was also sitting on the couch with Agathon, Alcibiades plops down between Socrates and Agathon, hugging and kissing the young poet before placing the crown on his head. After ordering a slave to take Alcibiades' sandals off, Agathon says there is room enough for three on the couch. Alcibiades asks who the third person is (213a-b). But before Agathon could answer, Alcibiades had already spotted Socrates. Leaping up, he exclaims, "Good lord, what's going on here? It's Socrates! You've trapped me again! You always do this to me—all of a sudden you'll turn up out of nowhere where I least expect you." He accuses Socrates of conniving his way onto the same couch with Agathon, "the most handsome man in the room" (213c).

The campy by-play between Socrates and Alcibiades that ensues provides a comic interlude with a serious point. Each man claims that the other man will beat him up (213d, 214d). Socrates asks for Agathon's protection, claiming that Agathon cannot imagine what it's like to be in love with Alcibiades; he can't say two words to, or even look at, another handsome man when Alcibiades is around without him getting jealous and becoming violent toward him. Alcibiades pledges that he'll never forgive Socrates for these statements and that he'll make the philosopher pay for this embarrassment, but then he repossesses some of the ribbons from Agathon's head so that he can make a crown for Socrates too. He claims that the philosopher will grumble later if

Agathon is crowned for his first victory and Socrates is not deemed worthy of such honor, even though he "has never lost an argument in his life" (213e).

Plato's audience should wonder why Socrates and Alcibiades are said to be jealous of one another. Is Alcibiades' reason for honoring Socrates here consonant with what he will report later in his speech about Socrates' attitude toward honor? Plato's audience is surely supposed to wonder about the relationship between ambition for power, represented by Alcibiades, and philosophy, represented by Socrates. Socrates' claim that Alcibiades is jealous might be a way for him to inoculate himself against any poison arrows that Alcibiades might unleash at the philosopher in his speech. But philosophic wisdom seems to be the source of a kind of power, and Alcibiades, ambitious for every kind of power, may very well be jealous of Socrates' autonomy. At the same time, Socrates probably does appear arrogant and jealous to Alcibiades, since Alcibiades' own infatuation with and envy of the philosopher makes demands on him in Socrates' name.

It is noteworthy also that here, and again after his speech, Alcibiades frames the contest with Socrates as a contest for Agathon (whose name, we recall, means "the Good"). The playfully suggested love triangle between Socrates, Alcibiades, and Agathon could potentially resolve itself in many ways. The supposed mutual jealousy between Socrates and Alcibiades would suggest that each of them regards Agathon as a rival for the other's affections; yet it soon becomes clear that they are rivals of each other, fighting over Agathon. One must wonder about the significance of the contest over "the Good" carried out between Alcibiades and Socrates. This contest is especially curious since in the process of attempting to win Agathon over Alcibiades will inadvertently settle the contest between Agathon and Socrates in favor of Socrates. At the same time, Alcibiades' courtship of Agathon will fail, leaving Socrates symbolically victorious in that contest as well. Perhaps Socrates' dual victory is meant to show that the love of wisdom surpasses mere political ambition in attaining the Good and surpasses poetry in exerting potentially beneficial effects upon noble youth. It is true that Socrates will ultimately fail with Alcibiades; but this fact must be balanced against the fact that according to Alcibiades no speaker has ever so profoundly moved him as has Socrates, and no one but Socrates has ever succeeded in making him feel ashamed.

Previously, each speaker on *Erôs* articulated his vision of the Good. Since the rivalry between Socrates and Alcibiades resumes after Alcibiades' speech, framing it like bookends, Plato's audience is probably supposed to realize that the contest between these two men is ultimately a contest for the Good as well. Here we might profitably recall the proverb Socrates recites to Aristodemus when he invites his associate to accompany him to the party, despite the fact that Aristodemus had not been invited by the party's host. Socrates said, punning on Agathon's name, "Good men go uninvited to a Goodman's feast" (174b). But Alcibiades is the only one who was not invited to the party by anyone. Recalling the problem raises the question of whether or not Alcibiades is a good man. The contest with Socrates over Agathon may be designed to highlight the sense in which all of the seekers are engaged in a contest over the Good, but especially to contrast the sense in which Agathon might be called "good" with the sense in which Alcibiades might be.

After putting some ribbons on Socrates' ("magnificent") head, Alcibiades sits back for a moment and then realizes that he is the only one drunk at the party. At this point he orders everyone to drink and get drunk, fills the large cooling jar with undiluted wine, drinks it all himself, and then has it refilled for Socrates. Following up on a theme first introduced by Eryximachus (compare 176c), Alcibiades says: "Not that the trick will have any effect on him; Socrates will drink whatever you put in front of him, but no one yet has seen him drunk" (214a). The contrast between being drunk and being sober is a recurrent motif in this dialogue whose title is "The drinking party." Notice how many times Alcibiades is referred to as being drunk (212d, 213a, 241c, 215a) (including several places at which he himself underlines the fact) and how this characterization contrasts with the stress on Socrates' sobriety (176c, 214a, 220a). According to Alcibiades' characterization of Socrates as a satyr and a flute player, Socrates, too, is a creature of Dionysos. It could be that Socrates never gets inebriated because he is already drunk with philosophy, this divine madness; the divine madness of philosophy might explain Socrates' apparent hubris, which is perhaps another aspect of his resemblance to a Dionysian satyr. It may be the madness of philosophy that makes him impervious to the elixirs of the god, reveling in his intoxicating mysteries without ever becoming inebriated. The audience is left to wonder about the kind of self-mastery that would allow Socrates to be just as much at home when the situation calls for drinking heavily as he is when it calls for abstaining altogether.

The reader should notice also that the first time *Socrates* mentions inebriation or sobriety is when Alcibiades finishes his speech and the philosopher exclaims, "You're perfectly sober, after all, Alcibiades" (222c). Yet Socrates' remark contradicts the other indications of Alcibiades' drunkenness (212d, 213a, 241c, 215a). What is the point of all this attention to Alcibiades' inebriation, and what is the point of Socrates' denial of it? On the one hand, Alcibiades' intoxication frees him from inhibition sufficiently that he can say what he really thinks about Socrates. But on the other hand although his faculties may be somewhat impaired, Socrates' claim that he is really sober suggests that Alcibiades' speech contains a great deal of truth.

As Socrates is drinking his jar of wine, Eryximachus objects, "This is certainly most improper. We cannot simply pour the wine down our throats in silence" (214b). He suggests some conversation or singing, calling what they are doing highly uncivilized, so Alcibiades asks the medical man to prescribe what is fitting. Eryximachus explains that earlier in the evening the guests had given speeches in praise of *Erôs*, and Alcibiades is the only one who did not have a chance to speak on this festive occasion. Since Alcibiades did not hear the previous speeches, and since he has obviously consumed more than his fair share of drink already, it is determined that it would not be fair to pit his "drunken ramblings" on the topic of *Erôs* against the "sober orations" of the other men. Alcibiades then returns to the earlier bickering with Socrates to continue the quarrel, saying that he hopes that Eryximachus had not believed anything Socrates had said about his jealousy, because the truth is just the opposite, according to Alcibiades. Socrates would beat him up, Alcibiades declares, if he were to praise anyone or anything else— even a God—while the philosopher is present (214c-d). Socrates objects to the charge that he places himself above the gods, a charge that amounts to impiety, one of the two formal charges that caused the philosopher to be put to death by Athens. "Hold your tongue!" he exclaims, and Alcibiades insists that Socrates can't deny that he (Alcibiades) would never praise anyone else while Socrates is around (214d).

In addition to providing a dramatic context that aids in interpreting Alcibiades' speech, this byplay furnishes the pretext for Alcibiades to give an encomium of Socrates rather than of *Erôs*. The effect of this substitution is to make Socrates—the philosopher who most seems to fit the description of the true erotic philosopher as Diotima describes him—actually come to stand in for or replace *Erôs* itself. In other words, it is as though Plato said to himself while he was composing the *Symposium*: "Now, just so my audience does not miss the point that Socrates is the embodiment of the highest *Erôs*, I shall follow the six encomia of *Erôs* by an encomium of Socrates." So rather than simply having Socrates tell us about *Erôs*, Plato shows us a certain kind of *Erôs* in its embodied form, in the dramatic depiction of Alcibiades' frustrated love for Socrates. Similarly, rather than just telling us about the true lover's journey, Plato depicts it for us, insofar as it can be thought of as exemplified in the behavior of Socrates in his Socratic dialogues. Most of the previous speakers had praised *Erôs* either from the perspective of the lover or from the perspective of the beloved, depending on the role they themselves play in their relationships. But Alcibiades' speech suggests that the truest Lover, the one who pursues his *Erôs* in the right way—namely, Socrates—is himself an object of adoration and love. Hence, the truest lover is simultaneously the most lovable. The one who acts the part of the lover in the right way becomes also an object of love for others. By having Socrates replace (or instantiate) *Erôs* as the object of praise in Alcibiades' encomium, Plato points to the profound connection between *Erôs* and its object. Because *Erôs* is a messenger from the gods to mortals, conveying some intimation of the object of desire through desire itself, *Erôs* the Lover can become *Erôs* the Beloved, *Erôs* that inspires and communicates something of the Beloved. The dimensions of Poverty and of Resource within *Erôs* are two sides of a single coin and cannot be divorced.[8]

Here, in the dramatic context of the *Symposium*, the substitution of Socrates for *Erôs* has the effect also of completing the circle. The discussion of

*Erôs* returns from the icy peaks reached at the pinnacle of Diotima's account to the incarnate, flesh-and-blood Socrates and his down-to-earth, plain-speaking manner of practicing philosophy. We shall see, too, that there is another side to Alcibiades' speech in praise of Socrates, a speech that the philosopher worries will be some kind of "mock eulogy" of him. For in addition to singing Socrates' praises and giving example after example of his awe-inspiring self-mastery, the speech supplies Plato's audience with one of the most powerful critiques of philosophy and of the character, Socrates as the exemplary philosopher, given anywhere in the dialogues.[9] Plato puts one of his most damning critiques of philosophy in the mouth of one of the most damnable characters of the period, Alcibiades. But Alcibiades is not simply a fool; his speech shows that he has an uncommon insight into the unique virtue of Socrates. Alcibiades' possession by Dionysus enables him to speak truths in spite of himself; however much the audience must bear in mind the speech's source, it does partially reveal Socrates, and not merely Alcibiades.

Alcibiades invokes his citizen's right to free speech (*parrhêsia*) in order to speak frankly to Socrates, even seeming to enter into a kind of truth-teller's agreement with him before delivering the speech. But since each man insists that the other is lying and that it is only from him that we will hear the truth, how might the audience know which man's claim to be telling the truth is true and which one is not? Is only one of them likely to be saying something true, or could both of them be telling the truth, perhaps according to different standards of truthfulness? What are we supposed to learn about Socrates and about philosophy from Alcibiades' encomium? And lastly, we might wonder, how does Alcibiades' speech fit when considered alongside the other speeches in praise of *Erôs*? What do we learn about *Erôs* from it?

To begin to answer these questions, we must scrutinize the exchange between Socrates and Alcibiades that precedes Alcibiades' speech. The preliminary back-and-forth between the two men is important here and reveals a great deal about how we are to hear and to judge Alcibiades' speech. Alcibiades and Socrates establish an agreement that provides that Alcibiades may tell the whole truth about Socrates; and we shall see that Socrates listens without interrupting the speech even at the many points at which Alcibiades invites him to correct the account if it is not true and correct.[10]

Alcibiades considers it to be a truth-teller's role to speak frankly, and he would seem to have consumed enough alcohol to have drowned any remaining inhibitions he might otherwise have had, permitting him to carry out this objective forthrightly. As soon as Eryximachus suggests that he use his turn to speak to praise Socrates, Alcibiades retorts: "What do you mean? Do you really think so, Eryximachus? Should I unleash myself upon him? Should I give him his punishment in front of all of you?" (214e). "Now wait a minute," Socrates says, "What do you have in mind? Are you going to praise me only in order to mock me?" Alcibiades answers, "I'll only tell the truth—please, let me," to which Socrates responds, "I would certainly like to hear the truth from you. By all means, go ahead." "Nothing can stop me now," Alcibiades announces, before telling Socrates that he can interrupt and correct any part of the account he regards as untrue (214e–215a).

Compare this exchange with a similar one in the following passage from Euripides' Electra, where Electra asks permission from her mother, Clytemnestra, to speak the truth. Clytemnestra tells Electra, "So, if you're anxious to refute me, do it now; speak freely, prove your father's death not justified." Electra follows the choral interlude by reminding her mother that she had given her permission to speak freely. "Mother, remember what you said just now. You promised that I might state my opinions freely without fear." Clytemnestra replies, "I said so, daughter, and I meant it." Electra is still fearful, however, that her mother will punish her once she has spoken, so she clarifies: "Do you mean you'd listen first, and get your own back afterwards?" Her mother assures, "No, no; you're free to say what your heart wants to say." Finally, Electra says, "I'll say it, then. This is where I'll begin."[11]

It would seem as though in both the exchange between Alcibiades and Socrates and the exchange between Electra and Clytemnestra, the two parties attempt to establish an explicit right to speak frankly by adopting the democratic right of free speech, or *parrhêsia*. Michel Foucault has shown that this right to say everything by employing "outspokenness" or "frankness" is typically utilized by someone of lesser power or standing toward someone of greater power or rank. In both of the above examples, the attempt to establish such an agreement seems intended to limit the risk of reprisals against the speaker. Outside of its political employment the consequences of speaking frankly were less likely to be physical reprisals, as Socrates claims to fear from Alcibiades, and more likely to consist in being judged or criticized harshly in return, as Foucault argues in his analysis of the transformation from political to ethical *parrhêsia*.[12] The fact that both Alcibiades and Electra adopt *parrhêsia* shows that each regards him or herself as the party of lesser standing and that each wishes to secure an agreement before speaking. Foucault shows that vestiges of this truth-teller's agreement still survive throughout medieval times, in the role of a messenger to the king. When a messenger says to the king, "Beg permission to speak freely sir," the messenger is agreeing to convey whatever news he has for the king as long as the king agrees not to cut off his head should the message be distasteful or worse. Such agreements are vital because the king needs messengers who will deliver news truthfully to him even when the news is not good, and the messenger requires the continued use of his head. So both have good reasons for entering into such an explicit contract or agreement.

Plato has Apollodorus, our narrator, characterize Alcibiades as using *parrhêsia* at 222c, where he refers to the extraordinary frankness employed in the speech. But, of course, what our narrator says provides information intended only for Apollodorus's unnamed auditor and, of course, for Plato's audience; it would not have been possible for any of the partygoers to hear this characterization. But if we are right about the reason for the verbal exchange cited above, the practice Apollodorus names would have been well known by Alcibiades' audience and probably taken for granted by them. What seems especially noteworthy here is that the nobly born Alcibiades, tall and hand-some, politically well-connected and wealthy—one of the three generals about to lead the Athenians to Sicily—considers it necessary to secure per-mission to speak freely from the lower-born, short, ugly, poor, and apolitical Socrates before adopting *parrhêsia* to deliver his speech.

It is possible that Plato wanted to alert his audience to the disagreement about what constitutes telling the truth that runs throughout the speech. For not only does this disagreement underwrite the byplay between Alcibi-ades and Socrates that precedes the speech, but it is underscored at six places in the speech itself (twice at 215b, and once each at 216a, 217a-b, 219b-c, and 220e). We have already noted the dialogue's attention to the contrast between Alcibiades' intoxication and Socrates' sobriety, but the contrast is connected to the broader contrast between two different ways of speaking the truth: Alcibiades' kind of truth-telling, guided by the motto "In wine, there is truth," and Socrates' ironical manner of telling the truth (something he promised to do when he said he would tell the truth in his own way 199a-b). Now the quid pro quo for Alcibiades' adoption of *parrhêsia* is that Socrates is free to tell him the naked truth in return, no matter how much it hurts. Alcibiades' speech, however, will underline the fact that it is often far from clear what Socrates believes, and that discovering the truth about this enig-matic philosopher requires that one "read between the lines." If one can do this, the philosopher's inner beauty and hidden truths may be disclosed. If not, he will be misunderstood or will at least seem aberrant, as he does to most characters and some commentators.

## THE SPEECH OF ALCIBIADES (215A–222C)

In order to praise Socrates Alcibiades says that he will have to use an image, an image employed to draw out the truth about the philosopher and not to mock him. He begins by recalling the little wooden statues of the Sylvan god, Silenus, which were rough and not very pretty on the outside, but which were split right down the middle and could be opened up to reveal inside beauti-ful, intricately carved images of the gods. He likens Socrates to one of these figures of Silenus. In this way, Alcibiades begins by drawing a distinction between the inner beauty of Socrates and the outer ugliness of this bizarre-looking man. The Silenus statues, he says, typically showed Silenus with a flute or with his pipes, and this will be an important feature of Alcibiades' second image. He next likens Socrates to the satyr, Marsyas, who challenged Apollo to a flute-playing contest and was skinned alive when he lost. (Is Alcibiades' charge meant to suggest that philosophy, as practiced by Socrates, requires one to risk, or get out of, one's skin?) It is important to recall again here that Socrates was almost universally characterized by the writers of Socratic conversations as having a large head with protruding eyes, an oversized forehead, and a wide nose. He was also known to be short, balding, and pot-bellied, but as strong as a horse. Many writers of Socratic dialogues assimilated Socrates' notorious ugliness to the satyr image. The philosopher's bizarre appearance is perhaps the only feature about which there is general agreement among the writers of Socratic conversations.[13] But as Alcibiades announces, the resemblance here between Socrates and a satyr goes much farther than mere looks (215b).

Alcibiades not only likens Socrates to a satyr, but he makes the following contrast as well: Socrates needs only words to enchant his listeners, whereas Marsyas needed his flute to play his divine, alluring music. Anyone who listens to this philosopher, Alcibiades explains, will be transported by his words, "completely possessed." Alcibiades says that he is not the only one who has experienced this effect. Accusing Socrates of being "impudent, contemptuous, and vile," he threatens to call witnesses to testify to the truth of this claim. In fact, he names (at 218b) all the other speechmakers to underscore the point that each of them knows very well what he is talking about. He will say to them that, as in the case of a snakebite, one will only talk about it to others who have had the same experience, because only they will understand what one has gone through. He says that he has been bitten by something much more "vicious" than a snake, namely philosophy, "whose grip on young and eager psyches is much more vicious than a viper's and makes them do the most amazing things" (218a). But in his own case, the effect of Socrates' words is even more intense, for it makes him feel frenzied and deranged, like the Corybantes[14] (215e), and produces in him a feeling that Alcibiades seems never to have experienced before: an overwhelming sense of shame.

In his testimonial concerning the effects of Socratic philosophizing, Alcibiades tells those gathered that he has "heard Pericles and many other good orators . . . but . . . they never upset me so deeply that my very own psyche started protesting that my life—my life!—was no better than the most miserable slave's" (215e). The brilliant military and political leader is forced by this customarily barefoot philosopher to admit that his life, in its present state, is not worth living, and that his political ambitions are a waste of time. At the same time, Socrates makes Alcibiades aware of the fact that the only matter that is really important is the care of himself, the attention to his own betterment that Alcibiades admittedly neglects. These admissions disclose at least as much about Alcibiades' character as they do about Socrates, and they explain perhaps why he admits to being driven to "stop my ears and tear myself away from him, for, like the Sirens, he could make me stay by his side till I die" (216a).

By his own admission, "Socrates is the only man in the world" who makes Alcibiades feel shame. This is because Alcibiades (again by his own admission) knows "perfectly well" what he should do but cannot bring himself to do it because he is so easily seduced by the adulation he receives in his political career. He loves the attention, and he is used to getting his way in all of his dealings, and yet the mere presence of Socrates serves to make him feel miserable about his life. It is as though Socrates is able to hold up a mirror to Alcibiades, and Alcibiades is revolted by the reflection he sees in it. The philosopher is clearly a lightning rod for Alcibiades' disappointment with himself, singularly capable of evoking shame in him. We shall see that this shame is so intense that it long ago drove Alcibiades to concoct a plan to reverse the balance of power between Socrates and him, as he will soon tell the group gathered at Agathon's house.

In their first conversation, dramatized in the *Alcibiades* I, or *Alcibiades Major*, Socrates told the nineteen-year-old Alcibiades that he must learn to rule himself and cultivate a concern for justice before attempting to rule others. In that initial conversation, Socrates tried to bring Alcibiades to see that his conceit of wisdom (the belief that he knows all he needs to know already) is out of place, and that he must properly prepare himself to meet his true rivals in the political arena. Socrates attempted to convince him that he must first learn to rule himself, if he hopes to become a free man. From Socrates' point of view, being tyrannized by one's desires or ruled by one's inclinations is as bad as, or worse than, being ruled by another person: in either case one is not free but a slave to someone or something. Their first conversation, which took place about seventeen years before the dramatic date of the *Symposium*,[15] concluded with Alcibiades pledging to become a follower of Socrates before Socrates corrects his seeming pledge of discipleship and evokes from the youth a promise to do what he needs to do to become a free man. But his testimony in the *Symposium* confirms that he did not do what he pledged to do, something Socrates suspected would happen, as he expressed at the end of their initial conversation (*Alc.* I 135e). It seems obvious that given the choice between self-cultivation and being applauded and praised by the multitudes in a political setting, Alcibiades chose then, and continues to choose, the latter (compare 216b).

The prerequisites for a successful and good political career, in Socrates' view, turn out to entail self-examination and dialogue so that one can both learn who one is and learn to care for one's self. Socrates believes that only by harmonizing all of one's desires into a coherent way of life and a consistent set of beliefs can one hope to attain happiness. Conflicting desires doom one to being unable to fulfill all of one's desires as we have seen before, since the fulfillment of some of these desires entails the frustration of others. If this conflict grows too large, one who harbors such incompatible or incongruous desires will not be able to rule one's self. In sum, then, Socrates believes that a person who manifests conflicting impulses, desires, beliefs, or values dooms himself to frustration and unhappiness, if not failure or death. Moreover, Socrates thinks that a person who cannot rule himself will be a poor (despotic, tyrannical) ruler of others. For Socrates, the care of the self must be undertaken prior to attempting to care for others.

Alcibiades' speech reveals much about his own character. He testifies to being ambivalent to the core, pulled one way toward his own betterment, and the other toward the gratification of his boundless honor-love. His shame in the face of Socrates' chastisement of him as a young man and his inability to keep his promises to Socrates also shows how sensitive Plato's dialogues are to the weakness of character that would cause someone to "know" what is good for him or her but to be unable to do it. This phenomenon, which Christian philosophers will later call "weakness of will" and which the Greeks called *akrasia*, is nowhere more evident than in Alcibiades' admissions to have violated his past agreements with Socrates to care for himself before attempting to rule the city.[16] It is likely that Socrates would treat Alcibiades' incapacity to follow his own best judgment as a form of ignorance, since he sometimes defends a strong intellectualist position, holding that "vice is ignorance" and therefore that "no one does wrong willingly" (cf. *Protagoras* 352b–360e; *Laws* IX, 860cff). In Socrates' view, if one really knows what is good (i.e., likely to contribute to one's ultimate well-being) one will do it, and if one does not do it, then one must not have truly known what is really good for him or her in all its implications and entailments.

According to Alcibiades, Socrates is like the satyrs in other ways as well, and since he has come this far, Alcibiades says that he's going to tell those gathered how Socrates really is. His powers, he says, are really extraordinary! "To begin with, he's crazy about beautiful boys" (216d). And he insists that he knows nothing, just like Silenus. But this is all just a mask or a veil, the outer exterior Socrates shows to others. Inside is a man who is really self-possessed and sound-minded in all respects. In fact, it couldn't matter less to Socrates whether a boy is beautiful, Alcibiades contends, for the philosopher cares nothing for the conventional goods people cherish and admire in others. In Alcibiades' opinion, Socrates regards these things as beneath contempt, because his life is just one big game of irony (216e). According to Alcibiades, this Marsyas spends his whole life ironizing and playing with people, but he doesn't really care a whit for the beautiful boys he will later spurn. In this part of his speech, Alcibiades is accusing Socrates of being haughty and condescending toward others, and of using irony as his shield. What does Alcibiades mean by Socrates' irony and how does this irony work?

Irony is less obvious than sarcasm, though in its simplest form the difference between them may not be readily apparent. Simple irony occurs whenever one says one thing and clearly means another, such as when one says, "Nice day, isn't it?" to someone one meets in the pouring rain. More complex irony occurs when a word or a phrase can have different meanings on different levels, in such a way that one can be heard or construed differently by different audiences. Concern for the verisimilitude of Plato's dramas—the concern that they "make sense" at the same time on the dramatic level and to Plato's audience—seems to necessitate the frequent use of such complex irony in many dialogues. What Plato wishes to say to his audience may be something that cannot be said directly by Socrates to his interlocutors. In some cases, Plato's message to his audience may have to be communicated through what remains unsaid between his characters, for various reasons, or it may consist in the things that are said but misunderstood by the characters to which they are said. Complex irony is more enigmatic than simple irony, and in some cases may not even be noticed as ironical at all. More enigmatic still is an almost impenetrable form of irony, in which the ironist straddles the ambiguity between shifting meanings or connotations. This most impenetrable kind of irony is no mere trope or double entendre, but rather a way of *being* an ironist rather than just *using* irony, a stance that may render it impossible for others to know what one really thinks or believes. It is this impenetrable kind of irony, which functions less to communicate with one's interlocutor than to mask or shield the ironist's deepest feelings, that Alcibiades is highlighting in his speech.[17]

Now, since the spoken word is delivered with the accompaniment of inflection, facial expressions, gestures, and body language, the more complex forms of irony convey meaning in several ways at once. It is well to remember that irony is a form of communication, a way of making a point, sometimes even a clear and obvious point; at the same time it can be a way of selecting one's audience, aiming a message at certain parties and over the heads of others. But at its highest levels, the circle of those privileged to understand the irony becomes smaller and smaller, and perhaps even dwindles down to the ironist alone, who thereby ceases to communicate, unless it be to some observant god.

Because, at its most complex, irony can be impenetrable to one's audience or interlocutor, irony can function to keep others at a distance. "Ironizing" always leaves an escape hatch through which the ironist can slip out. In this way, irony produces an unbridgeable gulf between the ironist and others. (In Plato's dialogues this gulf may exist at key places between Socrates and his interlocutors, and perhaps also between Socrates and Plato's audience.) For this reason, the ironist seems to remain always shielded or veiled, and this "reserve" may appear to others as a kind of arrogance or superiority, if they are discerning enough to detect his irony at all. This concealing of one's meaning seems haughty, a way of testing others and feeling superior to them. One must consider how such irony appears to those who dimly sense that they are its victims; they might understandably feel that they are being mocked. Worse still, irony in its most complex form, as Alexander Nehamas explains in *The Art of Living*, can be a form of dissimulation or dissembling.[18] Even more vexing to others is the way that irony leaves obscured precisely what aspect of something is being veiled, an obscurity Nehamas finds in Socrates' response to Alcibiades that is reported later in the speech. And because the words he does speak are susceptible to being construed in several different ways,

Nehamas follows Muecke in arguing that irony always affords the ironist the privilege of saying, "That is not what I meant, not really what I meant at all." At bottom, the impenetrability irony affords makes it impossible to pin down the ironist, so others always have the feeling of shadowboxing, of interacting with a moving target, since irony allows one to conceal one's truest thoughts and sentiments behind the mask irony supplies.

Alcibiades highlights several other examples of irony that are habitually employed by Socrates in Plato's dialogues: the way the philosopher regularly deprecates his own wisdom and seems to esteem the knowledge others have, the way he seems typically to equivocate when pressed on difficult questions that might jeopardize his disclaimers of knowledge and authority, and the way Alcibiades thinks he pretends to be in love with beautiful and promising boys (such as the young Alcibiades) as a ruse to seduce them to philosophy. Indeed, Alcibiades' description of Socrates in the *Symposium* is enough to make one wonder whether the highest philosopher as Plato understood him is capable of being understood by others, that is, whether he is necessarily ironical in all that he does and says precisely because he lives at a level that is entirely over their heads.

Alcibiades confesses that he himself was taken in by the philosopher's ruse, shortly after their first conversation (and before he and Socrates fought together in Potideia). The proud Alcibiades says that he thought Socrates was really interested in him, leading him to suppose that if he let Socrates have his way with him, the philosopher would teach him "everything he knows." Reenacting the theme that was first introduced when Socrates sat down next to Agathon upon his arrival at the party, Alcibiades admits to believing that he might gain wisdom and virtue by rubbing up against Socrates.[19] Assuming, as Agathon did, that knowledge flows by contact, like some kind of fluid, Alcibiades hopes that through intimate contact with Socrates the contagion of wisdom will infect him. He seems to think that by transacting some kind of trade or exchange with Socrates, he can receive a sort of psychic transfusion, securing instantly from Socrates what he has failed to pursue for himself up to this point, namely, the betterment of his character, that is, the improvement of his psyche.

Alcibiades goes on to tell the story of his several attempts to get Socrates alone. Saying that he must tell "the whole truth," he explains that the first time he engaged Socrates in conversation, the philosopher did not take advantage of the opportunity "to tell me whatever it is that lovers say when they find themselves alone" (217b). Instead, Socrates conversed with him in his usual manner and "at the end of the day he went off" (217c). Next, Alcibiades testifies to trying to arouse him through exercising together and wrestling with him—remember that the Greeks typically exercised in the nude—but Socrates was not affected by this ploy either (217c). Alcibiades explains that he finally succeeded in getting Socrates to accept a dinner invitation, but on the first occasion, the philosopher just went home after dinner and Alcibiades claims he was "too shy" to try to stop him (217d). The second time, he kept the philosopher talking late into the night and then sent the servants away. It was time to make his move. He notes the irony of the reversal of the standard roles in Greek pederasty[20] that occurred when he decided to chase the older and far from beautiful Socrates: "as if I were his lover and he my young prey!" (217c). More absurd still is the fact that, although Alcibiades perceives Socrates' inner beauty despite his superficial ugliness, and this attests to his ability to be motivated by something beyond mere physical eroticism, his attempt to relieve himself of his shame forces Alcibiades to reduce their contest to the most common terms and to base it on a kind of market exchange. For only at the physical level can he hope to get the better of Socrates.

By means of this plot to "attack" Socrates, the nakedly ambitious Alcibiades sets out to dominate or subjugate the only person who ever made him feel ashamed of himself. In so doing, Alcibiades makes plain that he is someone who conceives all human relationships in competitive, even adversarial, terms. His testimony here suggests further that Alcibiades did not really understand the philosopher, for if he had understood him, he would have known that Socrates was not a person who could be corrupted by sexual favors. That his effort to conquer Socrates is conceived by Alcibiades as just this sort of attempt is confirmed at 219e, where he exclaims: "I knew very well that money meant much less to him than enemy weapons ever meant to Ajax, and the only trap by means of which I had thought I might capture him had already proved a dismal failure."

Given what Alcibiades has already told the group about the shame the presence of Socrates produces in him, it seems obvious that the plot he concocted was designed to rid himself of his shame. Admitting as he does to being unable to do what he knows to be best for him, and given his reputation for being the kind of person who is disloyal and promiscuous in his interpersonal relations, it seems likely that Alcibiades wanted to sully the incorruptible Socrates as a way of knocking him off of his pedestal by evoking in the philosopher the common human desire for sexual gratification, thereby bringing him down to his own level.[21] If Alcibiades could only succeed in getting Socrates to desire him, then he would be in the driver's seat in their relationship, and he would have exposed the seemingly indomitable philosopher as no better than Alcibiades at maintaining his self-control and in adhering to his principles. Alcibiades probably thought that if he could bring Socrates to desire him, the philosopher would appear just as corruptible as he is, and in this way, the proud Alcibiades might regain his confidence and self-respect. And in getting Socrates to desire him, he would also gain the upper hand in another way, by gaining the kind of power manipulative people can wield when they know someone else cares for them. It seems clear from his speech that Alcibiades can only see their relationship as a competitive, zero sum game. As Alcibiades says, there is truth in wine.

After underscoring the fact that all of the previous speechmakers and Aristodemus too have experienced "the Bacchic frenzy of philosophy," this divine madness, Alcibiades returns to his story (218c). He was about to make his move on Socrates, telling him just what he had in mind. He had already set the scene, noting the dim lighting in the room, and the fact that the two were pointedly alone. He says that he told Socrates that he may have whatever he wants from him—his possessions, those of his friends, and his beautiful body—so much importance does he claim to place on "becoming the best man [he] can be" (218d). Alcibiades moves in for the kill when he says to Socrates: "With a man like you, in fact, I'd be much more ashamed of what wise people would say if I did not take you as my lover, than I would of what all the others, in their foolishness, would say if I did" (218d).

He characterizes Socrates' response as "highly ironic and typical." Socrates is said to have replied by telling Alcibiades that he'd better take a closer look in case he is mistaken about the beauty he thinks he sees in Socrates. And if the philosopher really did have the power to make Alcibiades better, then the young man, he says, is already more accomplished than he thinks he is to recognize this beauty. But in that case, however, if Socrates really does possess this power, then the exchange Alcibiades hopes to make would not be a fair one, and Socrates would be getting the short end of the stick, for this would be like trading real beauty for the semblance of beauty, or exchanging gold for bronze. In fact, it suggests to Socrates that Alcibiades is trying to "get the better of [*pleonektein*] him" in this attempted swindle (218e), which means he would be trying to outdo Socrates by getting more than his fair share. Finally, Socrates waxes poetic when he concludes, "The mind's sight becomes sharp only when the body's eyes go past their prime— and you are still a good long time away from that" (219a).

Notice that Socrates neither encourages Alcibiades in their game of cat-and-mouse nor does he reject him outright. He does not get up from the bed and leave Alcibiades' house.[22] Notice also how his ironic response makes it impossible to tell with any certainty whether Socrates does or does not possess this inner beauty that cannot be perceived with the eyes, whether the philosopher, then or at any other time, desired Alcibiades in the way the younger man wishes to be desired, whether Socrates, then or at any other time, experienced genuine love for young men such as Alcibiades, and whether he, then or ever, thought he had the power to make Alcibiades better. Readers may experience frustration at the impenetrability of the philosopher's rejoinder at the heart of Alcibiades "truthful" account. On the one hand, Alcibiades, propelled by the wine he has consumed, says he is going to tell the whole, naked truth about Socrates; but on the other hand, he presents the truth using Socrates' enigmatic words to him, the meaning of which is inextricably embedded in the philosopher's typically ironic manner of speaking. The opacity of Socrates' irony is perhaps what most frustrates Alcibiades, as the rest of his story of the night that he spent with Socrates seems to suggest.

On that night when Alcibiades and Socrates were alone, after he says that he disclosed his innermost thoughts to Socrates, offering himself and his possessions in trade for the philosopher's guidance, and after Socrates' initial, ironic reply, the befuddled Alcibiades tells Socrates that it is his turn to say what he thinks. Again, Socrates' response leads to misinterpretation by the younger Alcibiades. "You're right about that," says the philosopher, but he then adds: "In the future, let's consider things together. We'll always do what seems the best to the two of us" (219b). Proof that this response was misconstrued by Alcibiades comes from what he says next, telling the audience that Socrates' words made him think that his own arrows had found their target. Then he explains how he crawled over next to Socrates and put his arms around him, hoping to arouse him, but in fact they only lay there the whole night as if the philosopher were his father or older brother (219d). Plato's audience can clearly see that Socrates did not take the bait, but gave the impression of being uninterested in Alcibiades' offer. It becomes increasingly apparent that it is this rebuff that is the source of the outrage Alcibiades now feels toward Socrates. He exclaims:

> But in spite of all my efforts, this hopelessly arrogant, this unbelievably inso-
> lent man—he turned me down! He spurned my beauty, of which I was so
> proud, members of the jury—for this is really what you are: you're here to sit
> in judgment of Socrates' amazing arrogance and pride. . . . How do you think
> I felt after that? Of course, I was deeply humiliated. . . . No one else has ever
> known the real meaning of slavery! (219c-e)

Note Alcibiades' use of trial terminology and imagery here. His encomium of Socrates has transformed itself into an indictment of the philosopher, and Alcibiades wants to put him on trial for hubris. We must ask how this private, mock trial relates to the later public trial of Socrates for impiety and corrupting the youth. We must also ask whether this indictment by the drunken Alcibiades is not what was foreshadowed by Agathon's prescient threat that Dionysos would judge the philosopher and adjudicate between the young poet's wisdom and the philosopher's wisdom. This in turn should lead us to reflect on how the charges of the various trials are related. Readers should wonder: What is the connection between charging Socrates with hubris, impiety, corruption of the youth, and his peculiar claim to wisdom? We shall explore this question in our conclusion.

Returning to the text, Alcibiades now shifts gears and begins eulogizing Socrates. He admits that he couldn't help admiring "this utterly unnatural, this truly amazing man." What he seems most impressed with is Socrates' character and the extent of his self-control. (He considered it quite an accomplishment if someone could resist a dashing Don Juan like him!) Note also that Alcibiades attests that the "courtship" he has described occurred in the first year of their association, before they went off to fight together for Athens in Potidea (219e). The speech then recounts some remarkable examples that further attest to Socrates' self-mastery, his self-sufficiency, his bravery, and his sound-mindedness. Alcibiades recalls for his ad hoc jury how Socrates seemed impervious to the elements, how he demonstrated extreme, almost trance-like, powers of concentration (an example of which was glimpsed at the beginning of the *Symposium*), how courageously he fought in retreat, and how he even saved the younger man's life in battle, while refusing the honors due to him for that action. Socrates could go for days without food, but enjoy a good meal with the best of them. It was difficult to get him to start drinking, Alcibiades says, but when the occasion called for it, Socrates could drink everyone else under the table, and still no one had ever seen him drunk! (219e–221c)[23] Considering his own use of battle imagery to describe his relationship with the philosopher, it is striking that near the end of his encomium highlighting the courage and endurance of Socrates, Alcibiades testifies: "This was a very brave man, who would put up a terrific fight if anyone approached him" (221b). Given such a character, it is no wonder that Socrates did not fall for his cheap seduction ploy.[24] It is unlikely that Alcibiades could have succeeded in overpowering the philosopher, bringing to the battle only his good looks and a willingness to function as the compliant beloved. Those who know Socrates know that he does not accept gifts or fee payments in exchange for conversing with people, and they know that he also doesn't claim to have any knowledge to teach.

Alcibiades admits to attempting to exploit a shortcut to his own betterment and, at the same time, to relieve himself of the shame he has felt ever since Socrates first tried to humble him by showing him how unprepared he was, both in character and in knowledge, to meet his true rivals in the political arena. Socrates chastised the young and promising Alcibiades in their first conversation by accusing him of living in the midst of the "most extreme form of stupidity" (*Alc.* I 118b). In the light of what he now knows about Socrates, Alcibiades' story of the seduction plot reveals how little he then understood of Socrates and how badly he misjudged him. His miscalculation in this "plot" is probably attributable to his high estimation of himself and to the fact that he did not yet appreciate just how unusual Socrates was. Still, some of the most decisive events in the historical Alcibiades' checkered military and political career, not to mention his legendary love life, could be aptly characterized as miscalculations. One of these errors in judgment may even have caused his death, if one believes the reports that say that he was killed at the hands of an outraged family whose daughter he had seduced. If his audience at this symposium was supposed to act as a jury on the charges that Socrates is arrogant and hubristic, and Alcibiades says that they are (215b, 219c), then perhaps Plato's audience, in turn, is supposed to act as a jury in the dispute between them. Recall once more that Agathon had declared that Dionysos would be the judge in the dispute over wisdom between Socrates and him (175e–176a). Given what we know from other sources about Agathon's sexual promiscuity, one can imagine how he would have responded to the tempting Alcibiades.

Would Agathon have fared as well against Socrates in a contest for wisdom as he did in a contest for the best new tragedy? And how does Alcibiades want his audience to regard the philosophical way of life, as practiced by Socrates, a way of life he seems to be putting on trial here for a kind of hubris? Does he really think that Socrates is nothing more than a satyr in disguise? Perhaps Plato's device of putting the philosopher on trial here is meant to set in relief the profound hubris of all the other speakers, the hubris of having lived lives devoid of self-examination. Or perhaps Plato wishes to foreshadow the real trial of Socrates as a way of emphasizing the grave injustice eventually done to the philosopher and to philosophy by an Athenian jury.

Whatever reason or reasons Plato might have had for permitting Alcibiades to voice his criticisms of Socrates and of philosophy, his speech reveals at least as much about Alcibiades as it does about Socrates, and it reveals at least as much about the good qualities of Socrates as it does about the more questionable ones, such as his ironical posture toward others, the brutal way he sometimes appears to treat people in conversation, and the fact that he spurned Alcibiades' advances. Sympathizers of Socrates could argue, however, that by provoking Alcibiades to feel ashamed of himself, the philosopher was acting true to form, functioning as the gadfly for Alcibiades that he claimed to be for Athens as a whole (cf. *Ap.* 30e). These sympathizers might further say that the failure of Alcibiades to improve himself is not a failure of Socrates' message that he needs to do so; and yet the jury that sentenced the philosopher to death would probably hold against Socrates his associations with men such as Alcibiades and consider him guilty by association. The audience of Plato's *Symposium* is invited to consider the differences between the actions that brought Alcibiades and Socrates, respectively, into conflict with Athens. Alcibiades' speech confirms that the failure of this character is not a failure of Socrates, but of Alcibiades; there is no reason to think anyone else could have done as well as the philosopher does to point him in the right direction and to encourage him to master himself and to modulate his more tyrannical impulses. Yet Alcibiades' failure also shows that it is not easy to attain Socrates' degree of virtue, if even a man of Alcibiades' talents proved unable to do so.

Although viewed in one way, Socrates is not being criticized for his failure with Alcibiades, he does in a very real sense fail. He tries to better the youth and in a sense he does, for he makes Alcibiades acutely aware of his shortcomings, but the philosopher's counsel can do no more than this. It is possible that this failure is not meant to indicate a special limitation of Socrates and Socrates' way of doing philosophy, but rather is meant to underline a limitation of philosophy itself; and here is the sense in which this drama is a tragedy: philosophy itself has tragic limits, for wisdom, which should rule, is in a very real sense impotent. The impotence of wisdom (at least in terms of conventional notions of power) seems to be part of what Plato wishes to convey through his dialogues, together with the notion that wisdom should rule. Wisdom should rule, but in fact it cannot, at least not absolutely, at least not easily, at least not forever; and for the most part it is precisely what does *not* rule in human communities. The *Republic* makes this clear in its own way. And yet Plato leaves his audience with the distinct impression that the good and just life lived by Socrates is nonetheless preferable to the alternative. Alcibiades' entrance and speech does indeed bring the conversation back to reality from Socrates' flights into metaphysics through the teachings of Diotima; and the speech praises the strange eroticism of philosophy as the highest form of *Erôs*, embodied or instantiated in the exemplary person of Socrates. But viewed from another perspective, Alcibiades' encomium embodies the irrational forms of *Erôs* that actually flourish in the world. The tragedy of philosophy—the tragedy that is manifest in the light of what could be, in the light of the promise of Alcibiades and of Athens unfulfilled—is brought together with the comedy of those who are rendered ridiculous by failing to see their failings, by their oblivion in the face of the spiritual dimensions opened up by the philosophic *daimon*, and by their consequent overestimation of their own goods.

Alcibiades wraps up his long, sometimes seemingly rambling, encomium of Socrates by saying that there are many other things one could say about the specific accomplishments of this gadfly philosopher, but the most important thing he wants to stress is that Socrates is unique—like no one before or since. For every other human being, historical or mythical, one can find a parallel, explains Alcibiades. But no parallel exists for Socrates. He is so bizarre that he is not "even remotely like" anyone else. Thus, he recommends that rather than attempting to compare him to any human, one should liken him to Silenus, or the satyrs, as he himself does (221c-d). This reintroduction of the Silenus image affords Alcibiades the opportunity to illustrate another way in which the image fits Socrates.

His ideas and arguments, too, can be likened to the Silenus statues. His words, Alcibiades says, sound ridiculous, as coarse as the hides of the satyrs. He is always talking about horses and cobblers and such things on his way to "making the same tired old points" (221e). According to Alcibiades, the philosopher's arguments would seem laughable to those unfamiliar with him, and yet when they are opened up, when their meaning shines through, they are as beautiful as the little carvings inside the Silenus figurines. When one goes behind their crudity, Alcibiades concludes, they turn out to be the only arguments that make sense, arguments that are truly worthy of a god. The qualities this man possesses are then referred to as "of the greatest importance for anyone who wants to become a truly good man" (222a).

The speech Alcibiades delivers does not spare Socrates from reproach and it ends up acquitting him on any charge of corrupting the youth of Athens, youths such as this particular witness. In fact, Alcibiades could not have presented a better case to prove that Socrates is not responsible for his associate's misdeeds. The philosopher is described by Alcibiades as displaying both courage and moderation in the extreme: resisting his seduction attempt, demonstrating imperviousness to alcohol, extreme cold or heat, hunger, or fatigue, and bravely standing his ground in battle. At most, Socrates could be accused of pretending to play a conventional role in a homoerotic game of courtship and seduction with a view to transforming this relationship and guiding it toward different ends than those at which the conventional game aims. That is, Socrates begins pursuing Alcibiades as a lover pursues his beloved, but then turns the tables and makes Alcibiades desire him, not for his body but for the qualities of character he embodies. Alcibiades succeeds in exonerating Socrates for any minor indiscretions he may have committed by arguing that he is a truly good man, perhaps the only truly good and virtuous man.

Alcibiades' speech expresses his frustration at the way Socrates places the burden of self-transformation and self-care squarely on the younger man's shoulders. This point underscores the fact that teachers, mentors, guides, and parents can surely stimulate and attempt to induce the turnaround required to live a just and happy life, but since the turnaround must take place within the individual, only the individual herself can complete the project. Socrates sometimes went so far as to advise people concerning the path to be followed: he seems to do this, for example, in his first conversation with Alcibiades in the *Alcibiades Major.* The advice is always quite general, not concrete, because it must be broad enough to function as a beacon for the journey down the path. Socrates may say someone should "learn what needs to be learned" or "exercise themselves" or "begin to care for justice and virtue," as he said to Alcibiades in their first conversation, but the specific way in which one pursues Socrates' counsel and whether one is able to effectuate the proper self-care depends entirely upon the individual.[25] But the proper tools for the care of the self must certainly include self-examination and self-testing through philosophical conversation, a practice in which one must actively engage in order to derive lasting benefits. And nothing frustrates Alcibiades more than this fact. He would like someone else to make him good and wise; and hence he seeks a shortcut to his self-improvement through his plot to seduce Socrates.

Alcibiades concludes his eulogy by naming additional young men who were not present that had also experienced the bite of this viper-philosopher: Charmides, Euthydemus, and "many others" (222b). This serves as the occasion to warn Agathon away from Socrates, the erotic satyr-lover. Agathon should beware, warns Alcibiades, of his deception and guard his own emotions from the start, because "he presents himself as your lover, and, before you know it, you're in love with him yourself!" (222b).

## FINAL DIALOGUE (222C–223D)

After Alcibiades has finished speaking, Apollodorus interjects that his audience found Alcibiades' frankness amusing, since it "was obvious that he was still in love with Socrates." Socrates is the first one of the partygoers to respond to the speech, and he says that Alcibiades must be quite sober, if he could so cleverly conceal his true motive until the very end. But Socrates adds that they have not been fooled by the "little satyr play" Alcibiades has been putting on, imploring Agathon not to let anything come between them. Agathon points out that this is precisely what Alcibiades has done by sitting between them on the couch. In this way, the philosopher revives the contest he had earlier begun with Alcibiades over "the Good." This suggests that the disagreement about what constitutes telling the truth is at bottom not only a disagreement about two different ways of getting at the truth about something and disclosing it to others, but also about the Good, that is, about two very different conceptions of how one should live one's life. After some more bickering between Alcibiades and Socrates over Agathon, Alcibiades complains, "It's the same old story: when Socrates is around, nobody else can even get close to a good-looking man" (223a). When Agathon gets up to move to the other side of Socrates so that he can lie next to him, a second, larger group of revelers descends, "all of a sudden," on Agathon's house and chaos ensues. Everyone, it is said, was made to start drinking again, in no particular order.

Aristodemus reported that a number of the invited guests made their excuses and went home at this point. He also admitted that he fell asleep himself some time after that and slept for a long time, since it was winter and the nights were long. When he awoke, only Socrates, Aristophanes, and Agathon were still awake, passing around the cup of wine and talking. Thus in Aristodemus's account we seem to have another dramatic enactment of something we have previously heard, corroborating the amazing endurance Alcibiades had attributed to Socrates, a confirmation that the characterization of Socrates in Alcibiades' speech was no mere exaggeration, inspired by passion, but it was rather the very truth, freed by wine, that had lit that flame of love in the younger man's heart. The truth about Socrates is a truth filled with mystery, and like all mystery, it is a *daimonic* messenger, a hinting at something further undisclosed, a revealing and a concealing at once. So, the characterization of Socrates itself exemplifies the *daimonic* nature of *Erôs*, as does the dialogue as a whole.

Aristodemus had missed the first part of the discussion, but he heard enough to know that the philosopher was trying to convince the two playwrights that the same author should be capable of writing both comedies and tragedies. One suspects that Plato has tried to combine these two dimensions in writing the *Symposium*. We saw that he wrote speeches for both Aristophanes and Agathon that combined tragic and comic elements. We have now seen as well the comic and tragic elements in Alcibiades' speech—the comedy of his frustrated love for Socrates and the tragedy of philosophy's inability to prevail against common irrationality in political life, that is, the tragedy of Alcibiades' failed promise. Like a tragic hero, the beauty and nobility of philosophy is reaffirmed even as it meets its fate, a fate that comes through no fault of philosophy but which is rooted in the deep contradictions of the human condition. And the *Symposium* as a whole depicts as both comical and tragic the fact that human beings are desiring beings because humans are beings permeated by lack. By looking at *Erōs* from the various perspectives presented in the dialogue, seeing it manifested in the different ways of life each speaker represents, it also seems tragic that some people never get beyond the preoccupation with a beautiful body, while others appear comical, even ridiculous. The former, tragic ones never come to see that all beautiful bodies are of a kind, and so they therefore remain at the first step on Diotima's rising staircase. The latter are comic, because they attempt to ascend directly to the top of the staircase without going through the requisite steps that prepare one for the vision of ultimate reality.

Before Socrates could clinch his argument, however, the two poets fell asleep. Socrates had indeed outlasted all of the other original guests. Since dawn had broken, the philosopher got up and left. Aristodemus is said to have followed him, "as always." Socrates went to the Lyceum and washed up, then went to the marketplace and spent his day in conversation as he always did, before finally going home to sleep at the end of the next day. We will comment on these dramatic details in our conclusion.

CHAPTER 4

# Conclusion

In the following pages we draw together our observations about the dialogue in order to gain a synoptic view of it and to think about its meaning as a whole. In the course of this interpretation we have tried to justify the following claims about the *Symposium*:

1. In Diotima's teaching Plato presents the fundamental principles of his psychological thought.

2. Diotima's teaching links Plato's psychological thoughts with his metaphysical thought.

3. Diotima's teaching helps to explain the way Plato writes.

4. Therefore, on the basis of 1–3 above, one can claim that Diotima's teaching clarifies Plato's philosophy as a whole.

5. In the *Symposium*, Plato presents a novel conception of philosophy, the unique features of which have never been sufficiently appreciated, the view of philosophy as a form of *Erôs*, a *daimonic* messenger situated between the divine and mortal realms, partaking of both realms and responsible for their communion.

6. In connection with this unique conception of philosophy, the paradigmatic philosopher Socrates is presented as the embodiment of philosophical *Erôs*.

7. In the *Symposium* the philosopher is contrasted with other claimants to wisdom; but each of the characters also represents an alternative mode of *Erôs*. The contest of speeches about *Erôs* represents a contest of claims to wisdom and a contest of forms of *Erôs*.

8. The full teaching about *Erôs* is only seen when all the forms of *Erôs* presented in the *Symposium* are seen in relationship to one another and the philosophical *Erôs* is shown to emerge victorious.

9. As an especially important instance of the above, the characters of Socrates, Agathon, and Aristophanes dramatize the rivalry between

philosophy and poetry, and the philosopher is victorious over the poets as a result of his superior knowledge of *Erôs*, which enables him to understand both the tragic and comic dimensions of life.

10. Another especially important instance of the rivalry between competing forms of *Erôs* highlighted in the *Symposium* is the contest between philosophical and political *Erôs* represented by the relationship between Socrates and Alcibiades.

11. Alcibiades plays the role of Dionysian judging in the contest between Socrates and Agathon over wisdom, but, ironically, he does this by trying Socrates for hubris. In this way, the *Symposium* portrays Socrates brought to trial over his wisdom and over his hubris; and each of these trials is surely meant to gesture toward the actual trial of Socrates for impiety and corrupting the youth. Socrates' wisdom seems hubristic to those who are hubristic, and impious to those with false piety.

12. In relation to Alcibiades' intervention in the dialogue, Plato casts Socrates in the role of the Herms and casts Diotima's teachings in the role of the Mysteries that Alcibiades respectively desecrates and profanes, in an implicit allusion to the famous scandals of 415 BCE. By thereby associating Socrates and Diotima with traditional piety, Plato may be suggesting their kinship to the divine to his audience, and perhaps to some of them he may even be suggesting that Alcibiades' real sacrilege was his inability to heed Socrates and to participate in the Socratic art of love.

We follow up this summary of our interpretation with some further consideration of important details that contribute to the total effect of the dialogue, showing how these details relate to our main themes.

In the *Symposium*, Plato presents his audience with six speeches on *Erôs*, surrounded by two examples of it. The dialogue opened with Apollodorus professing his love of both philosophy and Socrates (a love reflected by Aristodemus); then, after the speeches on *Erôs*, Plato presents the dramatization of Alcibiades' *Erôs* for Socrates. One must ask if Apollodorus's love of Socrates and Alcibiades' love of Socrates are held up for admiration, or if they are simply testaments, along with the six speeches on *Erôs*, to the diverse and ubiquitous power of love.

In important ways, Alcibiades' "love" for Socrates is a very different sort of love from that of Apollodorus. The one lover, Apollodorus, claims to follow Socrates and to have been transformed by his love for him; and undoubtedly he was, although whether or not this transformation has the character he supposes is doubtful. The other lover, Alcibiades, feels admiration for Socrates coupled with shame at his own inadequacies. This shame causes his love to become tinged with envy and animosity, driving him farther away from philosophy, and provoking him to find a way to rid himself of this shame. Failing that, he must plug his ears and refuse to listen to what Socrates has to say. In some ways, the love Alcibiades experiences might seem superior to Apollodorus's brand of love, since perhaps Alcibiades has a keener insight into just how unique Socrates is and how difficult it is to follow in his footsteps. But although Alcibiades may have a keener sense of his own weaknesses of character than does Apollodorus, he also has a greater pride as well. As a result, Alcibiades' shame and the damaged pride that is its reverse side have paralyzed him and made him hostile to his own better judgment, preventing him from genuinely following Socrates. Apollodorus, on the other hand, is difficult to evaluate with so little textual evidence to go on, but one has the feeling that his devotion is the shallow devotion of a parroting acolyte consisting largely of the love of honor that he gratifies by setting himself apart from the crowd. That he insults his audience at the beginning of the dialogue (173a, 173d) foreshadows the arrogant way that Agathon later insults his guest, Socrates, in his speech.

Perhaps we are meant to contrast these two versions of the love of Socrates with a third, Plato's love for Socrates. Plato's love is embodied in the dialogue itself, a loving memorial to his departed friend that does not merely pay him homage but attempts to capture the uniqueness of his way of philosophizing. It is useful to remember that not only do the speeches in the *Symposium* discuss *Erôs* in all its manifestations, but the dialogue as a whole *exemplifies* particular loves as well: the love for Socrates, the love for the love of wisdom, and the love of wisdom itself. Moreover, if Diotima's teaching is correct, the *Symposium* must also exemplify Plato's love of the Good and Beauty as well; and even if Diotima's teaching is not correct, if *Plato* took it seriously *he* would have considered his dialogue an expression of these loves.

Turning to the six central speeches of the dialogue, we must not be taken in by an initial impression that the diversity of *Erôs* has been reduced to the love of older males for young boys. It becomes clear through the speeches of Eryximachus, Aristophanes, and Socrates especially that *Erôs* as they discuss it encompasses all human desire and even cosmological phenomena. Diotima's teaching about *Erôs* ties together the biological urge to procreate with the deep human impulse to create works of the spirit; and both of these are said to derive from a quest for immortality that even more primordially is a quest to "possess the good forever." This insight brings us into the realm of religion, for the good humans desire to possess is an eternal, timeless Good, belonging to the realm of the divine. Love of this Good fills the mortal, temporal realm, for the mortal realm is thoroughly conditioned by the lack of, and desire for, goodness. Human desires are diverse and can aim at either realm; people can desire the apparent goods of the changing world around them or people can desire the immutable goods of the Divine. Yet ultimately beneath this diversity is the priority of the timeless realm, for in the end a good beyond the relative world of becoming is the only good that can satisfy the deepest human longing. Like Aristophanes' original humans, people remain separated from their other halves, except that this other half is not just another human person; and even in the longing for it one finds a type of contact and communion with it, as Diotima makes clear.

Taken as a whole, the *Symposium* shows that there is an apparent diversity in the forms and objects of human desires; moreover, the different objects of *Erôs* have different ontological statuses, even while the desires for these diverse objects exist within the same being. The relationships between these desires have implications; it makes a great difference whether the diverse desires within a human being are harmonized or in conflict, and it makes a great difference which of them takes the lead. Humans desire temporal things only for the sake of happiness, and it appears that happiness depends on the mind's relation to a good that stands outside of time. The dialogue argues that these elements of the human condition combine to create the deepest secrets of human psychology. Human well-being or happiness, *eudaimonia*, involves an ordering or psychic harmony in one's self, and this ordering or harmony consists in the ranking or prioritizing of desires. It is the human condition constantly to be choosing between competing desires and the different values they represent. But desires are not all created equal; some desires have an intrinsic right to priority. Some things are really desired only for the sake of other things; that is, some goods are merely instrumental to the promotion of further goods, while others are more intrinsically valuable. To put desires in the wrong order, to emphasize or prioritize the wrong one, to make ends out of means, to allow the wrong desire to rule one's psyche, is to lessen or even destroy one's chance to achieve well-being. Which desires ought to be thought of as ends is determined by the consequences for the well-being of the psyche of prioritizing one set of desires over the other. Human well-being, that is, the human participation in the Good, is the arbiter of the proper order of desires in the human psyche, and thus the human Form, and/or the Form of the Psyche, is determined by the Form of the Good in a sense, as are all other Forms.

Human beings make contact with reality through the fact that at some level they do not create their own desires. We find ourselves having desires that constitute our subjectivity—yet these desires and the needs they reflect are not created by us out of thin air, and these desires aim at objects external to ourselves. These desires have limits. They have limits of definition, that is, the various objects of these desires delimit them and distinguish them from one another; but also, insofar as they have definite objects that would be capable of satisfying them, desires also have limits in the sense of natural termini that would constitute their fulfillment. Finally, desires have limits indicated by their relations to one another. For a person's limited energy is often channeled predominately toward the fulfillment of one desire to the exclusion of others, and it may be impossible to fulfill one desire without frustrating another. Each of these limits indicates an objective nature to subjective desire. Thus, there are objective implications to the fulfillment of desire, including the fact that each fulfillment has a potential effect on human character. To fulfill every desire at once may not only be impossible, the attempt to do so leads to disunity and conflict within one's self, or at least to an inadequate development of one's faculties. But prioritizing one desire over another is not going to have the same implications in each case. If one privileges the desires for temporal things, one ties one's self to a temporal, changing, uncertain level of reality. But human beings long for more, for a good that can be possessed forever. Human beings long for that which is eternal. Only by placing this desire for what is permanent and immutable over the desires for what is transitory can one attain the proper ordering of his or her desires that constitutes psychic health. For this reason, Diotima would certainly agree with the words of Christ: "Do not store up for yourselves treasures on earth, where moth and decay destroys, and thieves break in and steal. But store up treasures in heaven, where neither moth nor decay destroys, nor thieves break in and steal. For where your treasure is, there also will your heart be" (*Matthew* 6:19–21).

The relation between the lower stages and the higher stages of the lover's ascent described by Diotima is that the lower stages lead on to the higher stages, and also that the higher objects of love are usually causes of the objects desired on the lower level. The reason why the objects on the lower level have the qualities for which we desire them is owing to the objects on the higher level. But in addition to this causal relation, the objects on the higher level— and ultimately the Form of Beauty Itself—are made out to be the *ultimate* or *true* objects of desire, because they are that for the sake of which we desire the objects on the lower level. The causes in question assign to their effects properties that they themselves "possess" in some sense ( or really "are") in a superlative degree.[1] For instance, the beauty of the various beautiful bodies is a property they share in virtue of the Form of Beauty; in loving their beauty we are in a sense already loving that Form. The next stage on the ascent, the love of beautiful souls, is the love of something closer to the Form of Beauty (by virtue of the soul's ontological similarities to a Form and also by virtue of its unique way of relating to Forms, as the psyche can both participate in Forms and also somehow intuit them). And even the beautiful soul can be a cause (in the sense of efficient cause) of the beauty of the beautiful bodies. Likewise, the ascent to beautiful practices and studies is the ascent to things that shape the psyche and are efficient causes of its beauty, while being yet nearer ontologically to the Form of Beauty itself that is the ultimate cause of the beauty of all these things at all levels.

The relation of *Erôs* to beauty is complex; on the one hand, beauty is a means to an end. One wants to give birth in beauty as a means toward immortality, in the attempt to possess the good forever. Seen in this way beauty seems only desirable for the sake of the more ultimate object, the good. Therefore, Diotima replaces beauty with goodness as the object of desire, as she does at 204e, to move beyond an impasse in Socrates' understanding. Socrates' offhand remarks at (174a-b) seem to foreshadow this move by replacing the beautiful with the good, changing "going beautiful to the beautiful" to a case of good men going uninvited to the good. On the other hand, beauty seems to be reinstated as the object of desire by Diotima's account of the final vision (210e–211d).

Does this eternal reality of Beauty Itself even exist? Diotima speaks of it as though from experience, but Socrates does not claim to know about eternal things, even while he remains constantly in pursuit of them. He loves such things but he does not claim to possess them. All he claims to know about is *Erôs*, or desire. That is, he knows that he *desires* the eternal and he knows that what is not eternal falls short of the Beauty of which Diotima speaks, whether that beauty is real or, as he suggests of the wisdom his trance on the porch, a "dream" (ὥσπερ ὄναρ οὖσα 175e3–4).

The fact that Socrates embodies *Erôs* is connected with his being a master in the art of *Erôs*. To say that he knows *Erôs* is another way of talking about his human wisdom, his awareness of his own ignorance, since this awareness is inseparable from his longing for wisdom. Philosophic *Erôs* implies that one senses one's own ignorance, one's lack of and need for wisdom; yet understanding *Erôs* is the basis for philosophic insight into human nature. One can become wiser through reflecting on humanity's common lack of wisdom. Socrates as the master of *Erôs* represents the fact that philosophy can understand the human psyche through seeing all human longing in relation to its own longing. Socratic philosophy thus knows the psyche as a structure of longing and knows the psyche's possibilities as ways in which those longings can interact and combine. Socratic philosophy is a type of *Erôs* that understands *Erôs*. But this paradoxical kind of wisdom emerging from the very need for wisdom illustrates the in-between nature of *Erôs* and how erotic desire acts as a messenger from the object of desire, imparting something of its nature, or at least impressing its effect, upon the desiring mind. For Socrates' desire for wisdom in his awareness of his ignorance grants him a kind of wisdom, his "human wisdom." In the case of Plato's Socrates, Socrates' awareness of his ignorance is inseparable from some partial recollection of the Forms.

The dual nature of *Erôs* is seen in that desire connects humans to its object and yet exists precisely because of the absence, that is, the nonpossession, of that object. *Erôs* reminds humans of their distance from what transcends them, yet at the same time, it links them to the transcendent. The objects of *Erôs* are present and powerful in shaping life even in their absence, just as Platonic Forms are present in participation yet absent in their transcendence. Nothing is ever wholly divorced from its own Form, yet no particular is ever identical to its Form. Things in Becoming strive to be what they are; yet in being what they are they take their guidance from something beyond them—that whatness itself, which can never be reduced to one instantiation of itself. Thus, the dialectic of self and other in human *Erôs* has its general metaphysical analogue as well—each thing, in "striving" to be itself, that is, in continuing to exist in time, is related to an other, the "essence" that its existence expresses, that is, the Form in which it participates.

Socrates as the embodiment of *Erôs* has advanced to that kind of *Erôs* that seeks the ultimate principles of all things. His love for this knowledge points him toward that which transcends the world of change. His understanding of love and its various forms enables him to see the dim glimmers of longing for the eternal in every desire; all desires for changing things have an implicit reference to the unchanging beings for which those changing beings themselves are "longing"—that is, the time-transcendent character of their essence that they temporally instantiate. But Socrates' longing for the transcendent is unfulfilled; only the intimations of the transcendent embodied in *Erôs* itself reach Socrates. These intimations are *Erôs*'s messages from the divine, as desire takes its shape from that for which it longs and imposes that shape upon the desiring mind. Even in a mere hint or a question something of the nature of the object hinted at or asked about comes through, for the character of that object affects the structure of the hint or the question itself. A question is an intellectual desire, but the same observation can be made of desire generally; the character of desire and how it affects the psyche has everything to do with the character of the object desired. It is thus that desire is a messenger. It is as the heeder and prophet of these messages that Socrates becomes a man of irony and apparent hubris.

Socrates' life is dedicated to reminding people that they must recognize that they do not already possess what they need. They must acknowledge their need for a good that transcends any temporal good and any good they can provide for themselves. And this means that our strength as human beings lies in the very admission of our weakness and incapacity; our wisdom lies in the admission of our ignorance. It is precisely by admitting our lack of the Good, and thus discovering our *Erôs* for it, that *Erôs* can then function as a messenger that brings human beings closer to that supreme good. We must achieve a kind of nakedness—the humility brought on by a sense of our lack and our imperfection, an awareness of our ignorance—in order to enter into closer communion with the reality for which human beings ultimately long. Yet the intransigence of the philosopher's insistence that all be judged by the standard of the eternal and that all lesser goals are far less worthy, causes humility to appear to others as extreme arrogance and hubris.

The dialectic of self and other arises again here. On the one hand, human desire is egoistic, since people desire to possess their own good, that is, whatever they suppose will be to their personal advantage and will make them happy. On the other hand, if it is properly developed, *Erôs* leads people again and again to break the bonds of the self, because the true good they ultimately desire lies beyond the confines of the self and beyond anything they can acquire for themselves in this world. As Diotima stresses, we do not desire our own things except insofar as we suppose that they are good for us. Disagreeing with Aristophanes, who claimed that all human beings desire their own other half, implying a longing for what is one's own and what belongs to one's own self, Diotima teaches that human beings will even amputate a limb if they suppose its presence has become harmful. Hence, we desire a good *outside ourselves*, and yet we desire to *possess* this good; paradoxically, then, our desire has *both* egoistic and anti-egoistical dimensions. The tension between these two sides is what enables people to redefine their sense of self and their self-interest. The *Symposium* teaches that, as human beings, our sense of ourselves is bound up with our understanding of what is good for us, and as the latter changes, so must the former. This connection between our understanding of ourselves and our understanding of the good for which we are striving implies that the quest for wisdom is the quest for both self-knowledge and the knowledge of the good.

Our fundamental desire to make the good our own all too easily becomes distorted into the wishful attempt to make what is our own into the Good. In so doing, we take our folly to be wisdom and our narrow point of view, our prejudices, and our commitments become the standards by which we evaluate everything we encounter. We become trapped in a limited perspective, driven by narrow, egotistical or sectarian motives. The love of honor helps to constitute our sense of self, but also connects us to the larger groups from which we seek honor and recognition and from which we fear dishonor and disgrace. We define our selves and acquire our sense of honor and shame largely in terms of our identifications with and oppositions to larger groups and the activities in which they are engaged.

According to the teaching of Diotima, the highest human admiration is only rightly directed at the eternal reality that transcends human subjectivity and at those sages and exemplars among us who most embody that permanent reality. All forms of worldly admiration, the forms of the love of honor that aim at temporal power and prestige, are misdirected to the extent that they treat their objects as ultimate. Their objects have become false idols. Such is the idolatry of what Socrates calls "the great beast" in *Republic* VI—the common or vulgar conceptions of what is honorable or dishonorable manipulated by the sophists, based on ignorance of the kind that takes itself to be wisdom and takes external goods such as money, honor, or power to be the source of true happiness.[2]

The love of honor can inspire people to great deeds and great disasters. It can inspire creativity and good works, leading mortals to brave death and transcend themselves, to act for "higher" motives with no thought for narrow personal gain, but instead only for undying personal glory or the glory reflected back to one via the glorification of a cause. Yet obviously the greatest follies are also inspired by the same motives. Therefore, in Plato's dialogues, the spirited part of the psyche and its love of honor have such a bivalent role: spiritedness is a necessary prerequisite for the young philosophers of the *Republic* (375b), the ally of the rational part of the psyche (*Rep.* 440e–441a), and yet spiritedness can also impair one's judgment and have the most destructive personal and political effects.[3] It is probably because of Alcibiades' high spirit that Socrates is drawn to Alcibiades as to an especially promising youth; yet it is also on account of spiritedness that Alcibiades is drawn away from philosophy by desire for political honors. The illusions of spiritedness misidentify the good but constitute the point of view that actually rules in the world of politics. Certainly such illusions ruled Alcibiades and imperial Athens, creating the temptations that trapped Alcibiades and prevented him from living a life devoted to philosophic self-examination. Spiritedness can often be a form of *Erôs* unaware of the true aim of *Erôs*.

Nonetheless, Socrates' love of wisdom is, in a sense and up to a certain point, infectious. When the philosopher shows others that they are ignorant, he is showing them that they need wisdom, thereby introducing them to a lack in their character, and in the light of this they may well feel a certain shame, a shame that can impel them to seek wisdom. Insofar as one cultivates a love for the wisdom one now knows one lacks, the sense of shame will subside; even if one's sense of one's ignorance actually expands through further philosophical reflection, one at least knows that one is doing all that one can to remedy one's deficiency in wisdom, and one begins to have a sense of the value of that "human wisdom" of which Socrates speaks in the *Apology*, one's awareness of one's own ignorance—and, it should be added, even if it is not polite to say it, one begins to have a greater awareness of the ignorance of others as well. Clearly, Socrates' awareness of his own ignorance involves both a kind of humility and a kind of pride; thus, in imparting to others the awareness of their ignorance, and in modeling for them the proper way to respond to one's deficiency, Socrates is working on the spirited parts of their psyches. They are brought suddenly and involuntarily to an awareness of their ignorance, which causes shame and/or anger. But by following the Socratic exemplar, they can convert this shame into a well-justified humility in which one can take a kind of pride. Since Socrates' stance of ignorance has allowed him to gain victory over others, Socrates' stance even appeals to the interlocutor's love of victory. Yet the ultimate victory Socrates is seeking is victory over himself, or more precisely, over the kind of ignorance that is the self-deceptive pretense of wisdom; in other words, a victory over his own prejudices. The pride of this victory over one's own unsubstantiated beliefs is associated with the feeling of intellectual liberation. One has begun to break the chains that hold the prisoners in the Allegory of the Cave. There is a triumph in liberation that appeals to the spirited part of the psyche and its love of victory.

In addition to working on the spirited part and its love of victory, Socrates' art of love, that is, his dialectical practice, of course also addresses the rational part of the psyche and its love of wisdom. So besides applying the goad of shame and lure of pride, Socrates also arouses the wonder and curiosity of his interlocutors in order to lead them to seek wisdom. Plato's dramatization of the conversations of Socrates, therefore, seems centrally to aim at turning the love of victory toward the love of wisdom, and this harnessing of *philonikia* in order to cultivate *philosophia* may be the central goal of Plato's dialogues. The arousal of curiosity is a direct appeal to the *Erôs* of the rational part of the psyche. Socrates arouses this curiosity and wonder not only through his paretic arguments, but also through his own cryptic nature. Even Alcibiades is able to catch a glimpse of the "images of virtue" within Socrates—in part through an appreciation of Socrates' character, exemplified in virtuous acts, but also through a certain insight into his speeches. For Alcibiades notes that these speeches, like Socrates himself, appear one way on the surface, strange and coarse, but upon reflection and understanding begin to open up to reveal hidden, divine riches within, seeming finally to be "the only arguments that make sense." But perhaps it is the harmony between Socrates' speeches and Socrates' deeds that is most remarkable and most provocative of wonder (cf. *Laches* 188c–189a). What Plato shows his audience of Socrates' character in the drama of the *Symposium* is fully consonant with what Socrates (through Diotima) tells the audience, and Alcibiades confirms this portrait in his testimony.

According to the *Gorgias*, a "true art" does all that it does with a view to the good of its subject (*Grg.* 464–465a); the practitioner of such an art can explain all that it does with reference to that good. Moreover, the good is always some appropriate order, some appropriate arrangement and proportion of the elements of the things in question (*Grg.* 503e–504d). Thus, if one were to practice a good rhetoric, rhetoric as a true art, that rhetoric would have to look to the good of the psyche in all that it does (*Grg.* 504d-e). Since the good of a psyche is a proper ordering of the psyche, and since, as the *Republic* suggests, the psyche is properly ordered when its wisdom-loving element rules over its other elements (*Rep.* 583a, 586e, 589a-b), one would expect the practitioner of a good rhetoric to have speeches designed to put the wisdom-loving element in charge and to make the spirited part of the psyche the ally of reason, that is, to enlist the love of honor into the service of the wisdom-loving part of the mind. It is exactly this kind of "true art" that is constituted by Socrates' erotic art. Even as he suggests in the *Gorgias*, Socrates practices the true art of statecraft through a rhetoric that is not flattery but a true art aimed at producing the good of the mind (*Grg.* 521d-e). By making others aware of their need for wisdom and by provoking their shame, admiration, and wonder, Socrates inspires the philosophical life. Wonder is a form of *Erôs* characteristic of the learning and thinking part of the mind; curiosity is an intellectual desire. By stimulating curiosity and wonder Socrates awakens the *Erôs* of the rational part of the mind. At the same time, by embarrassing his interlocutors and upsetting their complacent self-images, Socrates reorients the spirited part of the mind, harnessing its forces for the quest of wisdom. Shame over one's own lack of understanding enlists the spirited part that feels the shame into the service of the learning part of the psyche that is subject to ignorance and curiosity.

Yet to tamper with other people's honor and pride is a dangerous form of therapy. In various dialogues, Socrates testifies to the animosity his philosophical practice can create. Even apart from the gadfly's irksome efforts to get his friends and fellow-citizens to question themselves, just because Socrates is devoted to a life that sets its sights beyond the political realm, his stance must seem negative and even accusatory to his contemporaries. To the extent that, like Alcibiades, they can appreciate the implicit argument against their values and ways of living made by Socrates' own exemplary life, they will begin to feel threatened by him even without being directly subjected to his refutations. This is why we see Socrates' ironic stance toward ordinary goods characterized by Alcibiades as the most outrageous insult. This is why Alcibiades puts Socrates on trial for hubris, an accusation that foreshadows the accusations of impiety and corrupting the youth that will later be brought against the philosopher by the city itself. (And the fact that Socrates' follower, Apollodorus, seems so haughty to his interlocutor in the opening of the dialogue seems to give some substance to the charge that Socrates has a bad influence on his companions.) These accusations—hubris, impiety, corrupting the youth—are distinct but related. Socrates' hubris lies in his quietly assumed mantle of superiority; his impiety lies in his seeming to question the gods or to teach new strange gods of his own; his corruption of the youth lies in his seeming to debunk the city's authorities. Yet it is obvious to the sympathetic reader of Plato that these real or apparent crimes are all explained and to some extent mitigated by Socrates' single practice and love—the love of wisdom and the skeptical, dialectical quest for truth.

Socrates understands the art of love because he understands his own ignorance and thereby his love of wisdom. He understands better than other mortals his unique way of being in-between, of being and not-being, of having and not having, and he sees the love of wisdom as the highest form of desire. Through Diotima's teaching he also understands how his desire is related to the desires for temporal gain or honor. Because he is aware of the various types of desire exemplified in life's many pursuits and has a sense of how these desires are to be ranked relative to one another, he sees philosophy's relationships to all other human endeavors. For he can see how the philosopher's desire for knowledge is related to the artistic and educational goals of the poets, to the celebration of piety or of conventional goods, to the desires for honor, and to the political goals of the city in general. One sees the Socratic understanding of these relationships depicted in Socrates' story of his response to the Oracle in the *Apology*. There we see how the philosopher's small, human wisdom contrasts with the putative wisdom of the politicians, the poets, and the craftspeople.[4]

In the *Symposium* we see philosophy's relations to these types exemplified in a different way: the politicians, the poets, and the technicians of narrow competence are represented by Alcibiades, the politician and general, Agathon and Aristophanes, the poets, and Eryximachus, the physician, respectively. The failure of most of these other points of view on the human good is that they shoot too low and aim at something fleeting—honor, super-ficial beauty, power, or a narrow expertise that often fails to understand its relation to the whole of knowledge. Philosophy, in contrast, understands the ultimate goal of *Erôs* and that this goal is timeless; philosophy is able to dis-tinguish the true goal from false idols. As for traditional piety spoken for by Aristophanes, its warning against hubris might all too easily extend to an antipathy toward philosophy, as it did in the case of Aristophanes' play *The Clouds*. Aristophanes' speech opposes the scientific speech of Eryximachus without being able to learn from it or to encompass any of its truths. Only philosophy as embodied in Diotima's *daimonic* account remains open to the mystery, while at the same time remaining comprehensive enough to weave all the truths of the other speeches into a coherent, dialectical whole. Socrates' philosophy can synthesize aspects of Aristophanes and Eryximachus, that is, the religious and scientific, as well as aspects of Aristophanes and Agathon, that is, the comic and the tragic.

The *Symposium* dramatizes the trial between Socrates and Agathon over wisdom, judged by Dionysus. Agathon's speech talks about wisdom, but he also attempts to have the most comprehensive speech by talking about all the virtues. It would seem a requirement of Socrates' conception of wisdom that wisdom would lead to all other virtues and that wisdom should be able to give an account of itself and all other virtues. Agathon's speech tries to discuss the wisdom of *Erôs* and he ascribes all other virtues to *Erôs* as well. In associating wisdom with an account of the other virtues in addition to other specific comments in his speech, Agathon is like a pale reflection of Socrates. Socrates often suggests that virtue is knowledge and in some dialogues wisdom seems to be knowledge of the good that would imply the other virtues. In the *Meno*, wisdom seems to be the ultimate vir-tue, the knowledge of how to use all other things well, including virtues such as courage (*Meno* 87e–89a); only if courage were used well would it truly be a genuine virtue. In addition the *Phaedo* suggests that the difference between genuine and sham-virtue is their underlying motivation, one might say their underlying *Erôs*; for genuine philosophical virtue does all for the sake of wisdom (*phronesis*), the "only correct coin, for which all these should be exchanged" (*Phaedo* 69a-b). Moreover, the ascription of both wisdom and the rest of virtues to *Erôs* specifically makes sense from the point of view of Platonic psychology. Although Socrates in the *Republic* seems highly critical of *Erôs*, according to the model of the tripartite soul discussed in Book Nine, all three parts of the psyche can be defined by what they desire (580d–581c); and it turns out that different objects of the various parts of the psyche are all potential objects of *Erôs* in the *Symposium*. *Symposium* 205d lists money making, love of gymnastics, and love of wisdom as forms of *Erôs*, and surely this list neatly corresponds to the desires of the three parts of the psyche. *Erôs* certainly can aim at sex like the appetitive part, at glory like the spirited part, and at wisdom like the calculative part. The ordered psyche that in the *Republic* is the unifying conception behind all the definitions of the virtues is the psyche in which the right part of the psyche rules the psyche. The ruling element in the psyche is the fundamental motivation for the sake of which all else in the psyche is done, as one can see from Socrates' discussion of the various types of psyche in the *Republic* (Bks. VIII and IX).

The upshot of these reflections is that for Socrates the properly ordered psyche is the philosopher's psyche, the psyche that desires wisdom and truth before all else. So it is *Erôs*, although *Erôs* of a particular kind, directed at a particular object, that constitutes the ordered soul and leads to all the virtues. One of the implications here is that wisdom may consist in either knowledge of the good or, failing such knowledge, a firmly held true opinion about the good or perhaps even the *desire* for knowledge of the good provided that that desire becomes the most authoritative desire in the psyche, placing the rational part of the mind that has this desire in command of the other elements in the psyche. Book Nine of the *Republic* makes it clear that the rational, learning part of the mind rules the mind if its desire for wisdom and knowledge rules the mind. This result is elegant, because it shows that the tripartite soul as discussed in Book Nine accommodates the three major possible candidates for wisdom considered in the dialogues—wisdom as the knowledge of the good, wisdom as true opinion about the good, and finally, wisdom as the Socratic awareness of ignorance and the erotic longing for wisdom that constitutes the "human wisdom" of the *Apology*. Interestingly, Socrates himself can be seen as embodying all three versions of wisdom; he certainly longs for a wisdom that he lacks, yet by virtue of knowing that he needs this wisdom he *may* possess actual knowledge of what is good (at least in the sense that he may actually *know* that seeking wisdom is good for him); yet even if it is not actual knowledge, his wisdom may involve a true opinion about the good—it may be a true opinion that seeking wisdom is good for those who lack it, that is, that philosophy is an appropriate way to care for the soul.

In drawing wisdom and the other virtues out of *Erôs*, Agathon may not be wrong, although of course his speech shows no real sign of insight into any of these points. In Socrates' speech, however, Diotima's teaching shows how genuine wisdom may arise from a certain form of *Erôs* and argues that all other genuine virtues arise from such wisdom. In addition, her teaching suggests the relation between the highest form of *Erôs* and its lowest forms. What she suggests is that all forms of *Erôs*—including the appetitive desire for sex and the spirited desire for honor—are aimed at the good; and the true and highest good for the psyche is the vision of the Beautiful Itself. So, Socrates uses Diotima's teaching to suggest that *Erôs* can lead to wisdom and all the other virtues. Socrates thereby associates wisdom and all the other virtues with *Erôs*, but in a very different way than Agathon had done. For Agathon, *Erôs* was a god possessed of wisdom and all the other virtues. For Socrates, *Erôs* is a *daimon* who neither merely possesses nor merely lacks what he seeks. Diotima will stress that *Erôs* lacks what it desires, but on the other hand *Erôs* is in an intermediate state, born of poverty and resource, functioning as a messenger between human poverty and divine resource and somehow partaking of both at once. The lover's ascent described by Diotima seems to be a change in the proportion of poverty and resource in *Erôs* (as one changes the proportion of the mortal and divine through changing the objects of *Erôs*). For although the movement up the ladder might be thought to be merely a change in the object of *Erôs*, when *Erôs* shifts from one object to another it is shifting in the direction of the cause or source of being, that is, in the direction of greater being. Hence, it is shifting toward the divine, toward the "resource" element in all human *Erôs*, the aspect of *Erôs* that partakes in or contains a trace of that for which it longs. But as long as *Erôs* remains *Erôs* the longing will never be utterly satisfied.

Given Agathon's speech and its attempt to talk about the relation between *Erôs* and wisdom and the other virtues, and Socrates' more successful attempt to do this, one can see these speeches as Agathon and Socrates "going to law" over wisdom. Then the drunken Alcibiades' speech on Socrates represents the judgment of Dionysus on the case.

Alcibiades is the messenger of Dionysus judging between them in favor of Socrates. But Alcibiades' way of affirming Socrates' wisdom involves accusing Socrates of hubris. This connection between Socrates' wisdom and his hubris is appropriate. Socrates' superiority over Agathon settles the question that was raised by Socrates' assertion that he wanted "to go beautiful to the beautiful" and by his adaptation of Homer which spoke of the good going uninvited to the good. Agathon is good in name only; Socrates is really good. Agathon is beautiful physically, but Socrates' true beauty, his beauty of psyche, is not physical and does not result from his having dressed for the party (although his desire to dress appropriately for the occasion is a sign of his inner beauty). In Alcibiades' judging between Agathon and Socrates in favor of Socrates there is also a struggle between Alcibiades and Socrates over Agathon (i.e., over "the good"). Socrates' and Alcibiades' *erotes*, and their ability to attract lovers, are pitted against one another. Socrates wins. Alcibiades' judging in favor of Socrates occurs in spite of Alcibiades himself.

The trial in the dialogue initiated by Alcibiades occurs only after Socrates has bested the others in a contest of speeches. Although Alcibiades had no part in that contest, he knew all too well its results, having been himself bested by Socrates in an earlier contest of wills. As he reveals in his speech, that contest was also a game of love, a game he had lost as he haplessly found their traditional courtship roles reversed and himself helplessly ("slavishly") in love with a godlike man whose very existence he is unable to live either with or without. One might think that the contest of speeches in its entirety enacts the trial by Dionysos of which Agathon spoke, saying that Dionysos would decide between himself and Socrates; but it is only with the introduction of Alcibiades that the god of inebriation, comedy, and masks returns to the scene. It is only in Alcibiades' speech that we are shown the Dionysian sides of the Apollinian Socrates, his satyr-like qualities and his masked mode of speaking. Interestingly, Socrates' Dionysian and Apollinian sides appear to be inextricably fused in his philosophical *Erôs*, one more duality encompassed by this hybrid *daimon*, offspring of *Poros* and *Penia*. Apollo, the god of the Oracle Socrates claimed as his inspiration, was a god of light, of reason, and of order. Dionysos is the patron of such satyrs as Marsyas and Silenus, the god of wine and of intoxication. Socrates' divine madness brought on by his philosophic *Erôs* contains elements of both. How can reason and intoxication, reason and inspiration, reason and madness belong together? The answer, suggested by Diotima's teaching and by the *Phaedrus*, appears in one word: *Erôs*. *Erôs* is the inspiration that animates reason and speaks to it prophetically, as the medium of "Platonic" recollection; the philosopher's wonder, filled with philosophic *Erôs*, seems like intoxication or madness, but it stimulates reason and even feeds it. There is a mystery at the heart of reason that reason longs to comprehend; this mystery even enables reason to exist. As Kierkegaard said: "The thinker without a paradox is like a lover without passion."[5]

In Alcibiades' speech, the praise of Socrates replaces the praise of *Erôs*. This replacement signifies that Socrates embodies *Erôs*. The vision of beauty itself that was the climax of Socrates' speech is replaced with a vision of Socrates in Alcibiades' speech, Socrates as the one who longs for the vision of beauty itself. Socrates had replaced Agathon's idea of a beautiful *Erôs*, possessing good, with the idea of a nonbeautiful *Erôs* longing for beauty and goodness. Similarly, Diotima's vision of the beautiful itself is replaced by Alcibiades' vision of Socrates, a man who the audience knows is longing to have the vision of the beautiful.

Socrates the philosopher has the rhetorical satyr's power, capable of speaking differently to different people without any necessary contradiction. His strange but seductive approach can even make the great Alcibiades ashamed of himself. But unfortunately neither mere protreptic nor subtle seduction is enough. The failure of Socrates' clever and well-crafted words reminds us that wisdom should rule, but in "the real world" it is usually all too impotent. It is precisely the appetitive and honor-loving parts of the psyche, forms of *Erôs* that are most common and the earliest to develop, that generally dominate in political life. The beauty of Socrates' speech cannot prevent the drunken Alcibiades from crashing the party and disrupting it, subverting what is left of the philosophical conversation and causing the mood of the party to resemble his own inebriated state. Of course, Socrates remains unaffected, just as he had been unmoved by Alcibiades' seductive charms. The detail that Socrates never becomes inebriated no matter how much he drinks illustrates that Socrates combines the Apollonian and the Dionysian, for his courtship with the god of wine is not exclusive of philosophical conversation. What really makes Alcibiades drunk is his inebriation by honor-love in the form of his overweening political ambitions; such wine never intoxicates Socrates. Socrates can drink the wine of leisure, but because he spends his leisure in the pursuit of wisdom, that is, in the love of the supreme Beauty and Goodness, he never gets drunk. His philosophy is divine madness, divine inspiration, a *daimonic* message from the divine; but it does not produce inebriation, but rather the ultimate sobriety. This sobriety depends on the fact that he couples his erotic longing for an absolute, immutable good with his awareness that human nature cannot *possess* such a good. In other words, the philosopher's *Erôs* remains true to both its parents, *Poros* and *Penia*, and thus to its own hybrid, or dual, nature.

It is to a consideration of the dual nature of *Erôs* that one must turn in order to understand Socrates' victory over the poets and how this victory has to do with the insight that his knowledge of *Erôs* gives him into the nature of comedy and tragedy. In defeating Agathon in the dispute over wisdom, Socrates defeats the poets. Through Diotima's teaching, Socrates' speech synthesizes the insights of Aristophanes and Agathon and at the same time synthesizes the comic and the tragic. Socrates' wisdom is superior to Agathon's because Socrates understands *Erôs* better. At the same time, *Plato* displays *his own* mastery of both comic and tragic discourse; he does this by weaving comic and tragic elements into the speeches of Aristophanes and Agathon. He also weaves comic and tragic elements into the *Symposium* as a whole, while offering insight into the theoretical ground of the connection between comedy and tragedy in his presentation of Diotima's teaching on *Erôs*. This deeper understanding of *Erôs* makes philosophy superior to comedy and tragedy—able to do justice to both the comic and tragic aspects of life.

A hint of the way Plato weaves together the comic and the tragic is seen in the fact that although philosophy is able to demonstrate its superiority to other walks of life, Plato never lets his audience forget that his Socrates is an ideal beyond the range of ordinary mortals. Many others have been "bitten" by the snake of philosophy and driven to madness with love of it and yet like Alcibiades have failed to live the kind of life lived by Socrates, the life of true philosophical self-examination. Socrates, as a *daimonic* being, a being in whom *Erôs* has come to its proper full development, is indeed a divine gift and a divine message. Recall that Socrates claims in the *Apology* that he is a gift to the city precisely because his life embodied the Oracle's message to human beings (*Ap.* 30d–31b). And yet he could not force others to hear the message; he had no power over them that could make them hear and heed it. We should remember the poignant question that Polemarchus asks rhetorically at the beginning of the *Republic*: "Could you really persuade us, if we don't listen?" (*Rep.* 327c). We could likewise ask: Could anyone truly teach anything to those not willing to learn? Could anyone truly convert another human being who is not ready and willing to be converted? The dramatic context and the choice of characters in the *Republic* suggests the tragic dimension of life; for, as the dialogue's original audience would have known, some of the participants in that conversation about an ideal city that "exists nowhere on earth" but "perhaps in heaven" (*Rep.* 592b) were executed by oligarchic and democratic regimes in real life (Polemarchus and Niceratus dying at the hands of the Thirty and Socrates, of course, at the command of the restored democracy). In the *Symposium*, it is the role of Alcibiades and the reminder of Socrates' failure with him, and ultimately of Alcibiades' failure to emulate Socrates, that indicates the tragic impotence of philosophy from the political point of view.

This tragic impotence on the political stage is compatible, however, with the unparalleled glory and worth of philosophy in human existence. Socrates' beauty is not diminished by the drunkenness of Alcibiades; indeed, in the somewhat unintended truthfulness of his self-revelations Alcibiades reflects, through his own shame and admiration, the greatness of Socrates. Socrates fails to bring Alcibiades to the life of philosophy, but Alcibiades, and all that he represents, fails to seduce Socrates. This mutual failure illustrates the relation between philosophy and political life and the tragicomic character of that relation. What is tragic is that the promise of Alcibiades and of Athens is lost, or that the victims of folly resist the authority of wisdom. But when the city executes Socrates, his death, and the life that led to it, transcends tragedy, for Socrates retains his happiness even in the face of death. The philosopher's life shows that human life in general is both tragic and comic; and yet precisely by embodying this tragicomic perspective on life, philosophy itself transcends the tragicomic, or perhaps transforms it into something else. Into what might it be transformed? Into a particular form of the life of serious play in honor of the gods celebrated in Plato's *Laws* (*Laws* 803c–804c), with philosophy at the center of that life, a perspective from which one can see at one and the same moment that human life is not so very serious *and* that it is necessary to treat it most seriously *anyway* (*Laws* 803b).

These thoughts about the tragicomic character of the philosophic perspective point toward the last scene at the drinking party: Socrates' presenting an argument to a comedian and a tragedian to show that the same playwright should be capable of writing both comedy and tragedy. Has Plato perhaps attempted this in the *Symposium*? We have already hinted that we think he has. Tragedy and comedy both have to do with the gulf between the eternal and the temporal that is hidden behind the encounter of humans with the limits of their own desires.[6] Ordinary comedy and tragedy are each generated in different ways by the tendency to ignore human limits and the resultant tendency to be crushed by them, in the form of Fate in the case of tragedy, or Folly in the case of comedy. The philosopher, by contrast, achieves the fullness of the human potential by engaging in a knowing struggle with these limits that acknowledges and respects them.

There is tragedy in human life in virtue of the fact that human life is a kind of being toward death, a recurrent theme in nineteenth and twentieth-century philosophy. Human life is ever incomplete, and its "completion" is brought about only by death. There is tragedy also to the extent that the very roots of our virtues are at the same time the roots of our vices; their common root is revealed by Diotima's teaching, for she suggests that all people, good and evil, desire to possess the good forever. To see that her claim is really this general, one has only to reflect on all the different sorts of desire she subsumes within her account—and on the fact that she explicitly says that everyone is a lover, including those who love money and sport—although only some are called lovers. Virtue parts from vice because the virtuous get farther along the scale of *Erôs* and come to have the right sorts of desire ruling in their life. But it is precisely because people desire to *possess* the good forever, that is, because people desire to make the good their *own*, that they so easily succumb to the false idolatry that causes them to regard *what is already their own* as the good itself. Put otherwise, this tendency in human beings leads them to take themselves too seriously, and, unable to laugh at themselves, they confuse their own folly with wisdom and believe they already know what they do not. Attempting to fill the void in themselves, that is, to satisfy the longings of *Erôs*, they will cling to any illusion of good.[7]

The tragic dimension of human life is clearly revealed through the human tendency to be ruled by the appetitive and honor-loving parts of the human character or *psychē* and by the fact that human beings remain temporal beings in spite of their longing for eternity. But the comic dimension of human existence also depends on this same disproportion between the eternal and the temporal in human existence, seen from another point of view. The comic aspects of life may also be bound up with a failure of logos, with the limits of reason and speech. The nineteenth-century statesman and philosopher Horace Walpole famously said, "Life is a comedy to those who think and a tragedy to those who feel." If he is right, then it follows that life is a tragicomedy to those who both think and feel.

The ridiculous are defined in the *Philebus* as those who overestimate their own goods (external goods, goods of the body, or goods of the psyche) when this overestimation is accompanied by weakness (49b). We find examples of this in most of the characters of the *Symposium*, beginning especially with Apollodorus, and certainly in the light of the *Symposium* we can see manifold examples of this in our own lives. But those whose overestimation of their own good is not accompanied by weakness but by strength are not ridiculous; Alcibiades, when he was sober, was not ridiculous. However, in this dialogue we see him inebriated, not sober; in this light, he does appear a bit ridiculous. Yet his presence is enough to remind us of the dangerous and tragic implication of what in this context appears as his comical foolishness; we know that when he sobers up and forgets about Socrates again, he will shortly come to betray Athens. Then he will be one of those who in the *Philebus* are called "powerful, fearful and hateful" (49b-c).

In the course of the dialogue we have also seen comic elements aplenty. To take a prime instance, consider Aristophanes hiccupping. The hiccups are comic, on the dramatic level, for what they do to Eryximachus's speech, but also, for Plato's audience, for turning of the tables on Aristophanes. Then there is the comic element in Aristophanes' speech, in its contrast between human pretensions and human reality. Comedy is in service to piety because of this unique ability to circumvent human defense mechanisms to bring out this contrast between pretensions and reality. It is appropriate for this comic defense of piety that it comes after the speech of the narrowly focused natural philosopher, Eryximachus, whose one-sided recollection of Empedocles' teaching was blind to the impact of strife on harmony and Love; hence, Aristophanes' speech balances out and redresses the one-sidedness of the nature-philosopher's speech and exposes his characteristic vice: a certain kind of hubris that consists in trying to know things beyond the mortal ken (i.e., "above the heavens and below the earth") and in abstracting from the ethical or normative dimension of life in the name of impartial truth ("examining the entrails of gnats," as in *The Clouds*, 155–68). Eryximachus does deal with the normative dimension to the extent that he offers prescriptions as a doctor; but he seems to claim a god-like knowledge of the fundamental principle of nature that subsumes an account of the good and evil of the human psychē within an understanding that would also account for hiccups. Perhaps Eryximachus also forgets the human need for the grandeur of the gods; he certainly seems to forget the power of myth and of the eruptive, chaotic dimension of the very *Erôs* he describes. What he says is not so much untrue as incomplete, even myopic. The aim of Aristophanes' speech is to remind us of the gods, the traditional Olympian gods, and of human weakness and inferiority when compared to the virtues humans ascribe to them.

Agathon's speech is also comic. Not only do his enormous pretensions contrast with his actual achievement, but also his efforts are made ridiculous by performative self-contradiction or ironic reversal: he does exactly the opposite of what he says he intends to do. He claims he will praise *Erôs* Himself rather than his effects, and yet he characterizes *Erôs* in terms taken entirely from the objects and effects of Love. Although he is a tragic poet, his speech seems comical in the vanity of his effort to model his account of *Erôs* after his view of himself. (Similarly, the comic poet Aristophanes' speech had contained a tragic dimension, in that it pointed to a certain insurmountable futility in human desire. But probably the Platonic Aristophanes is aware of this, as Plato seems to have paid Aristophanes the compliment of making his speech superior to Agathon's and to every other speech except that of Socrates.)

Alcibiades' speech was comical too, on account of his inebriation and his jealousy, envy, and love of Socrates, all of which seem to bubble up from him in the somewhat uninhibited, somewhat involuntary self-disclosure characteristic of drunken effusion. Yet of course, as we have suggested more than once, there is a tragic dimension to Alcibiades' revelations. They remind Plato's audience of the impotence of philosophy in the political realm, of the lost promise of Alcibiades and of Athens, and of the power and predominance in human existence of the forms of *Erôs* that, according to Diotima, are the farthest from an appreciation of *Erôs'* ultimate goal. It is tragic to devote one-self exclusively to the world of impermanence. Conversely, it is comical to presume to skip over the temporal world to go straight to timeless Being. In Diotima's teaching, contact with bodies in time is never denied its rightful importance and worth.

By juxtaposing the lofty heights of Diotima's "higher mysteries" with the intoxicated love, envy, and anger that Alcibiades directs at Socrates, Plato has set up a tension that mirrors the tension Diotima finds in *Erôs*. The eternal is adumbrated in, and the love of the eternal awakened by, her teaching; while the irrationality of a temporally directed *Erôs*, embodied in Alcibiades, is immediately laid beside it for comparison. This glimpse of the temporal and the eternal in human existence reflects the tension between the outer and inner sides of the enigmatic Socrates, between the mortal and divine elements in the *Erôs* he embodies, and between the ignorance and wisdom contained in the philosopher's *Erôs*. The *Symposium* awakens our *Erôs* for the mysteries of that divine, eternal Beauty and at the same time reminds us of our insuperable distance from it. Thus, the dialogue as a whole functions as a *daimon*, awakening our entreaties to the gods and giving us an intimation, through our own desire, of just what the desired object, the truth, might be like if only we could possess it. Yet, at the end of the *Symposium*, we are left without it. It departs from us like the vision Socrates has on the portico early in the evening, yet we are left pregnant with desire for it, full of the longing to continue Socrates' quest.

Alcibiades insists that Socrates' true beauty is hidden. And this hidden character is poignantly reflected by the fact that only Aristodemus, Apollodorus, and his unknown auditor, (and the reader of the dialogue) know how Socrates confirms Alcibiades' account of him by what he does after the party and on the following day. In the closing lines of the dialogue we are given confirmation that the account of Socrates in Alcibiades' speech is no mere exaggeration. The truth about Socrates is a truth filled with mystery, and like all mystery, it is a *daimonic* messenger, a hinting at something further that remains undisclosed, a revealing and concealing at once. But sometimes in the case of the deepest mysteries, their mysterious or wondrous character is itself concealed behind a veil of the trivial and the ordinary. Socrates on the day following the party will go about his ordinary life, despite having spent the previous evening without sleep, drinking and philosophizing until dawn; but only those few privileged to know both about the previous night and his activities on the following day can see anything extraordinary. The poise and vigor of Socrates, completely unaffected by the ephemeral world around him as he goes about his routine business on the day after the party at Agathon's house, betrays no glimmer, to the undiscerning eye, of the hidden light of virtue behind his coarse and homely exterior. But this quiet, secret virtue is what is truly miraculous about Socrates, a miracle hidden from view, like the images of the gods inside the figure of Silenus.

# Appendix: Intermediacy, Philosophy, and Recollection

## THE INTERMEDIACIES OF PHILOSOPHY AND RECOLLECTION: THE *APOLOGY* AND THE *MENO*

### THE *APOLOGY*

Consider the famous story of the Oracle from the *Apology* of Socrates. Socrates tries to explain the nature of the pursuits that have gotten him in trouble. He gives (ostensibly at any rate) an account of the origins of his philosophic quest.

Chaerephon makes an entreaty of a god, and the god responds with an oracle.[1] Socrates is sure that the oracle must be true somehow, but disturbed because he cannot imagine how it could be.[2] What he says here is pertinent: "For I am conscious [σύνοιδα] that I am wise [σοφὸς] neither to great nor a small extent" (21b4–5). Socrates later draws a conclusion from the first of his encounters: while he was interrogating his fellow Athenians about the wisdom they claimed to possess, Socrates realized that none of them, *including himself,* really knew anything "fine and good" (καλὸν κάγαθὸν 21d4). However, while they are unaware that they do not really have knowledge of fine and good things, Socrates *realizes* that he does not. It is of course no coincidence that just as Socrates does not know, neither does he think he knows; he does not think he knows precisely because he is *aware* of his lack of wisdom. But this awareness is what he takes to constitute his advantage and to make him wiser than the others (23a-b) are.

Indeed, when Socrates introduces the story he says he is going to explain a kind of wisdom that he has, which is the very wisdom that is supposed to account for his unsavory reputation. He calls it a "human wisdom" (ἀ·θρωπίνη σοφία 20d8), and adds that he probably really is wise in this human wisdom.

He speaks sardonically of others "who might be wise with some wisdom greater than human wisdom" (20e). Such wisdom, however, he does not understand, and a few lines later, when referring back to his "human wisdom" he adds the qualification that it might not be wisdom at all, suggesting that "[h]uman wisdom is worth little or nothing." Socrates suggests that the Oracle is not really saying that Socrates possesses wisdom, but that it merely uses his name, making an example of him as one who is aware that he is worth nothing with respect to wisdom (23a-b).

At this point we should note the following: Socrates is *conscious* of or *aware* of his ignorance; he *recognizes* (ἔγνωκεν 23b3) that he is worth nothing with regard to wisdom. If this is not knowledge in any strict sense, it must still be something akin to knowledge (at least to the extent that even correct opinion is akin to knowledge), for it involves at least awareness of his own actual epistemic situation. It is also implied that Socrates can detect when others do not know. For he bases his whole claim to distinction on the fact that the others think they know, but in reality just like Socrates they do not know. But his ability to make this distinction depends on his being correct in his assessment that they do not know. But if Socrates is truly ignorant of the matters he examines, one may wonder how he is in a position to evaluate them as being ignorant, that is, how he can tell that they do not possess a knowledge regarding these important matters that he also does not claim to know. How can Socrates, the ignorant, be sure that their accounts were not satisfactory? Perhaps Socratic cross-examination counts on making the interlocutor himself see the unsatisfactory character of each of his accounts; for presumably someone who knew a subject would not come to be dissatisfied with his own accounts. But there are interlocutors (e.g., Thrasymachus, and Callicles) who do not admit their accounts are really unsatisfactory and who seem to think that Socrates is being stubborn or engaging in trickery. If he were completely ignorant Socrates could not rule out the possibility that they were right. Nor can Socrates infer their ignorance from the mere fact that the interlocutors are unable to teach Socrates that what they say is true, on the presumption that those who know can teach what they know to others. For Socrates could just be a particularly bad student, incapable of learning. But Socrates obviously understands the subject well enough to be able unerringly to find contradictions in their views. Thus, he is not merely inferring the ignorance of his interlocutors from their inability to teach or from their tendency to become confused and dissatisfied with their own views; he is the one who finds the flaws that cause their dissatisfaction, and he finds them with the focus of a bloodhound. For this reason too, then, there seems to be a kind of knowledge involved in Socrates' ignorance, a knowledge that seems in some way to go beyond the awareness of his own ignorance. Socrates' awareness of his ignorance is said to be a kind of wisdom, a human wisdom. This human wisdom is said to be worth little or nothing in a context where it is clear that a contrast is being made with the wisdom of the god, who is said to be "really wise" (τῷ ὄντι ὁ θεὸς σοφὸς εἶναι 23a5–6). But compared to other human pursuits the pursuit that has led Socrates to this awareness of his ignorance is taken by him to be vastly superior and essential for human virtue and well-being (*Ap.* 22e).

As a result, Socrates is in a situation identical to the one the lovers of wisdom were said to be in the *Symposium*. For he does not possess wisdom, but he is also not so ignorant as to suppose that he knows what he does not. He is in-between wisdom and ignorance. His "interlocutors" are said to be in the position in which the ignorant are placed in Diotima's account. To put the matter in reverse, the position of Socrates, vis-à-vis wisdom and ignorance, is ascribed to philosophers as such in the *Symposium*. This fact must be a stumbling block to all interpretations that want to see the Socratic profession of ignorance in Plato as mere reportage of an idiosyncrasy of the historical Socrates.

Furthermore, as we noted above, Socratic Ignorance in the *Apology* seems to have an aspect of wisdom to it. It has a kind of ambiguity in this regard at least, since Socrates is able to refer to this very ignorance *as* a kind of wisdom. Since this wisdom is then contrasted with divine wisdom, the ambiguity of its status is reinforced: it is wisdom, but then again it is not. In this respect his situation is clearly similar to that of *Erôs* in the *Symposium*, who both lacks wisdom but in a sense partakes of it through his father's nature. Like *Erôs*, Socrates has wisdom in one sense, but not in another.

## THE MENO

There is another context in which this strange ambivalence or intermediacy betwixt knowledge and ignorance is prominent in the dialogues. This intermediacy occurs in connection with the so-called "doctrine of recollection." The idea of "recollection" (*anamnesis*) is brought up in the *Meno* to answer the following paradox: Learning is impossible. For one cannot learn what one already knows; and if one does not know something at all, one has no basis on which to begin to search, not knowing what is sought. Thus, whether one knows or does not know, one cannot learn (*Meno* 80d-e).

The paradox presumes that one either knows something or does not; if one could seek neither the known nor the unknown, it would not be possible to learn. Socrates responds by showing that the simple alternative "what is known" versus "what is not known," understood as the paradox presents it, is a false alternative; for the way out of the paradox suggested by Socrates is that there is a sense in which we do already know what we are seeking, but another sense in which we do not. The model used is that of memory. For what is stored in memory, in the moment before it is actually recollected, is in one sense "known" but in another sense not. If I am struggling to remember something, there is a sense in which I do know it (for the knowledge of it is inside me somewhere) but another sense in which I do not (for I have not at present succeeded in recollecting it). Socrates suggests the search for knowledge is analogous to recollection in this way. Even in order to ask questions about a topic one must have some understanding of what it is into which one inquires; yet clearly if one had complete knowledge of the thing in question one would have nothing to seek.

For instance, the interlocutors in the *Republic* must have some sense of what justice is, in order even to be able to formulate their proposed definitions of justice; yet it turns out that they do not have such an understanding of justice that they are able to define it adequately. Furthermore, when Socrates finds the flaw in a definition and points it out to them, in some cases both they and Socrates must possess a sense of what justice is in order to be able to appreciate that flaw. For instance, when Socrates uses a counterexample to reveal the inadequacy of the definition of justice as "telling the truth and paying what one owes" (at *Rep.* 331c), the force of the counterexample depends on both Socrates and interlocutors somehow understanding what does *not* count as justice. But they could not understand what justice is not without at least having some dim awareness of what justice is. One must always recollect in order to get inquiry started, in order in some sense to know what one is talking about, and in order to follow even negative arguments, such as Socratic refutations, etc. One must have a sense of what is right in order to see what is wrong, just as the *Phaedo* suggests that one must have a sense of the perfect in order to grasp the imperfect (*Phaedo* 74d-e). Hence, the metaphor of recollection provides another sense in which one might be said to be between ignorance and wisdom, or between ignorance and knowledge in general. For the notion of recollection implies that one both knows, in one sense, and yet does not know, in another sense, whatever one has not yet recollected. One possesses the knowledge and yet must seek it through recollection.[3]

In other dialogues (specifically the *Phaedo* and the *Phaedrus*), it is held that what one recollects in learning are the eternal, unchanging, invisible, incorporeal Forms that one has glimpsed as a disembodied psyche before the time of physical birth. But this metaphysical freight notwithstanding, Socrates touches upon a very common experience with this metaphor of recollection. Consider the moment when one struggles to find expression for a thought. There is a sense in which the thought itself somehow guides one in searching for words; thus, there is a sense in which one might be said to *already know* what one wants to say. But in another sense, since one has not yet found the words and is still groping, one might be said *not* to know what one wants to say. This experience points to a way in which one can be ignorant and knowing at the same time. It shows how one can be longing for something that one lacks—in this case, the right words—and how, even in that longing, one is able to have some hint of what one is seeking. This experience is also common in artistic creation; the artist knows what she is trying to achieve, in one sense, but in another sense, she is groping. The attempts to grasp the inspiration or to express the thought can fail; but then, when she sees that she has not expressed the idea, in order to *see* that she has not done so, she must possess some sense of the idea she has failed to express. Yet she is not aware of it explicitly, for she has failed to render it explicit; and yet she does know that she has fallen short of the idea she is seeking to express. This experience is similar to the case in which one struggles to recollect a name, and before having recalled it, is nonetheless sure that a name proposed by a friend is not the right one. Hence, one can say what is wrong in this case without being able to say what is right. These examples may help us to understand how Socrates is able to discover what is false without yet being able to give his own account of what is true.

From the foregoing, it should be fairly apparent that *Erôs* as discussed by Diotima is akin to the idea of Recollection. Like Recollection, *Erôs* is between ignorance and wisdom and combines both. Recollection is said to recollect eternal forms; and in the *Phaedrus* (249c–256e), *Erôs* is said to enable us to recollect Forms. In the *Symposium Erôs* is said to be a messenger bringing messages from the divine; Plato clearly associates the Forms with the divine in many dialogues. In the *Symposium Erôs* is also said to have inherited resources from his father, Resource; and clearly the Forms would be akin to the "Resource"-dimension of *Erôs*. Finally, Diotima's teachings of *Erôs* issues in the vision of a Form, and her account of the lover's ascent can easily be seen as an account of recollection.

Furthermore, the common experiences described above as being analogous to recollection also have a connection to the experience of *Erôs* as a messenger. The writer or artist who is guided by an unexpressed idea is also someone who *desires* to express that idea; and he or she is guided in these efforts by the object of desire. The artist's *Erôs* has become a messenger. This comparison is certainly appropriate to Plato's treatment of *Erôs*, because the *Phaedrus* describes *Erôs*, which is closely connected to recollection in that dialogue, as a "divine madness" akin to the "madness" of inspiration in poetry and prophesy. Moreover, *Erôs* is seen as the root of human creativity in the *Symposium*. Thus, Plato's dialogues themselves point to these analogies between the experience of (1) struggling to remember something, (2) creative inspiration, and (3) the inspiration of love. In all of these experiences, some latent or inchoate content motivates and guides the efforts to articulate it.

But it should be noted that the sense of being in-between involved in recollection would be common to *both* those who are ignorant but think that they know (the nonphilosophers) *and* those who are ignorant but aware of their ignorance (the philosophers). For according to the doctrine of recollection, *all* humans have forgotten knowledge buried inside them that they can learn to recollect. If so, this kind of "being in-between" is not the same kind of "being in-between" in which the philosopher as such finds herself, for she is in-between in virtue of her self-aware ignorance in a way that nonphilosophical humans are not. Nor is the intermediacy that one possesses in virtue of unrecollected knowledge in any obvious way identical to the way in which correct opinion is "in-between" knowledge and ignorance. For the person who has knowledge but hasn't recollected it is in a sense between knowledge and ignorance, but need not be so in virtue of some correct opinion and its form of "reasonless" contact with reality.

There is a kind of kinship between correct opinion, *Erôs*, and philosophy, however. Correct opinion has a kind of contact with reality, but it is unable to account for it with a *logos*.[4] According to the Platonic treatment of recollection, all humans have contact with reality and truth through unrecollected knowledge, but have not yet succeeded in bringing that knowledge to light. Bringing it to light may indeed involve at least the effort to express it by means of an account, that is, recollection may involve transforming a piece of correct opinion into knowledge by means of recollecting the Forms necessary to provide an account for it. Furthermore, philosophy as a kind of *Erôs* can be related to both recollection and correct opinion. The philosopher is a lover, as one desirous of wisdom; and this human desire, like all others, is a form of that *Erôs* which Diotima claims is a messenger spirit binding together the divine and the mortal, and that, varying the metaphor, she also says is the offspring of Resource and Poverty, an offspring that shares in the natures of both parents. There must be a kind of contact with reality that enables *Erôs* to be resourceful like his father, at the same time as there is a kind of distance or separation from reality implied by the side of *Erôs* that comes from his mother. So although these three notions of being in-between (correct opinion, recollection, and *Erôs*) are clearly distinct, they all imply the same notion of simultaneous contact with and separation from reality. They all exemplify the principle that "that which is neither shares in both." Moreover, although not every desire encompassed by the concept of *Erôs* can be regarded as "recollection of Forms" simply by virtue of the claim that *Erôs* is a messenger, it is fairly clear from both the discussion of divine madness in the *Phaedrus* and from Diotima's account of the lover's ascent that the advanced form of *Erôs* known as philosophy *does* involve the recollection of Forms, and that some inkling of such a recollection is present whenever the human heart stirs with love.

As noted above, since all learning is said to be recollection, it would seem that *everyone*, insofar as he or she learns, must be said to be "in-between knowledge and ignorance in a certain sense." But not everyone is a philosopher conscious of their lack of wisdom, so that not everyone is in-between wisdom and ignorance in the way the philosopher is. For if it were so, the philosopher could not be contrasted with the ignorant who are self-satisfied. On the other hand, however, everyone does experience some form of love, and all love is said to involve the duality referred to above and to be "in-between" the mortal and the divine. Thus, everyone is in-between in the ways that the nature of love and recollection suggest, but the philosopher comes to be "in-between" in a special way *precisely by becoming aware of these kinds of intermediacy*. For it is the philosopher who becomes aware of lack and simultaneously is guided by a sense of what is lacked. The very awareness of lack that the philosophers have impels them closer to the wisdom of the divine.[5] Finally, however dimly each person may "recollect" Forms in their sense of what things are and what words mean, only philosophers can recollect the Forms as such, that is, in full awareness that what they are grasping is of another order, not to be confusedly identified with the particulars through which Forms are expressed in the realm of Becoming.

As one can see from the above discussions, Diotima's account of the intermediacy of *Erôs* illuminates both the notion of Socratic Ignorance from the *Apology* and the notion of Recollection from the *Meno*. One could say that Diotima's teachings about *Erôs* form a bridge between Socratic Ignorance and the Platonic notion of recollection, two themes that otherwise seem to be part of two entirely different conceptions of philosophy. Diotima's account of *Erôs*, beginning with its acknowledgment of the intermediate and the Socratic nature of philosophy as such and culminating in the glimpse or the promise of a recollection of a Form, suggests that Recollection and Socratic Ignorance belong together; and the erotic and intermediate nature of philosophy revealed itself in both Socratic Ignorance and Platonic Recollection as well.

But, as we have already suggested, there is not just a single conception of intermediacy at work in Plato's texts. In the sections that follow, we show that there are in fact a variety of distinct intermediates that must not be conflated. And yet, for all their variety, these various sorts of intermediates are intimately interrelated. Plato has provided his audience with all the clues necessary to piece together a rich and suggestive picture of the various kinds of intermediacy exhibited by human existence, in all their layers and mutual involvements. Becoming aware of these various types of intermediacy and their relations to one another will serve to make evident Plato's continual fascination with the subject of intermediacy and to further clarify his thoughts on the subject of *Erôs*. To this discussion we now turn.

## THREE TYPES OF INTERMEDIACY

We shall distinguish three distinct intermediates in Diotima's teaching—correct opinion, *Erôs* in general, and philosophy as a particular form of *Erôs*. The fact that three cases are analogous in their status as intermediates should not lead us simply to conflate them. They are not the same. For instance, it is clear that the ignorance that is contrasted with correct opinion is a *more extreme* notion than the ignorance that is contrasted with philosophy. For ignorance was distinguished from correct opinion merely by the latter's ability to "hit upon being." Thus, the kind of ignorance in question is an extreme form of ignorance, so extreme that it implies the lack of any correct opinions.[6] Clearly, this form of ignorance is not one that any normal person possesses; it is clearly not the kind of ignorance Socrates possesses and not the kind he finds in his interlocutors, for both Socratic Ignorance and the ignorance that is contrasted with philosophy are of such a kind that the people possessing them could possess many correct opinions. So, in a single dialogue, in close proximity to each other, we are shown three different kinds of ignorance. The first is an extreme notion of ignorance that would seem to be distinct from correct opinion and imply that a person in such a state would have no true beliefs.[7] The second understanding of ignorance is that of a lack of wisdom that is unaware of its own nature as a lack, that is, that involves a mistaken belief in one's wisdom. But although their beliefs about themselves are mistaken, such people can have some true beliefs. One of their mistakes may even be to fail to distinguish their true beliefs from actual knowledge. An instance of this failure might be the poets Socrates discusses in the *Apology*, who mistakenly believe that their poetic inspirations represent their own wisdom rather than the wisdom of the gods; but if such poetic products are divine in inspiration they probably do contain truths that the poets may correctly opine. Therefore, the ignorance of those who are unaware of their own ignorance might still include some true beliefs, and so it is not the same ignorance that contrasted with correct opinion by Diotima, for this ignorance precludes any true opinion, any contact with being. Finally, these two kinds of ignorance are clearly distinct from the self-aware ignorance of the philosopher that embodies philosophical *Erôs*. The philosopher may possess correct beliefs; thus, his ignorance cannot be ignorance of the first variety. Nor can it be the second kind of ignorance, obviously, since philosophers are specifically contrasted in the *Symposium* with those who are ignorant in this second way, those who are neither good nor wise but believe themselves to be sufficient (*hikanon* 204a). Socrates also contrasts ordinary ignorance with his own form of ignorance in the *Apology*.

In each case there are good philosophical reasons given in the text why the intermediates in question must be intermediate, and in the case of each intermediate these reasons are distinct. Correct opinion cannot be identical with knowledge because it does not include the ability to give an account of itself, and it cannot be identical with ignorance because it has some contact with reality. *Erôs* must partake of the natures of both Resource and Poverty. As a *daimon*, it is intermediate between the mortal and the divine. Desire must be directed at something that is in some sense lacked by the desirer, and yet that object is somehow brought into relation to the desirer through the desire itself. The philosopher, like Socrates, must be intermediate because he could not seek wisdom if he already possessed it, and yet he must possess some kind of knowledge or awareness or wisdom in order to be conscious of his need for inquiry. One might well ask how the three intermediates that one can distinguish in Diotima's teaching—namely correct opinion, *Erôs*, and philosophy—are related to each other.

Socrates' awareness of his own lack of knowledge could be a correct opinion rather than knowledge, but it would be a special correct opinion, a correct opinion about one's own lack of wisdom and a correct opinion about one's consequent need to seek wisdom. So perhaps Socrates' wisdom is a correct opinion but not knowledge about the human good, namely, the possibly correct opinion that the human good consists in seeking knowledge of the human good.[8] The correct opinion that he lacks knowledge might have led Socrates to the correct opinion that his good consists in seeking the knowledge he lacks. But if so, then his correct opinion has succeeded in provoking his *Erós*, his longing for the good that he lacks. The philosophical awareness of one's own ignorance transforms the disposition of *Erós* in the psyche; for all humans long for something, but becoming aware of one's ignorance through dialectic directs one's longing in a specific direction.

Therefore, when Socrates examines others who are ignorant and unaware of their own ignorance, he tries to make them aware of their ignorance and to bring them into the state he himself is already in, making them desire wisdom, that is, making them philosophize. He produces this effect in part through an examination of opinions. This examination involves the attempt on the part of the interlocutors to give accounts of what they believe. Socrates is able to show that their accounts are faulty. Ultimately the interlocutors are shown to be unable to offer an account that will stand, and this inability is taken to prove their ignorance. The idea that ignorance involves the inability to give an account of some opinion should be familiar as part of Socrates' practice. In the *Symposium*, correct opinion is said to be unlike knowledge (and closer to ignorance than knowledge is) because of its inability to give an account of itself. Of course, many of the opinions of Socrates' interlocutors may be false, but in some dialogues we are left to wonder if the interlocutor's opinion is not in fact true, and what Socrates is doing is simply exposing their inability to defend it and by this means revealing their ignorance.

But although all the interlocutors remain ignorant in this sense of being unable to offer an adequate account, some of them do, temporarily at least, become aware of their ignorance through contact with Socrates. They then cease to be ignorant in a sense that implies a lack of awareness of their own ignorance, however temporarily. If one considers the kinds of ignorance distinguished above one can see that Socrates is taking his interlocutors from the second type of ignorance, one that is unaware of itself as ignorance and involves a mistaken belief that one knows what one does not, to the third type, the ignorance of the philosopher who understands that he lacks the wisdom of the Gods. This third type of ignorance, like the second, may involve the possession of true beliefs, but unlike the second form of ignorance, it always presupposes that such beliefs are clearly distinguished from knowledge, and that the philosopher is thus aware that she cannot be certain whether such beliefs are in fact true.[9] This third type of ignorance lies between wisdom and the second form of ignorance that involves the false belief in one's own wisdom. Furthermore, this third kind of ignorance, being aware that it is a lack of wisdom, promotes the philosophical *Erós* for wisdom. In doing so, it

redirects the *Erôs* that was already active in the interlocutor's psyche, directing it away from what they formerly desired when they believed they already
possessed sufficient wisdom, and directing it toward a clearer and truer conception of what is more immediately (and perhaps even ultimately) good for
them—namely, the quest for wisdom or the acquisition of wisdom to whatever extent it is possible.

One might well ask how the three intermediates that one can distinguish
in Diotima's teaching—namely correct opinion, *Erôs*, and philosophy—are
related to the intermediacy of Recollection. But before making this connection, we will consider further notions that in Plato's *Republic* are described as
intermediate (*metaxu*): opinion in general, and Becoming.

## THE INTERMEDIACIES OF OPINION
## AND BECOMING IN THE *REPUBLIC*

In *Republic* V, Socrates is talking about opinion as such (and not merely
correct opinion as Diotima did in the *Symposium*). According to Socrates,
opinion is said to be coordinate with something that partakes of both being
and nonbeing. This something turns out to be the world of change and relativity that most humans take for the whole of reality. In the *Timaeus* this
region of reality is referred to as "Becoming" (*genesis* 27d–28a). In *Republic*
V it is not the changing nature of Becoming in the ordinary sense of change
that Socrates emphasizes, but relativity or what is sometimes called "aspect
change" or "compresence of opposites." In Becoming one finds the ontological ground for the in-between state in which humans find themselves in connection with recollection and *Erôs*.

At *Republic* 475e, Socrates is about to begin his characterization of what
a true philosopher is, and what sort of education is necessary to fit the philosopher for the ruler's role. To this end, Socrates brings in the Forms:[10]

> And in respect of just and unjust, the good and the bad, and all the ideas or
> forms, the same statement holds, that each itself is one, but that by virtue of
> their communion with actions and bodies and with one another they present
> themselves everywhere each as a multiplicity of aspects. (476a)[11]

Socrates then explains what sets the true philosophers apart from the lovers of sights and sounds; the philosophers are those few who can see the nature
of the beautiful itself, etc. In this connection, the distinction between wakefulness and dreaming is introduced. Dreaming has to do with taking something that is like something else to be like it in a way in which it is not. For
instance, when dreaming that one is chased by a tiger, one typically *believes*
one is being chased by a tiger; thus, the dream-image of the tiger is mistaken
for a real tiger. The dream-image of the tiger is like a tiger in some ways, but
in other ways it is clearly not. Dreaming involves failing to distinguish the two
things in question; one so fails to notice the ways in which the image is not

like the original that one takes the image for the original. Note the ambiguity involved in the notion of dreaming: as an image is both like and not like an original—the thing about which one is mistaken is both like and not-like something else. Socrates uses the metaphor of dreaming to point toward a similar confusion made by the ordinary, nonphilosophical person: the failure to distinguish the Form from its associated particulars. Just as a kind of confusion of image for original happens in a dream when one believes that one is actually undergoing the experiences in the dream, thus taking images for reality, so those who make no distinctions between Forms and particulars are likewise confusing images for reality. But the true philosophers, in contrast, can make this distinction successfully and are thus comparatively "awake."

At 476d, knowledge and opinion (γνώμην and δόξαν) are then identified with the state of wakefulness and the state of dreaming, respectively (476d5–6). Socrates then asks Glaucon: "Does he who knows know [γιγώσκει] something or nothing?"(476e7). Glaucon answers that he knows something, whereupon Socrates asks: "Something that is or is not?" First we must note the two steps involved here: first, they rule out that knowing can be directed at nothing (οὐκ ὄν 476e10; μὴ ὄν 477a1) at all. Then, once they have agreed that it must be something rather than nothing, Socrates asks Glaucon to consider whether this is something that is in being or not. Glaucon says: "How could one know something that was not being?"

Next, Socrates anticipates by mentioning the possibility of something that could both be and not be, and says that it would lie between (metaxu) that which purely is (τοῦ εἰλικρινῶς ὄντος) and that which in no way is (τοῦ αὖ μηδαμῇ ὄντος 477a7). He then points out that if knowledge must be directed to being and ignorance to nonbeing, as they have agreed, then for something between being and nonbeing, they would have to find something between knowledge (ἐπιστήμης) and ignorance (ἀγνοίας) to be directed to it, if there happened to be some such thing (477b1).

Socrates next establishes that opinion (δόξα) and knowledge (ἐπιστήμη) are different. Socrates then introduces the idea that "powers" (δυνάμεως) can only be known by their objects and their effects (477c-d). He then gets Glaucon to agree to assign both knowledge and opinion to the genus of powers. When Socrates gets Glaucon to reiterate that knowledge and opinion are nonetheless not identical, Glaucon brings out another reason that they are not identical: "How could any one of intelligence affirm that the fallible and the infallible are the same?" (477e)

Socrates then says that knowledge must be of what is. But they hold it to be impossible for opinion to have the same object, because Glaucon takes them to have agreed that different powers must have different objects.[12] So, if *that which is* is the knowable, the opinable must be something else. But even false opinion cannot be directed at just nothing at all. So opinion can be directed neither to that which is nor to that which is not. Thus, opinion is neither knowledge nor ignorance (478c 3–4).

Compare and contrast what is said about opinion in general in this passage and what is said of correct opinion in the *Symposium*. There, correct opinion is distinguished from knowledge by the inability to provide an account. In the *Republic*, one reason why opinion in general cannot be knowledge is that opinion is fallible—it can be false. Knowledge must be true and infallible. Clearly, it is not the truth of knowledge that separates it from correct opinion, if correct opinions are also true; but it must be the infallibility of knowledge that distinguishes it, for even correct opinions, although they are true, may in a certain sense be fallible. Indeed, the fallibility of even correct opinions, in contrast to knowledge, may be tied to the feature that is said to distinguish correct opinions from knowledge in the *Symposium*, namely, that correct opinion is incapable of providing an account of itself. That is, a correct opinion affords no reasoning that demonstrates *why* the opinion is true and therefore warrants belief in it. Opinion is not knowledge because opinion, unlike knowledge, can come in two varieties, the true and the false (See *Grg.* 454d). But even false opinion is not about nothing at all, and so even a false opinion, just in order to be meaningful, must make some contact with Being.

But opinion is not knowledge not merely because it can be false as well as true; even when true, opinion is not knowledge because it is still fallible. But the fallibility of a correct opinion is connected to the fact that it is incapable of providing itself with an account that justifies it.[13]

Moreover, correct opinion, like opinion in general, must make some contact with Being; but correct opinion must make another kind of contact with Being above and beyond the contact with Being made by mere opinion. Just as opinion in general and correct opinion are distinguished from knowledge in ways distinct from one another in these two texts, they are also distinguished from ignorance in two different ways. Opinion cannot be ignorance since it is not aiming at nothing at all. To opine nothing would be not to opine. This idea suggests a kind of contact with being but of a more basic kind than that said to characterize correct opinion in the *Symposium*. In the *Symposium* discussion of correct opinion, it was in virtue of *truth* that true opinion has contact with Being; in the *Republic* discussion of opinion in general, it seems to be in virtue of mere *meaningfulness* that opinions in general, true or false, must possess some contact with Being.[14] This difference is not an incompatibility, however, since it is reasonable to think language has contact with Being through both meaning and truth; it is also reasonable to note that these two forms of contact must be distinguishable, since meaningfulness does not imply truth.[15]

The ignorance of Book 5 of the *Republic*, being coordinate with total nonbeing, is no ordinary ignorance. This conception of ignorance is an extreme or exaggerated conception similar to the one we found earlier in considering the ignorance distinguished from correct opinion in the *Symposium*. For ordinary ignorance does not preclude opinions—indeed, a person who has false opinions would be taken to be ignorant in an ordinary sense about those things concerning which she/he had false opinions. And as noted previously, the distinction between knowledge and correct opinion implies that one could be ignorant even of those things of which one has a correct opinion.

Having established opinion's place between knowledge and the extreme form of ignorance, Socrates recalls their earlier agreement that if something was such as both to be and not to be it would lie between that which purely is and that which wholly is not (τὸ τοιοῦτον μεταξὺ κεῖσθαι τοῦ εἰλικρινῶς ὄντος τε καὶ τοῦ πάντως μὴ ὄντος 478d6–7). The power coordinated with it would be neither knowledge nor ignorance, but something between knowledge and ignorance. Now, opinion appears to be such a power between knowledge and ignorance. So next Socrates turns to consider whether there can be something in-between that which purely is and that which entirely is not, namely, something that "partakes of both, to be and not to be, and could rightly be said to be neither purely" (το ἀμφοτέρων μετέχον, τοῦ εἶναί τε καὶ μὴ εἶναι, καὶ οὐδέτερον εἰλικρινὲς ὀρθῶς ἂν προσαγορευόμενον 478e1–3).

To sum up the argument: (1) knowledge is coordinate with Being and ignorance with Nonbeing. (2) There must be different coordinate objects to distinguish between different powers. (3) Opinion is a power distinct from knowledge, and falls in between the knowledge and ignorance. Hence the conclusion: There would seem to need to be something coordinate with opinion that falls between the objects of the powers on either side. This something could only be somehow between being and nonbeing. Socrates has then only to show that it can make sense to say that there is something with this status. In fact, he shows that what most humans would usually take to be reality, physical reality, has just this nature.

His explanation of the intermediacy of Becoming is important for the purpose of coming to a fuller understanding of the intermediacies of opinion, Recollection, and Erôs. The many beautiful and just things (the particulars) are characterized by relativity—they are beautiful at some times and not at others, in some ways and not in others. The sense in which they both are and are not is that they both are and are not F—where F is some property ascribed to them or some Form in which they participate. The Forms are "always F" because the Form just is identical with the F in question, the property itself. The Form *is* the property, *not* something that *has* the property. The Forms are also not the property-instance, that is, they are not the "property" in the sense of a mere attribute inherent in some substance. Rather the Form as property is what all the property-instances share that make them instances of the same property. The particular is nonidentical with the property F and *just for that very reason* is also non-F, even while having F as a property, that is, even while possessing a property-instance of the property F. This way of also not being F—not being identical to the Form F—is a condition of the possibility that the particular can fail to be F in any relation and or any time, that is, can fail to be F in every possible way. For clearly, had it been identical with the property it would have to be F at every place and every time; and the Form F is not merely F in some particular way, but is rather the ground for every possible way of being F, since all these possible ways of being F are F in virtue of some relation or other to the Form. One can recognize the familiar ambiguity known to students of Plato's metaphysics between the sense in which the property F or the Form of F is F, on the one hand, and the sense in which the bearer of the property F is F, on the other.[16]

So the sense in which Becoming is between being and nonbeing, and indeed a kind of mixture of them, is now made clear. This notion of the mixture of Being and Nonbeing depends upon the same kind of Nonbeing relied on in the *Sophist*—*not being F*, or *being different from F*. At the basis of all such *being different from F* is *being nonidentical to F*.[17]

Thus, we see two main kinds of difference: (1) nonidentity and (2) having different properties than something else. Nonidentity is more basic because it applies to the properties (or Forms) themselves and not just to things that have properties (or that participate in Forms). One distinguishes different particulars in terms of their different properties (their participations in different Forms), but one cannot distinguish the properties (the Forms) themselves this way. The properties are *not* themselves different because they *have* different properties, that is, the Forms are not different from one another by virtue of *participating* in different Forms. A property (or Form) F is different from other properties (Forms), G, H, etc. by virtue of being nonidentical with them. It is the nonidentity of the properties (Forms) themselves that enables all differentiation between bearers of properties (the participants in Forms) to take place. It may not be obvious that Plato is really distinguishing between these two kinds of difference in *Republic* V. But this distinction is bound up with the distinction between the realm of Being on the one hand and that which both is and is not, on the other. That which both is and is not is the realm of the many particulars that have some property F at a given time or in a given relation but do not have the property at other times or in other relations. The realm of Being is the realm of what is always F, for a given F, in the precise sense that F itself is always F in all its relations. But the Forms themselves are clearly distinct from each other, being nonidentical. And the particulars do seem to be identified and differentiated by the properties they possess. Their "mixed" reality is regarded as being in some sense dependent on the prior, more fundamental reality of the Forms. So it would seem that Plato is aware that nonidentity (by which we mean *being* nonidentical properties as opposed to merely *having* them) is the more fundamental kind of difference.

Hence, that which is neither being nor nonbeing but partakes of both is brought in to be the object of opinion. This mixture of Being and Nonbeing is meant to explain how opinion can be between knowledge and ignorance, that is, how opinion, while not aiming at *what is* in the way that knowledge does, can nonetheless also have *something* as its object (rather than pointing at utter nonbeing).[18] A consequence of this explanation is that the empirical world is not an object of knowledge but rather the object of opinion; presumably, the empirical world cannot be known in the strict sense because it is equivocal (changing and relative), so that whatever is asserted of it can never be absolutely true, where absoluteness implies independence of temporal and other coordinates. Anything one calls F is also not F in some way, except for F itself. For this reason the only "absolute" form of knowledge is what one can know directly about the Fs themselves (the Forms). One does have some understanding of what the property F itself is, and this understanding is independent of the question of whether anything instantiates F and where and when things do. It may be impossible to give an adequate account of F, and one may think that eternal truths about F are bound to be trivial; yet one does have a significant knowledge of F insofar as one can distinguish it from different properties G, H, etc. and from the particular things that are F in the sense of bearing F as a property. For example, one can distinguish fatness as such from a particular fat thing, and also fatness from other properties such as thinness, height, etc. A particular fat thing may be fat in some respects and not in others, or fatter at some times than at others. But fatness itself is neither fat nor thin, since it does not bear itself or its contrary as a property; rather it just *is* the property of fatness, different from other properties in terms of pure nonidentity and not by virtue of other properties it itself possesses.

In this section of the *Republic* Socrates sets out to contrast the knowledge coordinate with Forms with mere opinion, and therewith to justify the rule of those who possess knowledge. In order to do this, Socrates has had to present this account of that which lies between being and nonbeing. He calls it "the wanderer between being caught by the power between" (τῇ μεταξὺ δυνάμει τὸ μεταξὺ πλανητὸν ἁλισκόμενον 479d8–9). If, on Plato's view, Being is akin to divinity and Becoming is of the essence of mortality, then the *Republic* V discussion can be read as an ontological/logical presentation of what is presented in another, more mythic way in Diotima's speech. The Book V account illuminates the sense in which human *Erôs* finds itself in a region between. It should be quite clear that "That which both is and is not" involves both contact with and separation from the Forms. Thus, Becoming itself shares a feature with *Erôs*: for in its mixture of Being and Nonbeing it might be seen as a mixture of Resource and Poverty, having elements of both divine and mortal. A particular bears its attribute or property-instance as though it were a message from the Form in which it participates. But nonetheless, *Erôs* is more than just Becoming, as we shall see.

## VARIETIES OF INTERMEDIACY

We have seen at least six distinct intermediates: (1) correct opinion, (2) *Erôs* (these first two in the *Symposium*), (3) Philosophy (in the *Symposium* and

*Apology*), (4) Recollection (in the *Meno*, the *Phaedo*, the *Phaedrus*), (5) Opinion in general, and finally (6) Becoming, that which partakes in both being
and nonbeing (the last two in *Republic* V). In the case of all the kinds of
intermediacy that have appeared in these dialogues the in-between state is
not a merely neutral state, possessing neither of the attributes constituting
the extremes. Instead, it is conceived as a hybrid of the extremes, or at least
as possessing attributes it shares with each of the extremes. Correct opinion has one attribute that it shares with knowledge (contact with reality) and
another that it shares with ignorance (the inability to give an account). *Erôs*
is a hybrid of Poverty and Resource possessing the attributes of both of his
parents. The Philosopher/Socrates possesses both a kind of wisdom and a
kind of ignorance. Socrates calls his ignorance "human wisdom" as opposed
to divine wisdom (*Ap.* 20d-e), and even questions whether it should be called
wisdom at all (*Ap.* 20e). Yet it certainly makes him wiser than his interlocutors (*Ap.* 21d-e). Recollection is a way of knowing and not-knowing at the
same time; its in-between status is crucial to its being able to avoid the horns
of the dilemma in Meno's paradox. Opinion is coordinate with that which
both is and is not, that which partakes in both being and nonbeing. Becoming is said to be a mixture of Being and Nonbeing.

Despite these formal similarities, it is clear that we have distinct notions
of the intermediate here. Philosophers are specifically contrasted in the *Symposium* with the ignorant, and in this case ignorance is not a total blankness,
but rather the ignorant are conceived as possessing a certain opinion about
themselves. So the intermediate conception of philosophy/Socrates is not to
be identified with the intermediacy of opinion, since opinion lies between
total nescience and knowledge. And opinion as a whole obviously cannot be
identified with correct opinion; the latter is clearly only a species of the former. Of course, neither opinion nor one of its species can be identified with
the object of opinion, that which partakes in being and nonbeing. It is also
obvious this "ontological" intermediate is not to be identified with Socratic
Ignorance. Nor can the intermediacy of *Erôs* in general simply be identified with the intermediacy of philosophical *Erôs*, since all humans possess
*Erôs* without it usually taking a very philosophical form (even if Diotima's
identification of *Erôs* as a philosopher suggests that the particular species of
*Erôs* called philosophy is somehow deeply connected to and illustrative of the
nature of *Erôs* in general).

In each case there are good philosophical reasons given in the text as
to why the intermediates in question must be intermediate, and in the case
of each intermediate these reasons are distinct. (1) Correct opinion cannot
be identical with knowledge because it does not include the ability to give
an account of itself, and it cannot be identical with ignorance because it
has some contact with reality. (2) *Erôs* must partake of the natures of both
Resource and Poverty and, as a *daimon*, is intermediate between the mortal
and the divine; the intermediacy of *Erôs* is connected to the philosophical

point that desire must be directed at something that is in a certain sense lacked by the desirer, and yet is somehow brought into relation to the desirer through the desire itself. (3) Socrates, or the philosopher in general, must be intermediate because he could not seek wisdom if he thought he already possessed it, and yet must possess some kind of knowledge or awareness or wisdom in order to be conscious of his need for inquiry. (4) Recollection must be able to escape between the horns of the dilemma found in Meno's paradox since learning would be impossible if one had to learn either what one already knew or else something of which one was so ignorant that one possessed no standard by which even to begin the search. (5) Opinion cannot be identical with knowledge because it can be false and yet it cannot be ignorance (in an extreme sense) because it too has some contact with reality. It is clear that the kind of contact with reality a specifically correct opinion has must be something over and above the contact that it has simply in virtue of being an opinion, or else the distinction between opinion and correct opinion would collapse. Finally, (6) the reason why the many particulars in the world of Becoming must be seen as intermediate is not as simple and clear-cut, but with a little reflection it can be understood. The relativity of the particulars, the fact that they can possess a property F in one relation and not in another, is what is said to constitute their intermediacy. They are being contrasted with a complete lack of properties, nonbeing, on the one hand, and with the properties themselves (i.e., the Forms), which are necessarily always identical to themselves, on the other. Whether or not Plato endorses the views of any of the characters speaking in these texts, one can see that he has presented six different intermediates, together with good or at least plausible philosophical reasons for considering them to be intermediates.

Moreover, these distinct intermediates are necessarily related. Philosophy is impossible without opinions to examine and without the distinction between knowledge and opinion. Without that distinction the philosopher could not be contrasted with those who have the false opinion that they know what they do not. Furthermore, such a false opinion about oneself can be obtained by confusing correct opinion with knowledge; therefore, to possess the kind of wisdom Socrates seeks, it is clearly not enough to possess correct opinion. Consequently, it is not only the contrast between knowledge and opinion that is essential for philosophy, but also the more specific contrast between knowledge and correct opinion. The philosopher would like to eliminate false opinions and transform true opinions into knowledge.

Next, it is obvious that any account of opinion in general must apply to correct opinion in particular, and that any account of correct opinion leaves a space for an account of opinion in general. If opinion alone had turned out to be intermediate, one could infer that correct opinion was intermediate in the same way (being a species of opinion), but one could not infer anything about what constitutes its specificity as a correct opinion. If correct opinion alone had turned out to be intermediate, one could not infer anything about opinion in general. As it is, correct opinion must share in the kind of inter-mediacy possessed by opinion in general, but then must possess a distinct intermediacy of its own over and above it. Clearly, one of these accounts alone would leave a gap to be filled in by the other; putting them together, one achieves a fuller, more complete view of the matters in question. In both cases the intermediate in question is said to have a kind of contact with real-ity. But in the case of opinions in general (which can clearly be either true or false), the contact is a contact by virtue of *meaningfulness*, whereas in the case of correct opinion an *additional* kind of contact is clearly required. A correct opinion must also be meaningful and so it possesses the former sense of contact, but in addition it is somehow more in touch with reality than false opinion, and so it possesses a second kind of contact with reality as well that constitutes its correctness.

The sixth intermediacy—that which both is and is not—is required to explain how the intermediacy of opinion is possible. What makes it possible for opinion to have a kind of contact with being while yet being fallible is that opinion is directed toward something that partakes of both being and nonbeing. Recall that the intermediacy of Becoming is constituted by the fact that a thing that possesses property F is not identical to property F and so can possess that property in one relation and not in another. This fact means that when a particular is said to be F in a simple unqualified way, there is always a question of how this assertion is understood, for if true, it will be true in only specific senses (and at specific times) and false in others. Since the bearers of properties possess these properties without being identical to them, their relationship to them is in a certain sense contingent, namely, in the sense that there is no necessity that they possess these properties in every relation (including temporal relations) in which they are considered. To the extent that the bearing of properties is contingent, there is no rational account pos-sible that will guarantee that a particular will have a given property, and thus any claim about particulars in Becoming is without rational warrant; nothing compels such a claim to be true, and if it is only shown to be true by sensation, the evidence in question is still a matter of contingency and requires one to take the senses on trust; whereas a rational account of relations among Forms themselves deals with necessary relations among the properties and not con-tingent relations between the properties and changeable bearers of proper-ties. Insights into the relations between the properties or Forms themselves grasp necessity and compel assent, but no longer necessarily pertain to the changing world of Becoming; for this reason knowledge is coordinated with the realm of Being or Forms and only opinion is coordinated with the realm of Becoming with its relativity and contingency.[19] One sees here the ground of the difference between necessary a priori truths and contingent, empiri-cal truths, and with respect to contingent claims, the ground of both true propositions and false propositions; for propositions are true when a thing has the property it is asserted to have in a certain relation and false when it does not. In case of propositions about Forms, a proposition is true and necessary when a given Form has the necessary formal relation to another Form that it is asserted to have, and false (necessarily false) when it does not. If such a proposition is true, the necessity on which it is based can render it knowledge if that necessity is noetically beheld. In the case of contingent claims, that is, matters of opinion, a proposition is true when a particular that is asserted by the proposition to bear a given property in a given relation does indeed do so, and false when it does not do so. In either case there is some "contact" with being, since the propositions in question refer to the property F, although in the case of the contingent, empirical claim there is also a reference to a changing bearer of properties; the property itself, referred to in each case, is a species of Being, a Form. But we can also see that a *correct* opinion has an *additional* "contact" with Being insofar as the correct opinion is not merely referring to a real property or Form, but in addition is also *correctly depicting its possession by a particular*. Reflecting on the sixth intermediacy, that which partakes of both being and nonbeing, not only explains the intermediacy of opinion, its difference from knowledge and mere ignorance, but even serves to clarify the difference between the intermediacy of opinion in general and that of correct opinion in particular. Similarly, falsity is explained by a claim attributing to a particular a property it does not possess, or attributing to it possession of that property in a relation in which it does not possess it (in the case of empirical claims), or in the case of an a priori claim, asserting a formal relation between properties or Forms that does not in fact obtain. As the *Sophist* explains, falsity can remain meaningful in either case because one's thinking and assertion still pertain to the being of the Forms and the becoming of particulars even if one is misconstruing the relations of these elements; falsity is not referring to nothing, but construing what is in a way other than it actually is.

But we should here bring in a seventh intermediate: the psyche of the universe itself. According to the *Timaeus*, the psyche is compounded of both Being and Becoming. The Forms of the Same, the Different, and Being are combined in the psyche in two versions, one indivisible and changeless, and another that is divisible and comes to be (*Tim.* 35a-b). But if the psyche is composed of Being and Becoming, and if Becoming is a mixture of Being and Nonbeing, one could say that the psyche consists of two parts Being to one part Nonbeing. What this idea indicates is that the psyche, unlike merely physical becoming, *has an additional mode of contact with Being*, that is, with the Forms. For the psyche does not merely participate in the Forms; it can also become *aware* of the Forms in which it and material entities participate. The psyche does not merely participate in Forms, but displays intentionality, that is, directedness at Forms over and above mere participation in them, a directedness, or an additional kind of "participation" by means of consciousness. It is the intermediacy of the psyche that explains the distinction between the intermediacy of *Erôs* and the intermediacy of Becoming as such;

for *Erôs* is the very nature of the psyche. The psyche is a *daimon*, partaking of the mortal in its association with change and of the divine in its association with unchanging Forms (see the *Phaedo* 79c-e). Each particular in Becoming, in participating in its Form, is in a sense "directed" at Being; but the psyche in desiring its own good through all of its more specific desires is also always directed at Forms, in two ways: (1) the psyche desires some particular in virtue of some quality that the particular receives via participation in a Form, but also (2) in desiring that particular the psyche always desires its own good, and desires to possess that good forever; and in desiring to possess its own good forever, the psyche is in fact desiring an additional contact with the Forms, including the vision of Beauty Itself that presumably can lead on to the Form of the Good. It is because the reality of Becoming points toward unchanging Being in its very participation in the Forms that the psyche's *Erôs*, sensitive to both Being and Becoming, can long for the Being reflected in Becoming and can thus feel the desire for eternality of Being, that is, the desire to "possess the good forever" of which Diotima speaks. This desire for something eternal, for the Beings that are only hinted at by Becoming, is the erotic root of Recollection.

Recollection occurs when *Erôs'* hybrid or bivalent nature makes known to the psyche its lack and the lack of all things in Becoming, thereby acting as a "messenger from the divine." Recollection is nothing other than just these messages from the divine, that is, from the Forms, imparted by *Erôs*. These messages are themselves dual and ambivalent, in that Recollection remains partial, just as in the Allegory of the Cave the philosopher's eyesight must pass by degrees through intermediate stages of brightness and darkness in the paths both out of and back into the Cave of becoming. The philosopher, lying between the ignorance of false wisdom and the true wisdom of the Gods, is the one whose *Erôs* has awakened the recollective power of the psyche. In the nonphilosopher the messages speak merely of the physical realm and only confusedly and implicitly of the Forms reflected in it; in the philosopher, possessed of the philosophical *Erôs* for wisdom, the messages of *Erôs* speak more clearly of the higher realm of Being at which the physical world only hints. It is these clearer messages of *Erôs* that constitute philosophical Recollection. Yet, since the philosopher remains human and erotic, the recollective messages of *Erôs* never translate the philosopher into the realm of the gods or provide him with divine status. Yet owing to the intermediacy of Becoming and the closer connection to Being found in the intermediacy of the psyche, as a result of the intermediacy of opinion by which the psyche relates to the intermediacy of Becoming, owing to an even closer connection to Being possessed by true opinion and the still closer connection to Being found in the recollective messages of *Erôs*, it is possible for humans to be more or less aware of the difference between Becoming and Being, and more or less aware of the difference between knowledge and mere opinion (whether true or false opinion). This possibility enables the philosopher to exist, as the one who is most aware of these differences and therefore erotically strives to achieve a closer contact with Being by passing from mere opinion to knowledge.

All human beings find themselves "in-between" with the intermediacy of *Erôs* and even with the intermediacy of Recollection. For *Erôs* itself, which all humans possess, is said to be in-between, and Recollection implies that in a sense all humans are "between ignorance and knowledge," in that it implies that they have knowledge in one sense that in another sense they do not. There is thus a sense in which all humans are in-between, and this state is clearly a different sense than the sense that is characteristic of Socrates, the philosopher, or in the sense that the *Symposium* locates philosophers, since Socrates in the *Apology* and philosophers (as such) in the *Symposium* are contrasted with the nonphilosophers who make up the bulk of humanity. One can call this intermediacy that all humans share the intermediacy of the human condition as such.[20] But this intermediacy of the human condition is best seen as a compound of other intermediates and a potentiality for one of them. In other words, (1) all humans are particulars with contingent properties and thus partake of both being and nonbeing. Moreover, (2) all humans have psyches that are compounded of mixtures of Being and Becoming (according to the *Timaeus*); in addition, (3) all humans have opinions and some correct opinions, and (4) all humans possess erotic desire, an *Erôs* that is a messenger between the divine and mortal realms (whether or not humans are aware of that messenger role). Finally, (5) humans, or at least some of them, have the *capacity* (whether or not it is ever actualized in a given case) to *recognize* their need to strive to replace their opinions with knowledge; that is, some humans can become more aware of their erotic need, awakening and developing their *Erôs* and climbing with it up the stages of Diotima's erotic ascent. Humans may possess the intermediacy of Becoming, the intermediacy of the psyche, the intermediacy of *Erôs*, the intermediacy of opinion and the intermediacy of correct opinion. With luck, some at least can come to experience the intermediacy of the philosopher through philosophical *Erôs* and Recollection.

## FORMS AND INTERMEDIACY

Clearly, Plato was interested in intermediacy, interested enough to make his characters discuss various notions of it in various texts. It is also clear that these distinct intermediacies fit together into a more comprehensive, coherent picture. On the one hand, one finds an outline of the intermediacy of the human condition that involves the intermediacies of Becoming, the psyche, *Erôs*, opinion, and correct opinion; on the other hand, one finds an outline of the intermediacy of philosophy and Recollection, the intermediacy of the philosopher who examines opinion and seeks to pass from opinion to knowledge. It seems clear that other well-known Platonic images of the philosophic process, such as Socratic midwifery or journeying out of the Cave, could be brought in to enrich this picture. Indeed, one might also discuss further levels of intermediacy, such as the intermediacy of *dianoia* between *doxa* and *nous*, and with it the intermediacy of the dianoetic objects, the so-called "mathematical intermediates"; and one could go on to discuss the image of the Divided Line in this perspective. But in this context, it is enough to have shown that Plato's texts offer this rich, complex, and yet coherent picture of various forms of intermediacy. For these accounts of the various forms of intermediacy are *necessarily* related to the idea of Forms. There is no way to understand what is meant by a Form in the dialogues without understanding the contrast between Being and Becoming, that is, between the Forms and the many particulars that participate in them. That means that in order to understand a Form one must contrast it with the kind of intermediacy found in the *Republic* V, the intermediacy of that which both is and is not. Furthermore, one cannot understand the Forms without understanding their epistemic implications, and that implies the difference between opinion and knowledge (as the passages from *Republic* V and *Timaeus* 51d–52d and their context make clear). The Forms are that for which philosophical *Erôs* longs and that which philosophical recollection recollects; their pursuit of the knowledge of Forms is what sets the philosopher apart from the nonphilosopher. Hence, the Forms discussed in Plato's texts *are just one part of a larger picture, a picture in which the main emphasis is on intermediacy.*

The Forms seem to be brought in to enable us to understand this intermediacy, to isolate or account for one aspect of it. In any case, since the Forms are necessarily related to the intermediacy of the human condition, the Forms are also necessarily related to the theme of Socratic Ignorance. They are not just related in the weak sense that both of these ideas appear in Plato and might have been parts of divergent views that he held at various points of his life. The hypothesis of Forms is part of the explanation of the difference between knowledge and opinion; Socratic Ignorance depends on the distinction between knowledge and opinion. One might think that this only shows that Plato discusses the same topic, knowledge versus opinion, in two different ways at different points of his career. But there are links between the various kinds of intermediacy. Plato's Diotima seems to make a kind of loose analogy between correct opinion and philosophy as Socratically ignorant by discussing their analogous forms of intermediacy in close proximity to each other in the *Symposium*, notwithstanding the fact that they are clearly distinct intermediates. Hence, one of the Platonic characters makes an analogy between two of the intermediates distinguished above. One of these intermediates, correct opinion, is further clarified by the *Republic* discussion of opinion in general. And the nature of opinion in general is explained in the *Republic* by means of a contrast between the kind of being possessed by the Forms, on the one hand, and the intermediacy of the many particulars, on the other. So we could say that these intermediates are linked in a chain, in which two of the links, between correct opinion and Socratic Philosophy in the *Symposium* and between opinion and its object in *Republic* V, are links evident in the texts themselves. It matters not for our argument that the former link is only an analogical one, for that is sufficient to demonstrate authorial awareness of the relevant connection. The one link not "in" the texts but joining the text of the *Symposium* with the account in the *Republic* is the logical link between correct opinion and its genus, opinion in general. This connection is of course one that Plato saw, as demonstrated by the fact that the explanation of the intermediacy of opinion in the light of the intermediacy of Becoming seems to provide a ground for clarifying the distinction between opinion and correct opinion.

Furthermore, both a conception of philosophy as Socratically ignorant and a vision of the Forms appear in close conjunction as part of the teaching of Diotima. It is the height of implausibility to suggest that these features both appear in this dialogue because this dialogue is "transitional" and so incorporates elements from different stages in Plato's philosophical thinking.[21] One would have to suppose that Plato put these ideas together without being able to connect them in his consciousness. The mutual coherence of these diverse notions of intermediacy tells against that possibility.

The relationship between the Forms and their associated particulars is the ground of all the varieties of intermediacy noted above. The Forms are both present and absent, ontologically speaking, in the realm of Becoming. Becoming is seen as mixture of Being (Forms) with Nonbeing. The particulars around us are said to participate (*metechein*) in the Forms, and yet none of them is the Form; in several respects each particular falls short of the Form. The particulars in a sense both have and do not have the characteristic engendered in them by the Form. The Form is present in all its particulars by participation, but it transcends the particulars at the same time, and so in a very real sense is present in none of them. The Forms are both in contact with the particulars that participate in them, in some figurative and nonspatial sense of contact, and distant from them as well, in some figurative and nonspatial sense of distance. They are immanent in one respect and transcendent in another.

This ontological fact regarding the relation of Forms to the world of Becoming and to humans as denizens of that world has an epistemic consequence. For our knowledge is a part of Becoming as well in a certain sense (Cf. *Symposium* 208a-b). When one considers each of the dialogues in which the Forms are prominent, one can see that the *distance* of the human mind from the Forms is being emphasized at least as much as its *partial contact* with them. Consider the following brief characterizations of the role of the Forms in the dialogues in which they prominently appear:

*Phaedo*—Epistemic distance from the Forms in emphasized here, for Socrates holds that in this life one cannot get a secure grasp on Forms and that one may be closer to them when the soul is liberated from the body. Upon reading the *Phaedo*, it is unclear whether the hypothesis of Forms is more important as a dogma on which to base belief in immortality or as a hope meant to encourage one in the face of death.

It is interesting that in both the *Phaedrus* and the *Symposium* the Forms are connected with the theme of love. As the ultimate object of Love the Forms appear as what is absent and lacked, and therefore as only "present in the mode of absence." One's awareness of Forms in this life comes only by means of dim recollection, indirect for the most part, though this indirect awareness goads the mind toward philosophy, which seems to promise the possibility of a more direct awareness of reality.[22]

In the *Republic*, the epistemic distance from a grasp of the Forms is again emphasized, not only by the fact that Socrates is himself no philosopher-king, even though he introduces such knowers of Forms; Socrates' distance from the knowledge required of philosopher-kings is also set at a remove by the incredible educational program described as being necessary to assure that the philosopher-rulers have a grasp of eternal, unchanging reality through the *Eidē*. This educational program is one that cannot have been completed either by the Platonic Socrates or even by Plato himself. Socrates' insistence upon it makes clear the kind of discipline and study that separates humans, even lovers of wisdom, from the knowledge of the Forms.

In the *Parmenides*, the "Forms" are a pet theory of the young Socrates that is attacked by the elder Parmenides. Then Parmenides suggests and illustrates a method for enabling Socrates to defend his thesis. But this method again emphasizes epistemic distance from, that is, current incomprehension of, the Forms. For not many would be capable of the exercise that Parmenides undertakes, nor be capable of its general application as a philosophical method, nor would many understand its application to the problems raised in the first part of the dialogue. Plato seems to set a barrier between the Forms and claimants to knowledge, a challenge to true philosophers—a barrier that is very high and hard to scale.

In the *Philebus*, the effect does not seem to bring the Forms closer, but instead to posit the methodological ideal of using collection and division to grasp the "one and the many" in each area of study. This procedure for attaining this ideal—even after the fecund suggestion that a "different device" may be needed—again places the knowledge of Forms off in the distance, since it sets out a rigorous path entailing *real work, as yet unaccomplished*, in the path of all would-be students of philosophy. Plato is again using his "metaphysics" *to set tasks, complex and perhaps lifelong tasks upon which any claim to knowledge must be contingent*. The effect is again to emphasize the epistemic distance between humans and the Forms, even while pointing out a manner of approaching them.

In the *Timaeus*, as in *Republic* V, the ontological distance between humans and Forms is established in the famous contrast between Becoming and Being. This distance is a distance that, however, at the same time implies relationship and even a kind of contact. Plato seems to be depicting the relationship between the perfect and the imperfect, demonstrating that this relationship involves both contact and distance.

So in the Platonic texts in which Forms make a prominent appearance, their *distance* from human understanding is emphasized at the same time as is their *involvement* in the everyday world. The notion of *intermediacy* is always present, and important, wherever the Forms are, even if words for intermediacy do not appear.

# Notes

## INTRODUCTION

1. All quotations from the *Symposium* in English are taken from the Nehamas and Woodruff translation unless otherwise noted.

2. Charles Kahn sees that "Plato's theory of *erōs* provides an essential link between his moral psychology and his metaphysical doctrine of Forms" and discusses this connection admirably in his *Plato and the Socratic Dialogue: The Philosophical Use of a Literary Form* (Cambridge: Cambridge University Press, 1996), 258, and chapter 9 and chapter 11, 340–45, passim.

3. Vlastos distinguishes the "elenctic" Socrates of the so-called "early" dialogues from a more "Platonic" Socrates characterisic, he thinks, of Plato's "middle" period. We are skeptical of his view, for reasons that will become clear in what follows. See Gregory Vlastos, *Socrates: Ionist and Moral Philosopher* (Ithaca: Cornell University Press, 1991), especially chapters 2 and 3. Also see our "Eros as Messenger in Diotima's Teaching," in *Who Speaks for Plato; Studies in Platonic Anonymity*, ed. Gerald A. Press (Lanham, MD: Rowman and Littlefield, 2000).

4. Christopher Rowe, ed., *Plato: Symposium*, (Aris and Phillips, 1998) 205–206.

5. This claim has been doubted by some commentators, but we defend it in what follows.

6. A very interesting recent account of the Socratic writings is found in the first chapter of Kahn's *Plato and the Socratic Dialogue.*

7. For a concise summary of the history of Plato interpretation and the possibility of a "Third Way" between dogmatism and skepticism, see Francisco J. Gonzalez's Introduction to *The Third Way* (Lanham, MD: Rowman and Littlefield, 1995).

8. See, for instance, Vlastos, *Socrates, Ironist and Moral Philosopher.*

9. See, especially, Gerald A. Press, ed., *Who Speaks for Plato? Studies in Platonic Anonymity* (Lanham, MD: Rowman and Littlefield, 2000).

10. We do not mean to imply that all of Plato's dialogues would lend themselves to oral presentation, but only that the Athenians of Plato's day may still have regarded listening to oral discourse as a more familiar and customary activity than silent reading. In

the *Phaedrus*, Phaedrus is trying to memorize a speech so he can rehearse it to Socrates, until Socrates asks him to simply read it. Indeed, the dialogue form as a literary form seems to pay tribute to the high value of face to face oral communication by depicting it, and the relative superiority of oral discourse is even discussed by Socrates in the *Phaedrus*. Elinor J. M. West develops the image of a written text as akin to a musical score, as well as the image of weaving a tapestry that is partly old and partly new, in "Plato's Audiences, or How Plato Replies to the Fifth-Century Intellectual Mistrust of Letters," in *The Third Way: New Directions in Platonic Studies*, ed. Francisco J. Gonzalez (Lanham, MD: Rowman and Littlefield, 1995).

11. See the critique of writing in the *Phaedrus* (275c–277a).

12. Cf. *Seventh Letter* 341c-d.

13. See Drew Hyland, *Finitude and Transcendence in the Platonic Dialogues* (Albany: State University of New York Press, 1995).

14. *Apology* 30e–31a, *Theaetetus* 149a–151d, and *Meno* 80a-b.

15. Our list is intended to be suggestive rather than exhaustive.

16. Some commentators have taken Eryximachus to be the symposiarch. See Christopher Gill's introduction to his translation of *The Symposium* (London: Penguin, 2003), xii–xiii; Jamey Hecht, *Plato's Symposium: Erôs and the Human Predicament* (New York: Twayne, 1999), 87; K. J. Dover, *Symposium* (Cambridge, Mass: Cambridge University Press), 11. Dover appeals to the following passages to make this case: 176b5–177e6; 189a7–1c; 193d6–194a4; *213e9ff.*, 214a6–e3. We follow Anderson in holding that Phaedrus is the symposiarch, exercising his authority at 194d and 199b-c. Daniel Anderson, *The Masks of Dionysos: A Commentary on Plato's Symposium* (Albany: State University of New York Press, 1993), 17–18. Although it is Eryximachus, who proposes that they give speeches on the topic of *Erôs* and attempts to lead the celebrants to moderation on this second night of partying, we think there is good evidence for believing that Phaedrus is the symposiarch, despite Eryximachus's several attempts to take over this role. Eryximachus himself attributes to Phaedrus the evening's topic, calling him the "father of our subject" (177d). This point may also explain why Phaedrus speaks first, even though Eryximachus seemed initially to be functioning as the master of ceremonies. Going first would have the effect of freeing Phaedrus thereafter to focus on his duties as symposiarch. It is notable also that Phaedrus addresses himself to the other guests as a whole, while several of the subsequent speakers address themselves directly to Phaedrus. Pausanias, for example, begins and ends his speech by addressing Phaedrus (180c, 185c). He concludes: "Phaedrus, I'm afraid this hasty improvisation will have to do as my contribution on the subject of Love." Agathon, too, ends his speech by presenting it to Phaedrus: "This is how I think of Love, Phaedrus" (197c). At 194d, Phaedrus, true to the office of symposiarch, interrupts Agathon to warn him against answering Socrates' question, lest they get sidetracked and cause everyone to miss the rest of the speeches. Socrates, too, addresses Phaedrus at the end of his speech (212b). And at 199b, Socrates asks permission from Phaedrus to question Agathon. Finally, Aristodemus is said to have referred to "Phaedrus and the others" (199b), just as Socrates later refers to "Phaedrus and the rest of you" (212b). Absent express textual identification of anyone as the symposiarch, we believe that Rosen is wrong in naming Eryximachus as symposiarch rather than Phaedrus. Stanley Rosen, *Plato's Symposium* (Indiana: St. Augustine's Press, 1999), 290. Allen's view is more nuanced. He calls Eryximachus the

"unelected master of ceremonies" and notes the physician's several attempts to take over the proceedings. See R. E. Allen, *The Dialogues of Plato*, Vol. 2: *The Symposium* (New Haven: Yale University Press, 1993), 16.

17. For more on these homoerotic mentoring relationships, see K. J. Dover, *Greek Homosexuality* (Cambridge: Harvard University Press, 1978). We will discuss the relevant special features of these relationships at the appropriate point in our commentary.

18. Empedocles argued that two great forces—*philotēs* or Love and conflict or strife—combine to move the universe. Readers of the *Symposium* must decide how well Eryximachus understands Empedocles and to what extent Aristophanes may be reformulating Eryximachus's account in such a way as to reflect better the thought of Empedocles, as Anderson rightly argues that he does.

19. It is never clear whether his jurors think Socrates is a Sophist who teaches others, and therefore is charged with the corruption of the young, or whether they think he is some kind of "nature philosopher" who studies "things in the heavens and below the earth" and is therefore guilty of impiety, or both. Socrates is concerned in his defense to refute both of these characterizations of his practice in the city. The philosopher takes pains in his defense to underscore that it will be his (largely anonymous, except for the comic poet Aristophanes) "early" accusers who will be hardest to refute and will likely be the cause of his undoing, if he is convicted (*Ap.* 18b-c).

20. Diskin Clay reports that the first translation into French of the *Symposium* (Louis Le Roi, 1558) ends with Diotima's final words, not even bothering to translate the speech of Alcibiades or the enigmatic final scene. Diskin Clay, "The Tragic and Comic Poet of the *Symposium*," in *Essays in Ancient Greek Philosophy*, Vol. 2, ed. John Anton and Anthony Preus (Albany: State University of New York Press, 1983), 186–202.

21. In addition to betraying Athens and being charged (in absentia) with acts of impiety, Alcibiades had his property confiscated and is believed to have been killed by the family of a girl he seduced or was stoned to death at about the time of Apollodorus's retelling of the *Symposium* story. For what is known about him (Alcibiades III of Phegous), see Debra Nails, *The People of Plato: A Prosopography of Plato and Other Socratics* (Indianapolis: Hackett, 2002), 12–20. Nails details three different occasions on which Alcibiades was recalled from his command during the Peloponnesian War. See also, Steven Forde, *The Ambition to Rule: Alcibiades and the Politics of Imperialism in Thucydides* (Ithaca: Cornell University Press, 1989) and John Finlay, "The Night of Alcibiades," *The Hudson Review* 47, no. 1 (1994): 57–59.

22. The other two being Critias and Charmides. Readers of Plato's *Charmides* will recall that Charmides was Plato's maternal uncle. Critias was the uncle of Charmides. They later became part of the group of Thirty Tyrants, or oligarchs, who overthrew the democracy for a year (from 404 to 403).

23. See Xenophon, *Memorabilia* I.2, where Xenophon attributes the public outrage against Socrates to Socrates' associations with Alcibiades and Critias.

24. Leo Strauss, *On Plato's Symposium* (Chicago: University of Chicago Press, 2001), 15–16. It is certainly true that the main topic of the banquet depicted in the *Symposium* is *Erôs*, but the main topic of the dialogue *as a whole* is not simply *Erôs* but the *speeches* on *Erôs* by Socrates and the other participants. Apollodorus's auditors in the frame narration seem more interested in the speechmakers than they are in *Erôs*

per se. Strauss's observation is at least in part meant to draw attention to the significance of Socrates' denial of the divine state of *Erôs*.

25. Mark L. McPherran, *The Religion of Socrates* (University Park: Pennsylvania
State University Press, 1999), 135–36.

26. In the teaching of Diotima recounted in Socrates' speech, *Erôs* comes to cover
the full range of human experience. *Erôs* here signifies what the poet Robert Bly called
"that great river of desire" that runs through every human being.

27. Most commentators agree that the speeches on *Erôs* involve the characters
praising themselves. See for instance, Robert Wardy, "The Unity of Opposites in Plato's
Symposium," in *Oxford Studies in Ancient Philosophy*, Volume XXIII, ed. David Sedley
(Oxford: Oxford University Press, 2002), 17.

28. See ch. 1 of Kahn, *Plato and the Socratic Dialogue*.

29. For his view that Socrates is "unerotic" or "defectively erotic," see Rosen, *Plato's
Symposium*, xiii, xvii, xviii, xx, 4–5, 38, 65, n.14, 232–34, 250–52, 277, 279, 311, 317, 320,
342. Cornford, on the other hand, thought that Socrates was a man of erotic passion
and that one of the purposes of the *Symposium* was to correct the misleading impression of asceticism one might have derived from the *Phaedo*. F. M. Cornford, "The
Doctrine of *Erôs* in Plato's *Symposium*," in *The Unwritten Philosophy and Other Essays*
(Cambridge: Cambridge University Press, 1950), 68–69.

30. Strauss, *On Plato's Symposium*, 262.

31. Ibid., 28.

32. Many commentators have seen the special importance of the contest between
philosophy and tragedy in the *Symposium*, for example Edmund L. Erde, "Comedy and
Tragedy and Philosophy in The Symposium: An Ethical Vision," *Southwestern Journal
of Philosophy*, 7 (Winter 1976): 161–64; Jamey Hecht, *Plato's Symposium: Eros and the
Human Predicament*, 57; Strauss, *On Plato's Symposium*, 7–8, 34, 245–48; James Rhodes,
*Eros, Wisdom, and Silence: Plato's Erotic Dialogues* (Columbia: University of Missouri
Press, 2003), 197–98, 200, 300. See also Rowe, *Plato: Symposium*, 8–9, 164; Robert
Lloyd Mitchell, *The Hymn to Eros: A Reading of Plato's* Symposium (Lanham, MD:
University Press of America, 1993), 13.

33. For a discussion of the profanation of the Mysteries and the desecration of the
Herms, see Nails, *The People of Plato*, 17–20. Nails says that Phaedrus was accused of
profaning the mysteries but not of desecrating the Herms (233–34). Eryximachus was
accused of profaning the mysteries but may or may not have been accused of desecrating the Herms (143–44).

34. Strauss sees Socrates as the one who really profaned the Mysteries. Strauss,
*Symposium*, 14–15, 24, 40.

35. Strauss finds a model for the *Symposium* in Aristophanes' *The Frogs*. In *The
Frogs*, Dionysus goes to Hades and judges a dispute between Euripides and Aeschylus.
Part of their dispute involves differing estimates of Alcibiades. In *The Frogs* "Dionysus
chooses Aeschylus, the man favorably disposed toward Alcibiades." Thus, Strauss concludes that "Plato pays Aristophanes back" by showing how "the man who is made the
point of reference in a contest between tragic poets decides at the *Symposium* in favor
of Socrates . . ." Strauss, *Symposium*, 26–27, 41, 252, 257. Hecht also sees Alcibiades as
representing the Dionysian arbiter between Socrates and Agathon. Alcibiades' placing

the ribbons on Socrates' head is a sign of the philosopher's victory. Hecht, 85, 87. See also Rhodes, 368, 371, and Anderson, 101.

36. There is disagreement regarding the question of exactly who in the *Symposium* is "profaning the mysteries." Socrates' speech presents "mysteries"—the prophet Diotima is clearly modeled on a hierophantic priestess and uses the language of the Mysteries—but these mysteries do not seem to be the mysteries of Eleusis. So one might suppose that Socrates is mocking the Eleusinian mysteries with his imitation of them. Also, Socrates seems to reveal Diotima's "mysteries" to his friends without putting them through any overt initiatory process, so one might suppose that he is profaning Diotima's mysteries by revealing them to the uninitiated. On the other hand, Socrates himself may be a hierophant initiating his friends by means of his speech. But since Alcibiades will also employ the language of the mysteries in his speech about Socrates, it is arguable that his drunken behavior and speech profane the mysteries that had just transpired before his entrance. So is Socrates profaning the mysteries or is Alcibiades doing so? According to Rhodes, it is not Socrates who profanes the mysteries, but Alcibiades. Rhodes, 399. Like most other commentators, Wardy also sees Alcibiades' revelations about Socrates as a "profanation of the mysteries." Wardy, 11. See also Hecht, 91–92. Strauss thinks it is Socrates who really profaned the mysteries, but Strauss also sees Alcibiades' entrance as related to the profanation of the Mysteries. Strauss, *Symposium*, 14–15, 23–24, 40, 252. Hecht sees the likening of Socrates to satyr statues as a reference to the desecration of the Herms. Hecht, 89.

37. Commentators frequently note the instances of foreshadowing of Socrates' later trial for impiety and corrupting the youth at 175d-e and 219c5. For instance, Hecht, 35. Strauss, *Symposium*, 273. Rosen, *Symposium*, 20–21.

38. Most commentators see that *Erôs* is likened to Socrates in this dialogue and that much in the dialogue associated Socrates with *Erôs*, but not all agree that this fact is meant as an indication that Socrates is truly erotic. Dorter provides a detailed account of all the ways in which Socrates is likened to *Erôs*. Kenneth N. Dorter, "A Dual Dialectic in the "*Symposium*," *Philosophy and Rhetoric* 25, no. 3 (1992): 253–70, esp. 264, 270, n.15. See also Rowe, *Symposium*, 175–76; Mitchell, *Hymn to Eros* 166–67, 220.

39. See Stephen Halliwell, "Philosophy and Rhetoric," in *Persuasion: Greek Rhetoric in Action*, ed. Ian Worthington (London: Routledge, 1994), 241.

40. Good examples of such concerns in Plato's work can be seen in *Apology*, *Republic* Book I, *Phaedo*, *Gorgias*, and *Laws*, Bk. X.

41. Cf. *Republic*, Book II, and *Euthyphro*. The whole drama of the *Apology* shows Plato's awareness of the problem. See also, *Republic* 537d–539b.

42. Rowe, *Symposium*, 160.

43. See, e.g., *Republic* 435c-d. Hyland, Gonzalez, and others have noted that definitions are never unequivocally successful in the Platonic dialogues. See Hyland, *Finitude and Transcendence in the Platonic Dialogues*, chapter 7: "What About the Ideas?," 165–95, and Francisco J. Gonzalez, *Dialectic and Dialogue: Plato's Practice of Philosophical Inquiry* (Evanston: Northwestern University Press, 1998), passim, but esp. chapter 9, "Conclusion: Dialectic in the Seventh Letter," 245–74.

44. See Giovanni Reale, *Toward a New Interpretation of Plato*, trans. John R. Catan and Richard Davies (Washington, DC: The Catholic University of America Press, 1997), and Thomas A. Szlézàk, *Reading Plato* (London: Routledge, 1993).

45. See Francisco J. Gonzalez's "Introduction" (A Short History of Platonic Interpretation and 'The Third Way'), in *The Third Way: New Directions in Platonic Studies*.

46. Gonzalez exhibits the need for a *tertium quid* in the following characterization of the state of Plato interpretation: "The skeptical interpretation can account for the form of Plato's writings only by minimizing their positive philosophical content, while the 'doctrinal' interpretation can uncover their content only at the cost of considering their form little more than a curiosity and even an embarrassment" (13).

47. The question is discussed in Cicero (*Academica*, Book One, circa first century BCE); Sextus Empiricus (*Outlines of Pyrrhonism*, I. 33) and Diogenes Laertius, *Lives of Eminent Philosophers* (both from second–third centuries CE), and the anonymously written "Introduction to Plato's Philosophy" (sixth century CE). The last three writers conclude that Plato was not a skeptic, but their discussions do illustrate that the issue was raised in the ancient world and that there were proponents of a skeptical reading of Plato.

48. Diskin Clay reminds us that the second edition (1970) of the *Oxford Classical Dictionary* contains an entry on "Plato" authored by two different Oxford philosophers, one of whom (J. D. Denniston) writes one numbered section on Plato's "style," while the other, Richard Robinson, writes fifteen numbered sections on Plato's arguments. In the third edition of the *OCD* (1996), however, the entry on "Plato" written by Julia Annas makes no mention of his style or form. Diskin Clay, *Platonic Questions: Dialogues with the Silent Philosopher* (University Park: Pennsylvania State University Press, 2000), xi.

49. Stanley Rosen, "Is Metaphysics Possible?" *Review of Metaphysics* 45 (1991): 242, and Rosen's, *The Question of Being: A Reversal of Heidegger* (New Haven: Yale University Press, 1993), 29, 59, 78. See also Drew Hyland, "Against a Platonic 'Theory' of Forms," in *Plato's Forms: Varieties of Interpretation*, ed. William A. Welton (Lanham, MD: Lexington Books, 2002).

50. *Rep.* 336e–337a, 337e, 368b, 354b-c, 505a, 506b–507a.

51. A similar characterization of philosophy is found in the *Lysis* and *Apology*, as we shall show in what follows.

52. As far as one can tell from the available evidence, not all writers on Socrates made much of Socrates' profession of ignorance. Of the most extensive portraits of Socrates, those of Aristophanes, Xenophon, and Plato, only Plato makes important use of this supposed biographical fact. Among the fragments of the other Socratics we are aware of only one passage from Aeschines' *Alcibiades* dialogue that makes reference in an interesting way to Socrates' ignorance, and interestingly, that passage seems to connect ignorance to *Erôs*, just as we, following earlier commentators, will do in the balance of our commentary. On the Socratics and the theme of *Erôs*, see Charles Kahn, 21. Kahn thinks that the fact that this passage from Aeschines seems to echo Plato's portrayal of Socrates in the *Apology* shows that this profession of ignorance is "a well-documented attitude on the part of the historical Socrates."

53. See, especially, Gonzalez, *Dialectic and Dialogue*, 168.

54. Scholars such as Stanley Rosen, Kenneth Sayre, Francisco Gonzalez, and most recently, James M. Rhodes have held this position. Stanley Rosen has often pointed out that there is no "theory of ideas" in Plato's dialogues. "There is no general concept of a form or idea in the Platonic corpus. Each version of the ostensible theory of forms must be studied in its own right, not assimilated into a nonexistent comprehensive doctrine." Stanley Rosen, *Plato's Sophist: The Drama of Original and Image* (New Haven: Yale University Press, 1983), 50. Ultimately, Rosen considers the so-called "theory of ideas" to be "an invention of nineteenth century historical scholarship, based not upon the Platonic dialogues but upon Aristotle." Rosen, *Question of Being*, 29.

Rhodes considers modern views of "Plato's silence" and finds three major options, only two of which recognize Plato's silence. One view, the esotericists, believe that Plato is silent about what he could have said; the view Rhodes prefers is that Plato is silent only because there are truths that go beyond language or at least writing in some way. In dealing with such "ineffable" or "nonpropositional" truths Plato has no choice but to be silent and attempt to express them only indirectly through philosophical dramas that can lead the student's mind along the path to the eventual acquisition of these ineffable truths for themselves. Rhodes, 40–108. One should compare Hyland's analysis of philosophical speech as not an effort to reduce *noesis* to *dianoia*, but as the attempt to use speech to go from one irreducible *noesis* to another. Hyland, *Finitude and Transcendence*, 181–85.

The significance of nonpropositional knowledge is also highlighted in Kenneth Sayre, "Why Plato Never Had a Theory of Forms," in *Proceedings of the Boston Area Colloquium in Ancient Philosophy*, ed. John J. Cleary and William Wians (Lanham, MD: University Press of America, 1993), Vol. 9, 167–99, and more recently *Plato's Literary Garden: How to Read a Platonic Dialogue* (Notre Dame: University of Notre Dame Press, 1996). For a recent and particularly valuable discussion of the notion of nonpropositional knowledge, see Francisco J. Gonzalez, *Dialectic and Dialogue*.

55. See Gonzalez, *Dialectic and Dialogue*, ch. 2.

56. Other intermediacies discussed in Plato's dialogues include the intermediacy of opinion in general, the intermediacy of Becoming, and the intermediacy of mathematics. See our Appendix for a discussion of various forms of intermediacy.

57. Pierre Hadot, *What Is Ancient Philosophy?*, trans. Michael Chase (Cambridge: Harvard University Press, 2003).

## CHAPTER 1. INTRODUCTORY DIALOGUE (172A–178A)

1. Since the narrator is never Plato himself, even these narrated dialogues are still imitative poetry in which the author never speaks in his own voice. Thus, all the dialogues are examples of the very kind of imitative poetry about which Plato's Socrates complains in the *Republic*.

2. Plato also often provides commentary on portions of his text by having one character analyze or interpret or comment on what has transpired. Of course, in all these cases, one must not simply assume that Plato endorses the commentary, but in all cases it represents something that he intended his audience to hear.

3. Nussbaum thinks it possible that the Glaucon of the *Symposium* is the Glaucon of the *Republic*, but notes that in any case the name would suggest "anti-democratic

associations." Martha Nussbaum, *The Fragility of Goodness* (Cambridge: Cambridge University Press, 1986), 170. Rhodes thinks that both Glaucon and subsequent auditors (probably oligarchs), may be investigating and desiring to stop their political enemies; they are not philosophically curious, but politically anxious about a possible coup being planned by their enemies. Rhodes, following Nussbaum, thinks the frame is set in the time of the "Alcibiades fever" of 405–404. Rhodes, 190–92, especially 192, n.12.

4. Hamilton thinks Plato is trying to make his account more plausible by "appealing to the authority of apparently unimpeachable witnesses." Walter Hamilton, ed. and trans., *Plato, The Symposium* (New York and London: Penguin Classics, 1951), 10. But Dover notes that the frame dialogue could have been put to contrary purposes, for it might either lend veracity to the story or else make literal veracity irrelevant. Dover, ed., *Symposium*, 9. Waterfield comments on the narrative complexity of the dialogue. He says: "[B]y drawing so much attention to how far we are from the symposium, [Plato] is actually inviting us to think what it would be like to have been there." Robin Waterfield, *Symposium* (Oxford: Oxford University Press, 1994), xx–xxi. Gill remarks that the frame suggests the "'erotic' attraction of the search for the truth" and "the difficulty of gaining even partial and indirect access to the truth (or rather, to the *search* for truth)." Gill, *Symposium*, xviii–xix. Cobb notes: "One effect of [the frame] is to direct the reader's attention to the lives of the speakers during the years since the banquet . . ."; he also indicates that it may be used "to illustrate the process of immortality as Socrates describes it in his speech. . . . ," citing 209c-d, since the event is immortalized through reproduction. William S. Cobb, *The Symposium and The Phaedrus: Plato's Erotic Dialogues* (Albany: State University of New York Press, 1993), 62. Rhodes notes that the frame casts the *Symposium* as a whole as an exercise in *anamnesis*. Rhodes, 194.

5. Hamilton thought of Apollodorus as "Socrates' Boswell." Hamilton, 10. Others have more subtle views. Rosen thinks that we are supposed to notice Apollodorus's fanaticism and that it qualifies his report, but that he is ambiguous, not all bad. Rosen, *Plato's Symposium*, 12–15. Anderson thinks Apollodorus lacks real comprehension and is concerned merely with form. Anderson, 111. Hecht thinks Apollodorus is devoted to Socrates rather than philosophy. Hecht, 29.

6. For a fuller analysis of the setting and arrangement of guests in Agathon's banquet room, see Peter H. von Blanckenhagen, "Stage and Actors in Plato's *Symposium*," *Greek, Roman and Byzantine Studies*, 33, no. 1 (1992): 54–68.

7. See also his further remarks at 173c-d.

8. Hecht describes Aristodemus as ethically "small" because he "believes that by wearing no shoes one enhances one's greatness." Hecht, 29. Strauss notes that in Xenophon's *Memoirs of Socrates*, 1.4.2–19, Aristodemus appears as one who ridicules the sacrifices and divination, "a man of hubris." Strauss thinks it is relevant to the assessment of Apollodorus's and Aristodemus's characters that they "leak" the story of the party. Strauss, *Symposium*, 13–14, 21, 24. Rhodes also characterizes Aristodemus as "a voluble atheist." See also Rosen, *Plato's Symposium*, 18. Osborne, in contrast, sees Aristodemus as a successful student. She says: "He seems to stand for one who, by following Socrates, has already arrived. . . . He is the real lover who has already mastered the technique." Catherine Osborne, *Eros Unveiled: Plato and the God of Love* (Oxford: Clarendon Press, 1994), 98.

9. Commentators generally agree on the approximate date of the banquet, fixed as it is by its proximity to the known date of Agathon's victory. Nehamas notes that the party falls between the productions of Aristophanes' *The Clouds* and his *Thesmophoriazousai*. Alexander Nehamas, *Virtues of Authenticity: Essays on Plato and Socrates* (Princeton: Princeton University Press, 1999), 304. According to Nussbaum, the banquet occurs in January of 416/15, when Agathon was under thirty years old, Alcibiades was thirty–four, and Socrates fifty-three. Nussbaum, *Fragility*, 168, 170. (See also Hamilton, 9; Strauss, *Symposium*, 14–15; Waterfield, xx–xxi; Nehamas, *Virtues of Authenticity*, 303; Rowe, *Plato: Symposium*, 10–11; Mitchell, *Hymn to Eros*, 4–5; and G. K. Plochmann, "Hiccups and Hangovers in the Symposium," *Bucknell Review* (1963): 4). Disagreements begin over the time of the retelling of the story of the banquet by the narrator Apollodorus in the frame dialogue. Nails places the frame around 400 BCE (Nails, 314–15). Strauss thinks the frame occurs in 407 when Alcibiades had returned to Athens, as does Rosen (Strauss, *Symposium*, 14–15, 24, 40; Rosen, *Plato's Symposium*, 15). Rowe thinks the frame conversation takes place not long before 399 BCE. Nehamas places the frame sometime between 406–400 BCE. We know that Agathon left Athens in 407, that Socrates was put to death in 399, and that Socrates is referred to in a way that indicates that he is still living at the time of Apollodorus's retelling; thus, Plato may have intended the two rehearsals of the story by Apollodorus to be set sometime between these two dates. Martha Nussbaum believes that the renewed interest in this event, which took place more than a decade earlier, was prompted by news of the death of Alcibiades (sometime in 405 or 404). She disagrees with Bury, who put the date of Apollodorus's retelling in 400. She opts for the hypothesis that it is 404 BCE just before the assassination of Alcibiades. She seeks an explanation of why the story of this old party becomes of interest at just this time, such that two different inquiries are made about it in two days. She speculates that it may have been during the time near the end of the war when the beleaguered city was rife with false rumors of Alicibiades' return. The Athenians still hoped Alcibiades would come back even after their second rejection of him (she points to Aristophanes' *The Frogs*, 1422–25). She notes that "the friend" who inquires about the party "two days" after Glaucon did is clearer about when the party happened, and she speculates that the friend may have heard news of the death of Alcibiades (Nussbaum, *Fragility*, 168–70). Rhodes sides with Nussbaum in putting the frame in 404 (Rhodes, 34, 190). See also Waterfield, xx–xxi; Mitchell, *Hymn to Eros*, 3.

10. Mitchell, *Hymn to Eros*, 6.

11. *Symposium* 178e–179b3, 182b, and193a are the passages that seem to contain allusions to historical events that show that Plato must have written the *Symposium* after 385 BCE. Dover dates the composition of *Symposium* to 384–379. Dover considers that *Symp.* 178e–179b3 could be a reference to the Sacred Band of Thebes, formed around 378, and that 182b6ff. could refer to the King's Peace in 387/86 that "recognized the Persians' claims to the cities in Asia." Finally, 193a2ff could refer to the Spartans breaking up the Arcadian city of Mantinea in 385. See Dover, *Symposium*. Nehamas (303–304) says that Phaedrus in the dialogue speaks only hypothetically of regiments of lovers (178e–179b) and concludes that the dialogue was written before 378 BCE when Thebes actually created the "Sacred Band." Nehamas, *Virtues of Authenticity*. Hamilton (9) places the date of composition not earlier than 385 BCE. We are agnostic regarding the compositional chronology, preferring to take our clues from any dramatic dating Plato provides.

12. At the end of the dialogue we learn that Socrates goes to wash up after leaving Agathon's house the next morning, before making his way to the marketplace for another day of philosophical conversation. Rojcewicz and others have argued that the fact that the philosopher bathes before and after the party is meant to suggest a kind of purification process. Richard Rojcewicz, "Platonic Love: Dasein's Urge Toward Being," *Research in Phenomenology* 27 (1997): 103–20. Osborne suggests that the preoccupation with bare feet and footwear is meant to draw attention to a contrast between being close to the earth or down to earth and being elevated or insulated. Osborne discusses all the places in the text where either shoes or bare feet are mentioned. Osborne, *Eros Unveiled*, 97–100.

13. Osborne claims that Socrates has dressed up "to play the part of Agathon's lover at Agathon's party." She likens his style to that of Agathon's *Erôs*. Osborne, 91, 98.

14. Strauss notes that Socrates in effect alters the proverb about the good going unbidden to the good in his assertion that he desires to go beautiful to the beautiful, and suggests that this play with the words *kalos* and *agathos* announces the problem of whether the ultimate object of *Erôs* is the beautiful or the good. Strauss is interested in the contrast between the good and the beautiful. Strauss, *Symposium*, 28. Rosen does more with the context of the Homeric quotation (which he identifies as coming from *Iliad* X, 222–26). He also makes much of the connection to the *Protagoras* where the same quotation is also used, and the other connections to the *Protagoras*. Stanley Rosen, *Plato's Symposium*, 24–25. Both Rosen and Strauss see hubris in Socrates' use of the adage; and Rosen thinks that it is invoked at Aristodemus's expense. Rosen, *Plato's Symposium*, 22–23; Strauss, *Symposium*, 28. Usher sees Socrates' remark about "going beautiful to the beautiful" as a "comic incongruity" of a kind characteristic of satyr plays and a foreshadowing of Plato's critique of beauty in the dialogue. M. D. Usher, "Satyr Play in Plato's Symposium." *American Journal of Philology* 123 (2002): 221. Hecht finds the proverb's usual form in fragment 289 of the comic poet Eupolis, which he quotes as follows: "Good men go of their own accord to bad men's feasts." Hecht points to the parallel between the two uses of "*kalos*" in Socrates' assertion that he wants to go beautiful to the beautiful and the two uses of "*agathos*" when he speaks of the good going uninvited to good men's feasts. He notes that Menelaus was not really portrayed by Homer as a feeble fighter, but was called a feeble fighter by a lying god who was trying to get Paris to fight him. Hecht also notes that Homer's *Odyssey* is about a good man coming unbidden to the feasts of bad men (the suitors of Penelope). Perhaps Socrates is comparing himself to Odysseus, he suggests. Hecht, 30–32. See also Rowe, *Plato: Symposium*, 131.

15. Cobb thinks that Socrates' remarks likening his own wisdom to a mere dream are ironic. Cobb, 62. But we think they are examples of "complex," not simple irony. Socrates is ironic when he praises the "wisdom" of others, suggesting the superiority of their wisdom to his own. But Socrates is appropriately humble regarding his lack of the kind of wisdom that he seeks, even while realizing that the vast majority of humans, perhaps all, are in the same situation. His greater awareness of the common human ignorance is what constitutes the "human wisdom" of which he speaks in the *Apology* (*Ap.* 20d). There *is* irony, however, in the idea that his awareness of his ignorance does count as *a kind of wisdom* that renders him *superior* to others, and his humility regarding his very real ignorance in no way prevents him from recognizing this point of superiority and being frank about it at his trial.

16. In Homer, the words of this quotation appear in a context in which Diomedes asks for a companion to spy on the Trojans. Rhodes sees the quotation from Homer at 174d2–3 as an indication that Socrates regards Agathon and his associates as an enemy camp. Rhodes, 185, 201 with n. 26. See also Rosen, 23–24; Mitchell, *Hymn to Eros*, 104, 206.

17. This episode is also suggestive, as Bloom notes, for the way it shows Socrates uncoupling himself from Aristodemus in order to pursue his thoughts, before he is made later to engage in a discussion of the desire for "coupling," the longing that leads people to want to be linked or made whole through the conjoining of separated halves. Allan Bloom, *Love and Friendship*, (New York: Simon and Schuster, 1993), 450.

The trances of Socrates have prompted much speculation. Taylor viewed Socrates' trances as mystical experiences related to the revelation of Beauty Itself discussed by Diotima. A. E. Taylor, *Plato, The Man and His Work* (Cleveland: Meridian Books, 1961), 211–12, 232–34. Cobb disagrees with Taylor, holding that there is no reason to see the trances as mystical. Cobb, 62. Strauss emphasizes the mystery of Socrates' silent meditations and that they suggest that Socrates was secretive. Strauss, *Symposium*, 42. Anton thinks it possible that the trances are part of Socrates' struggle to internalize Diotima's teachings. John P. Anton, "The Secret of Plato's *Symposium*." *The Southern Journal of Philosophy* 12 (Fall 1974): 288; Rosen notes that Socrates is cognizant enough to decline the slaveboy's request to come in. Rosen, *Symposium*, 25–26. Osborne oddly takes Socrates' lagging behind on this occasion as a sign that because Socrates has dressed for the occasion, Aristodemus is representing the true Socratic way and so must take the lead. Osborne, 91, 99. It could be that Osborne is making a mistake similar to the one Aristodemus may have made, namely, investing too much importance in mere appearances. Granted that Plato, as author, is free to use the appearances of his characters to represent symbolically whatever he wants, it is at least as plausible that he wanted to express something favorable about Socrates through depicting Socrates' willingness to depart from his accustomed attire on a special occasion. Plato may have been trying to show Socrates' relative freedom from affectation and independence from externals. Certainly, Socrates in this dialogue is no less philosophical for not wearing his "philosopher costume."

Also, on the subject of Socrates' trances, we would note that it is possible that Socrates is *both* lost in thought and communing with ineffable truth, contemplating a temporary and partial noetic vision of elusive Forms. Any nonpropositional insight is "mystical" in a weak sense, if all one means by "mystical" is "irreducible to rigid concepts" or "incapable of being fully expressed in words." This interpretation has the virtue of taking seriously the magic aura with which the author seems to have invested him by means of the dramatic detail, and yet at the same time enabling one to hear seriously what Socrates says at 175e, when he claims that his wisdom is "paltry" and "disputable," "being like a dream," and to detect a note of sadness in it. To think that Socrates is thus not entirely ironic in denigrating the value of his own wisdom (no doubt in comparison with the wisdom of the gods, not in comparision with the false wisdom of men), in no way prevents one from finding the pointed irony in his attribution of wisdom to Agathon in the words that follow.

18. Stanley Lombardo and Karen Bell, trans., in John M. Cooper, ed., *Plato: Complete Works*, D. S. Hutchinson, associate ed. (Indianapolis: Hackett, 1997).

19. See also *Prot.* 338b–e, 347c–348a.

20. Catherine Osborne's work alerted us to this pivotal theme. See Catherine Osborne, *Eros Unveiled*.

21. Commentators often note that the language of litigation here foreshadows the future trial of Socrates. See, for example, Hecht, 35. Rhodes thinks that Agathon has prearranged the whole speechmaking contest and is envisaging victory in this contest when he makes this remark to Socrates. Rhodes, 205–206.

22. Anderson, *Masks*, 104.

23. Contra Phaedrus, Cobb asserts that poetic works on love did exist prior to the *Symposium*, citing choruses in the *Antigone* and the *Hippolytus*; but Taylor, objecting to Bury's earlier reference to these same passages, notes that these can hardly be called eulogies. Cobb, 63, with n.7 on 187; Taylor, 211, n. 2.

## CHAPTER 2. SIX SPEECHES ON LOVE (*ERÔS*)

1. See Andocides, "On the Mysteries," 15–16.

2. Strauss thinks that "love of immortal fame … has a certain kinship to spiritedness in the *Republic* but is not identical to it …" Strauss, *Symposium*, 57. It is true that the spirited element in the psyche discussed in the *Republic* can manifest in other ways than the love of honor; but that the love of honor is one of its most significant guises is surely seen in the fact that Socrates so closely associates this element with the love of honor in a crucial argument in Book IX. 580d–583a, esp. 581a-b. Moreover, the various emotions that fall under the province of this part of the psyche—anger, shame, pride, fear—are closely interrelated and closely connected to the virtue of courage, among other things, which may be what motivates the idea that these passions "belong together" as a single psychic "element."

3. Rowe, *Plato: Symposium*, 138; Mitchell, *Hymn to Eros*, 20–22.

4. Anderson thinks that the speeches of Phaedrus and Eryximachus make clear how these two could have become involved in the mutilation of Herms. Given his announcement that he and Phaedrus have little tolerance for alcohol, Anderson imagines a drunken Phaedrus persuading a drunken Eryximachus to follow Alcibiades on a rampage. Anderson writes, "Phaidros had claimed that the beloved is the one who stimulates action on the part of the lover (as Phaidros stimulated Eryximakhos to propose the speeches in honor of *Erôs*)." Anderson, 39. In this light, it is especially telling that Phaedrus's speech suggests that Phaedrus only fears getting caught. Strauss and Rhodes both regard Phaedrus as a "valetudinarian." Strauss, *Symposium*, 52; Rhodes, 207. Strauss also regards Phaedrus as an "avant-gardist," a young man of the Greek Enlightenment. According to Strauss, because Phaedrus subjects *Erôs* to "the criterion of gain," his is "the lowest of all the speeches." But Strauss also notes similarities between Phaedrus's position and that of Socrates, for example, that the beloved is placed higher than the lover than both of them. Strauss, *Symposium*, 55–56. See also Rosen, *Plato's Symposium*, 35–36.

5. "*Agapē*" in the Christian sense signifies something closer to "charity" as caring for the psyche of another, or "caring for the whole person," than either sexual desire or romantic love. For a comprehensive examination of these concepts, see Anders Nygren, *Agape and Erôs: The Christian Idea of Love*, trans. Philip S. Watson (Chicago: University of Chicago Press, 1962). For a contrasting view of Nygen's work, see Lowell D. Streiker,

"The Christian Understanding of Platonic Love: A Critique of Anders Nygren's *Agape and Erôs*," *Christian Scholar* 47 (1964): 331–40. Finally, see James V. Schall, S.J., "The Encyclical: "Gods Erôs is Agapē" (http://www.ignatiusinsight.com/features2006/schall_encyclical_jan06.asp).

6. See Anderson, 25 and Strauss, 54. While not as renowned as the relationship between Pausanias and Agathon, Eryximachus and Phaedrus seem also to be linked erotically. At the beginning of the *Symposium*, after Eryximachus counsels the mostly hungover partygoers to practice moderation on this occasion, Phaedrus says that he "*always* follows" Eryximachus's advice (176d). And at 177a-c, Eryximachus says that Phaedrus is *constantly* complaining that no song of praise has been composed in honor of *Erôs*, the God of Love. Their comments suggest an ongoing association between them, as does the fact that they were accused together of profaning the Mysteries. At *Protagoras* 315c, Eryximachus and Phaedrus are mentioned together with some others, listening to the sophist Prodicus. We follow Anderson (15–16, 39), Rosen (*Plato's Symposium*, 8), and others in regarding them as lovers. Rosen points out that, since Socrates is "linked" with both Aristodemus and with Alcibiades, only Aristophanes, who will describe Zeus's bisection of human beings, is unaccompanied. Strauss suggests that *Plato* is Aristophanes' lover. Strauss, *Symposium*, 254. Rosen disagrees. Rosen, *Plato's Symposium*, 16, 33–34, note 95.

7. It is noteworthy that an army organized around Phaedrus's ideal actually existed in Thebes for about forty years (from 378 to 338), so Plato could have heard of the existence of the formidable "sacred band" that is reported by Plutarch to have gone undefeated until they were crushed in 338 BCE.

8. By custom, it also appears that sexual relations were supposed to be "intercrural" (between the legs). In his *Symposium*, Xenophon's Socrates says, "The boy does not share in the man's pleasure in intercourse, as a woman does; cold sober, he looks upon the other drunk with sexual desire." K. J. Dover, *Greek Homosexuality*, 52.

9. Both Plato and Aristotle take up the virtue of courage first, Plato here and in the *Laws*; Aristotle in his account of virtue or excellence in his *Nicomachean Ethics*. That courage should be treated first is probably meant to indicate that without courage, none of the other virtues would be able to guide one's actions in a time of crisis. So having courage seems to be necessary for having (or holding onto) any other virtues or principles at all. Discussing courage first might also indicate that it is the virtue most readily understood by the audience. Thomas Smith emphasizes the idea that Aristotle and Plato are interested in critiquing the traditional Greek conception of courage or "*andreia*," a word Smith translates as "manliness," owing to its etymological relation to the word for "man," *andros*. Thomas Smith, *Revaluing Ethics: Aristotle's Dialectical Pedagogy* (Albany: State University of New York Press, 2001), 89 and accompanying n.4. Smith sees this notion as lying at the core of "the conventional Greek understanding of human excellence" (292), a conception he calls "virtue-as-virility" and which is associated with a culture of honor and self-assertion. According to Smith, the pedagogy of Aristotle's *Nicomachean Ethics* responds to and criticizes these prevailing attitudes in the mind's of Aristotle's audience (33–64). Surely, similar considerations are relevant in the case of Plato's *Symposium*. In Plato's *Laws*, courage is explicitly ranked lowest in the list of cardinal virtues (*Laws* 631a, c-d), but it is also discussed there *first*, before the other virtues.

10. Bloom, 459.

11. Mitchell, *Hymn to Eros*, 34.

12. The erotic association between Pausanias and Agathon (made fun of by Aristophanes at *Symp.* 193b-c) seems to have been renowned in Athens. Xenophon also mentions the relationship between them in his *Symposium* (VIII.32). In the *Protagoras*, Socrates sees Pausanias with Agathon and says, "I shouldn't be surprised if Pausanias were in love with him" (*Prot.* 315e). There is no evidence that their relationship was ever terminated, and Dover cites Aelian, *Varia historia* 2.21 to support the claim that "when Agathon emigrated to Macedon, Pausanias followed." K. J. Dover, *Plato: Symposium*, 89. Dover notes that the sustained relation between Pausanias and Agathon is unusual for the Greeks (177d, 193b-c). Dover, *Plato: Symposium*, 3. Wardy points out that even though Pausanias departs from convention by engaging in a long-term adult-adult relation with Agathon, Pausanias accepts the lover-beloved distinction. Wardy, 14–15. One wonders how the asymmetry of the relationships would manifest between two adult men.

13. Bloom notes the irony of these relationships, namely that the young beloved has the more noble motive compared with the older *erastēs*, in his discussion of the *Symposium*. See Bloom, *Love and Friendship*, 466–68.

14. See Anderson, 30, Hecht, 49, Strauss, 54. Says Hamilton: "It is possible to see in Pausanias the clever pleader for homosexual license, who employs high-sounding but sophistical reasoning to justify the satisfaction of physical desire" (14). Hecht (50–51) notes that Pausanias wants a law that most favors lovers like himself: "clever speakers, older, uglier and committed to a single partner." But see Rowe, *Plato: Symposium*, 140 for a more charitable view.

15. As Rhodes puts it: "Pausanias arranges for the putatively noble pederast to get his gratification risk-and-cost-free. The *erastēs* ends with no enforceable responsibilities at all" (224). Rosen also discusses the ironic tension between the goals of the lover and the beloved in the relationship. Rosen, *Plato's Symposium*, 87–88.

16. Hecht (54) calls Aristophanes' hiccups "perhaps the most famous hiccups in Western literature ..." Few today would treat this issue as lightly as A. E. Taylor, who said of Aristophanes' hiccups: "There is nothing here which calls for a 'serious' explanation" (216). Some commentators are more interested in the meaning of hiccups themselves, whereas others focus more on the significance of the change in the order of the speeches that results. Cobb suggests three possibilities regarding Aristophanes' hiccups: (1) Plato is getting back at Aristophanes for *The Clouds*; (2) the incident makes fun of Eryximachus, who is forced to give "medical advice of a rather trivial sort"; or (3) the incident is making fun of Pausanias, because 185c could be read as saying that "something else" that might have caused the hiccups was Pausanias's speech. Cobb endorses the last possibility in particular, but also suggests that all three could be correct (66). All three of these views have had defenders; R. G. Bury, *The Symposium of Plato* (Cambridge: W. Heffer and Sons, 1964), xxii–xxiii lists them (cited by Cobb, 188, n.16). Wardy (19) takes the incident to be a deflationary comment on Pausanias but also a counterpoint to Eryximachus. Anderson thinks that hiccups are the intervention of Dionysus (whom the speakers had tried to exclude by drinking temperate and sending away the flute-girl) (11–12). Rhodes thinks that Agathon has secretly prearranged the contest including the seating order and that Aristophanes' hiccups upset his plans. Rhodes (207, 227) postulates *Erōs* as a supernatural cause. Rhodes also sees the hiccups as Plato's revenge for *The Clouds*, a "gentle satirizing" of Aristophanes (264–65).

17. For instance lines 171ff, in which a lizard defecates on Socrates.

18. On the role of bodily functions in Aristophanic comedy, see also Hecht, 54–55.

19. As Cobb notes. Cobb, 66. See also Mitchell, *Hymn to Eros*, 49.

20. Commentators have widely different views of the quality of Eryximachus's speech. Konstan and Young-Bruehl develop a positive interpretation of Eryximachus's speech and see it as the best of the non-Socratic speeches on *Erôs*. See David Konstan and Elisabeth Young-Bruehl, "Eryximachus' Speech in the *Symposium*," *Apeiron* 16 (1982): 41–46. Hamilton (15), in contrast, calls Eryximachus "a pompous and oracular pedant" and says that "it is by way of contrast that his poor speech is put between the better speeches of Pausanias and Aristophanes." Wardy (5) calls Eryximachus "the bland aficionado of technical control of *Erôs* as happy reconciliation, total pacification." Rhodes (231) finds in Eryximachus "a radical Asclepiad technism . . . that intends to dominate nature and the gods."

21. See Konstan and Young-Bruehl, 41–46. In contrast to the usual minimization of Eryximachus's speech, Konstan and Young-Bruehl conclude that their analysis "points to a degree of systematic exposition and intellectual rigor in the speech that is incompatible with sheer parody. Of all the contributions in the *Symposium* apart from that of Socrates himself, it is the only one which rivals, for example, Protagoras' great speech in the dialogue named for that sophist, in philosophical significance and coherence" (44).

22. Cf., for example, Empedocles Fr. 90, which reads: "So sweet seized on sweet, bitter rushed to bitter, sharp came to sharp, and hot coupled with hot" (quoted in Anderson, 35). Anderson goes on to point out that Eryximachus also fails to notice how this principle, in Empedocles' view, suggests the long-term victory of Strife over Love.

23. Wardy (7–8) notes that Eryximachus's view of Heraclitus seems to comprehend only one kind of harmony that Heraclitus considers, and Wardy refers to *Sophist* 242e2–243a2, which he takes to show that Plato was aware that there was another way of interpreting Heraclitus, establishing that Plato's reading of Heraclitus is not as limited as that of Eryximachus. Dorter (265) also thinks that Eryximachus misunderstands Heraclitus; Eryximachus does not truly harmonize extremes but merely avoids them. Rosen says: "Eryximachus goes beyond both Heraclitus and Empedocles in suggesting that man is able to reduce strife to harmony" (*Plato's Symposium*, 112).

24. Compare *Laws* 658e–659a.

25. The inappropriateness of using pleasure as the standard of good music is also discussed in the second book of the *Laws* and in the discussion of true and false arts in the *Gorgias* (463b–465d).

26. Eryximachus's view seems very much in accord with *Laws*, Book X, 906a-c.

27. Socrates will use Diotima's teaching to argue that *Erôs* is always directed at the good or at least at what seems good to the one desiring. Even when love is directed only at what seems good, it is really aiming for the true good but simply missing it through error; were it not so, the fact that the false goods *seem* good would not be essential to their desirability. Even though in one sense humans always seek the true good, there is of course another sense in which human desire can be directed at various things, including wrong or inappropriate things. This tension between apparent goods and real goods is a significant feature of the psychology that runs throughout Plato's dialogues,

a feature that even seems to be exploited by Socrates in his refutations. According to this logic, when one loves any object one is always seeking the true good through it; thus, in a sense one's desire is divided. For on the one hand, one loves and wants the object at which one's desire is actually directed, that is, whatever *seems* good to one. But on the other hand, one desires only "whatever is truly good for one" and desires the present object *only* because one believes that it is a means to what is really good for one. This view of the true object of *Erôs* is connected to the Socratic paradox that no one willingly does evil. For the paradox, as Socrates understands it, only means that if one were to recognize with one's whole being that the thing one desires is not going to lead to one's benefit, one would cease to desire it. (It requires additional argument to show that moral evil is always detrimental to the psyche.) Thus, a thirsty person might desire to drink turpentine only until she realized what it was, or a hungry person might desire an artificial fruit only until he realizes it is plastic. The original desire remains, for one is still hungry or thirsty, but knowledge has redirected hunger or thirst away from the turpentine and the plastic fruit; the thirst was never for turpentine qua turpentine and the hunger was never for plastic fruit qua plastic.

The true good that humans seek is always their self-advantage, yet paradoxically this self-advantage leads beyond the self; in this mystery lies the religious character of *Erôs* that will emerge in Diotima's speech.

28. For a careful and succinct analysis of Eryximachus's indebtedness to Empedocles, see Anderson, 31–39. Anderson cites a range of sources that support the likely hypothesis that Empedocles practiced and wrote on medicine. Our analysis of the relation of the speeches of Eryximachus and Aristophanes has benefited greatly from Anderson's analysis in ch. 3 of *Masks*.

29. Strauss speaks of Eryximachus's "loveless art." According to Strauss, Empedocles' doctrine is "purely theoretical" and "looks at the whole with perfect detachment from human needs . . ." (*Symposium*, 98, 108).

30. Rhodes (238–39) sees Aristophanes' joke about Eryximachus's cure as a serious counterexample to Eryximachus's theory.

31. As Hecht notes (100).

32. Strauss (95) thinks that the change in order between Eryximachus and Aristophanes suggests that they are somehow interchangeable. The change puts Socrates and the poets together, and also places the strong drinkers together. (It would have been impolite for Agathon to have put the three best speakers together on purpose.) It also puts Aristophanes in the central position of the speakers on *Erôs*. The body asserts itself after Pausanias had tried to put it in place; it gives Eryximachus a chance to show that he is a physician. Strauss (95–96) notes that Eryximachus claims to build on the beginning made by Pausanias, and that Pausanias, Eryximachus, and Aristophanes, defenders of pederasty, form a triad. Dorter thinks that one of the points of the hiccups incident is to suggest that Aristophanes' and Eryximachus's speeches are connected. He also thinks that the hiccups are a way of displaying the body's imperfections through its susceptibility to ailments. See Dorter, 261–62, and n.10 on 269. Plochmann (9–10) criticizes those who think that the point of the hiccups is primarily the alteration in the speech order, for there is no reason why Plato could not have had the speeches in any order from the beginning. Plochmann suggests that the hiccups are a "disharmony of the diaphram, which in the *Timaeus* is listed as the point of separation between the respective seats of

the appetitive and the ambitious part of the soul." In Plochmann's view this disharmony suggests a "maladjustment of bodily love and ambition" such as is also seen in Aristophanes' account of the four-legged men. He also says that "Aristophanes was hiccuping from a surfeit of speeches," and he also suggests that even the contents of the Aristophanes' and Eryximachus's speeches may have been switched, to the extent that each discusses love as the other might have been expected to do, for Eryximachus talks about love in general as "a universal and blind passion" and Aristophanes talks about the origin or "phylogenesis" of love. But given the level of appeal to *technē* and natural philosophy in Eryximachus's speech, and the mythic and comic nature of Aristophanes' speech, this particular suggestion by Plochmann seems off the mark.

33. Bloom (478) thought that Aristophanes' speech was "the truest and most satisfying account of *Erôs* that we find in the *Symposium.*" Hamilton (16) says that it "constitutes almost the most brilliant of all [Plato's] accomplishments as a literary artist." Diskin Clay calls it "one of the most important speeches in the *Symposium.*" Clay, "Tragic and Comic Poet," 189. To Nussbaum, Aristophanes' speech, together with that of Alcibiades, present the most serious challenges to the teachings of Diotima that Socrates recounts in his speech. Nussbaum (173, 187, 197–99) thinks that Plato has put into Aristophanes' mouth a presentation of the love of the individual that critiques the apparently more metaphysical love in Diotima's teaching.

34. There is a form of sexual reproduction outside the body in some animal species in which the female lays the eggs upon the ground and the male deposits sperm in them, as in the cicadas referred to by Aristophanes at 191b. Rhodes (272) raises the question how the original double-women reproduced before the creation of sexual intercourse.

35. Rhodes (267, 271, 275) implies that the circle-men are supposed to resemble male sexual organs.

36. Aristophanes says (190b-c) that Homer's story about Ephialtes and Otos was originally about them (*Iliad* V, 385, *Odyssey* xi, 305*ff*). Ephialtes and Otos were giant brothers who bound the god Ares in chains and threatened to scale the heavens to make war on the Olympian Gods.

37. See Hyland, *Finitude and Transcendence*, 113–14.

38. See K. J. Dover, "Aristophanes' Speech in Plato's *Symposium,*" *Journal of Hellenic Studies* 86 (1966): 41–50.

39. Other commentators have seen Aristophanes' speech as masking a very impious position. Strauss regards Aristophanes' suggestion that "*Erôs* deserves the greatest worship because he is the most philanthropic of all gods" as the proposal of a "religious revolution." Strauss, *Symposium*, 122. Strauss thinks that Aristophanes' "crucial point" is that "you cannot understand *Erôs* if you do not see in it the element of rebellion." Strauss says: "[T]he *Symposium* as a whole, and especially Aristophanes, questions the Olympic gods, the gods worshipped by the city." Strauss, *Symposium*, 128. Rhodes (268–69) reads the Platonic Aristophanes as a hater of the gods, but one who believes the gods are too powerful to overthrow and therefore advocates a protective piety.

40. Thus, Anderson thinks that in a surface defense of homoeroticism, in which he argues that male/male relations are most manly, Aristophanes is actually mocking Phaedrus, Eryximachus, and Pausanias (and perhaps implicitly Agathon).

41. Given Agathon's portrayal in Aristophanes' *Thesmorphoriazusae*, the reference to Pausanias and Agathon's manliness is probably a joke. See also Strauss, *Symposium*, 146, and Nails, 10.

42. Anderson (40) notes that Eyrximachus's speech had ignored the role of strife and that Aristophanes' speech acts as a corrective to this oversight. Plochmann (10) views Aristophanes as a *parody* of Empedocles.

43. Rosen contrasts Aristophanes's story with Homer's tale about Hephaestus's binding of Ares and Aphrodite as a punishment. As Rosen notes, whereas Aristophanes says all would want to be joined, this would effectively destroy both partners. Rosen, *Plato's Symposium*, 153.

44. See Hyland, 117; Wardy, 21 with n.36; Strauss, *Symposium*, 134–35; Nehamas, *Virtues of Authenticity*, 307; Nussbaum, *Fragility*, 173–75; Dorter, 270, n.13; Rosen, *Plato's Symposium*, 134, 143, 158; and Henry G. Wolz, "Philosophy as Drama: An Approach to Plato's *Symposium*," *Philosophy and Phenomenological Research* 30 (March 1970): 323–53.

45. The question of whether it is better merely to *seem* just or really to *be* just is the central question of Plato's *Republic*. In *Republic* II the case is made that it is better merely to seem just while in fact being unjust; the image of the Ring of Invisibility is used to pose the question why one should be just if the fear of punishment is taken out of the picture. Glaucon and Adeimantus ask Socrates to show them what justice and injustice are and what they each do to the psyches of those who possess them. They want him to defend the life of justice on this basis, removing the mere appearance of justice from consideration; they would like him to show that the just life is better even without the reputation for justice, and even if it is saddled with the reputation for injustice instead. This challenge is tantamount to requiring that justice and injustice be shown to have an objective value apart from the power of human opinion to assign them a status. This problem provides the backdrop, and a main goal, of the bulk of ethical and political thought of *the Republic*, Bks. II–IX. By the end of Book IX, Socrates seems to have convinced his interlocutors that real justice, being an ordered state of the psyche that constitutes its true well-being, is valuable in itself (though also for the effects it produces). He seems to have convinced them as well that it is no profit to anyone to conceal an unjust psyche, just as it benefits no one to conceal a bodily sickness in order to avoid having to treat it. Believing that being honored is more important than actually being honorable, that is, that good reputation is more valuable than true virtue, would have to count as a defect of the spirited part of the psyche that ought to function as reason's ally. See Rowe, *Plato: Symposium*, 138.

46. But at 180b7, Phaedrus says love *is* the oldest, as noted in Rowe, *Plato: Symposium*, 137.

47. See Rhodes, 284; Hecht, 68; Waterfield, xxiv–xxv; Cobb, 69; and Rosen, *Plato's Symposium*, 163.

48. Waterfield, xxiv–xxv; Hamilton, 18.

49. P. Christopher Smith, "Poetry, Socratic Dialectic, and the Desire of the Beautiful," *Epochē* 9, no. 2 (Spring 2005): 233–53.

50. Thanks to Mark Moes for reminding us of this line.

51. See *Rep*, Bk. IX, 580d–581c.

52. Mark Moes, "Spiritual Pregnancy and Socrates' Refutation of Agathon in the *Symposium*" (Typescript, 2005): 1–2.

53. See, for example, William A. Welton, ed., *Plato's Forms: Varieties of Interpretation* (Lanham, MD: Lexington Books, 2002), especially Francisco J. Gonzalez, "Plato's Dialectic of Forms" and Drew A. Hyland, "Against a Platonic Theory of Forms."

54. Rosemary Desjardins has developed the idea that Plato's dialogues are themselves examples of "serious play." Rosemary Desjardins, "Why Dialogues? Plato's Serious Play," In *Platonic Writings, Platonic Readings*, ed. Charles L. Griswold Jr. (New York: Routledge, 1988): 110–25.

55. Commentators who see the comic dimensions of the tragedian Agathon's speech include: Nehamas, *Virtues of Authenticity*, 308; Wardy, 21–22; Dorter, 270, n.13; and Paul Shorey, *What Plato Said*. (Chicago: Chicago University Press, 1933): 144–46.

56. Hecht (41) notes that Socrates' remark about the Gorgon's head at 198c alludes to Odysseus's descent to Hades; thus, Socrates casts himself in the role of Odysseus yet again. Hecht (96) notes many allusions in the dialogue that seem to associate Socrates and Odysseus in some way. Socrates is both like and unlike Odysseus. Rhodes (297–98) also notes the Odysseus motif: "The entire *Symposium* is a conversation of Odysseus-Socrates with the dead in Hades." Strauss also notes the comparison between Socrates and Odysseus and speaks of Socrates' "Odyssean rhetoric," citing Xenophon's *Memoirs of Socrates*, 4.6.13–15. Strauss, 178–79.

57. In the *Gorgias*, Socrates lists four true arts, two for the body (exercise and medicine) and two for the psyche (legislation and justice). These true arts aim at the good or the well-being of the body and the psyche, respectively. "Rhetoric" by contrast is cast as one of the "false arts" collectively called "flattery" (*kolakeia*); the branches of flattery are also four, in imitation of the true arts: ornamentation and cookery (in place of the true arts of the body), sophistry and rhetoric (in place of the true arts of the psyche). Flattery in all its forms aims at mere pleasure in abstraction from well-being, mere immediate gratification without regard for health or virtue. Although Socrates initially places rhetoric among the species of flattery, he later indicates the possibility of a good kind of rhetoric that would aim at the well-being of the psyche (and so presumably would be an instrument of the arts of legislation and justice, jointly known as "statesmanship"). The possibility of a philosophical rhetoric emerges also in the *Sophist*, with the talk of a "sophist of noble descent" (231d) and in the *Phaedrus*, where Socrates speaks of a *true* rhetorician who practices the art of rhetoric rather than the "knack" of flattering (*Phdr.* 270c–274b), and the importance of rhetoric and poetry in Plato's thinking and writing becomes clear in reading *the Republic*, the *Laws*, and to some extent, any of the dialogues. The criticism of imitative poetry in *Republic* X sometimes misleads commentators into believing that Plato is simply an enemy of rhetoric and poetry, but this conclusion is far too simplistic, as anyone reading Aristophanes' *Symposium* speech should realize. The rivalry between philosophy and poetry with which Plato is concerned (in the *Symposium* as elsewhere) does not preclude the philosopher's respect for and use of poetry and rhetoric. Like any form of power, poetry and rhetoric become dangerous when they are divorced from, or substituted for, philosophical reflection and self-examination.

58. This contrast between long speeches and Socratic conversation is also prominently made in Plato's *Gorgias* and at *Protagoras* 334d–338e.

59. Furthermore, someone might distinguish between those things that one does not possess, or that one *lacks*, and those things that one *desires* or *needs*; all things one desires might be lacked, but not all lacked things are desired or needed. Love wouldn't have to *desire* good things merely because Love *lacked* them if one could imagine Love not *needing* anything good. Apart from perfect beings such as the gods, who already possess the good, Socrates apparently cannot imagine anything not needing the good. It is reasonable, however, to think that the good is needed necessarily by whoever lacks it; for the very ideas of need and good are bound together if what is meant by "need" is not just any subjective desire but what is necessary for well-being (*eudaimonia*). One might also say that the "good" is by definition whatever is truly *needed* for one's well-being.

60. Strauss finds this remark extremely ironic in its dramatic context. He says that it would be very easy to challenge the truth (presumably if it is undefended or incompetently defended, as it often is) but very hard to challenge Socrates (presumably because Socrates is such an excellent verbal wrangler). Strauss, *Symposium*, 182.

61. In the *Theages* (128b), Socrates says that he knows nothing except the subject of love, and adds: "although on this subject, I'm thought to be amazing, better than anyone else, past or present" (Nicholas Smith, trans.). The connection between the ugly Socrates and the theme of love appears to have been a commonplace of Socratic literature. In Xenophon's Socratic writings, in addition to his own *Symposium*, there is also the wonderful exchange between Socrates and Theodote in *Memorabilia* (3.11) that shows a wily Socrates as the ultimate seducer who knows how to size up his interlocutors and to make himself the object of their affections. This scene features another unlikely role-reversal as the beautiful courtesan Theodote is made to desire the homely Socrates for his wisdom. According to Charles Kahn (Kahn, 4, 14–15, 18–23), the Socratic dialogues of Antisthenes, Phaedo, Euclides, and Aeschines (of which only fragments remain—in Euclides' case, only titles) show some evidence of a common interest in the theme of "[t]he roles of friendship and *Erôs* in philosophy" (4). Most interesting is the case of Aeschines, whom Kahn regards as being, "[f]rom the literary point of view . . . that originator of the notion of Socratic *erōs*" (18). In his dialogue entitled *Alcibiades*, Aeschines provides his own commentary on the relationship between Alcibiades and Socrates. In this dialogue, as in the *Alcibiades* I, Socrates states that he benefits Alcibiades not by art (*technē*) but by divine dispensation (*theia moira*). See also Plato's *Meno* 99e, where the same expression is employed. Divine dispensation is then identified with the power of the afflicted to be benefited by their own desire (*epithumia*). Socrates compares his own love (*erōs*) for Alcibiades with Bacchic possession, which enables those possessed to "draw milk and honey from wells where others cannot even draw water." Aeschines' Socrates concludes: "And so although I know no science or skill [*mathēma*] which I could teach to anyone to benefit him, nevertheless I thought that in keeping company with Alcibiades I could by the power of love [*dia to eran*] make him better" (quoted in Kahn, 21). Socrates' love is associated with divine possession and providence, as manifested in the beneficial power of philosophical companionship. In Aeschines' *Aspasia*, Socrates claims Aspasia, the courtesan-mistress of Pericles, as his teacher in virtue, and the implication may be that he received instructions from her on matters of love (24 and accompanying n. 24). (Socrates claims to be instructed by Aspasia in rhetoric in Plato's *Menexenus* 235e; perhaps this claim itself may be counted as another implicit connection between love and rhetoric in his texts). In Aeschines' dialogue, Socrates recommends Aspasia as a

teacher of virtue and rhetoric, and defends his recommendation by examples that to some extent, as Kahn notes, "involve the power of love" (24). Kahn sees the Diotima of Plato's *Symposium* as being "in many ways Plato's response to Aeschines' Aspasia." (26). With reference to one particular episode in the dialogue, in which Socrates reports that Aspasia cross-examines, or "Socratically questions" Xenophon and his wife by way of marriage counseling, Kahn notes that "in her 'Socratic' role" she represents the principle that one can be made better through the power of love (27). Kahn concludes: "We thus have several different versions of . . . [the] deep, somewhat mysterious link between *erōs* and the urge to *aretē* . . ." (27).

62. Some commentators see the deep connection between Socrates' profession of ignorance and his claim to know the art of love. Bloom, 432; Rhodes, 352; and David Roochnik, *Of Art and Wisdom*. (University Park: The Pennsylvania State University Press, 1999), 239–45. See also, Hyland, *Finitude and Transcendence*; Mitchell, *Hymn to Eros*, 17; Rowe, *Plato: Symposium*, 136.

63. The fact that Diotima questions Socrates, using his characteristic mode of philosophic examination in her lessons to him, suggests a connection between the art of love she teaches him and Socratic cross-examination. Did he perhaps learn his dialogical method from her, along with the art of love, maybe even as part of it? Interestingly, Socrates' method of questioning is likened to midwifery in the *Theaetetus*, and midwifery, being concerned with reproduction, would seem to fit nicely into Diotima's teachings. If Socratic Ignorance, as the longing for knowledge and wisdom, is a form of *Erōs*, and Socratic philosophizing is a form of therapy for the psyche that functions by stimulating the psyche's longing, strengthening reason's desire for wisdom until it rules over appetitive desire and guides the desire for honor, then it would seem Socrates' favored method is part and parcel of his art of love. Note how this art would seem (ideally speaking) to function by making others like Socrates—seekers ignorant of the good who, by inquiring into it, somehow come to embody it. (Examples of Socrates making others like himself can be found at *Meno* 80a-d, 100a; *Euthydemus* 278e–282d, 288d–292e; and the *Cleitophon*.) But for some reason, it is difficult for others to persist in Socratic inquiry to the point of actually becoming more than superficially like Socrates, as the cases of Aristodemus and Apollodorus seem to show. For a recent analysis of Socrates' failure to turn promising pupils toward philosophy, see the Introduction to Gary Alan Scott, *Plato's Socrates as Educator* (Albany: State University of New York Press, 200), 1–12.

64. It is further evidence that the midwife's art that Socrates claims for himself in the *Theaetetus*, having to do with spiritual procreation, is also part of this art of love that Diotima's teaching will in fact include an account of biological and spiritual reproduction. Anton (291) thinks the younger Socrates of the *Symposium* is hubristic when he claims to know erotic matters. But Rhodes (352) believes (as do we) that Socrates' profession of ignorance can be reconciled with his claim to knowledge of an art of erotics. Roochnik also overcomes the supposed conflict between Socrates' profession of ignorance and his claim to understand erotic matters by connecting Socrates' knowledge of *Erōs* with his knowledge of his own ignorance. Roochnik, 239–45.

Nussbaum contrasts "Socratic knowledge of the good" with "the lover's understanding." Nussbaum, *Fragility*, 190. But in our view, the so-called "Socratic knowledge of the good," with the *Republic* in mind, might better be called "the Socratic *dream* of a knowledge of the good." If Nussbaum were to take more seriously the ignorant

Socrates' apparently inconsistent claim to a knowledge of the art of love, she might be able to imagine how the "knowledge of the good" and "the lover's understanding" with its focus on particularity come together in Socrates' erotics. For the only "knowledge of the good" Socrates seems to have is his awareness of his need for philosophy, owing to his awareness of his ignorance; and this double awareness seems to constitute what the *Apology* calls his "human wisdom." But we would argue that this wisdom is a "lover's understanding" of a sort; not only is Socrates utterly passionate in his pursuit of wisdom, but he views his philosophical companions through the eyes of love by virtue of their shared pursuit of wisdom. Contra Nussbaum, this love is also a love of individuals, although it is not merely that, and it enables Socrates to have an intimate understanding of his companions (as evidenced, for instance, at *Phaedrus* 228a-c). See Rowe, *Plato: Symposium*, 7, 188, 195.

65. Most modern scholars have been of the opinion that Diotima is a fictional character, but there are interesting arguments on both sides of the question of her historicity. A. E. Taylor argued that Plato does not typically populate his dialogues with fictional characters, although there are gaps in the historical record that would preclude us from confirming (or disconfirming) the historicity of certain characters, such as Callicles (Taylor, 224). For a good discussion of this question, see David Halperin, "Why Is Diotima a Woman?" in *One Hundred Years of Homosexuality and Other Essays on Greek Love* (New York: Routledge, 1989), esp. 119–24.

It is interesting to note that if Diotima is a historical figure, one is faced with the question of how accurately her views are depicted by Plato. If one assumed they were recounted accurately, then one must choose between two options: Either (1) her teachings regarding beauty itself are really not teachings about a "Form" (or "Idea"), or (2) Diotima would be the earliest source for what has been called Platonic metaphysics, insofar as it represents a distinct philosophy from Pythagoreanism.

66. Anderson, 53. Nussbaum, on the other hand, sees the story about Diotima having postponed the plague as a way of conferring her with authority. Nussbaum, *Fragility*, 177.

67. See Thucydides, *History*, Bk. II, 13–16; 47–54. Thucydides, who was himself struck by the plague, blames its severity on the crowded conditions within the city's walls in which people were forced to live after the war began.

68. Osborne, Nussbaum, and others question the preeminent place of Diotima's speech as an access to Plato's thought. Osborne, 57, with n.17; Nussbaum, *Fragility*, 197–99; see also Rosen, *Plato's Symposium*, 29; Gill, xx.

69. In the *Parmenides*, the philosopher for whom the dialogue is named critiques a theory of Forms put forth by a young Socrates; in the *Sophist*, the *Visitor* from Elea criticizes previous philosophers, including advocates of Forms. Socrates in the *Protagoras* argues from the assumption that the good is pleasure (353c–356c), whereas Socrates in the *Gorgias* opposes this view (495d-e).

70. This policy accords with canons for rhetoric laid down by Socrates in the *Phaedrus* (259e–263e), a dialogue that, like the *Symposium*, conjoins issues of love with issues of rhetoric.

71. There are various opinions concerning the question of why Plato chooses to make Socrates appeal to a woman. Rhodes (303–305) thinks Diotima is a woman to counter the misogyny of the others and because she represents "the spiritual analogue

of biological feminine receptivity as the way to human perfection." Anderson (10, 51, with n.1, 162–63) also thinks she might constitute an implicit challenge to the privileging of male homosexual relations in the previous speeches, but also points out that the fact that Socrates uses a woman to administer the lesson would have been "irksome" to the others. Cobb (64, 71–72) emphasizes how shocking it would be to Plato's original audience to see Socrates as inferior to a woman. He suggests that Diotima may be a woman because the main metaphor used in her account is that of pregnancy and birth. He considers the possibility that she is made a woman because Plato does not endorse the views he puts into her mouth. He also considers the possibility that she may be made a woman because she is presented as a priestess in a mystery-religion. But the possibility that Plato "means to challenge the dominant male chauvinism of his day is highly debatable." Rosen (163) refers to Aristophanes' *Thesmophoriazusae* 136 where Agathon is called a womanish man, a weakling. According to Rosen, although Agathon is effeminate, he makes the strongest claim, identifying himself with the god. It is in order to combat this, that Socrates uses a "mannish woman," Diotima. Not only does Wardy (2, 26, 42) think that Diotima is a fiction, he thinks she is not even fully a woman since, he says, she has "a man's soul." He holds that Diotima should not be regarded as Plato's mouthpiece. See also Halperin, "Why is Diotima a Woman?"

72. F. M. Cornford referred to "the immortality and divinity of the rational psyche, and the real existence of the objects of its knowledge—a world of intelligible Forms separate from the objects our senses perceive" as the "two pillars" of Platonism. *Plato's Theory of Knowledge* (London: Routledge and Kegan Paul, 1935 . Reprint, Indianapolis: Bobbs-Merrill, 1957), 2. But in speaking of the link between these so-called pillars above, we prefer to think that one of these pillars is constituted by the full richness of Plato's psychological thought.

73. The connection between love and recollection in Plato is interesting for many reasons, not least of which is the way it forms a bridge between the irrational and the rational. Inspiration, divine madness, and desire are not simply realities that destroy reason, that violate it or that stand beyond its limits; rather, they lie at its foundations and nurture it, enabling it to be what it is. In Plato what transcends reason is reason's mysterious source, accessible only via intimations (in poetry, myth, or prophecy) that must be subjected to reason in order to be purged of error and that reason must properly interpret if they are to be understood. Perhaps no philosopher has ever had a subtler understanding of the relation between reason and desire.

74. The claim that according to Diotima's teaching *Erôs* includes all forms of human desire is controversial. In particular, it conflicts with an important alternative interpretation offered by Charles Kahn in his *Plato and the Socratic Dialogue*. We will discuss Kahn's view and differences with him in what follows.

75. And yet the meaning of "*Erôs*" will later be so expanded that one wonders whether by that part of Diotima's account she would still be able to hold that *Erôs* is just one *daimon* among others.

76. On Diotima's account, it is not completely clear whether the ignorant are really ignorant of their ignorance or merely apathetic about it; but even such apathy or carelessness would, in Diotima's view, constitute a form of ignorance. She explains that such people are content with themselves and do not think that they need anything, although they in fact do, and thus there are at least in some sense "ignorant of their

ignorance": whatever they may think about their own ignorance, they do not think of it as pointing to a need.

77. One finds another example of Plato positioning philosophy in this in-between region (characterized by the "positive ignorance" or "negative wisdom" of Socrates) in the *Lysis*.

> "And therefore, whatever is neither bad nor good is sometimes not yet bad although an evil is present, but there are times when it has already become such."
>
> "Very much so."
>
> "Then whatever is not yet bad, though an evil is present, this presence makes it desire good. But the presence which makes it bad deprives it of the desire, at the same time as the friendship of the good. For no longer is it neither bad nor good, but it is bad. And a good thing, as we showed, is not a friend to a bad one."
>
> "Certainly not."
>
> "Because of these things, then, we might say also that the ones who are already wise, whether these are gods or human beings, no longer love wisdom. Nor, on the other hand, would we say that those love wisdom who have ignorance in such a manner as to be bad. For we wouldn't say that anyone bad and stupid loves wisdom. There are left, then, those who while having this evil, ignorance, are not yet senseless or stupid as a result of it, but still regard themselves as not knowing whatever they don't know. And so therefore, the ones who are not yet either good nor bad love wisdom; but as many as are bad do not love wisdom, and neither do those who are good." (*Lysis* 217e4–218b3, Bolotin trans.) See also Gary Alan Scott's review of Pierre Hadot, *What is Ancient Philosophy?* (Cambridge: Harvard University Press, 2002). *The Review of Metaphysics* 68, no. 1 (September 2004): 180–81, and a longer version of this review in *Ancient Philosophy* xxiv, no. 2 (Fall 2004): 524–30.

One might say that the gods do not require a guide, while the completely ignorant do not feel a need for one. On the theme of guides and followers in the lover's education in the *Symposium*, and in the drama of the dialogue, see Catherine Osborne, *Eros Unveiled*, 86–99.

78. The issue is further complicated if one points out that Diotima's teaching is recounted by Socrates, apparently the same Socrates who so frequently professes his ignorance in other dialogues. It might be thought that it is Socrates who is imputing his own characteristic ignorance to philosophy as such, and that Diotima is simply an invention of the character Socrates, an invention he employs as a mask. But whether Diotima is truly his teacher or merely his mask, the same problem will exist. The problem in question is that to which we have previously referred in discussing the problem of reconciling Socrates' claim to an art of love with his profession of ignorance, or alternatively, the problem of how to reconcile "Platonic" talk of Forms with the "Socratic" insight into human ignorance. Commentators usually and quite naturally want to resolve what they experience as an intolerable tension or outright contradiction by affirming either the "skeptical" or the apparently "positive" or "dogmatic" side of Plato. Anderson, for instance, connects love and dialectic in the following way: Dialectic is the process of becoming aware that one is wearing a mask; one sees that what one thought was oneself is not really oneself. But love is a process of growth that comes by

removing masks; hubris, by contrast is a belief in an immutable self, a refusal to remove the mask, which Anderson regards as a failure in self-knowledge. He sees Diotima's teaching as implying the lack of any immutable self. According to Anderson's view, there would seem to be no difference between self-knowledge and continual self-trans-formation. Since he reads this view into Diotima's teaching and into the *Symposium* and the *Meno*, he believes that Plato's true epistemology is incompatible with the theory of Forms and the doctrine of recollection as traditionally interpreted. Anderson, 8–9. But this interpretation does not consider the extent to which the idea of Forms only makes sense in the context of a belief in flux and relativity of the world of Becoming. Far from being incompatible, Diotima's "flux-doctrine," including the view that knowledge as a state of the psyche exists only via continual replenishment, is inseparable from the idea that some principle of identity transcends the flux, constituting the similarities that enable the "offspring" to be the heirs of their antecedents. If discussions of the Forms in the dialogues presupposed that philosophers could purely and permanently grasp Forms, and by this means truly escape the realm of Becoming, then there might be some incoherence in Diotima's view, or some disagreement of it with the hypothesis of the Forms. But the idea of the Forms tends to be used in the dialogues to empha-size flux of Becoming and the in-between status of the human condition. The noetic nonpropositional vision of Forms does not really lift one out of the flux, except in a relative sense. Although such a vision transcends language in the sense that it cannot be exhaustively expressed, it is only through a temporal dialectical process that works with *logoi* that the vision can be attained or approximated. It is through their relation to such a process, with all its limits and imperfections, that such visions find their value.

79. We bracket for our present purposes any consideration of the validity of the reasoning leading up to this conclusion. It may very well be the case that Plato is not trying to present valid arguments for these conclusions here, but simply trying to display a philosophically pregnant vision of things in a powerful and suggestive man-ner. The real test of this vision may not lie in the somewhat playful arguments offered here, but in their deeper meaning, a meaning that can only be teased out of them by further reflection.

80. See *Meno* 80a-b. For a good discussion of this and other passages that suggest the magical power of Socrates, see Jacqueline de Romilly, *Magic and Rhetoric in Ancient Greece* (Cambridge: Harvard University Press, 1975), 33–37.

81. In the *Meno*, Socrates uses the doctrine of recollection to respond to Meno's paradox about the impossibility of learning. His strategy is to suggest that one *does* in a sense already know what one is seeking, but one has forgotten what is in some way still stored within the mind.

82. Kahn, 276.

83. Ibid., 276–77.

84. The case of *Erôs* and *poiesis* here are examples of general terms with a con-ventional usage that does not properly correspond to the corresponding Forms. Surely, these examples suggest that Plato does not really think that Forms neatly correspond to each general term in natural language when those terms are used in their conventional senses. There may (or may not) be a Form for every general term, but it apparently does not follow that the participants of that Form are just those entities denoted by a general term taken in its conventional sense. Diotima, at any rate, if she spoke in terms

of Forms here, would be acknowledging that there are participants in the Form of Love and the Form of Poetry that are not covered by the conventional usage of these terms.

85. These three examples would be objects of the three parts of the psyche.

86. As one might conclude from an examination of the affinity argument in the *Phaedo* (78b–80b). and the account of the creation of psyche in the *Timaeus* (35a).

87. Kahn points out that each part is also said to have its own *epithumia*, and he contrasts this with other places in which *epithumia* means only specifically appetitive desire. But Kahn thinks that when Plato uses *epithumia* more broadly, it is his most general term for desire. He disagrees with our view that in the Diotima passages, *Erôs* is being offered as a general account of desire. See, Kahn, 262, on the scope of *epithumia* and on Plato's nontechnical vocabulary of desire. On our disagreement with Kahn, we will have more to say at the appropriate place.

88. Of course, Plato is not rigid about this; he treats human desire differently depending on the problem he is exploring at the time. No one model exhaustively describes human beings, so he uses different models for different purposes. Some of the models for the psyche Plato employs include: the Chariot (*Phaedrus*), the Chimera (*Republic*), a jar which may be leaky or intact (*Gorgias*), a mirror (*Alcibiades* I), a marionette of the gods (*Laws*), a wax block or an aviary (*Theaetetus*), a writer and a painter (*Philebus*).

89. As evidence for this claim, consider Socrates' account of *nous* in the *Phaedo*; consider Timaeus's account of the motives of the Demiurge in the *Timaeus*, and consider the definitions of the virtue of wisdom in the city and wisdom in the psyche in the *Republic*.

90. Kahn (260) sees that "criminal desires can rule in a soul only by corrupting the rational part, the *logistikon*, so that it accepts as the good (or, in the case of *erôs*, as the good-and-beautiful) whatever these lawless desires propose as their object." We agree with Kahn that Diotima's teaching can be interpreted so that it supports the Socratic paradoxes; where we diverge from Kahn will be discussed in a subsequent note.

91. See Strauss, *Symposium*, 147, 173, and Thomas Pangle, "Interpretive Essay" in *The Laws of Plato* (New York: Basic Books, 1980), 441–45.

92. We borrow this line from the movie *Koyaanisqatsi*, where it is used in another context altogether.

93. Osborne (102) notes a shift in emphasis in Diotima's teaching that occurs when the need to possess the good becomes "a need to possess immortality in order to gaze for ever on the beautiful itself." Here, she says, "the emphasis changes from *possessing* the beautiful to gazing on beauty and goodness itself." As a result of such gazing one is said to "beget" true virtue. Thus, rather than trying to "possess" beautiful things one is simply "begetting" them. Hecht (75) thinks that "begetting in beauty" is "a deeper purpose" than "perpetual possession of the Good"; begetting in beauty is no "mere holding" but rather "is creative." But, it would seem that the begetting is a means to or a mode of the perpetual possession of the good, once one understands that *what it means for a human to perpetually possess the good is to beget in the beautiful*. If one brings together in this way "perpetual possession of the good" with "begetting in beauty" the problem Hecht (73–75) raises with reference to Nietzsche, namely, the question of whether human desire is finite or infinite, is in a way resolved. For an activity that has

its end in itself is in a way infinite, and yet is still complete. It is true that this human "immortality" as endless begetting is contrasted with the immortality of the divine, but as appropriate to human beings such "processive" immortality ought to be fulfilling to them when pursued properly at its highest level, at least in theory.

94. We deliberately refrain from capitalizing "good" and "beauty" here because we are not referring to Forms, but to the concrete entities participating in these Forms that are the proximate objects of human desire.

95. Hackforth held that the *Symposium* is incompatible with the dialogues that seem to allow for personal immortality. R. Hackforth, "Immortality in Plato's *Symposium*," *Classical Review* 64 (1950): 43–45. Luce argued that Diotima's teaching in the *Symposium* is compatible with the idea of personal immortality. See J. V. Luce, "Immortality in Plato's Symposium: A Reply," *Classical Review* 66 (1952): 137–41. Price sides with Luce. A. W. Price, *Love and Friendship in Plato and Aristotle* (Oxford: Oxford University Press, 1989), 30–35. Sheffield sides with Hackforth (25–26, n.35). Kahn (345, n. 20) thinks that Plato's allusions to immortality at 208b4 and 212a7 show Plato's consistency on the issue of immortality and that the full account is not presented in the *Symposium* owing to considerations of dramatic context. Cobb (76, 80–81) reads 212a as counterfactual, but he admits it is syntactically ambiguous. If it were a contrary-to-fact conditional, then it would be a further denial of personal immortality. In any case, Cobb's point is that it is no basis for wriggling out of what otherwise seems to be Diotima's clear denial of immortality. Rowe holds that Plato "gives up" psychic immortality here for the sake of argument. (Christopher Rowe, "Socrates and Diotima: *Erôs*, Immortality and Creativity," in *Proceedings of the Boston Area Colloquium of Ancient Philosophy*, v. XIV (1998) eds. John J. Cleary and Gary M. Gurtler, S.J., 249, with n.22). Konstan, in his reply to Rowe, points out the effect of Diotima's account of personal identity on the issue of personal immortality. Diotima's view calls into question personal identity, demonstrating that one's connection with one's future self is just as tenuous as is one's connection with one's own progeny. Konstan suggests that true immortality is connected to timelessness. He also argues that the claim that all humans desire immortality is not as implausible as Rowe believes. (David Konstan, "Commentary on Rowe: Mortal Love," in *Proceedings of the Boston Area Colloquium of Ancient Philosophy*, v. XIV (1998) eds. John J. Cleary and Gary M. Gurtler, S.J., 263, 265). Warner holds that Diotima's view of personal identity legitimizes her extension of the notion of "immortality." Martin Warner, "Love, Self, and Plato's *Symposium*," *Philosophical Quarterly* 29, no. 117 (1979): 29, 338. Hecht (76–77) too points out that Diotima's observations about personal identity, regarding both the mind and the body, have the effect of quelling any disappointment over the fact that the immortality available to mortals is not personal immortality. Anderson (74, 77–81, 85) thinks that the self as static is an illusion that inhibits the self as process. He says: "[I]n a profoundly ironic twist to the argument, the effort to preserve oneself brings to an end the process that the self is—precisely because 'keeping it exactly the same forever, like the divine (208a-b) is contrary to the mortal nature, and necessarily destructive of it.'" Accordingly, Anderson thinks that an immortality of "immutability" would be death, since it would end the "process" that is life. Only Diotima's "immortality of process" makes sense to him. Cornford ("Doctrine of Erôs," 76) also suggests that at the highest stages of the ascent the passion of *Erôs* is no longer for immortality in time, but for the "immortality" of timelessness. Strauss (*Symposium*, 251) holds that the *Symposium* abstracts from consideration of the immortality of the

soul. The immortality suggested at the end of Diotima's speech is only "the beholding of the immortal." Rhodes (343) believes we cannot find a genuinely Platonic doctrine of immortality in the dialogues. Rowe ("Socrates and Diotima," 250) thinks that Diotima's discussions of immortality are meant to be ironic. Rosen (*Plato's Symposium*, 253–54) also notes "the absence of any doctrine of personal immortality." For further references to the literature, see also Wardy, 36, n.67.

96. Different manuscripts have different readings of the word in question; some manuscripts give "*adunaton*" whereas others have "*athanaton*" coupled with "*de allēi*." So one must ask whether Diotima is saying "in no other way is it possible" for the mortal to partake of immortality, or whether she is saying that "the immortal has another way" of being. We take the former reading for granted now, but consider in the next note how one might interpret the passage if one accepts the other reading.

97. In the previous note we pointed out that one must ask whether Diotima is saying "in no other way is it possible" for the mortal to partake of immortality, or whether she is saying that "the immortal has another way" of being. If she is saying the latter then she means that the mortal shares in immortality only through reproduction—replacing the old with the new—whereas the immortal (i.e., the divine) "has another way" (ἀθάνατον δὲ ἄλλῃ 208b4), namely, it is "always the same in every way" (τῷ παντάπασιν τὸ αὐτὸ ἀεὶ εἶναι 208a8), that is, the truly immortal stands outside of time.

98. Perhaps Diotima is a "perfect sophist" because she understands the roots of the love of honor. For sophists are associated with the power of rhetoric, and the power of rhetoric is concerned with the manipulation of the love of honor. A perfect sophist would understand the ground of the impulse that makes effective rhetoric possible.

99. A full accounting of Plato's thoughts on honor-love would be a prodigious undertaking. Platonic images for this element in the psyche include the lion in the image of the psyche as a Chimera (from *Republic* IX), and the white horse in the image of the psyche as a Chariot (from the *Phaedrus*); and in addition to the discussions associated with these images, one would have to study the many explicit statements of characters about spiritedness, honor-love, and related concepts, and also examine the *characterization* of characters in their dramatic interactions in the dialogues to determine what the drama itself might convey about spiritedness.

100. Diotima here leaves the loves of women completely out of account, which seems odd because of the broad construal of love earlier that included even animals, and also because Diotima is herself a woman. But in patriarchal ancient Greece it may have seemed to many that the significant human desires are usually the desires of males, despite the inclusion of the exceptional woman Alcestis in the earlier examples and despite the existence of immensely significant female characters in ancient poetry. But one need not assume that the irony of having a woman talk about love in a context that is exclusively male is lost on Plato; but if it is not, it remains to be considered what he intends by this irony.

101. Sheffield (3–4, 13–15, with n.20) does not believe that the "psychic pregnancy" of men should be thought as mere fertility. Rather, there is already embryonic knowledge and virtue inside the human psyche, whether it manages to give birth to true virtue or only mere images of virtue. According to Sheffield (25), the lover does not require something external to impregnate him, but only to help him deliver his conception. She compares and contrasts the idea of psychic pregnancy with the idea of recollection.

She points to certain limits of the recollection model that Plato avoids with the psychic pregnancy model. But there remains the question of how to understand Plato's use of these two models. Should we think that these are theories about which he changed his mind? Or are these simply metaphors that he uses judiciously to bring out different aspects of the subject in different contexts, without taking any of them too literally or expecting them to capture fully the truth? We think they are more likely the latter.

102. Cornford thinks the division between higher and lower mysteries is Plato's way of marking the limits reached by *the* historical Socrates. Cornford, "The Doctrine of Erôs," 75. Taylor (229, n.1) emphatically disagrees with this interpretation. See also the recent counterargument in Sheffield, 9.

103. That beauty can appear in many different, and even contrary, physical manifestations is perhaps also displayed by a humorous passage from the *Republic* (*Rep.* 474d–475a), in which Socrates describes how the lover of boys can find all kinds of different boys equally beautiful in different ways.

104. Plochmann (17) identifies the Form of Beauty with the Form of the Good from *Republic* VI, as does Taylor (231). Hamilton (21, 24) too identifies the ascents of the *Republic* and the *Symposium* and also the Forms of Beauty and of Good. White, on the other hand, argues against two claims: (1) that Beauty is the primary object of love, and (2) that the Form of Beauty is identical to the Form of Good. F. C. White, "Love and Beauty in Plato's Symposium," *Journal of Hellenic Studies* 109 (1989): 143, 153–54. Against the first claim, he points out that the real object of *Erôs* is the lasting possession of the good; thus, beauty is only a means to the good. Beauty and beautiful things are objects of love but they are not the final or ultimate object of love. Against the second claim, he points out that Beauty and Good could be coextensive without being identical (156, n.19). Nye does not think that Beauty Itself is a Form at all. Andrea Nye, "The Subject of Love," *Journal of Value Inquiry* 24, no. 2 (April 1990): 140.

105. We follow Nehamas's interpretation of self-predication statements, as does Rowe. Rowe, *Plato: Symposium*, 198.

106. The importance of the idea of a proper arrangement or "harmony" of elements to the idea of the good may be inferred from: *Gorgias* 503e–504d, *Rep.* 443d–444e, *Phaedo* 93b–94a, *Philebus* 64d–65a. The idea that being a unity that enables a thing to be and renders it intelligible is indicative of the essence of Goodness is an interpretation derived from the apparent analogy between Good in relation to Forms, as conveyed by Socrates' image of the Sun (*Rep.* 507a–509b), on the one hand, and the Forms in relation to their particulars, on the other. According to this interpretation, the Good can have participants that are not Forms through the mediation of the goodness of Forms, that is, particular things become good to the extent that they are "harmonized" by the appropriate Forms. They become "good" in a secondary, or instrumental, sense to the extent that they aid something else in coming to be harmonized by its Form.

107. For perhaps the best (and most famous) discussion of the Form of the Good as the ultimate Form, see *Republic*, Bk. VI, 504e–509c. Cf. also *Philebus* 64c–66d.

108. Kahn (341) sees Socrates' trances as explained by Diotima's account of the vision of Beauty: "From the point of view of the dramatic structure of the *Symposium*, the doctrine of metaphysical Form is presented as a revelation designed to explain what Socrates is really in love with, where his thoughts are directed in these repeated episodes of personal detachment from his surroundings." Taylor (225, 230–32) thinks the

vision of the Form of Beauty is a mystical experience. Dover thought that the knowledge of the Form of Beauty was "ineffable." Cobb (5, 77) disagrees: "[T]he objects of reason cannot be ineffable," concluding that the erotic ascent cannot be "a transcendence of knowledge or reason." For Cobb, the knowledge of the Form of Beauty "is open to rational understanding and can be stated as a general principle."

In contrast, Rhodes (360–61) thinks the vision of the Beautiful is the same experience recounted in the *Seventh Letter* at 341c7. He concludes: "*Erôs* leads us to a wisdom that is silent because it is ineffable, not because it is secret." For Rhodes Beauty Itself is absolutely transcendent, so much so that he seems not to bear in mind sufficiently the problem of participation; for it would seem that participation would also imply that the Forms possess a certain degree of immanence as well.

Although Anderson regards the vision of the Beautiful as "beyond philosophy and discourse," Anderson (58, 62–64, 148) finds the simultaneously transcendent and immanent nature of the Forms to be contradictory. He holds that Plato was aware of these contradictions and wanted to make his audience aware of them too. For Anderson, the experience Diotima is trying to describe is a knowledge of a different order than, and incompatible with, that implied in what Anderson takes to be her earlier definition of knowledge. We do not agree with Anderson's attribution to Diotima of a "definition of knowledge." We do agree that there is a distinction in Plato between propositional and nonpropositional knowledge and we think that Anderson is too dismissive of this idea (see, e.g., Anderson, 64). Gonzalez, *Dialectic and Dialogue*, gives the finest treatment of the theme of nonpropositional knowledge of which we are aware.

Anderson (82–85) thinks there is no place for Platonic recollection in the *Symposium* and even supposes that it is excluded by Diotima's view of knowledge as processive in nature. Anderson thinks that the simplicity of Beauty means that it cannot be partially remembered. But Anderson does not consider the possibility that a "partial" recollection of a Form might be the insight into a Form only as bound up or involved with other Forms and various particulars and so obscured by them. One should not be misled by the expression "partial recollection" into supposing that it implies that one only recalls "part" of a Form. For one might remember a Form in its simplicity and unity, but only as obscured by its involvement with other Forms and the various particulars that instantiate it. Recollection on this view would be akin to purification, or abstraction, or idealization (which also involves the attempt to disentangle a Form from other beings and thereby "purify" it). One should also recall that Plato's discussions in other texts seem to imply that knowledge can be a matter of degree, for that is what is suggested by his metaphors of light or vision in the Allegory of the Cave in the *Republic*. There it is quite clear that things can be gradually more and more illuminated by degrees and that the budding philosopher comes to see them gradually more and more clearly.

Part of what makes this issue difficult is confusion over what kind of knowledge is supposed to result from a process of recollection. Should it be propositonal or nonpropositional? Should it consist in a good definition or analysis or only in the dispositional ability to provide one? If it is a noetic vision of a Form in abstraction from all of its involvements, such "knowledge," although it might be the only true knowledge in the strict sense, would not be as directly "useful" in human life as a true opinion would be. Yet such knowledge might be indirectly useful by improving the quality of the propositional knowledge and true opinions available.

109. Sheffield (18–19) is able to argue that the ascent is not just a process of successive generalization by bringing in the concept of psychic pregnancy. One does not generalize from souls to arrive at institutions and laws. There is a causal link between the levels of the ascent as well, although some generalization is involved in certain of the transitions between stages. Sheffield (25–26) also discusses comparisons and contrasts between the imagery of psychic pregnancy and the imagery of recollection. Nye (142) disagrees with the "ascetic" reading of the ascent passage: "It is not the *heterosexuality* or the physicality of romantic love that requires progression to more inclusive loving relations, it is the obsessively narrow quality of romantic love." Nye sees Diotima's view as deeply incompatible with Plato's thought in other dialogues. Waterfield discusses the influence of the ascent passage on mystical literature. Waterfield, xxviii–xxix. See also Gill, xxxii, n.62. Both cite the following: Plotinus *Enneads* 1.6. 8–9; Origen *De Principiis* 2.11.7; Augustine, *Confessions* 9.10.

110. Rowe, "Socrates and Diotima," 256.

111. Michael Despland, *The Education of Desire: Plato and Philosophy of Religion*. Toronto: University of Toronto Press, 1985.

112. Gill considers that Diotima's status as a divinely inspired prophet who knows things beyond the human ken has the effect of underlining "the general Platonic theme that philosophical inquiry ..." by contrast "... consists in a continuing search for knowledge of objective truth rather than its achievement" (Gill, xx). For Hyland, Diotima speaks "with the authority of, but also from the finite standpoint of, religious revelation" (Hyland, *Finitude and Transcendence*, 215). Dorter (263–64) sees Socrates as mediating between piety and wisdom with the love of wisdom.

113. The possible functions served by Socrates' appeal to Diotima that have been recognized in the secondary literature include: to soften Socrates' critique of Agathon by putting the young Socrates in place of Agathon (Cornford); to enable Socrates to preserve his claim to ignorance by appealing to another's knowledge: (Cornford, Gill); to enable Socrates to avoid praising an image of *Erôs* that bears such a resemblance to himself (Hamilton); to enable Socrates to act as a narrator who can also comment on her teaching (Rowe); to present views that are not those of the historical Socrates, but perhaps those of Plato (Nehamas); to make use of her status as a prophet to enable her to speak about divine matters, matters about which she does not have to claim philosophical knowledge (thus also, from a philosophical point of view, setting a limit to her authority) (Gill, Hyland). Cornford, "The Doctrine of Erôs," 71; Gill, xxviii–xxix, with n.51; Hamilton, 19–20, 27; Hyland, *Finitude and Transcendence*, 215; Nehamas, *Virtues of Authenticity*, 304; Rowe, "Socrates and Diotima," 251, n.24. In Rosen's view Socrates' conquest of Agathon involves a compromise with Agathon/poetry. Socrates "accomodates his own mythos of Diotima to the need for peace between poetry and philosophy." Thus, for Rosen, "Diotima is not a thinly disguised Plato but a purified Agathon." Rosen, *Plato's Symposium*, 159, n.3, 203.

114. For further analysis concerning the status of Diotima, see David Halperin, "Why is Diotima a Woman?" and our *"Erôs* as Messenger in Diotima's Teaching."

115. If Diotima is a mystagogue, is Socrates profaning her secret teachings by revealing them to the others? Many commentators have seen in Alcibiades' subsequent entrance an allusion to the "profanation of the mysteries" of which Alcibiades, Eryximachus, and Phaedrus were accused. Leo Strauss sees the *Symposium* as presenting the

"true story" of this profanation, according to which Socrates is the culprit and "Alcibiades was completely innocent." Leo Strauss, *Symposium*, 24, 230.

116. The contrast between these different points of view on love, or more specifically, on friendship, underwrites much of the argumentation of Plato's *Lysis*.

117. This example follows the discussion of *akrasia* by Socrates at *Protagoras*, 352b–357e.

118. Or perhaps one should say that the highest study is the study of the Good Itself, as indicated in the *Republic*, and that the study of Beauty Itself leads on to the study of the Good Itself, culminating in a vision of the Good. Note that the same logic applies at this step of the ladder as well: what makes the study of beauty beautiful is its object, Beauty Itself; any study is shaped by its object, and the objects of the highest studies for Plato are Beauty and Goodness.

119. See *Laws* IX, 859c and context, *Republic* X, 607b–c and context.

120. Osborne (52–85, 86–116, 222–26) defends Plato from the criticisms of Anders Nygren and Gregory Vlastos. Osborne sees the *Lysis* as undermining the usual interpretation of Diotima's teaching in the *Symposium*. According to her the acquisitive theory of love that Anders Nygren found in the *Symposium* is shown to be unsatisfactory in the *Lysis*. For this reason, Osborne (52–58, 223–26) does not believe that Diotima can be taken as Plato's mouthpiece. In her view, "the conclusion reached in the *Lysis* makes the uncritical, acquisitive reading of the *Symposium* impossible."

To ask about the motives for love is inappropriate, argues Osborne (63), for love is itself a motive. Love is not something itself motivated "by non-loving considerations." She argues that "because we can discern an exchange of benefits in relations of love . . . we are tempted to see those benefits as a causal explanation of the relationship." But it is a mistake to do so, she thinks. Osborne makes one aware of the following "chicken-egg" problem: Does one love before one desires, or must one desire in order to love? Most precisely, is love itself a desire or are certain desires simply sometimes concomitant with love or caused by it? But in our view, Diotima's notion of *Erôs* is that of a fundamental desire that grounds all others and that is really the desire for happiness, a desire that may be consciously or unconsciously held. But it turns out that the highest happiness will consist in beholding the transcendent and in striving to beget in beauty under the influence of its inspiration. One does not possess the transcendent object of desire—one only beholds it. Yet one still does desire something from it, the happiness achieved via its contemplation, as well as the begetting that would result from this vision. It is perhaps too difficult a question to answer whether on this view it is a nonacquisitive love for a vision of the Form that grounds all acquisitive desire, or whether it is an acquisitive desire for personal happiness that makes one desire this vision in the first place.

121. Some commentators consider the possibility that the speeches are hierarchically arranged, so as to form an ascent leading to Socrates' speech. Cobb, 64, with n.12; Friedländer, *Plato*, Vol. 3, 11–27; Dorter (255) finds two complementary orders of ascent in the speeches, an ascent of conceptions of goodness in the actual order of presentation, and an ascent of accounts of *Erôs* in the order in which Socrates refers to his predecessors' speeches. Plochmann also regards the order of the speeches as twofold: one order in terms of the order of presentation, and the other in terms of the relation to Socrates' speech. According to the second order, Socrates' speech is

"at the hub of a wheel." Plochmann (16–17) distinguished nine steps on the "ladder of love" and sees all the other speeches as representing or misrepresenting combinations of these stages; only Socrates' speech gets the stages right. According to Plochmann (12–13), each speech features its own pair of contraries: Phaedrus (lover versus non-lover), Pausanias (the heavenly versus the vulgar loves), Eryximachus (the healthy versus the sick), Aristophanes (love between the like versus love between the unlike), Agathon (the ugly versus the beautiful). Socrates' speech finds something intermediate between these contraries. At the same time, each speech features different virtues: Phaedrus (courage), Pausanias (temperance), Eryximachus (temperance or justice), Aristophanes (justice), while according to Agathon love is all the virtues, and Socrates identifies love and wisdom. The role of Alcibiades' speech is to show how the virtues are manifested in Socrates. For Nehamas, the first three speeches praise love for its effects, whereas the second three begin an inquiry into its nature. Nehamas, *Virtues of Authenticity*, 306–307. For Strauss, the first three speakers subordinate *Erôs* to something external to it, in the case of Phaedrus, gain, in the case of Pausanias, moral virtue, and in the case of Eryximachus, *techne*; the next three speakers do not subordinate *Erôs* to anything outside of *Erôs* but find its end within *Erôs* itself. For Aristophanes *Erôs* aims at ugliness (the ugliness of the original nature) and for Agathon it aims at beauty; whereas for Socrates it aims at neither, but at the good. Strauss, *Symposium*, 54, 89. Strauss sees Phaedrus's speech as isolated from the rest, which then consists of two triads: Pausanias, Eryximachus, and Aristophanes, who, as lovers, each try to defend pederasty (Strauss indicates that, unlike the other two, Aristophanes' love is not for individuals), and Agathon, Socrates, and Alcibiades. He sees Phaedrus's speech, with its love of gain, as reflecting on a lower level Socrates' love of wisdom or the good. Strauss, *Symposium*, 54–55, 262. Phaedrus and Agathon, the beloveds, do not defend pederasty. Strauss, *Symposium*, 96, 120, 216, 262. Strauss points out that while Aristophanes represents the love of one's own, Agathon represents the love of the beautiful; Diotima's teaching in a way synthesizes the two, because both are needed, but in a way that deliberately abstracts from the lower of the two, the love of one's own, downplaying its importance. Strauss, *Symposium*, 173. This claim fits in with Strauss's general notion that every Platonic dialogue is deliberately constructed to represent only a partial point of view on its topic. According to Strauss, Socrates' understanding of praise (198d) demands that he remain silent about the seamy side of love. Strauss, *Symposium*, 176. Rosen calls attention to the curious fact that Aristophanes' speech is between two exchanges with Eryximachus, as Agathon's speech is between two exchanges with Socrates. Rosen's interpretation of this circumstance is that it signifies that Eryximachus lays siege to the city, while Socrates encompasses poetry. Rosen, *Plato's Symposium*, 164. Our own view of the significance of the relation of the speeches will be made clear in what follows.

122. Allen points out that the speeches in the *Symposium* have a "ring structure," a structure used successfully by Plato in *the Republic*. He writes: "Phaedrus makes *Erôs* a god, and the oldest; Pausanias makes him two gods; Eryximachus makes him two natural forces; Aristophanes makes him a single natural force in men; Agathon, returning to Phaedrus, makes him a single god, but the youngest. This structure is so effective that, though the individual speeches, with the exception of Aristophanes', have severe logical and stylistic weaknesses, the overall effect is one of great brilliance, and the reader is left with a sense of intellectual satisfaction. The whole is golden, despite the dross of the parts; it is pure alchemy of style" (R. E. Allen, *Symposium*, 11–12).

## CHAPTER 3. THE ENTRANCE AND SPEECH
## OF ALCIBIADES (212C–222C)

1. "Oh glistening and violet-crowned and famous in song, bulwark of Hellas, glorious Athens, fortunate city" (quoted in Martha Nussbaum, *Fragility*, 193).

2. Pindar, *Olympian* 2.25.

3. According to Anderson, Alcibiades is Dionysus—the ivy is associated with Dionysus, violets with Aphrodite and also Athens. Anderson (101) also thinks there is an implicit identification between *Erôs* and Dionysus here. According to Rhodes (368), the violets in Alcibiades' wreath symbolize Dionysus's subordination to Aphrodite. Socrates' victory over Agathon is symbolized by Alcibiades/Dionysus giving some ribbons to Socrates (212e7–213e3–4). Hecht (85, 87) also sees Alcibiades as representing the Dionysian arbiter between Socrates and Agathon. See also Strauss, *Symposium*, 257. As mentioned previously Strauss sees in Aristophanes' *The Frogs* a model for the *Symposium*. In *The Frogs* Dionysus goes to Hades and judges a dispute between Euripides and Aeschylus. In the *Symposium* Alcibiades is in the Dionysus role. Strauss, *Symposium*, 26–27, 41, 252.

Many commentators see Alcibiades as playing the role of Dionysus or one possessed by Dionysus, in making the judgment in Socrates' favor. See, for example, Rhodes, 367–68; Strauss, *Symposium*, 257; Usher, 224. Anderson (13–15) sees many different "judgments of Dionysus" in favor of Socrates. Such Dionysian judgments include the fact that the drunken Alcibiades chooses to praise Socrates rather than *Erôs*; the fact that Socrates' speech proves superior to those of the other symposiasts; Alcibiades' observation about Socrates' superior tolerance for alcohol; Socrates' proximity to Dionysus suggested by Alcibiades' comparisons of Socrates to satyrs; Alcibiades' taking back part of the crown of ribbons he has given to Agathon and giving them instead to Socrates; the fact that revelers crash the party, preventing Socrates' scheduled praise of Agathon; and finally, the fact that the philosopher has out-argued and out-drunk the two poets at the end of the dialogue. Hecht (35) also takes the fact that Socrates is able to drink Agathon under the table as one sign that Dionysus judges in Socrates' favor. We think these are all plausible and compatible interpretations of "judgment of Dionysus."

4. Nails, 10–17; Hecht, 7–12.

5. For a sense of how the Platonic Socrates regards Athenian imperialism, see *Gorgias* 518e–519a, where Socrates is speaking to Callicles regarding the famous Athenian statesmen Pericles, Cimon, Themistocles, and Miltiades (revered figures who spanned the political spectrum of the time):

> You're singing the praises of the people who gave the Athenians lavish treats and indulged their desires. They're reputed to have made their city great, but no one notices that these men from Athens' past made her bloated and rotten, by stuffing her, with no sense of restraint or right, full of trumpery like harbors, dockyards, fortifications, and tribute payments. So when the retribution I spoke of comes, in the form of weakness, people will blame the advisers who happen to be there at the time, and will sing the praises of Themistocles and Cimon and Pericles, who should be held responsible for their troubles. (Waterfield trans.)

If one examines this passage in the context of the *Gorgias* as a whole it becomes clear what the problem with such "statesmen" is: they serve ambitions for power and material gain, but ignore the care for the psyche's virtue that was central to Socrates' concerns.

6. We accept the *Alcibiades* I as genuinely Platonic, relying on its acceptance for more than two thousand years before scholars, such as Ast and Schleiermacher, in the nineteenth century began calling it into question. Alfarabi, for example, regarded this dialogue as the jewel among Plato's works. The ancient commentators gave it the subtitle "On the Nature of Man," and even early scholars who disputed the authenticity of other dialogues did not question the authenticity of the *Alcibiades* I. For a discussion of this issue, see the Introduction to Thomas Pangle, *The Roots of Political Philosophy: Ten Forgotten Socratic Dialogues* (Ithaca and London: Cornell University Press, 1987), especially 15.

7. *Republic* 494c–e appears to be referring to Alcibiades, so aptly does its description fit him. Plato has Socrates ask Adeimantus:

> What do you think someone like that will do in such circumstances, especially if he happens to be from a great city, in which he's rich, well-born, good-looking, and tall? Won't he be filled with impractical expectations and think himself capable of managing the affairs not only of the Greeks but of the barbarians as well? And as a result won't he exalt himself to great heights and be brimming with pretension and pride that is empty and lacks understanding? (*Rep.* 494c–d)

8. Nehamas notes a problem with the identification of Socrates and *Erôs*; according to Diotima's view of *Erôs*, Socrates as *Erôs* should be the pursuer, not the pursued. Yet the paradigmatic lover also becomes an object of love. Hence, Socrates is the consummate erotic and as such becomes an object of love. Nehamas, *Virtues of Authenticity*, 312–13. We think this double identity of Socrates as lover and beloved is a point of especial significance. That participation in the Form of the Good that Socrates embodies is in a sense the very thing that all humans are seeking (unbeknownst to them); for it is the true version of the good life. But since that good life consists in the Socratic quest, Socrates' *Erôs* as pursuer is precisely the way humans can attain to the object of pursuit. See also Wardy, 16–17.

9. The best examples of such critiques in other dialogues are found in Callicles' criticisms of Socrates and of philosophy (*Grg.* 482c–483a, 484c–486d) and Thrasymachus's criticisms in *Republic*, Bk. 1 (336b–d, 337a, 337e, 338b). See also the whole of the *Clitophon*.

10. Mitchell, *Hymn to Eros* 177, 183, 212.

11. Euripides, "Electra," in *Medea and Other Plays*, 141, lines 1046–60.

12. Michel Foucault, *Fearless Speech* (Los Angeles: Semiotext(e), 2001).

13. Paul Zanker goes so far as to argue that this Socrates figure becomes a kind of idealized inversion of conventional norms of beauty. See Paul Zanker, *The Mask of Socrates: The Image of the Intellectual in Antiquity* (Berkeley: University of California Press, 1996), esp. 24–36, 61–62.

14. The Corybantes were the ministers of Cybele, but were sometimes associated with the Curetes who were sent by Rhea to guard the infant Zeus on Crete and to cover his cries by making a clashing din, so that the baby could be saved from his child-devouring father, Chronus. Worship of Cybele involved dance and the music of the drum, pipe, and cymbal that was supposed to have a healing effect on those who became swept up in its frenzy. See E. R. Dodds, *The Greeks and the Irrational* (Berke-

ley: University of California Press, 1966), 77–80, and Mark O. Morford and Robert J. Lenardon, *Classical Mythology* (Oxford: Oxford University Press), 40, 201.

15. We know that the first conversation with Alcibiades occurred when the youth was "not yet twenty years old" (*Alc.* I 123d), so this would make 433 the dramatic date of the *Alcibiades* I.

16. The most prominent of these agreements is expressed at the end of the first *Alcibiades* (*Alc.* I 139e).

17. See Pierre Hadot, "The Figure of Socrates," in *Philosophy as a Way of Life*, (Oxford: Blackwell Publishing, Ltd. 1995), 147–78. By preserving his authorial anonymity, Plato seems to mirror this kind of irony of his central characters. This aspect of Plato's work has inspired many interpretations, from the divergent forms of esotericism characteristic of Leo Strauss and his followers, on one hand, and the Tübingen school, on the other, to Kierkegaard's notion of indirect communication and Nietzsche's notion of the mask, as he applied it to Socrates and Plato. For two different kinds of "esotericism" in Plato interpretation, see Szlézàk, *Reading Plato* and Leo Strauss, *The City and Man* (Chicago: University of Chicago Press, 1964).

18. Alexander Nehamas, *The Art of Living: Socratic Reflections from Plato to Foucault* (Berkeley: University of California Press, 1998), 19–98. The analysis in this section is indebted to Nehamas's treatment of irony, beginning with his refusal to regard Vlastos's notion of complex irony as not complex enough to capture the equivocity in the character and speech of Socrates. On irony, see also, D. C. Muecke, *The Compass of Irony* (London: Methuen, 1969) and S. Kierkegaard, *The Concept of Irony with Continual Reference to Socrates* (Princeton: Princeton University Press, 1992).

19. Usher (207) sees the story of Alcibiades' attempted seduction of Socrates as being an adaptation by Plato of the story of King Midas and the satyr Silenus, in which Alcibiades plays the role of Midas and Socrates the role of the satyr. Yet ironically, Alcibiades, crashing that party with his komus of revelers appears as satyric. Usher, 207, n.12. As Usher notes, the values that Alcibiades represents—wealth, beauty—are among the traditional aristocratic values celebrated in sympotic poetry. Thus, it is doubly ironic for rich and beautiful Alcibiades, drunken at a symposium, to report on Socrates' contempt for wealth and beauty, and with this context in mind the charge that such contempt counts as hubris becomes clearer (208–09).

20. See also 222b. Many commentators remark on this role reversal, for example: Usher, 214, n.45; Wardy, 15; Hecht, 53, 94; Waterfield, xviii; Hamilton, 28; Nussbaum, 188–92; Strauss, *Symposium*, 270.

21. See our essay, "An Overlooked Motive in Alcibiades' *Symposium* Speech," *Interpretation* 24, no. 1 (Fall 1996): 67–84, for a fuller analysis of this strategy.

22. Anderson (123–24) makes this point in his commentary. He regards the fact that Socrates neither leaves nor forces Alcibiades to leave as proof that Socrates is not struggling with his passions. He also suggests that it is Alcibiades' duplicity that forces Socrates to respond in the way he does.

23. In the dramatic action of the *Symposium* as well, Plato permits his audience to see that Socrates, legendary for his moderation, has drunk all of the other partygoers under the table.

24. The debate in the secondary literature over the claims of some commentators that Socrates is "frigid" or "unerotic" tends to consider both the teaching of Diotima—whether or not it truly requires one to leave behind the love of individuals—and of Socrates himself, especially his behavior in this incident with Alcibiades. Regarding the former question—the implications of the teachings of Diotima—Vlastos argued that this teaching, which he took to be indicative of Plato's view of love, left no room for the love of individuals. Vlastos, "The Individual as an Object of Love in Plato," in G. Vlastos, *Platonic Studies* (Princeton: Princeton University Press, 1981, 1–34. A. W. Price, in "Loving Persons Platonically," *Phronesis* 26 (1981): 25–34, and in *Love and Friendship in Plato and Aristotle*, 45–49, disagrees with Vlastos's view, as do Hyland, (*Finitude and Transcendence*, 123–26) and Donald Levy, "The Definition of Love in Plato's "*Symposium*," *Journal of the History of Ideas* 40 (April–June 1979): 287–88, among others. Nussbaum sees Alcibiades' speech, with its use of imagery focusing on the particular details of Socrates' character, as a Platonic self-criticism of the earlier Platonic view enshrined in Diotima's teaching, a view that Nussbaum also thinks leaves behind the love of individuals. Duncan also sees Alcibiades' and Aristophanes' speeches as indicative of the importance of the love of individuals and embodying a critique of Diotima's teaching, but much like Hyland, he seems to think Plato is deliberately presenting the two equally necessary sides. Roger Duncan, "Plato's *Symposium*: The Cloven Erôs," *The Southern Journal of Philosophy* (Fall 1977): 15, 288. Hyland is also in disagreement with Vlastos's view, and more subtly with Nussbaum's view as well. Hyland, *Finitude and Transcendence*, 123–26. Anton too (284, n.6, 288–91) regards Socrates as an imperfect lover, although Anton does not suppose that Socrates wholly lacks *Erôs*, nor does Anton express criticism of Diotima's view. Rather, at the time of Agathon's party, Socrates had merely not yet assimilated her teaching. The Socrates of the *Symposium* is hubristic when he professes to know erotic matters. The Socrates who professes ignorance will be a more mature Socrates, chastened by his failure with Alcibiades. We would argue however, that Socrates' claim to know the Art of Love may be another way of saying that Socrates is aware of what he lacks. Hecht (89) claims that Alcibiades' comparisons between Socrates and statues of the satyrs suggests both Socrates' "frigidity" and the desecration of the Herms. (Yet we would note that since the statues in question are *statues of satyrs*, beings that are notoriously erotic, it may very well be that Socrates' erotic quality is being emphasized.) Hecht suggests (92–93) that Alcibiades may exaggerate Socrates' "frigidity" to lessen his own shame at having failed to seduce him. Usher (218) interprets Socrates' frigidity to Alcibiades as a reaction to Alcibiades' ugliness of soul in line with Diotima's remarks about beauty and procreation at 206d4–7. Rhodes adamantly disagrees (204–205, 349–57, 400) with Nussbaum, Vlastos, Rosen, and others who suppose that Socrates is erotically deficient. Anderson (ix) also comes out firmly against Rosen and Nussbaum. For Anderson, Socrates' rejection of Alcibiades is not a rejection of love. According to Anderson, Alcibiades fails because of his "duplicity" and "unworthiness." Socrates is not antierotic, as Rosen and Nussbaum think. Yet, their views may be indicative of what Alcibiades thought of Socrates. (Anderson, 101, n. 1 on 174, and 124, with n.38 on 178). For Anderson, Diotima is advocating neither celibacy nor promiscuity; the one who makes the ascent is still capable of appreciating the differences between beautiful bodies and ugly ones. Diotima's view allows for reciprocal or mutual love, and for symmetry as well as asymmetry in the love relationship. Anderson, 60, with n.22, 65, n.27, 72–73.

On the larger question of the erotic character of Socrates in general, Leo Strauss's remarks are ambiguous. At one point Strauss says that Socrates was not a lover and connects this claim to the fact of his not having written Strauss, 252–53. In addition, Strauss speaks of the "pettiness" Socrates thinks is involved in the love of individuals. Strauss, *Symposium*, 119. At another point, Strauss also seems to agree that Socrates is unerotic and not really ignorant. *Symposium*, 260, 267–68. And yet according to Strauss's twelve-part classificatory scheme, Socrates falls simultaneously under two categories: "Old-manly-lover" and "old manly beloved." Strauss, *Symposium*, 253–54. Moreover, near the beginning of his discussion of the *Symposium*, Strauss asserts: "Socrates, far from being an unerotic man, is the erotician" (*Symposium*, 7), and later says that Socrates is erotic "on the highest level" (29). Yet, Strauss agrees that there is a depreciation of *Erôs* (he means "*Erôs*" in the ordinary sense of sexual desire) at the end of Diotima's speech, but thinks that the *Phaedrus* contains "an unqualified praise of *Erôs*." To this extent his view seems akin to Nussbaum's on this point. *Symposium*, 248. Rosen, however, is unambiguous on this point; he sees Socrates as "unerotic" or "defectively erotic." *Plato's Symposium*, xiii, xvii, xviii, xx, 4–5, 38, 65, n.14, 232–34, 250–52, 277, 279, 311, 317, 320, 342).

25. See, for example, *Alc.* I, 120b, 123d-e, 124b, and 132b. That Alcibiades must cultivate a concern for justice and virtue is the main message of the entire dialogue, for justice is the matter about which Alcibiades has neither learned from another nor discovered for himself, according to Socrates.

## CHAPTER 4. CONCLUSION

1. But this idea need not mean that what one loves in the Form of Beauty is a *property of being beautiful that it possesses*, as though Beauty Itself were merely a beautiful thing; rather, what one loves in Beauty is the property of Beauty that Beauty Itself *is*, that is, the nature that all the property-instances of beauty share or to which they are all related in some way or another.

2. The connection between the "great beast" and the notion of idolatry appears in the work of Simone Weil.

3. The dangers of spiritedness uninformed by philosophy are apparent in many places in the dialogues. See *Rep.* Bk.VIII (548d–549b) for some explicit criticisms of the excessively spirited person. The critique of the Cretan and Spartan modes of government and education in *Laws*, Bk. I and II, is also pertinent on this point. See *Laws* 630d–631a, 666e–667a.

4. Socrates' "small wisdom" is contrasted with the conceits or arrogance of those with only narrow technical competence. Socrates, in contrast, knows his limits, which means that he understands that there is a point beyond which his mortal wisdom cannot go; he knows that he must remain humble, so far is he from god-like omniscience. Plato would surely have us reflect also on the relationship between philosophy and piety, in that Socrates does not merely reject the oracle, nor does he simply accept it at face value. Instead, he regards it as mystery into which it is his divinely-appointed philosophical duty to inquire. If even a divinely inspired oracle must be examined and inquired into, then Socrates would seem to have a deeply ingrained skeptical sense. It is as if he would counsel: "Don't take anything at face value, not even the words of a god."

Yet Socrates also seems to be predisposed to find a way in which the Oracle is *true*, to interpret it so as to find its *truth*, which he seems predisposed to believe as truth. Frequently Socrates will *reinterpret* what he does not directly critique, as in his handling of the definition of justice attributed to Simonides in *Republic*, Bk. I, or in his treatment of the traditional gods and heroes in Bks. II and III. (Likewise, the Athenian Stranger reinterprets the Dorian "law of laws" in *Laws*, Bk. I.) The strategy seems to be: "If we assume that this authority is representative of wisdom and goodness, then we can use our own best, self-critical, rational understanding of wisdom and goodness to determine the *proper interpretation* of this authority." Thus, it might seem that the ultimate divine revelation for Socrates lies in his own logos. But this is all further complicated by Socrates' claims about his *daimonion*, and the question of the relationship of this unique *daimonion* to that *daimon* all humans share: *Erôs*. Socrates is a kind of rationalist, (i.e., a believer in reason,) but his rationalism is unique in that it remains in touch with mystery, a mystery that does not threaten reason but rather lies at its source and nourishes it. Reason retains ultimate authority, but only in virtue of its willingness to listen to and think about the mystery; similarly, Socrates becomes Socrates as we know him only because of his willingness to take the Oracle seriously; he questions it not to dismiss it, but to understand it.

5. Sören Kierkegaard, *Philosophical Fragments* (Princeton: Princeton University Press, 1985), 46.

6. Our reflections on the relations between comedy, tragedy, and philosophy in Plato were influenced by Drew Hyland, *Finitude and Transcendence*, and also by Kierkegaard's *The Concept of Irony*.

7. An interesting discussion of these false ways of "honoring the self" is found in one of the legal preambles of Plato's *Laws*, Bk. V, 726a–732d.

## APPENDIX

1. It is interesting to note that Socrates blames his involvement in philosophy on the response of an oracle. In other words, the origin of his philosophic life begins with precisely the kind of interaction that is the province of the *daimonic* as described in the *Symposium*. Of course, philosophy also begins in Socrates' wonder over this *daimonic/* oracular event.

2. This condition in which something seems to have two opposed properties at once seems in a famous passage of the *Republic* (523a–525a) to constitute the sine qua non of that perplexity that leads the mind away from the realm of the senses to the realm of true being. It is worth mentioning that in the realm of the intermediate (*metaxu*) as conceived in both the *Symposium* and the *Republic*, there is ample cause for such perplexity, because things generally have opposed properties owing to their very intermediacy. This will become clearer in our discussion of the *Republic* in the Appendix.

3. Recollection itself has an additional odd feature: it never seems to be complete. Witness Socrates' use in the *Meno* of the square root of eight as the paradigm for an answer brought about by recollection. Any value given for the square root of eight is an approximation; the square root of eight can never be adequately expressed. Again, just as the *Phaedo* (at 74d-e) suggests that one must have a sense of the perfect in order to

grasp the imperfect, even if one never perceives anything in the world that is truly perfect, but only perceives approximations, so too mathematicians have an understanding of the square root of eight that enables them to make ever closer approximations to it without ever being able to express its value exactly. If Plato thought of the geometrical solution that Socrates works out with the slave-boy in the *Meno* as a second best expedient to which one resorts owing to the impossibility of finding any corresponding numerical value, this second best expedient might be parallel to the use of images and myths in the dialogues to express truths that exceed the grasp of a more straightforward logos.

4. Knowledge here seems to demand a "logos" or account. This point suggests propositional knowledge, yet there is ample evidence that Plato acknowledges and even emphasizes in certain respects nonpropositional knowledge. But the demand for a logos could be interpreted in a way consistent with the belief in the priority of nonpropositional knowledge, however. Diotima suggests that knowers can give accounts, and we presume she means accounts that are in some way adequate. This characterization need not imply, however, that such accounts are in every way adequate, but only that they are accounts the ignorant would be unable to give. The accounts given by someone possessing nonpropositional knowledge, while never being adequate to the essentially nonpropositional insight, would presumably be more adequate accounts than would those given by the ignorant.

5. The best evidence that the connection between *Erôs* and Recollection we are making is not a fanciful interpretation is the fact that Love and Recollection are connected so closely by the *Phaedrus*.

6. There is also a similarly exaggerated conception of the opposite extreme, seen in the notion of "the wisdom of the gods": a knowledge that few actually possess, if anyone except the gods does possess it.

7. This notion of ignorance is similar to the notion of ignorance seen in *Republic* Bk. V, in which ignorance appears as a kind of faculty coordinated with nonbeing. Perhaps this nonbeing is the "altogether not" of which one cannot speak, according to Parmenides. See *Sophist* 258e–259a. where the contrary (*enantion*) of being is distinguished from what is not in another sense—otherness. The ignorance coordinated with total nonbeing would seem to preclude having not merely correct opinions, but any opinions at all.

8. For evidence that Plato is aware of the apparent circularity of this formulation, see *Rep.* 505b-c; for evidence that such circularity stimulated his thought, see *Euthydemus* 288d–292e. See also the *Clitophon*.

9. Interestingly, when one gains the ability to distinguish a true opinion from knowledge, that is, when one realizes that one does not know it, one becomes uncertain whether or not it is true. This fact raises the possibility that a firmly held true opinion may occasionally be better for someone than a Socratic awareness of their own ignorance; true opinions have great practical benefits and, whatever their deficiencies in other respects, are seemingly equal to knowledge in their ability to successfully guide action (*Meno* 96d–97d). This theme is rich and could be easily tied to the whole Straussian problem of "the city and man" (see *Rep.* Bk. VII, 537e–539d).

10. As is well known, the Forms are decisive in Socrates' account of the philosopher here. If we understood the grasp of Forms to be incompatible with the Socratically

ignorant nature of philosophy, the account of the nature of philosophy in the *Republic* and in the *Symposium* would seem to be radically opposed.

11. His language here suggests that Forms can participate in one another, but that this does not change their ultimately independent—"itself by itself"—nature. We think this shows that there is no serious difference between a so-called "middle-period" theory of Forms and a later theory in this respect.

12. This inference seems to leave out the possibility that these powers could also be distinguished by what they accomplish (a possibility that seems to be acknowledged at 477d). But perhaps the reasoning is that in the case of cognitive powers, what is accomplished is just the grasping of the object.

13. In some cases, this inability to provide an account could be due to the ignorance of the holder of the opinion; in other cases, however, the inability to provide an account might have to do with the nature of the object of opinion. To the extent that the object of opinion is a particular in the realm of Becoming, no account could ever be enough to warrant unqualified belief in it; for the very nature of its object, a changing mixture of Being and Nonbeing, would provide no basis for an account that would provide sufficient warrant to convert the belief into knowledge. In fact, the only case in which the inability to provide an account of a correct opinion could be owing merely to the ignorance of the opinion holder would be a case in which the opinion could be construed as an opinion of the Form, an opinion that happens to be correct of the Form, but which is still based on an unwarranted generalization from particulars and not on an insight into the Form itself. In this sense, the opinion still has Becoming for its object, because it is directed at particulars, but in another sense the opinion is a correct opinion (but not knowledge) about a Form. If one examines the argument for Forms at *Timaeus* 51d–52d, one sees it is based on the necessity of a distinction between knowledge and true opinion. The reasons given for the distinction between knowledge and true opinion are (1) knowledge comes through instruction, true opinion comes through persuasion; (2) knowledge involves a true account while true opinion lacks any account; (3) knowledge remains unmoved by persuasion, but true opinion can be changed by persuasion; (4) everyone has true opinions, but only gods and few people have knowledge. If one reflects on these distinctions, one sees that they connect closely to the difference between knowledge and true opinion that comes out in our previous discussion: knowledge must be infallible, but true opinion, although true, is fallible. But what is it about the true account involved in knowledge that makes such a difference and that makes the difference between instruction and mere persuasion? Clearly, the true account makes the knowledge infallible. But why should such infallibility have to count as evidence for the reality of Forms? It is because it is only the existence of Forms and the possibility of knowing them that provides the necessity involved in rational inference; only the necessity involved in rational inference ensures infallibility and makes the difference between instruction and persuasion. If the world had only contingent truths in it, no evidence would be stronger than perceptual evidence—it would be opinion that might happen to be true but also might not, depending on how the world is contingently arranged. If there is to be necessity that provides for the security and infallibility of rational inference, there must be something in reality that the mind can grasp that includes necessary relations among its elements—and for Plato, for whom the empirical world is a Heraclitean flux, only the Forms fit that description.

14. Cf. the *Parmenides* 135b-c, on Forms as conditions of discourse. Cf. also *Cratylus* 440a-c, where the underlying thought is similar.

15. Indeed, these two sorts of contact with being are in effect distinguished by the Eleatic Stranger in the *Sophist*. By showing how it is possible in a sense to speak of what is not and distinguishing this sense from another sense in which it is not possible, the Eleatic Stranger describes a way in which it is possible for even false discourse to relate to being, although obliquely. Far from disagreeing, the Eleatic Stranger shows how it is possible for what Socrates is saying in *Republic* V to be true. That is, he shows how it is possible for opinion to be different from mere ignorance through retaining some connection to being, even when it speaks of "what is not." Actually, the *Sophist* and *Republic* V both contain two forms of "what is not": total nonbeing and the nonbeing of difference. The "what is not" accepted in the *Sophist* is not the total nonbeing that is coordinate with ignorance in the *Republic*, so there is no disagreement. The total nonbeing coordinate with ignorance in the *Republic* is the nonbeing of which we cannot speak or think, rejected at *Sophist* 259a. The "what is not" of which one can speak in the *Sophist* is the same as the nonbeing of which Becoming partakes, which turns out, as we shall see, to be difference; the argument of the *Sophist* regarding nonbeing is presented in *Republic* V in a truncated or condensed form.

16. That is, the distinction between the Is of identity and the Is of predication, or between identity on the one hand and participation on the other. Far from being confused about this distinction, Plato's discussions of the Forms make this very distinction for us, except in contexts where he expects us to find it. If there seem to be problematic cases of self-predication in Plato this is for the same reason that a number of other sophistical paradoxes appear in the dialogues: to lead us into perplexity and to make us more dialectical.

17. Of course, the Forms are also different from one another, and so the sort of nonbeing that is difference would seem to apply to them as well as to things in Becoming. Did Plato recognize in the *Parmenides* that a kind of aspect-change or relativity might apply even to the Forms? Without knowing the answer to that question, we can at least say that the particulars are between being and nonbeing in a more radical sense owing to their temporality. This observation makes it more interesting to note that it is nonetheless not temporality, but relativity, that seems to be emphasized as characteristic of particulars in *Republic* V.

18. We should note that the sense of "knowledge" used in this passage is extraordinary because it seems to imply we can only have knowledge about Forms and not about the world of change. This point is not a real problem, however, because it is easily shown that Plato recognizes different senses of "knowledge." For instance, math and the arts are knowledge in one respect but not in another (cf. *Republic* VI, 511d; *Philebus*, 61d-e; the *Apology* 22d; and elsewhere). In a strict sense then knowledge may *not* be available about the empirical world (cf. also *Timaeus 29b-d*) but this is not too strange as long as we are clear that we are using knowledge here in a strict and even technical sense. Interestingly, *Republic* 511d states that *dianoia* is *metaxu* between *nous* and *doxa*, and thereby seems to indicate yet another grade of intermediacy, distinct from those we are examining here. But as such a *dianoia*, even mathematics is then not knowledge in the *strictest* sense.

19. One should refer to the argument for Forms at *Timaeus* 51d–52d and our discussion of it in note 13 *supra*.

20. Undoubtedly, Plato's most famous image for human intermediacy is that of the Cave. During the initial imprisonment in the Cave one is still related to the world outside, but only distantly, through images and the light of the fire. Of course, the journey out of the Cave and back into it represent various stages of philosophical intermediacy.

21. Or for that matter, Vlastos's view, according to which the *Symposium* is a full-fledged middle-period dialogue in which we have two different portrayals of Socrates, characteristic, according to Vlastos, of two different periods of Plato's career. See *Socrates, Ironist and Moral Philosophy* 33, 47, along with our critique of Vlastos in "Eros as Messenger in Diotima's Teaching."

22. It is unclear whether this more direct awareness is fulfilled and even in the rare case where it may be it might very well take the form of a nonpropositional awareness. The criticism of writing in the *Phaedrus*, especially if seen in the light of the *Seventh Letter*, has been thought to suggest this. For two views, see Kenneth Sayre, *Plato's Literary Garden* and Fransico J. Gonzalez, *Dialectic and Dialogue.*

# Works Cited

Allen, R. E. *The Dialogues of Plato*, Vol. 2, The *Symposium*. New Haven: Yale University Press, 1993.

———. "A Note on The Elenchus of Agathon: Symposium: 199c–201c." *The Monist* 50 (1966): 460–63.

Anderson, Daniel E. *The Masks of Dionysos: A Commentary on Plato's Symposium.* Albany: State University of New York Press,1993.

Anton, John P. "The Secret of Plato's Symposium." *The Southern Journal of Philosophy* 12 (Fall 1974): 277–93.

Bacon, Helen. "Socrates Crowned." *Virginia Quarterly Review* 35 (1959): 415–30.

Blanckenhagen, Peter H. von. "Stage and Actors in Plato's Symposium." *Greek, Roman and Byzantine Studies* 33, no. 1 (1992): 54–68.

Bloom, Allan. *Love and Friendship*. New York: Simon and Schuster, 1993.

Bury, R. G. *The Symposium of Plato*. Cambridge: W. Heffer and Sons, 1964.

Clay, Diskin. *Platonic Questions: Dialogues with the Silent Philosopher*. University Park: The Pennsylvania State University Press, 2000.

———. "The Tragic and Comic Poet of the Symposium." In *Essays in Ancient Greek Philosophy*, Vol. 2, ed. John P. Anton and Anthony Preus. Albany: State University of New York Press, 1983.

Cobb, William S. *The Symposium and The Phaedrus: Plato's Erotic Dialogues*. Albany: State University of New York Press, 1993.

Cooper, John M., ed., *Plato: Complete Works*. Indianapolis: Hackett, 1997.

Cornford, Francis M. "The Doctrine of Eros in Plato's Symposium." In *The Unwritten Philosophy and Other Essays*, ed., W. K. C. Guthrie. Cambridge: Cambridge University Press, 1968 (1950).

———. *Plato's Theory of Knowledge*. London: Routledge and Kegan Paul, 1935. Reprint, Indianapolis: Bobbs-Merrill, 1957.

de Romilly, Jacqueline. *Magic and Rhetoric in Ancient Greece*, Cambridge: Harvard University Press, 1975.

Desjardins, Rosemary. "Why Dialogues? Plato's Serious Play" In *Platonic Writings, Platonic Readings*, ed. Charles L. Griswold Jr. New York: Routledge, 1988 (Reprint: The Pennsylvania State University Press, 2001).

Despland, Michael. *The Education of Desire: Plato and Philosophy of Religion.* Toronto: University of Toronto Press, 1985.

Diogenes Laertius. *Lives of Eminent Philosophers.* Trans. R. D. Hicks. 2 vols. Loeb Classical Library. Cambridge: Harvard University Press, 1958.

Dodds, E. R. *The Greeks and the Irrational.* Berkeley: University of California Press, 1966.

Dorter, Kenneth N. "A Dual Dialectic in the *Symposium.*" *Philosophy and Rhetoric* 25, no. 3 (1992): 253–70.

Dover, K. J., *Greek Homosexuality.* Cambridge: Harvard University Press, 1978.

———, ed. Plato: *Symposium.* Cambridge: Cambridge University Press, 1980.

———. "Aristophanes' Speech in Plato's *Symposium.*" *Journal of Hellenic Studies* 86 (1966): 41–50.

Duncan, Roger. "Plato's Symposium: The Cloven Eros." *The Southern Journal of Philosophy* 15 (Fall 1977): 277–90.

Erde, Edmund L. "Comedy and Tragedy and Philosophy in the Symposium: An Ethical Vision." *The Southwestern Journal of Philosophy* 7 (Winter 1976): 161–64.

Finlay, John. "The Night of Alcibiades." *The Hudson Review* 47, no. 1 (1994): 57–79.

Forde, Steven. *The Ambition to Rule: Alcibiades and the Politics of Imperialism in Thucydides.* Ithaca: Cornell University Press, 1989.

Foucault, Michel. *Fearless Speech.* Ed. Joseph Pearson. Los Angeles: Semiotext(e), 2001.

Friedländer, Paul. *Plato*, Vol.3. Trans. Hans Meyerhoff. Princeton: Princeton University Press, 1958.

Gill, Christopher. *Plato, The Symposium.* London: Penguin, 1999.

Gonzalez, Francisco. *Dialectic and Dialogue: Plato's Practice of Philosophical Inquiry.* Evanston: Northwestern University Press, 1998.

———."Plato's Dialectic of Forms." In *Plato's Forms: Varieties of Interpretation*, ed. William A. Welton. Lanham, MD: Lexington Books, 2002.

———, ed., *The Third Way: New Directions in Platonic Studies.* Lanham, MD: Rowman and Littlefield, 1995.

Hackforth, R. "Immortality in Plato's *Symposium.*" *Classical Review* 64 (1950): 43–45.

Hadot, Pierre. *What Is Ancient Philosophy?* Trans. Michael Chase. Cambridge: Harvard University Press, 2003.

———. *Philosophy as a Way of Life: Spiritual Exercises from Socrates to Foucault* Trans. Michael Chase. Ed. Arnold I. Davidson. Oxford: Blackwell, 1995.

Halliwell, Stephen. "Philosophy and Rhetoric." In *Persuasion: Greek Rhetoric in Action*, ed. Ian Worthington. London: Routledge, 1994.

Halperin, David M. "Why Is Diotima a Woman?" In *One Hundred Years of Homosexuality and Other Essays on Greek Love.* New York: Routledge, 1990.

Hamilton, Walter., ed. and trans. *Plato, The Symposium.* New York and London: Penguin Classics, 1951.

Hecht, Jamey. *Plato's Symposium: Eros and the Human Predicament,* New York: Twayne, 1999.

House, Dennis K. "Review of R.E. Allen, trans. *The Dialogues of Plato,* Vol. 2: *The Symposium,* New Haven: Yale University Press, 1991." *Phoenix: The Journal of the Classical Association of Canada* 48, no. 1 (Spring 1994): 75–76.

Hyland, Drew. *Finitude and Transcendence in the Platonic Dialogues.* Albany: State University of New York Press, 1995.

———. "Against a Platonic 'Theory' of Forms." In *Plato's Forms: Varieties of Interpretation,* ed. William A. Welton. Lanham, MD: Lexington Books, 2002.

Kahn, Charles. *Plato and the Socratic Dialogue: The Philosophical Use of a Literary Form* Cambridge: Cambridge University Press, 1996.

Kierkegaard, Soren. *The Concept of Irony with Continual Reference to Socrates.* Trans. Howard V. Hong and Edna H. Hong. Princeton: Princeton University Press, 1992.

———. *Philosophical Fragments.* Princeton: Princeton University Press, 1985.

Konstan, David. "Commentary on Rowe: Mortal Love." In *Proceedings of the Boston Area Colloquium of Ancient Philosophy,* XIV (1998), ed. John J. Cleary and Gary M. Gurtler, S.J., 260–67.

Konstan, David, and Elisabeth Young-Bruehl. "Eryximachus' Speech in the *Symposium.*" *Apeiron* 16 (1982): 41–46.

Kurlansky, Mark. *Salt: A World History.* New York: Penguin, 2002.

Leslie, Shane. *Plato's Symposium or Supper.* London: Fortune Press, 1946.

Levy, Donald. "The Definition of Love in Plato's Symposium." *Journal of the History of Ideas* 40 (April–June 1979): 285–91.

Lombardo, Stanley, and Karen Bell, trans. "Symposium." In *Plato: Complete Works,* ed. John M. Cooper, D. S. Hutchinson, assoc. ed. Indianapolis: Hackett, 1997.

Luce, J. V. "Immortality in Plato's Symposium: A Reply." *The Classical Review* 2, no. 3/4 (Dec. 1952): 137–41.

McPherran, Mark. *The Religion of Socrates,* University Park: Pennsylvania State University Press, 1999.

Mill, John Stuart. On *Utilitarianism.* Indianapolis: Hackett, 2001.

Mitchell, Robert Lloyd. *The Hymn to Eros: A Reading of Plato's* Symposium. Lanham, MD: University Press of America, 1993.

Moes, Mark "Spiritual Pregnancy and Socrates' Refutation of Agathon in the *Symposium*" (Typescript, 2005).

Morford, Mark P. O., and Robert J. Lenardon. *Classical Mythology,* Third Edition. New York: Longman, 1985.

Muecke, D. C. *The Compass of Irony.* London: Methuen, 1969.

Nails, Debra. *The People of Plato: A Prosopography of Plato and Other Socratics.* Indianapolis: Hackett, 2002.

Nehamas, Alexander. *Virtues of Authenticity: Essays on Plato and Socrates.* (Princeton: Princeton University Press, 1999.

———. *The Art of Living: Socratic Reflections from Plato to Foucault.* Berkeley: University of California Press, 1998.

Nussbaum, Martha. *The Fragility of Goodness.* Cambridge: Cambridge University Press, 1986.

Nye, Andrea. "The Subject of Love." *Journal of Value Inquiry* 24, no. 2: (April 1990) 135–53.

Nygren, Anders. *Agape and Eros: The Christian Idea of Love.* Trans. Philip S. Watson. Chicago: University of Chicago Press, 1962.

Osborne, Catherine. *Eros Unveiled: Plato and the God of Love.* Oxford: Clarendon Press, 1994.

Pangle, Thomas. *The Roots of Political Philosophy: Ten Forgotten Socratic Dialogues.* Ithaca and London: Cornell University Press, 1987.

———. "Interpretive Essay." In *The Laws of Plato.* New York: Basic Books, 1980.

Plochmann, G. K. "Hiccups and Hangovers in the Symposium." *Bucknell Review* 11 (1963): 1–18.

Press, Gerald. A., ed. *Who Speaks for Plato? Studies in Platonic Anonymity.* Lanham, MD: Rowman and Littlefield, 2000.

Price, A. W., *Love and Friendship in Plato and Aristotle.* Oxford: Oxford University Press, 1989.

———. "Loving Persons Platonically." *Phronesis* 26 (1981): 25–34.

Reale, Giovanni, *Toward a New Interpretation of Plato.* Trans. John R. Catan and Richard Davies. Washington, DC: The Catholic University of America Press, 1997.

Rhodes, James. *Eros, Wisdom, and Silence: Plato's Erotic Dialogues.* Columbia: University of Missouri Press, 2003.

Rojcewicz, Richard. "Platonic Love: Dasein's Urge Toward Being." *Research in Phenomenology* 27 (1997): 103–20.

Roochnik, David. *Of Art and Wisdom.* University Park: The Pennsylvania State University Press, 1999.

Rosen, Stanley. *Plato's Symposium.* Indiana: St. Augustine's Press, 1999.

———. *The Question of Being: A Reversal of Heidegger.* New Haven: Yale University Press, 1993.

———. "Is Metaphysics Possible?" *Review of Metaphysics* 45 (1991): 235–57.

———. *Plato's Sophist: The Drama of Original and Image.* New Haven: Yale University Press, 1983.

Rowe, Christopher J., ed. *Plato: Symposium.* Warminster: Aris and Phillips, 1998.

———. "Socrates and Diotima: Eros, Immortality and Creativity." In *Proceedings of the Boston Area Colloquium in Ancient Philosophy* XIV (1998), ed. John J. Cleary and Gary M. Gurtler, S.J.

Sayre, Kenneth. *Plato's Literary Garden: How to Read a Platonic Dialogue.* Notre Dame: University of Notre Dame Press, 1996.

————."Why Plato Never Had a Theory of Forms." In *Proceedings of the Boston Area Colloquium in Ancient Philosophy*, ed. John J. Cleary and William Wians, Vol. 9. Lanham, MD: University Press of America, 1993.

Schall, James V., S. J. "The Encyclical: God's Eros is Agape" http://www.ignatiusin sight.com/features2006/schall_encyclical_jan06.asp

Scott, Gary Alan. *Plato's Socrates as Educator*. Albany: State University of New York Press, 2000.

————. Review of Pierre Hadot, *What is Ancient Philosophy?* Cambridge: Harvard University Press, 2002. *The Review of Metaphysics* 58, no. 1 (September 2004), 180–81.

————. Review of Pierre Hadot, *What is Ancient Philosophy?* *Ancient Philosophy* Vol. xxiv, no. 2 (Fall 2004): 524–30.

Scott, Gary Alan, and William A. Welton. "An Overlooked Motive in Alcibiades' *Symposium* Speech." *Interpretation* 24, no. 1 (Fall 1996): 67–84.

————. "Eros as Messenger in Diotima's Teaching." In *Who Speaks for Plato; Studies in Platonic Anonymity*, ed. Gerald A. Press. Lanham, MD: Rowman and Littlefield, 2000.

Sheffield, F. C. C. "Psychic Pregnancy and Platonic Epistemology." *Oxford Studies in Ancient Philosophy* 20 (Summer 2001): 1–33.

Shorey, Paul. *What Plato Said*. Chicago: University of Chicago Press, 1933.

Smith, P. Christopher. "Poetry, Socratic Dialectic, and the Desire of the Beautiful." *Epochē* 9, no. 2 (Spring 2005): 233–53.

Smith, Thomas. *Revaluing Ethics: Aristotle's Dialectical Pedagogy*. Albany: State University of New York Press, 2001.

Strauss, Leo. *On Plato's Symposium*. Chicago: University of Chicago Press, 2001.

————. *The City and Man*. Chicago: University of Chicago Press, 1964.

Streiker, Lowell D. "The Christian Understanding of Platonic Love: A Critique of Anders Nygren's *Agape and Eros*." *Christian Scholar* 47 (1964): 331–40.

Szlézàk, Thomas A. *Reading Plato*. London: Routledge, 1993.

Taylor, A. E. *Plato, The Man and His Work*. Cleveland: Meridian Books, 1961.

Usher M. D. "Satyr Play in Plato's *Symposium*." *American Journal of Philology* 123 (2002): 205–28.

Vlastos, Gregory. *Socrates: Ironist and Moral Philosopher*. Ithaca: Cornell University Press, 1991

————. "The Individual as an Object of Love in Plato." In G. Vlastos, *Platonic Studies*. Princeton: Princeton University Press, 1981.

Wardy, Robert. "The Unity of Opposites in Plato's Symposium." In *Oxford Studies in Ancient Philosophy*, ed. David Sedley, XXIII (Winter 2002): 1–61. Oxford: Oxford University Press, 2002.

Warner, Martin. "Love, Self, and Plato's *Symposium*." *Philosophical Quarterly* 29, no. 117 (1979): 320–39.

Waterfield, Robin. *Symposium*. Oxford: Oxford University Press, 1994.

West, Elinor J. M. "Plato's Audiences, or How Plato Replies to the Fifth Century Intellectual Mistrust of Letters." In *The Third Way*, ed. Francisco J. Gonzalez. Lanham, MD: Rowman and Littlefield, 1995.

White, F. C. "Love and Beauty in Plato's Symposium." *Journal of Hellenic Studies* 109 (1989): 149–57.

Wolz, Henry G. "Philosophy as Drama: An Approach to Plato's *Symposium*." *Philosophy and Phenomenological Research* 30 (March 1970): 323–53.

Woodruff, Paul, and Alexander Nehamas, eds. and trans. Plato, *Symposium*. Indianapolis: Hackett, 1989.

Zanker, Paul. *The Mask of Socrates: The Image of the Intellectual in Antiquity*. Berkeley: University of California Press, 1996.

# Index